Victory in Italy

By the same author

Wall of Steel: The History of 9th (Londonderry) HAA Regiment, RA (SR); North-West Books, Limavady, 1988

The Sons of Ulster: Ulstermen at war from the Somme to Korea; Appletree Press, Belfast, 1992

Clear the Way! A History of the 38th (Irish) Brigade, 1941–1947; Irish Academic Press, Dublin, 1993

Irish Generals: Irish Generals in the British Army in the Second World War; Appletree Press, Belfast, 1993

Only the Enemy in Front: The Recce Corps at War, 1940–46; Spellmount, Staplehurst, 1994

Key to Victory: The Maiden City in the Second World War; Greystone Books, Antrim, 1995

The Williamite War in Ireland, 1699–1691; Four Courts Press, Dublin, 1998

A Noble Crusade: The History of Eighth Army, 1941–1945; Spellmount, Staplehurst, 1999

Irish Men and Women in the Second World War; Four Courts Press, Dublin, 1999

Irish Winners of the Victoria Cross (with David Truesdale); Four Courts Press, Dublin, 2000

Irish Volunteers in the Second World War; Four Courts Press, Dublin, 2001

The Sound of History: El Alamein 1942; Spellmount, Staplehurst, 2002

The North Irish Horse: A Hundred Years of Service; Spellmount, Staplehurst, 2002

Normandy 1944: The Road to Victory; Spellmount, Staplehurst, 2004

Ireland's Generals in the Second World War; Four Courts Press, Dublin, 2004

The Thin Green Line: A History of the Royal Ulster Constabulary GC, 1922–2001; Pen & Sword, Barnsley, 2004

None Bolder: A History of 51st (Highland) Division, 1939–1945; Spellmount, Staplehurst, 2006

The British Reconnaissance Corps in World War II; Osprey Publishing, Oxford, 2007

Eighth Army in Italy 1943–45: The Long Hard Slog; Pen & Sword, Barnsley, 2007

The Siege of Derry 1689: The Military History; Spellmount, Stroud, 2008

Only the Enemy in Front: The Recce Corps at War, 1940–46 (revised p/bk edn); Spellmount, Stroud, 2008

Ubique: The Royal Artillery in the Second World War; Spellmount, Stroud, 2008

Helmand Mission: With the Royal Irish Battlegroup in Afghanistan 2008; Pen & Sword, Barnsley, 2009

In the Ranks of Death: The Irish in the Second World War; Pen & Sword, Barnsley, 2010

The Humber Light Reconnaissance Car 1941–45; Osprey Publishing, Oxford, 2011

Hobart's 79th Armoured Division at War: Invention, Innovation and Inspiration; Pen & Sword, Barnsley, 2011

British Armoured Divisions and Their Commanders 1939–1945; Pen & Sword, Barnsley, 2013

Victory in Italy

15th Army Group's Final Campaign

Richard Doherty

Pen & Sword
MILITARY

First published in Great Britain in 2014 by
Pen & Sword Military
an imprint of
Pen & Sword Books Ltd
47 Church Street
Barnsley
South Yorkshire
S70 2AS

ISBN 978-1-78346-298-8

A CIP catalogue record for this book is available from the British Library

Typeset in Ehrhardt by
Mac Style Ltd, Bridlington, East Yorkshire
Printed and bound in the UK by CPI Group (UK) Ltd, Croydon,
CRO 4YY

Pen & Sword Books Ltd incorporates the imprints of Pen & Sword
Archaeology, Atlas, Aviation, Battleground, Discovery, Family History,
History, Maritime, Military, Naval, Politics, Railways, Select,
Transport, True Crime, and Fiction, Frontline Books, Leo Cooper,
Praetorian Press, Seaforth Publishing and Wharncliffe.

For a complete list of Pen & Sword titles please contact
PEN & SWORD BOOKS LIMITED
47 Church Street, Barnsley, South Yorkshire, S70 2AS, England
E-mail: enquiries@pen-and-sword.co.uk
Website: www.pen-and-sword.co.uk

Contents

Dedication

To the memory of all who served in Operation GRAPESHOT,
especially those who lost their lives.

And some there be, which have no memorial; who are perished, as though they had never been; and are become as though they had never been born; and their children after them. But these were merciful men, whose righteousness hath not been forgotten. Their bodies are buried in peace; but their name liveth for evermore. The people will tell of their wisdom, and the congregation will shew forth their praise.

That their dust may rebuild her a nation,
That their souls may relight her a star.

Maps and Figures

Maps

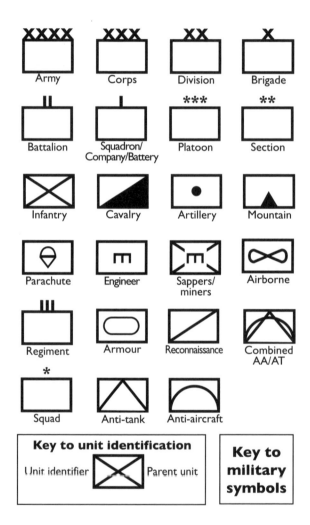

Army

Corps

Division

Brigade

Battalion

Squadron/
Company/Battery

Platoon

Section

Infantry

Cavalry

Artillery

Mountain

Parachute

Engineer

Sappers/
miners

Airborne

Regiment

Armour

Reconnaissance

Combined
AA/AT

Squad

Anti-tank

Anti-aircraft

Key to unit identification

Unit identifier

Parent unit

Key to military symbols

Note: maps have been simplified to show only essential detail and contours, many waterways and roads have been omitted since their inclusion would have made the maps so cluttered as to be of little value. The reader will be aware that Fifth Army, and some elements of Eighth Army, attacked from the high ground of the northern Apennines onto the plain of the Po, or the Lombardy Plain, and that Fifth Army then advanced into the Alps.

Further detail is available on Touring Club Italiano 1:200,000 maps 2 (Lombardy), 3 (Trentino Alto Adige); 4 (Veneto, Friuli Venezia Giulia) and 6 (Emilia Romagna); or 1:400,000 map 1 (Italia settentrionale/Northern Italy).

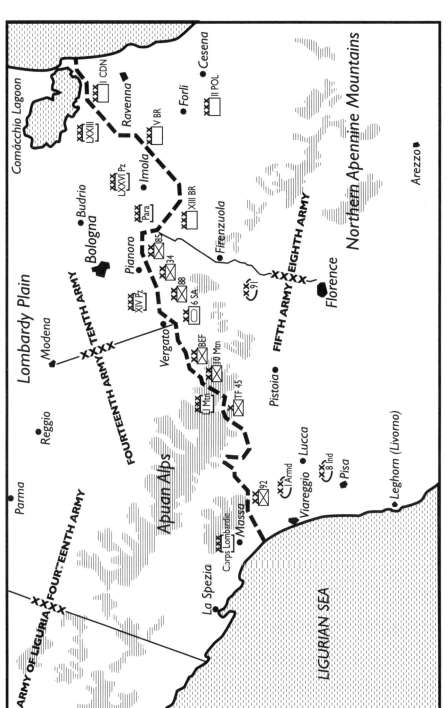

Map 1: Dispositions of opposing forces, April 1945.

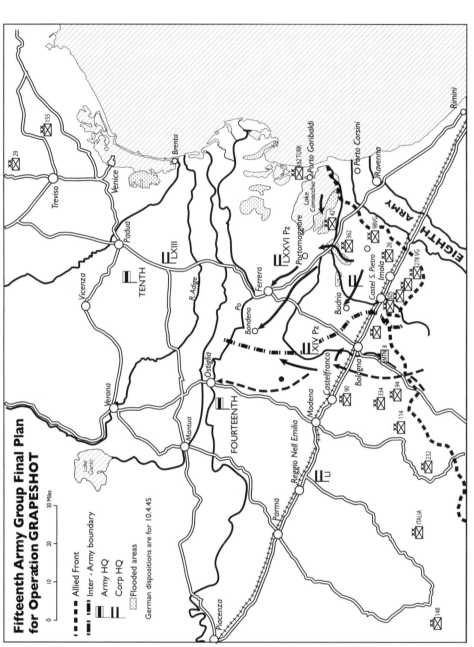

Map 2: 15th Army Group final plan for Operation GRAPESHOT.

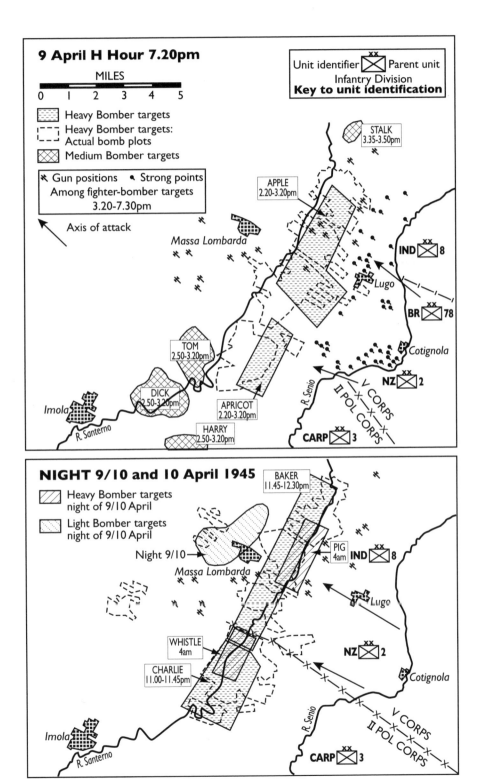

9 April H Hour 7.20pm

MILES

0   1   2   3   4   5

Heavy Bomber targets

Heavy Bomber targets: Actual bomb plots

Medium Bomber targets

Gun positions   Strong points
Among fighter-bomber targets
3.20-7.30pm

Axis of attack

Unit identifier Parent unit
Infantry Division
Key to unit identification

STALK
3.35-3.50pm

APPLE
2.20-3.20pm

IND 8

Massa Lombarda

Lugo

BR 78

TOM
2.50-3.20pm

Cotignola

DICK
2.50-3.20pm

NZ 2

Imola

R. Santerno

APRICOT
2.20-3.20pm

R. Senio

V CORPS

II POL CORPS

HARRY
2.50-3.20pm

CARP 3

NIGHT 9/10 and 10 April 1945

Heavy Bomber targets
night of 9/10 April

Light Bomber targets
night of 9/10 April

BAKER
11.45-12.30pm

Night 9/10

Massa Lombarda

PIG
4am

IND 8

Lugo

WHISTLE
4am

NZ 2

CHARLIE
11.00-11.45pm

Cotignola

Imola

R. Santerno

R. Senio

V CORPS

II POL CORPS

CARP 3

Map 3: Operation BUCKLAND: Allied bomber attacks on Eighth Army's front.

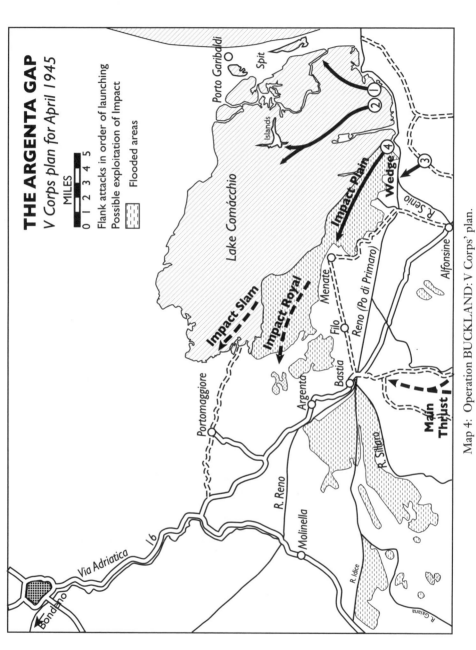

Map 4: Operation BUCKLAND: V Corps' plan.

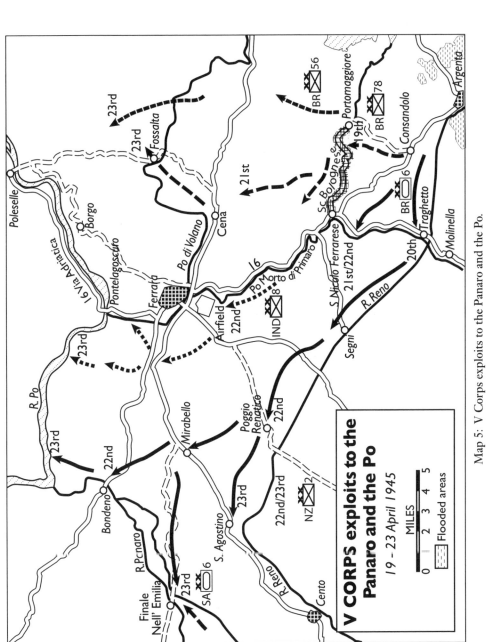

Map 5: V Corps exploits to the Panaro and the Po.

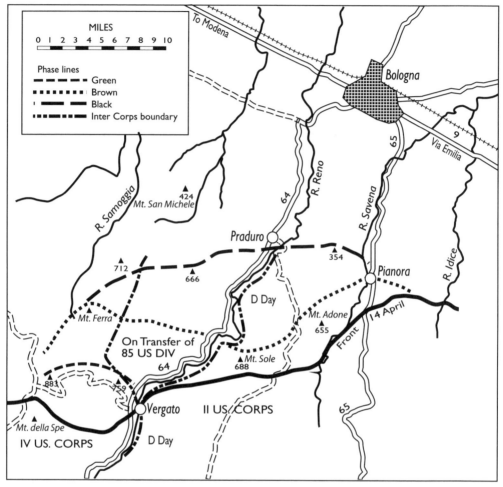

Map 6: Fifth Army plan for Operation CRAFTSMAN.

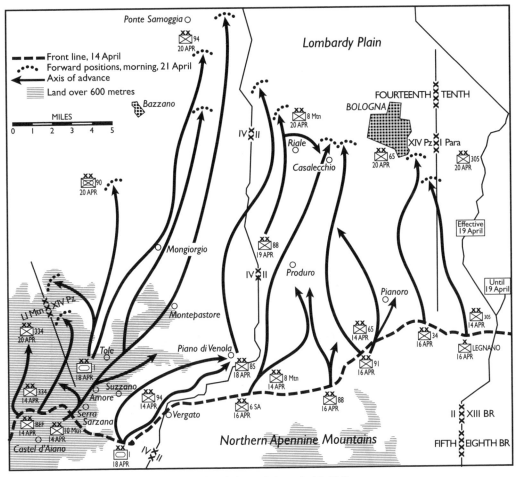

Map 7: Breakthrough into the Po Valley.

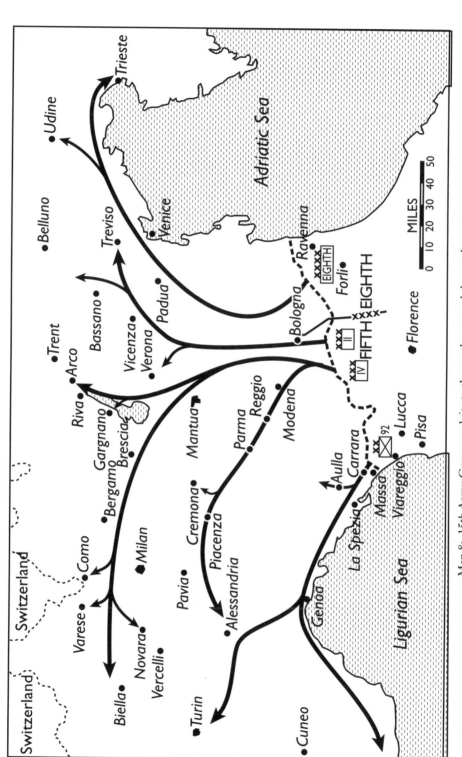

Map 8: 15th Army Group exploits to the north-east and the north-west.

Figures

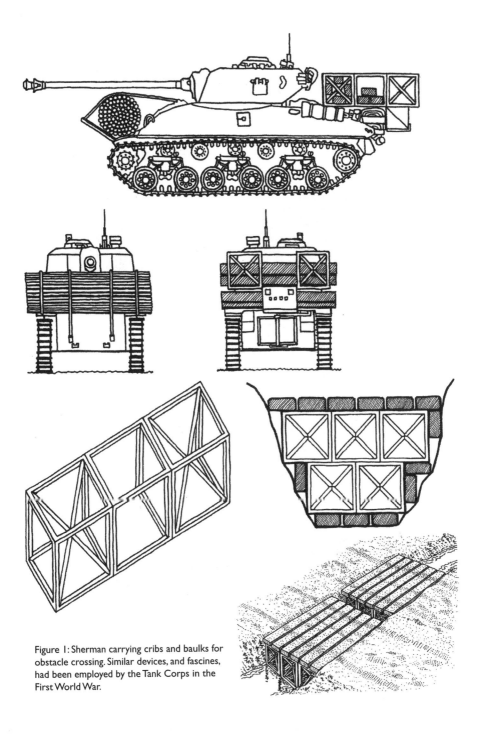

Figure 1: Sherman carrying cribs and baulks for obstacle crossing. Similar devices, and fascines, had been employed by the Tank Corps in the First World War.

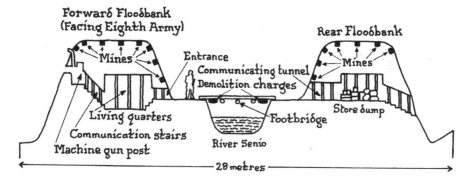

Figure 2: A cross section of the Senio defences showing how the floodbanks were adapted by both sides in the final winter of war.

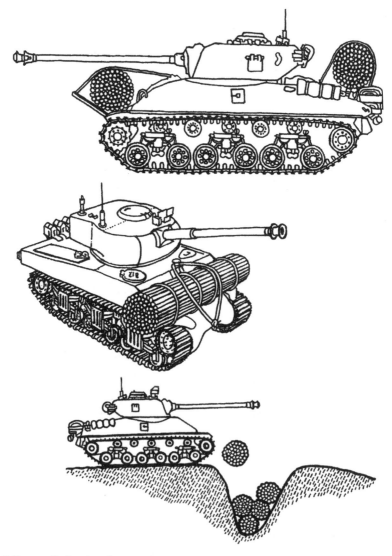

Figure 3: Sherman Firefly adapted to carry fascines so that it could cross waterways without the muzzle of its 17-pounder digging into the far bank.

Acknowledgements

Researching and writing a book such as this would not be possible without the help of many individuals and organizations over a number of years. I am indebted to all who helped with this book in any way and acknowledge their assistance with gratitude.

The campaign covered in this book is not well known. In fact, when I first thought of producing a study of it there was, to my knowledge, only one book dealing with this remarkable campaign; published in 1980, it was written by Brian Harpur, who was a participant. Having known many who fought in that final campaign in Italy, and having studied the Italian campaign over many years, I felt that it was time that a new book was produced.

When I put the idea of this book to Brigadier Henry Wilson, Publishing Manager at Pen and Sword, he was quick to give it his support. My first debt of thanks, therefore, is to Henry for his belief in this book, as well as his encouragement and support throughout the project. This is the seventh book he has commissioned from me and, over the years we have worked together, Henry has become a good friend whose advice and insight I value.

Pen and Sword authors are used to the high level of professionalism that the company puts into its books, but that does not mean that the production team should be taken for granted, and so I place on record my thanks to Matt Jones, especially for his patience and good humour, to Jon Wilkinson for his jacket design work and Mat Blurton of Mac Style for his design work on the book itself.

The term 'national treasure' is much used, and abused, but there is no doubt that, among the United Kingdom's true national treasures, the National Archives rank highly, as do the Imperial War Museum and the National Army Museum. All three have been invaluable sources of information for me. In particular, the National Archives holds the war diaries of the British formations and units that took part in Operation GRAPESHOT and, as ever, the staff members in the search and reading rooms were courteous, efficient and professional. The same may be said of the Imperial War Museum where I used both the Department of Printed Books and the Department of Documents. I must make a special mention of the late Rod Suddaby, who was always a mine of information and ever willing to help researchers. Sadly, Rod died on 26 June 2013, while this book was being researched. Although he had retired as Keeper of the Department of Documents, which was very much his creation, the results of his work at the IWM will be a lasting monument to him and a wonderful asset for generations of historians and researchers.

Bob O'Hara and his team of researchers at the National Archives have also been very helpful, providing information from war diaries and other sources when I have been unable to get to London. My visits to Kew are always enriched by meeting Bob and by our discussions on many topics over a cup of tea or coffee.

Libraries Northern Ireland also provided research material and I am especially indebted to the staffs of the Central Libraries in Belfast and Londonderry. The Linen Hall Library, Belfast, was also very helpful in tracking down and obtaining long out of print volumes that I needed for my research and I am grateful to the Linen Hall staff for their assistance. I would also like to thank the Library and Information Services staff at Headquarters 38 (Irish) Brigade, Lisburn, and the Prince Consort's Library at Aldershot for the loan of several difficult to find volumes of military history, especially those of the United States Fifth Army and a number of US Army divisions. In addition, Major (Retd) Noel Nash MBE deserves to be included in this list for his enthusiastic support and assistance.

Thanks are also due to Dr Andrzej Suchcitz, of the Polish Institute and Sikorski Museum, Prince's Gate, London, and Dr Tomasz Piesakowski for their assistance and advice. Dr Piesakowski is a veteran of the Italian campaign who served in the 13th Rifle Battalion in 5th Kresowa Division. His experiences as a prisoner of the Soviets were horrendous and gave me a fresh insight into the determination of the soldiers of General Anders' II Polish Corps.

I have long admired Lieutenant General Sir Richard McCreery, the final – and, in my estimation, finest – commander of Eighth Army and it was a delight to have the support and assistance of his son Bob, as well as that of his biographer, my fellow historian Richard Mead, whose work on Sir Richard, *The Last Great Cavalryman*, is a model of what the biography of a great commander should be. Particular thanks are, therefore, offered to Bob McCreery and the McCreery family and to Richard Mead.

Andy Shepherd and I have been acquainted for several years and I value his views on matters military. I asked Andy to read the various drafts of this book as it progressed and to provide his criticisms. His input was invaluable and has helped shape the final book, and for that I am very grateful. It was Andy Shepherd who put me in touch with Squadron Leader James Owens, Royal Australian Air Force, whose insights on aerial reconnaissance and deep knowledge of the subject were a great help. Jimmy transferred from the Royal Air Force to the Royal Australian Air Force as this book was in progress and I agree with Andy Shepherd's assessment that the UK's loss is Australia's gain.

There is no greater expert in the history of armoured warfare and of armoured fighting vehicles in the United Kingdom than David Fletcher MBE. Formerly the historian at the Tank Museum, Bovington, David is now enjoying a very busy retirement and is still more than willing to provide answers to obscure questions. As with several of my previous books, David was a willing and very useful ally in this work. He was able to tell me that the Churchill Ark bridging tank, although deployed in Normandy, does not appear to have been used in north-west Europe but there is no doubt that it was used extensively in northern Italy. However, neither of us has an answer to the question 'what does Twaby stand for?'

Ken Ford, another historian and friend, provided some of the photos used in the book and I am grateful to Ken for these. Lieutenant General Sir Philip Trousdell KBE CB, formerly Colonel of the Royal Irish Regiment, allowed me to use extracts from an account written by his father, the late Colonel P. J. C. Trousdell OBE, of his service in Italy, which included this campaign.

Mrs Barbara Downey, née Doherty, and her sisters kindly gave me a copy of a photograph of their late father, Lance Sergeant Rex Doherty MM, with permission to publish it in the book. Rex Doherty earned the Military Medal in March 1945 along the Senio line but, as with so many of those who had behaved gallantly, did not talk of what he had done. I am glad to be able to include a photograph of such a courageous and modest man. My thanks also go to Barbara's husband, Terry, a classmate and neighbour from boyhood days.

For information on the United States forces, I extend sincere thanks to Gordon L. Rottman, a US Army veteran and historian of considerable repute, for his willing assistance and preparedness to answer a wide range of questions on the forces serving in Italy during the Second World War. Thanks also to Ian Blackwell, fellow historian and Pen & Sword author, for his support and for providing me with additional material on the US forces and the Brazilian Expeditionary Force, as well as some of the NARA photos which appear in this book.

In Italy I had the benefit of advice and guidance from a number of individuals. Dottore Pier Paolo Battistelli and Professore Piero Crociani, both widely-published and much respected military historians, in Italian and English, assisted me in my research in the Italian military archives in Rome as well as providing much information from their own knowledge and publications. No question was too obscure for them and I am very grateful for all their help, and their hospitality in Rome. Pier Paolo put me in contact with Signor Piero Compagni and Signor Sanzio Guerrini of the Senio Line Museum in Alfonsine, both of whom also went out of their way to help me. *Tenente Colonnello* Filippo Cappellano, head of the *Archivo dell'Ufficio Storico dello Stato Maggiore Esercito*, himself an accomplished and published military historian, was a welcoming host at the archives and I thank him also. Since the *Archivo* is within a military establishment, non-Italians must apply for security clearance to visit and my thanks are due to Anita Krol of the UK Embassy in Rome for her efficient assistance in arranging that clearance.

My life-long friends Lucia Bedeschi-Radcliffe and Marina Radcliffe, and Marina's husband Paolo Petri, were welcoming hosts in Rome and have always shown me the greatest kindness on my visits to the Eternal City. To them I owe a very special word of thanks: *Mille grazie*.

Studying the ground over which a battle was fought is critical to understanding the battle. Being able to study it with serving soldiers who have a special interest in it is a privilege and one that I have enjoyed on several occasions in Italy and elsewhere. I had studied the ground over which Fifth Army fought and was planning a trip to north-eastern Italy to study Eighth Army's ground when I had a request from 2nd Battalion Royal Welsh to join them as historical advisor on a battlefield study over that very ground, from the Senio Line to Trieste, following 2nd New Zealand Division's advance. It was a privilege and an education to be able to do so, and I extend warm thanks to all those who took part in the study but especially to Lieutenant Colonel Chris Barry, Commanding Officer, and Major Owen Pritchard, who organized the study. I hope that all who took part found it useful. I certainly did. I should add that Piero Compagni and Sanzio Guerrini joined us on the Senio and had the Senio Line Museum in Alfonsine opened for us on a day that it would normally be closed, and their support and advice added value to the study. Piero also introduced us to the superb bi-lingual publication by Marco Belogi and Daniele Guglielmo, *Spring 1945 on the Italian Front*, an atlas of the campaign which is the subject of this book. So much can come out of studying the ground. My sincere thanks to all involved in that study.

The maps and figures in this book were prepared by Tim Webster, who has worked with me on other books and is well attuned to my foibles. My thanks to Tim for his excellent work.

Finally, I owe special thanks to my wife, Carol, my children Joanne, James and Catríona, and my grandchildren, Cíaran and Joshua, for their patience, support and understanding without which this book would not have materialized.

Richard Doherty
Co. Londonderry
July 2014

Prologue

As the drone of thousands of radial aero engines increased, 12 Anti-Aircraft Brigade's 3.7-inch heavy anti-aircraft guns opened fire. Their task? Not to engage the approaching aircraft, but to fire smoke shells marking a line in the sky, a bomb line, indicating the targets for the bombs nestling in the planes' bellies. The bombers were Boeing B-17 Flying Fortress and Consolidated B-24 Liberator four-engined machines of the Mediterranean Allied Strategic Air Forces (MASAF). Their targets were the front-line positions and troops of Colonel General von Vietinghoff-Scheel's German Army Group C.

Although some Axis aircraft were still operating in northern Italy, this was the last major use of British heavy anti-aircraft guns in the theatre, in

> a new and rather tedious mission: a line to mark the front for Allied bomber aircraft ... indicated by the shell-bursts of linear concentrations, fired at 15,000 feet at 30 second intervals. Since the programme might last as long as one-and-a-half hours of virtually continuous firing, special stocks of ammunition were needed as were arrangements to relieve detachments. The result was, naturally, overheated barrels and accelerated wear.[1]

The bombs dropped by those 825 heavy bombers totalled 1,511 tons, mostly 20lb fragmentation bombs but including some 100lb general-purpose bombs. Although few casualties ensued, telephone communications in the German forward area were destroyed. B-25 Mitchell tactical bombers also struck at targets close to the Santerno river. When the Fortresses, Liberators and Mitchells had completed their phase of the operation, fighter-bombers of the tactical air forces, the British Desert Air Force (strictly 1st Tactical Air Force, but the old DAF title, preferred by the airmen, continued in use) and the US XXII Tactical Air Command made the first of a series of attacks along the front. Allied artillery also pounded German positions as 15th Army Group prepared to launch Operation GRAPESHOT, its final attack in Italy, an offensive that would see Army Group C not simply defeated, but destroyed.

The offensive included both Eighth British and Fifth US Armies hitting hard at the enemy in one of the finest examples of manoeuvre warfare carried out by the western Allies. In the course of Operation GRAPESHOT the Allies gave the Germans a master class in such warfare. But, like all master classes, this owed its success to skilful planning, preparation, training, husbandry of matériel, co-operation between arms, and inspiring leadership. In the following chapters we shall examine these and other factors that led to victory in Italy.

Note

1. Routledge, *Anti-Aircraft Artillery*, p.284.

Chapter One

The story of Operation GRAPESHOT really begins long before the opening shots of Eighth Army's Operation BUCKLAND. Since GRAPESHOT marked the final phase of the Italian campaign, it is no exaggeration to say that its story began with the Allied landings in Italy in September 1943 following the brief Sicilian campaign in July and August of that year. Initially, the strategic objective of the Italian campaign had not been clear, and the Americans were not as committed to it as the British, who saw continuing the war in the Mediterranean as part of a process of closing the ring on Germany. This friction would touch the progress of the campaign and become a major problem on a number of occasions, affecting both the manpower committed and the supply of essential equipment to Italy. Indeed, friction between British and American politicians and planners would influence affairs in Italy until the end of the war.

The Germans did not try to hold on to the southern area of Italy, but their commander, Field Marshal Albert Kesselring, organized a fighting withdrawal to a defensive line across the peninsula: the Gustav Line. The most famous feature of the line was Monte Cassino, on which sat the historic monastery of Saint Benedict. During the cold, wet winter of 1943–44 the Allies' advance was stopped by the Gustav Line's determined defenders. Breakthrough attempts were made by the US Fifth Army, which included X British Corps, commanded by Major General Richard McCreery, but the Germans held the line tenaciously.

In January 1944 a plan to break through the Gustav Line and simultaneously land an assault force at Anzio behind the German lines resulted in heavy losses in the attacking forces along the Rapido river (on the Gustav Line) and at Anzio. At the latter, VI US Corps was sealed into its bridgehead by a German army. Further breakthrough attempts, including the bombing and destruction of the monastery in February and of the town of Cassino in March, also failed.

Not until May 1944, after Eighth Army had sidestepped across Italy to act in concert with Fifth, did the Allies pierce the Gustav Line. This was followed by the shorter Hitler Line battle before both armies set off in pursuit of the retreating Germans, while VI Corps broke out of the Anzio beachhead. Rome was liberated on 4 June, but Mark Clark, Fifth Army's commander, had chosen to ignore the orders of General Alexander, the Army Group commander, to roll up and destroy one or both of the German armies, thereby shortening the war in Italy. There followed a period of elation as Fifth and Eighth Armies pursued the Germans north of Rome, along the Tiber valley, to the shores of Lake Trasimene.

At Trasimene, where Hannibal had destroyed Flaminius's army in 214 BC, Kesselring's men made a determined stand that forced the Allied advance to a halt. But this was only a delaying action as Kesselring sought time while his engineers completed the Gothic Line defences. A further delaying action was fought along the Arno river before Fifth Army liberated Pisa and Eighth Army Florence. By late summer 1944, the German Tenth and Fourteenth Armies stood ready for the Allies along the Green, or Gothic, Line.

Alexander's plan to break through the Gothic Line and onto the plain of Lombardy and the Po valley was intended to bring the war in Italy to an end in 1944. That it did not succeed was due to several factors. Principal among those was the focusing of Allied strategic attention on the campaign in north-west Europe, which led to a reduction of Fifth Army's strength to provide formations for a landing in southern France, Operation DRAGOON, including the French Expeditionary Corps, with its skilled mountain fighters, as well as several US formations. Thus Alexander was deprived of the superiority in numbers required for a successful offensive, especially one in such difficult terrain. Even so, he came close to success, using a deception plan that fooled the Germans about the timing and location of each army's attacks. On this occasion, the differing strategic vision of British and American planners had a baleful influence on the campaign. Had the French Expeditionary Corps been available for Operation OLIVE it could have played a major role in achieving Alexander's objectives.

But there was no French Expeditionary Corps and no breakthrough onto the northern plain. Although battered badly, the Germans maintained their defensive cohesion. Alexander's Operation OLIVE may have splintered and broken the door of those defences, but it had not smashed it down. Once again, Allied armies were committed to difficult fighting in the Apennines. Tantalizingly, they could look down on their objective, the flat lands of northern Italy where defence would be more difficult. They were not to reach that land in 1944.

Operation OLIVE began on 25 August and Eighth Army, which opened the assault, made good progress initially. However, the Germans were quick to move reinforcements – three divisions, one each of infantry, panzers and panzer grenadiers – to the threatened sector. In turn, the deployment of those three divisions against Eighth Army played into Alexander's hand. Alex had planned a two-pronged attack with Fifth Army following up Eighth's right hook with a left hook. In fact, German redeployment allowed the initial phase of Fifth Army's advance to be carried out against little resistance as Lemelsen's Fourteenth Army was pulled back from its original positions, allowing Fifth Army's leading elements to move easily 'as if on autumn manoeuvres through countryside dotted with ochre-coloured villages set amid ripening grain fields, orchards and vineyards'.[1]

The British *Official History* suggests that OLIVE ended on 21 September as Eighth Army crossed the Marécchia river in heavy rain. Jackson, the official historian, wrote that Eighth Army had reached its 'promised land', but was to find mud rather than the milk of good tank 'going' and frustration rather than the honey of rapid exploitation. Leese could rightly claim in his report, written immediately after the offensive on 26 September that [Eighth] Army's achievement was 'a great one'. It had crossed the Apennines secretly and on time. It had gate-crashed 'the powerful Gothic Line defences at very small expense and before the enemy was ready'. Moreover, it had defeated eleven German divisions in sustained battle and had broken into the plains of the Romagna.[2]

Four days after writing his report, Lieutenant General Sir Oliver Leese, who had succeeded Montgomery as Eighth Army commander on 1 January 1944, promoted to command an army group in South East Asia, handed over command of Eighth Army to Lieutenant General Sir Richard McCreery. Previously commander of X Corps, McCreery had fought in Italy since the corps landed at Salerno as part of Fifth Army in September 1943. At the time of this handover, no official announcement was made in London. Not until a month later did the British public learn that Leese had departed and that McCreery was his successor. By the time the news was made public, McCreery had already visited every formation in Eighth Army and many of their units. His appointment was welcomed by many who had served with him. Gerald Templer, formerly one of his divisional commanders who was recovering from injury in England, wrote to congratulate him, reminding him that he (Templer) had predicted that McCreery would become an army commander, while General Sir Claude Auchinleck, the C-in-C, India, who had sacked McCreery in North Africa, also wrote to say that he believed Eighth Army 'could not be in better hands'.[3]

Eighth Army's change of command was not the only one at this time. On the other side, concern was being expressed by Kesselring and von Vietinghoff about the leadership and management of I Fallschirmjäger Corps whose commander, General Schlemm, a Luftwaffe officer, was believed to have mishandled some infantry divisions under his command, including 44th, 98th and 334th. Following visits to 98th and 334th Divisions, von Vietinghoff told Kesselring that he believed that they 'had been burnt up too quickly by an unapproachable and ruthless Corps Commander, who had insisted that newly-arrived troops mount counter-attacks before they had time to settle down'. Nor did Schlemm demonstrate the sensitivity demanded by the prevailing tactical situation. So it was that, on 20 October, Schlemm was informed that Göring was transferring him to command a new fallschirmjäger corps in north-west Europe. His place as commander of the fallschirmjäger corps in Italy was to be taken by Richard Heidrich, previously commander of 1st Fallschirmjäger Division.[4] On 23 October Kesselring himself was removed from the picture when he was injured seriously as his staff car collided with a heavy artillery piece; he was out of action for several months and General von Vietinghoff took command of Army Group C in his absence.[5]

In the United States the Head of the UK Military Mission, Field Marshal Sir John Dill, was in the final stages of the disease that would claim his life on 4 November. With Dill's death came further change in the Mediterranean. Churchill decided to send General Wilson, Supreme Allied Commander in the theatre, to Washington to succeed Dill, and to promote Alexander to field marshal (backdated to 4 June, the date of the liberation of Rome, to maintain his seniority over Montgomery in the Army List, the latter having been promoted on 1 September. Wilson also became a field marshal, on 1 January 1945). Alexander was appointed to Wilson's old job, leaving a vacancy at the head of the army group in Italy, to which Mark Clark was promoted.[6] News of his new appointment was conveyed to Clark at Fifth Army HQ at dawn on Thursday 25 November, Thanksgiving Day, in a message delivered by his British signals officer. Since the latter would only come on such an errant at that hour if the matter were important, Clark was prepared for 'trouble' but was pleasantly surprised to see a smile on the signals officer's face. The message came from Churchill and read:

> It gives me the greatest pleasure to tell you that the President and his military advisers regard it as a compliment that His Majesty's Government should wish to have you command the 15th Group of Armies under General Alexander, who becomes Supreme Commander owing to the appointment of General Wilson to succeed Sir John Dill in Washington. I am sure we could not be placing our troops, who form the large majority of your command, in better hands, and that your friendship, of which you told me, with General Alexander will be at once smooth and propel the course of operations.[7]

Churchill had been impressed with Clark on first meeting him, describing him as the 'American Eagle'. He seems to have been unaware of Clark's antipathy towards the British troops under his command, a factor influencing his thinking as he propelled 'the course of operations'. However, Clark's prejudice would be offset by the close co-operation and trust between his army commanders.

Clark's role as commander of Fifth Army was assumed by Lieutenant General Lucian King Truscott Jr, an appointment made by the US authorities on Alexander's recommendation. Truscott had commanded VI Corps at Anzio, impressing Alexander considerably. Fifth Army's official history suggests that Truscott 'had been slated to command Fifteenth Army before his return to Fifth Army in Italy'.[8] In becoming the new army commander, Truscott was promoted over both corps commanders in Fifth Army, Geoffrey Keyes and Willis D. Crittenberger, who had been senior to him. Truscott had much in common with McCreery: both were cavalrymen and shared a sense for the battlefield that would be demonstrated to good effect in the months ahead.

With a new command team in place in Italy, this is an appropriate point to examine the principal characters in the drama to be staged in northern Italy in April 1945 as Operation GRAPESHOT: Alexander, Clark, McCreery and Truscott.

Sir Harold Alexander, one of Britain's best-known generals, was Churchill's favourite commander. Commissioned in the Irish Guards, he had served with distinction throughout the Great War, gaining an outstanding reputation for courage and rising to command a brigade. His star continued to rise after the war, as he saw considerable active service in several theatres. A divisional commander at the outbreak of the Second World War, he took 1st Division to France in the British Expeditionary Force and commanded with such competence that he was promoted to lead I Corps in the final days of the campaign. His reputation was probably sealed in Churchill's eyes when he ensured that he was the last member of I Corps to leave the beaches at Dunkirk, even cruising off the beaches and through the harbour in a small motorboat calling through a loudspeaker 'Is anyone there?' in both English and French. He became a national hero, and subsequently took over Southern Command. Churchill sent him to Burma to oversee the British retreat to India and, in August 1942, selected him to succeed Auchinleck as C–in–C, Middle East.

Alex, as he was known, played a critical role in the final battle of El Alamein and the campaign in Tunisia, by which time he was commanding 18 Army Group. Continuing as an army group commander, now 15 Army Group, in the Sicilian campaign, he had two highly egotistical army commanders to deal with, Montgomery of Eighth Army and Patton of Seventh US Army. Alexander remained as the army group commander throughout the Italian campaign and again had two thrusting egos with which to deal as army commanders, Montgomery, until the end of December 1943, and Clark, commanding Fifth Army. Although Alex supported Clark when the latter seemed to lose his confidence at Salerno, Clark disobeyed Alexander's orders as the Allies broke through the Gustav Line and out of the Anzio beachhead by making Rome his objective rather than the destruction of one or both of the German armies. Clark continued testing Alexander's undoubted skills of diplomacy until the end of the campaign. Those skills were needed to command a coalition force with personnel from over twenty different nations. In this, Alexander found his métier and was arguably the finest man for that role.[9]

Mark Wayne Clark, son of an officer in the United States Army, entered West Point in 1913. Commissioned four years later, he went to France with 11th Infantry Regiment of 5th Division, but was wounded seriously on his first day in the line. He recovered but saw no further action. For the ambitious Clark this was a setback, but he remained in the army after the war, earning a reputation for efficient administration and good judgement. Having attended the Command and General Staff College at Fort Leavenworth, he was also marked out for advancement in the event of the United States going to war; the rapid expansion that would be called for in such circumstances needed officers with Clark's staff training. And so it turned out. As a staff officer of 3rd Infantry Division he came to the attention of the commander of that division's 5 Brigade, Brigadier General George Marshall, later to become Chief of Staff of the US Army.

When the Japanese attack on Pearl Harbor thrust America into the war, Clark was a brigadier general, having leapfrogged several officers with more service. Further promotion came in 1942 when he was raised to major general, appointed to command II Corps and then became Deputy Supreme Commander, Allied Force Headquarters, London. In that role he undertook a secret mission by submarine to Algeria to discuss the planned Allied invasion of French north-west Africa, and continued negotiating with the Vichy French after the Operation TORCH landings on 8 November 1942. Promoted to lieutenant general on 11 November, eleven days later he signed an agreement with Admiral François Darlan, the Vichy leader recognized by the Allies as political head of French North-West Africa. (Darlan was assassinated by an anti-Vichy gunman on Christmas Eve 1942.)

On 4 January 1943 Lieutenant General Clark was appointed to command the newly-created Fifth Army, which he led into action at Salerno in Operation AVALANCHE in September and in the advance up the Italian peninsula. His relations with his British counterparts, Montgomery and, later, Oliver Leese, were strained at times and he disliked McCreery, who commanded the British X Corps in Fifth Army. With the liberation of Rome in June 1944 he displayed his penchant for publicity; he was always keen to portray Fifth Army as 'General Clark's Fifth Army'. As we shall see, when appointed to command 15th Army Group, he continued to regard McCreery and Eighth Army with disdain, considering that Fifth Army should take the main role in the spring offensive.[10]

Sir Richard McCreery was commissioned in 12th (The Prince of Wales's Royal) Lancers in 1915 and earned the Military Cross commanding his troop on 9 November 1918, two days before the war ended. His achievement was all the more remarkable since he had been wounded so seriously in April 1917 that it was feared that he might lose his right leg. However, surgeons were able to save his leg, although not the toes of his right foot. Thereafter, he walked with a pronounced gait. Between the wars, he rose to command his regiment, attended Staff College and was an enthusiast for mechanization, becoming familiar with the problems of mechanized warfare in a desert setting when 12th Royal Lancers went to Egypt in 1936.

McCreery crossed to France with the BEF in 1939 as GSO I of Alexander's 1st Division; his relationship with Alex was good and teamwork in the divisional headquarters was excellent. In January 1940 McCreery was promoted to command 2 Armoured Brigade in 1st Armoured Division, although the division was still in Britain and did not arrive in France until May 1940. However, McCreery led 2 Armoured Brigade in action and earned an excellent reputation, being appointed DSO for his leadership of his brigade's rearguard action between the Somme and Seine rivers, fought in very difficult circumstances. Back in Britain, he was promoted major general and became GOC 8th Armoured Division, which he led and trained to a very high standard. Subsequently, he was posted to Egypt and, in March 1942, became General Auchinleck's principal adviser on armoured warfare. Although the two were later not to see eye to eye on the organization of armoured formations, as a result of which Auchinleck removed McCreery, between them they ensured that Eighth Army had sufficient tanks to meet Rommel's advance after the fall of Tobruk and to fight Panzerarmee Afrika to a standstill along the El Alamein line in July 1942.

When Alexander succeeded Auchinleck in August 1942 he appointed McCreery as his chief of staff. The team that had inspired 1st Division was once again in operation. It was McCreery's suggestion that led to Montgomery recasting his break-in plan for Operation SUPERCHARGE in November, although, typically, Monty claimed it as his own idea. When Brian Horrocks was wounded in June 1943, McCreery succeeded him as commander of X Corps, which was to be an assault formation, under command of Fifth US Army, for the Salerno landings. Throughout the Italian campaign, and despite the friction of working under Clark's command, McCreery's courage and leadership had few equals, so much so that he was chosen to succeed Leese as commander of Eighth Army.[11] His handling of the aftermath of the Operation OLIVE offensive earned much admiration and was one of the factors inspiring John Strawson, himself a veteran of the Italian campaign, to describe McCreery as 'the greatest cavalry soldier of his generation and at the same time that rare coalition of a brilliant staff officer and higher commander'.[12]

Lucian King Truscott Jr holds a unique place in the history of the United States Army as the only officer to command a regiment, division, corps and army in the Second World War. He joined the army in 1917, after the United States declared war on Germany, taking advantage of an officer training programme that crammed into three months what West Point did in four years. Not surprisingly, such officers were dubbed 'ninety-day wonders'. Truscott was commissioned into the cavalry and assigned to the 17th Cavalry, with whom he served in the United States and Hawaii, thus not seeing any combat service. Nonetheless, he proved an outstanding soldier and was promoted rapidly in what was a small army (in 1932 the US Army numbered only 119,913 enlisted men). A captain in 1920, he did not achieve his majority until 1935, the result of the army being so small, and became a lieutenant colonel in 1940. Between 1925 and 1931 he was, first, a student and, later, an instructor at the Cavalry School; then followed six years in the same pattern at the Command and General Staff College.

Lieutenant Colonel Truscott came to the attention of Colonel Dwight D. Eisenhower when he joined IX Corps as assistant G 3, impressing Eisenhower so much that the latter thereafter selected him for important appointments. In May 1942 he was promoted brigadier general and assigned to the British Combined Operations HQ. So inspired was Truscott by the British Army commando units (there were, as yet, no Royal Marine commandos) that he created a US Army equivalent, which he styled 'Rangers', the first of whom fought at Dieppe in Operation JUBILEE in August 1942. Three months later, Major General Truscott commanded the force that took Fort Lyautey in French Morocco and, during the subsequent Tunisian campaign, served as Eisenhower's deputy with responsibility for training, before taking command of 3rd Infantry Division in March 1943.

Truscott's leadership and training made 3rd Division one of the most outstanding US Army formations of the war. He trained his soldiers to move fast, instigating the famous 'Truscott Trot' that emulated Confederate General Stonewall Jackson's 'foot cavalry' of the American Civil War. The first demonstration of the division's speed came in the Sicilian campaign when Truscott informed his combat team commanders that the division would advance to Palermo in five days, and be the first Allied troops to arrive there. Palermo was about a hundred miles away, with the first forty over mountains rising to over 4,000 feet and the entire journey on twisting roads over steep gradients and with many bridges that the enemy might demolish. The final stretch was also over the range of hills enfolding Palermo. Truscott's target was achieved. Palermo fell to US troops. In 1944, when VI US Corps' commander in Anzio, Major General John P. Lucas, was relieved, Truscott succeeded him and proved an inspiration to American and British soldiers alike. He led the corps' advance from Anzio and, had Clark not redirected VI Corps, breaking Alexander's orders in so doing, his men might have trapped large numbers of retreating Germans and shortened the war in Italy.

In August 1944 Truscott's corps took part in Operation DRAGOON, the landings of southern France. Once again VI Corps moved rapidly, this time up the Rhône valley. After his promotion to lieutenant general in September, Truscott handed over command of VI Corps and, although nominated to command Fifteenth Army, was appointed to succeed Clark as Fifth Army commander. When he left VI Corps it had already reached Alsace, having pushed into the fortified Vosges mountains.[13]

While all these changes were taking place, fighting continued as both Allied armies attempted to push their way onto the plain. In Fifth Army's eastern sector, four US divisions, the veteran 34th, plus 85th, 88th and 91st (forming II Corps), were pushing slowly through the Apennines, at heavy cost in casualties, towards Bologna. From 1 to 16 October, they sustained 5,699 casualties and took 3,666 German prisoners, but were only eight and a half miles closer to their objective. With total US casualties for the period at 6,329, it was clear that II Corps could not continue suffering such a drain of manpower.[14] Also involved in the struggles in the Apennines was XIII British Corps, temporarily under Fifth Army command. XIII Corps, too, had a difficult time and sustained heavy casualties, including the first soldiers to suffer from exposure as autumn turned to winter in the mountains.

While Fifth Army was thus engaged in the Apennines, Eighth Army was fighting across a series of river obstacles. On taking command, McCreery was ordered by Alexander to continue the advance on the axis of the Via Emilia, Highway 9, which runs in a straight line from Rímini to Bologna through Forlí and Faenza (the longest stretch of straight road in Europe). Unlike Leese, however, McCreery adopted tactics more suited to the terrain in the wettest time of the year in Italy. Employing his Indian soldiers' mountain-fighting skills to infiltrate the higher reaches of the river obstacles, he used the topography to advantage rather than fighting against the grain of the country. Regrouping his forces also ensured steady progress. By the end of October McCreery had taken his command onto the flat lands of the Romagna. However, he had decided that the commander of I Canadian Corps, General E. L. M. 'Tommy' Burns, was 'not thrusting enough' and relieved him, placing Charles Foulkes, GOC of 2nd Canadian Division in north-west Europe, in command. This change of leader improved morale in the Canadian Corps; Burns was not an inspiring commander.[15]

Eighth Army's advance continued into November, as McCreery had no wish to establish static positions that might tempt his soldiers to adopt defensive attitudes.

Forlí was liberated and the van of the army thrust towards Faenza, which Hitler had ordered to be defended at all costs. With I Canadian Corps being rested before returning to action in December, most fighting fell to V Corps and II Polish Corps. When the Canadians returned to operations, three corps (X Corps was non-operational since its tactical headquarters had gone to Greece) became available and three attacks were launched: I Canadian targeted Ravenna in Operation CHUCKLE, V Corps Faenza, and II Polish flanked through the hills on V Corps' left. All were successful. On 4 December the Germans abandoned Ravenna and were driven from Faenza on the 16th. Five days later they were also evicted from Bagnacavallo, some two miles north-east of Faenza. Thus a large German salient south of the Senio had been eliminated (another remained but would be dealt with in January), ending Eighth Army's last significant advance in 1944. McCreery's men were across the Lamone river on a wide front, but their foe had settled into a new defensive line along the Senio.[16]

In Fifth Army General Truscott assumed command on 16 December after a farewell ceremony for Clark at Army HQ.[17] This was the day on which the Germans launched their counter-offensive in the Ardennes, popularly known as the battle of the Bulge, and Clark was concerned that there could be a parallel attack in Italy, especially as Intelligence had indicated a build-up of enemy forces facing Fifth Army's lightly-held western sector. The Ardennes offensive suggested possible counter-attacks on other fronts, with the German build-up opposite Fifth Army's western sector perceived as indicating that an assault was planned in the Serchio valley, thereby threatening the army's principal logistics base and port at Livorno, or Leghorn.

The front line in the Serchio valley was only twenty miles north of Lucca, a major supply centre for Fifth Army, and no more than forty-five from Livorno. Two brigades, 19 and 21, of 8th Indian Division, resting near Lucca, were ordered to the Serchio valley 'in case of need'.[18] Other reinforcements included two regimental combat teams (RCTs) of 85th Infantry Division, as well as 'some additional artillery and tank battalions' (five artillery and two tank battalions and, from II Corps, a chemical battalion with 4.2-inch mortars), which were deployed to the coast; 1st Armored Division was ordered to Lucca and placed in army reserve. These reinforcements were still moving into position when the Germans struck on 26 December.[19]

The German offensive, Operation WINTERGEWITTER (Winter Storm), took the form of a number of attacks by some half-dozen battalion-sized battlegroups with limited objectives. Two American battalions, 1/370th Infantry Regiment and 2/366th Infantry, took the brunt of the attacks and broke. Both units were composed of black soldiers, whose morale was low due to systemic racial prejudice in the American forces, reflecting American society; 370th Infantry Regiment was part of 92nd Infantry Division, referred to at the time as 92nd (Negro) Division, while 366th Regiment was attached to that division between late-November 1944 and late-February 1945 (it was disbanded in March 1945). General Crittenberger, to whom Truscott had given responsibility for the coastal sector, deployed 19 and 21 Indian Brigades to stop the Germans, which they did effectively. Having blocked the attack, the Indians took the offensive, with close air support from fighter-bombers of XXII Tactical Air Command, and, by the 30th, had restored the situation, taking back the ground lost to the enemy. Of the offensive Truscott wrote:

> It was fortunate that the Germans did not make any greater effort in the Serchio valley than they did. Elements of four German divisions had been identified in these actions, but none of them involved more than combat groups with limited objectives. It seems likely the Germans were making a reconnaissance in force which they might have exploited if additional troops had not been encountered there. We were relieved that this was so, for a major attack could have been embarrassing or even gravely dangerous.[20]

The acting commander of Fourteenth Army, General von Tippelskirch, had intended the attack as a morale booster for his troops by proving that they could still launch a successful offensive while providing a diversion against any renewal of the American drive on Bologna. Mussolini, now leader of the Italian Social Republic, based at Salò on Lake Garda, had sought a more powerful attack, employing two Italian and two German divisions, but failed to have his way.[21]

In January 1945 the Canadians went into action for the last time with Eighth Army. Although the Allied armies had been ordered to adopt a stance of offensive defence, McCreery interpreted that as permitting operations to improve his positions for the intended spring offensive. This allowed him to plan the elimination of the remaining German lodgements south and east of the Senio, something he believed should be done as soon as possible. The weather was on Eighth Army's side with a hard frost coming down as 1944 gave way to 1945, making the ground firm enough for armour to operate. I Canadian Corps attacked on 2 January and, over five days, advanced ten miles to gain the southern shore of Lake Comácchio and the base of the spit separating the lake from the Adriatic. Although the Germans counter-attacked, their efforts came to nothing under heavy fire from the Perth Regiment and elements of an ad hoc force, formed around HQ 9 Armoured Brigade, holding the coastal sector, plus attacks by Desert Air Force aircraft. Almost a thousand Germans were lost to that fire, and air strikes, before their commanders called off the counter-attack.[22]

South-east of Bagnacavallo and north of Faenza the Canadians cleared another German salient in conjunction with 56th (London) Division. While 2 Canadian Brigade took Granarolo on the night of the 3rd, the Londoners attacked from the left. Operation CYGNET included the first use of Kangaroo armoured personnel carriers (APCs) in Italy as a battlegroup of 10th Royal Hussars, 2nd Royal Tanks and 2/6th Queen's advanced.[23] The Kangaroos, improvised by removing the turrets from Canadian Ram or American Sherman tanks, or the armament from M7 Priest self-propelled howitzers, carried the Queensmen, who were thus able to keep pace with the armour; the war diary of 2/6th Queen's refers to the Kangaroos as 'Sherman carriers'.[24] Fifty-three Kangaroos, manned by 4th Hussars, deployed and played a significant part in the operation's success. Such was the speed with which the infantry moved that the Germans were taken by surprise and many were soon being ferried back under escort in the Kangaroos to 56th Division's rear lines. For the infantry the APCs provided four important advantages: 'protection while on the move; better communication, especially with the gun tanks; carrying capacity for ammunition and personal kit; and a feeling that, at last, something had been done to help them in their hard, tiring and dangerous work.'[25] The surprise achieved by CYGNET was such that 11th (HAC) Regiment RHA noted that it was 'supported by a small fireplan due to limited ammunition'.[26] While artillery support may have been small, the Desert Air Force, taking advantage of favourable weather conditions, flew 1,100 sorties in support.[27]

McCreery was an enthusiastic proponent of the Kangaroo, first used by the Canadians in north-west Europe. However, the commander of Second British Army, General Sir Miles Dempsey, had turned down a proposal from Lieutenant General Sir Richard O'Connor, VIII Corps' commander, to introduce them into British service as early as July 1944.[28] No such prejudice was shown in Eighth Army; Kangaroos played a critical part in operations in 1945.

Having completed the elimination of these salients, Eighth Army was positioned to strike towards Ferrara and Bologna, a manoeuvre that would cut the German line of retreat to the Po. With the terrain offering more opportunities for mobile warfare, and APCs affording the infantry greater mobility and flexibility, the destruction of the German armies in Italy became a more realistic proposition.

On 1 January 1945 Fifth Army's 'front lines were still essentially the same as on 26 October' and adverse weather had hindered attempts to advance towards Bologna.[29] Although constrained by the same 'offensive defence' policy as McCreery, Truscott considered plans to advance on Bologna along either Highways 64 or 65. In doing so, he was under pressure from Clark who was still determined to take Bologna. On Highway 64, leading elements of Fifth Army were over twenty miles from the city, while on Highway 65 they were within a dozen miles of it:

> The terrain favoured an advance down Highway 65; the road net was the best in the Army sector; and only the bristling array of defences which the Germans had prepared on all the dominating ground along the highway could be counted as a serious disadvantage.[30]

Highway 64 would take an advancing force through a less well-fortified area, 'held out the possibility of a close envelopment of Bologna from the northwest and afforded means of supplying five divisions'. However, safe use of the road could be guaranteed only by securing the long north-running ridge line from Monte Belvedere to Monte Pigna and Monte Pero. As with Highway 65, the Monte Sole area 'would have to be captured to permit extensive advance down Highway 64'.[31]

Clark's plan for the capture of Bologna, the PIANORO plan, was almost an obsession, and Truscott had come 'to learn that General Clark was very sensitive to any criticisms or suggestions pertaining to [it].'[32] However, realizing that the Allied ammunition shortage left Fifth Army with a reserve for no more than fifteen days of offensive operations, Truscott recommended that the attack be cancelled and 'that we contain the enemy on our front with limited-objective attacks involving not more than a division at any one time'.[33] Reluctantly, Clark accepted that there should be no major offensive until the ammunition situation improved; Field Marshal Alexander agreed that the PIANORO attack should be cancelled.[34]

Approval was granted, however, for two limited-objective divisional-strength attacks on Fifth Army's front, one by '92nd Infantry Division in the coastal sector to test further the battleworthiness of the colored troops, the other in the IV Corps sector to capture Mt Belvedere and improve our positions west of Highway 64'.[35] As approval was being given for these operations it was also decided that XIII British Corps would revert to Eighth Army command, although 6th South African Armoured Division was to remain under Fifth Army command.

Fifth Army's history indicates that the operation undertaken by 92nd Division was intended to open up Highway 64 and keep the enemy 'under pressure and off balance'.[36] The attack began on 4 February with a series of drives in the Serchio valley and on the coastal plain. At first, operations in the valley made some gains against the Italian garrison, but counter-attacks by German troops forced the attacking 365th and 366th Regiments back almost to their start lines by the 11th. On 8 February both 370th and 371st, supported by two tank battalions, attacked along the coast but sustained many casualties against stout resistance. By the 11th this attack had also petered out. In neither case was the enemy forced to commit other than local reserves. 'From the conduct of the attack our command was forced to conclude that the troops of the 92nd Division could not be utilized in a serious offensive.'[37]

The second limited-objective offensive, undertaken by the recently arrived 10th Mountain and 1st Brazilian Divisions, met with much more success. Launched on the right flank of IV Corps, west of Highway 64, this 'reflected the preliminary planning for the spring offensive'.[38] Facing 10th Mountain Division was a daunting task: clearing about eight miles of high ground dominating the upper reaches of Highway 64, from opposite Porretta to points south-west of Vergato. On 18 February the attack began with men of 10th Mountain scaling the near-vertical 1,500-feet Serrasiccia-Campiano cliff; by the 25th the division had taken Monte Belvedere (3,737 feet) and Monte della Toraccia in what Fifth Army's historian described as 'a dashing attack' that inflicted heavy losses on 232nd Grenadier Division. On the right, the Brazilians took the third major mountain in the area, Monte Castello. Both formations pushed on north-eastwards in a second phase, clearing the ground from Monte Grande d'Aiano to Castelnuovo. Once again, the defenders, 114th Jäger Division, suffered heavily, their casualties including about 1,200 men taken prisoner.[39]

By 7 March Fifth Army had gained almost all the ground included in the list of limited objectives. That momentum could have been continued, but Truscott decided that further advances might overextend the exposed flank and draw enemy attention to the sector, thereby prompting the Germans to increase the fortified positions west of Highway 64. The army's salient had been widened, with IV Corps' right flank almost abreast of II Corps' left. Consolidation now took place along ridges and peaks that would serve as excellent jumping-off positions for the spring offensive, especially as the ground in front of Fifth Army, although rugged, sloped gradually down to the plain of the Po, some twenty miles away. At this time, the Germans also returned to reserve 29th Panzer Grenadier Division, which had been brought forward to face any further American attack.[40]

For Fifth Army the rest of the month was spent regrouping in readiness for action when spring arrived. Its front line was much as it had been at the end of October, except where 10th Mountain and the Brazilians had taken ground from the Germans. With XIII Corps returning to Eighth Army command, the length of front held by Fifth Army was reduced to less than a hundred 'actual ground miles'.[41]

Notes

1. Fisher, *Cassino to the Alps*, p.319.
2. Jackson, *Victory in the Mediterranean*, Pt III, pp.299–300.
3. Mead, *The Last Great Cavalryman*, pp.161–2.
4. Jackson, *Victory in the Mediterranean*, Pt II, p.392.
5. Ibid., p.422.
6. Jackson, *Victory in the Mediterranean*, Pt III, pp.69–70.
7. Clark, *Calculated Risk*, p.380.
8. Starr, *From Salerno to the Alps*, p.369.
9. Summarized from: Doherty, *Ireland's Generals in the Second World War*, pp. 48–61; Nicolson, *Alex*; & Alexander, *Memoirs*.
10. Summarized from: Clark, *Calculated Risk*; & Blumenson, *Mark Clark*.
11. Summarized from *Mead*, op. cit.
12. Strawson, *The Italian Campaign*, pp.183–4.
13. Summarized from: Jeffers, *General Lucian Truscott's Path to Victory* & Truscott, *Command Decisions*.
14. Starr, p.363
15. Mead, pp. 162–3.
16. Jackson, Pt III, pp. 114–17; Blaxland, *Alexander's Generals*, p. 231; Doherty, *Eighth Army in Italy*, p.167.
17. Truscott, p.453.
18. Ibid., p.455.
19. Ibid.
20. Ibid.
21. Jackson, Pt III, p.127; Fisher, pp.408–10.
22. Molony, *Victory in the Mediterranean*, Vol. VI, Pt I, pp.448–9.
23. Jackson, Pt III, p.127.
24. NA, WO170/5060, war diary, 2/6 Queen's, 1945.
25. Jackson, op. cit., p.58.
26. NA, WO170/4831, war diary, 11 (HAC) RHA, 1945.
27. Jackson, p.157.
28. Baynes, *The Forgotten Victor*, pp.204–5. The Kangaroo APC was eventually adopted by Second Army.
29. Starr, p.371.
30. Ibid., p.382.

31. Ibid.
32. Truscott, p. 451.
33. Ibid., p.456.
34. Ibid.
35. Ibid., p.456.
36. Starr, p.383.
37. Ibid., p.383.
38. Ibid.
39. Ibid.
40. Ibid., p.384.
41. Ibid.

Chapter Two

The winter months had seen much activity away from the front lines: Fifth and Eighth armies, having suffered heavily in the autumn fighting, needed rebuilding. Manpower shortages, however, threatened that process as formations were withdrawn from Italy for service elsewhere. This problem was as old as the Italian campaign itself: some original formations, British and American, had only been 'on loan' for the initial phase before moving to the UK at the behest of the strategic planners. From Eighth Army, 7th Armoured Division had been repatriated after a brief spell on the Italian mainland, while 50th (Northumbrian) and 51st (Highland) Divisions had gone back after the Sicilian campaign. The Americans lost 82nd Airborne Division to north-west Europe after the fighting at Salerno.

The process continued during the campaign as the strategic planners' attention focused more and more on north-west Europe. Fifth Army had been reinforced by General Juin's French Expeditionary Corps (*Corps expéditionnaire français*), a formation whose mountain-fighting skills proved invaluable in breaking the Gustav Line; but the Allied high command decided that the corps should be transferred to a new Franco-American army for Operation ANVIL, the landings in southern France. Originally planned to coincide with Operation OVERLORD on 6 June 1944, this was delayed until 15 August and renamed DRAGOON. The loss of Juin's corps left Fifth Army short of manpower, especially for the fighting in the Gothic Line and the struggle to break out of the Apennines onto the northern plain. As a result, XIII British Corps was transferred to Clark's command.

When General Marshall, returning from the Yalta conference, visited 15th Army Group HQ in Florence in February 1945, he made it clear that American commanders regarded Italy as a secondary theatre. However, he emphasized that the armies there should maintain a posture that would ensure as many German divisions as possible being retained in Italy rather than being transferred to fight either the Red Army or the western Allies.[1] That posture would have to be maintained with existing forces: no new formations were available to reinforce 15th Army Group. Any new formations that might become available would go to north-west Europe.

Although Truscott lost XIII Corps on 18 January on its return to Eighth Army, he had received 10th Mountain Division, which had arrived in Italy in late-December with over 14,000 men. The penultimate US division to arrive in Europe, 10th Mountain began deploying from 8 January, under command of IV Corps.[2] Also under Fifth Army command was the Brazilian Expeditionary Force (*Força Expedicionária Brasiliera, or FEB*), a single infantry division (1st Infantry Division) with support and service elements, including a contingent of nurses. (Brazil also provided a fighter squadron that served with the USAAF's 350th Fighter Group (*1º Grupo de Aviaçã de Caça*, or *1º Grupo de Caça*: 1st Fighter Group) and a light aircraft squadron (*1º Esquadrilha de Ligação e Observação*: 1st Liaison & Observation Squadron). Approximately 26,000 Brazilians sailed to Europe to serve with the Allies. The first elements of the FEB had arrived in July 1944 and a Brazilian RCT (Regimental Combat Team, the equivalent of a British brigade) entered the line in mid-September, with the complete division in place under its GOC, *General-de-Divisão* (Major General) Joao Batista Mascarenhas de Moraes, in the Reno river area.[3]

With the Brazilians and 10th Mountain in his order of battle, Truscott had the strength of ten divisions under his command, nine complete formations and the manpower equivalent of a tenth: six American infantry divisions, 1st Brazilian, two armoured divisions (1st US and 6th South African), plus the equivalent of another division in American and Italian troops. By 31 March Fifth Army was disposed with IV Corps, under Crittenberger, from the Ligurian Sea to the Reno, holding more than two-thirds of the army's front line, and II Corps, under Keyes, with 1st US Armored Division, 34th and 91st Divisions, and the Italian Gruppo Legnano from the Reno to Monte Grande. In II Corps reserve was 88th Division: both 6th South African Armoured Division and 85th Infantry were in Army reserve. Late in March, 442nd Infantry Regiment returned to Italy from France, rejoining Fifth Army for the spring offensive.

Eighth Army lost even more formations over the winter. German withdrawal from Greece created a crisis that developed into major civil unrest and led to the deployment of Allied troops in Operation MANNA. Those Allied troops were taken from Eighth Army and included 23 Armoured Brigade, 3 Greek Mountain Brigade, and 2 Parachute Brigade. Eighth Army was the only possible source of troops for Greece, especially as the British government had agreed to send a force to the country to prevent civil war, or a communist takeover, and maintain order until elections were held. The first formations were followed by 4th Indian Division, which was flown to Greece, and by 139 Brigade of 46th Division with the remainder of the division joining them later; 4th British Division was also despatched. Tactical HQ X Corps, under Lieutenant General John Hawkesworth, deployed to act as Headquarters British forces in Greece. Thus McCreery had lost the strength of a corps. Worse was to follow when, in February 1945, he was told that I Canadian Corps would be transferred to north-west Europe. This was a great loss as, time and time again, the Canadians had shown themselves to be courageous, effective and well led, demonstrating a particular aptitude for river crossings. Indeed, McCreery had considered the Canadians an essential element of his order of battle for the offensive.[4]

Even worse news came with the order that three British divisions would follow I Canadian Corps to 21st Army Group. However, this order was modified after Field Marshal Alexander made representations to Brooke, the CIGS, to retain British formations in Italy to allow 15th Army Group to make a decisive strike that would lead to victory; Alexander sent Clark's chief of staff at 15th Army Group HQ, General Al Gruenther, to intercede with Brooke. As a result, only one of the three planned divisions left Italy: this was 5th Division, known popularly as the Cook's

Tour Division since it had served in many theatres; 5th Division had only returned from Palestine to relieve 1st Division when it received orders to move again. The divisions 'saved' for Eighth Army were 1st and 46th; the former was to move to Palestine to rest and re-organize, while the latter deployed to Greece and would not return to Italy in time for the offensive.[5]

However, there were some new or recent arrivals. One of the three Indian armoured divisions had been scheduled for transfer to Italy although only its infantry brigade, 43 Gurkha Lorried Infantry, made the move, joining 1st Armoured Division from July 1944 until that formation was disbanded when the brigade transferred to other commands. The Gurkha brigade had been in Persia and Iraq Command, from which also came 14th/20th Hussars, a regiment that had thus far seen no action in the war and was keen to earn at least a single battle honour (in the event, it received three: Bologna, Medicina and Italy 1945).[6] The recently formed Jewish Hebron Brigade Group also arrived while 2 Commando Brigade, which had been 2 Special Service Brigade until December 1944, returned to Eighth Army command. Three Italian *Gruppi di Combattimento*, or combat groups, joined Eighth Army's fold: these were the Cremona, Folgore and Friuli Groups. (Another group, Legnano, went to Fifth Army, as we have seen, while two more, Mantova and Piceno, did not see action.)[7]

By March 1945 Eighth Army deployed three British divisions (6th Armoured, 56th (London) and 78th Infantry), two Indian (8th and 10th), two Polish (3rd Carpathian and 5th Kresowa) and 2nd New Zealand. McCreery also had a miscellany of brigades including 2, 7 and 9 British Armoured Brigades, 2 Warsaw Armoured Brigade, 21 and 25 Tank Brigades, 43 Gurkha Brigade, 2 Commando Brigade and 2 Parachute Brigade. These formations were commanded by V Corps (56th, 78th, 8th Indian and 2nd New Zealand Divisions, Gruppo Cremona, 2 Armoured Brigade, 9 Armoured Brigade, 21 Tank Brigade and 2 Commando Brigade); X Corps, which returned from Greece in March (Jewish Brigade Group and Gruppo Friuli); XIII Corps (10th Indian Division and Gruppo Folgore); II Polish Corps (3rd Carpathian and 5th Kresowa Divisions, 2 Warsaw Armoured Brigade, 7 British Armoured Brigade and 43 Gurkha Brigade); 6th Armoured Division and 2 Parachute Brigade were in Eighth Army reserve. This gave 15th Army Group a total of seventeen divisions, including three armoured, and the equivalent in brigade-strength formations of several more divisions, plus four Italian combat groups, each of two-brigade strength with artillery, support and service units.[8]

Against this, the Germans could field no fewer than twenty-one German and four Italian fascist divisions, although these were generally weaker in manpower than their Allied counterparts. Other than 26th Panzer, 29th and 90th Panzer Grenadier, and 1st and 4th Fallschirmjäger Divisions, most were restricted in their mobility while Allied air superiority hampered daytime movement, except in weather that grounded aircraft. The importance that the Germans still gave to northern Italy was demonstrated by the transfer of 710th Division from Norway early in 1945, even though Allied armies were already on Germany's borders. (The division proved doughty opponents to 10th Mountain in their assault on Monte Belvedere.) Kesselring, who had been the German commander in Italy, but who had been injured in a car crash in late-October 1944, returned to Italy in late-February, only to be called back to replace von Rundstedt as C-in-C, West in March. His successor as C-in-C, South was von Vietinghoff, recalled from the Baltic, who took up his new command on 23 March. Since Italian partisans had proved a major problem to the Germans and their fascist allies, a large internal security force, virtually another army, under SS General Karl Wolff was deployed; this equated to about ten divisions and included Cossacks, Slovaks and Spaniards, as well as Germans.[9]

Although little is known about them in the United Kingdom, Italian partisans played an important role in the campaign to liberate their country, especially in northern Italy. The resistance movement in Italy grew up almost spontaneously from 'groups of politicians in the cities and small bands of ill clad, poorly equipped men in the hills'. From many backgrounds – professionals, peasant farmers, communists, ex-soldiers and idealistic youths – they shared a common goal: to fight the German forces occupying Italy, and the rump of Mussolini's fascist state.

Politically it was of great significance: to the Italians it was a symbol of national unity and desire to break with the recent past, and to the Allies it was a possible core around which a provisional government might be established in northern Italy and public order maintained when the German forces withdrew or capitulated. Militarily its importance is more difficult to assess.[10]

The six principal anti-fascist political parties formed a co-ordinating Committee of National Liberation (CNL) in the main cities; these included committees in German-occupied cities such as Milan. On 9 June 1944 the Milan committee combined its forces as the *Corpo Volontari della Liberta*, the Corps of Volunteers of Liberty, which led to an agreement to merge all partisan groups into a single army. The Italian government and the Allies were informed of the Milan decision and chose Major General Raffaele Cadorna, who had commanded Ariete Armoured Division, as military adviser to the Milan committee. Cadorna was parachuted into northern Italy on 12 August 1944.[11]

Frictions within the partisan movement – two left-wing parties (the Communist and the Action parties), with the most organized and strongest forces, became the driving force – led to a struggle with the Allies over the movement's political identity, the Committee wanting to maintain this and the Allies wishing to control it. Nor did difficulties in communicating with the partisans help; in this respect, complex arrangements made by the Allies were a factor. The Allies were slow to take advantage of the resistance movement, especially as plans to support such a movement in Italy were overtaken by a decision at the Tehran Conference in December 1943 to support the Yugoslav partisans, and then the French resistance in the build up to the Normandy landings; Poland was also given preference over Italy in August 1944 at the time of the Warsaw rising.

Although support was provided for the Italian partisan movement, it was not as much as might have been expected. However, it increased in late-1944. Weather conditions caused a decrease in January 1945 but the level rose thereafter. No accurate figures can be given for the overall strength of the partisan army, which was estimated at 145,000 in September 1944, probably its peak figure, and some

50,000 after the winter of 1944–45. Providing supplies, including uniforms, for this force strained Allied resources. (The British authorities provided uniforms that were British battledress dyed black – presumably in the belief that the partisans would be operating only by night and that the Germans would respect a uniform and not execute captured partisans out of hand.)[12]

Vietinghoff's command was disposed in three armies, two German and one Italian: Tenth and Fourteenth Armies and the Army of Liguria, commanded respectively by Generals Traugott Herr, Joachim Lemelsen and Alfredo Guzzoni. (Marshal Rodolfo Graziani, former governor general of Libya, was overall commander of Mussolini's forces; he had been the sole Italian marshal to remain loyal to Il Duce when the latter was deposed in July 1943.) The Army of Liguria, deployed on the French frontier, included three of the four Italian fascist divisions (Italia, Littorio and San Marco) while the fourth (Monte Rosa) was in Fourteenth Army, in a sector considered an unlikely target for an Allied attack. While the German armies were as well supplied as possible, and had been reinforced, they were very short of petrol and, of course, had precious little air support, the Luftwaffe being only a shadow of its earlier self. The *Aeronautica Nazionale Repubblicana*, the Italian National Republican Air Force (ANR), no more than a group in strength, disposed two fighter and one bomber *gruppi*; the fighter *gruppi* each included three squadrons but the bomber *gruppo* was smaller. A third fighter *gruppo*, named for the great Italian First World War air ace Francesco Baracca (whose famous *Cavallino Rampante*, the black prancing stallion, became the logo of Ferrari), never became operational. In the battles of April 1945, Axis air forces were virtually powerless and the ANR's last interception missions were carried out on 19 April.[13]

Although much weaker than before, the Axis armies still presented a formidable challenge. The defences they had created demanded a major effort to overcome, and the attackers did not have the desired three-to-one superiority for success. As ever in Italy, the Germans had demonstrated that they could put up an effective defence, taking a high toll of the attackers. Although they must have realized that the war was nearing its end, and that their cause was lost, they continued fighting tenaciously. Some were not so sure, and there was a small trickle of deserters, as indicated in the war diary of G Branch, HQ XIII Corps on 1 February.[14] Nonetheless, Kesselring commented about morale being much better than he had expected when he returned to Italy and noted that, even in private, there was no talk of 'throwing up the sponge'.[15] Reflecting on this, one historian of the campaign wrote:

> It is astounding that the morale of the Germans did not crack when they found such skilled and completely fresh troops as the 10th Mountain and such eager and fast improving ones as the 1st Brazilian driving them from their mountain strongholds, after journeying from the bottomless well of manpower across the Atlantic.[16]

Overcoming the German defences in northern Italy required careful and original planning but the Allied commanders were not to be found wanting, nor were they lacking in devising ways of overcoming the many problems facing them as they made their plans to defeat the enemy.

While the Germans endured major problems in manpower and matériel during that final winter they were not alone in this. Both Fifth and Eighth Armies suffered shortages of artillery ammunition, the withdrawal of manpower, as we have seen, and problems with morale, leading to large-scale desertions. At this point, it is appropriate to look at these problems, examine some of the reasons for them, and consider how they were resolved.

The manpower crisis hit both Allied armies and seemed to threaten the viability of any offensive in spring 1945. We have seen how the emphasis on north-west Europe drained personnel from Italy, especially from Eighth Army. Until early in the Italian campaign, Eighth Army could rely on receiving reinforcements and replacements from the UK, but that source had been turned off during 1944. As British forces built up in the UK for the liberation of France, commanders in the Mediterranean were warned that no further drafts would be sent to them. This policy was decided upon in February 1944, and the Mediterranean commanders were told that their last infantry reinforcements would sail from Britain in May. From then onwards reinforcements and replacements would have to be found within the Mediterranean; the last replacements from Britain were posted to battalions in July. It had been anticipated that, by September 1944, there would be a worldwide deficiency in British manpower of about 42,000, with half of that occurring in the Mediterranean.[17]

When General Sir Oliver Leese wrote in his report after Operation OLIVE that Eighth Army had broken into 'the powerful Gothic Line defences at very small expense and before the enemy was ready' his infantrymen would not have agreed with him. Infantry casualties during OLIVE had led to the disbandment of 1st Armoured Division, the disbandment of 18 and 168 Brigades, the reduction to cadre of two regular battalions, and the disbandment of four TA or war-raised battalions.[18] Moreover, the degree to which infantry battalions had suffered was marked by the reduction of most of those in Italy to three rifle companies; before long those battalions retaining four rifle companies would lose their fourth companies through attrition, reducing the manpower of an infantry battalion from thirty-six officers and 809 men to thirty officers and 700 men.[19] During Operation OLIVE Eighth Army had sustained over 14,000 casualties, mostly in the infantry. With over 1,700 men killed, half of all infantry casualties had occurred in British units; II Polish Corps suffered over 3,500 casualties.[20]

Such were the fortunes of war that as the UK well of reinforcements dried up another opened. Allied airpower was so much greater than that of the Axis that the Luftwaffe and ANR no longer presented a major threat to Allied ground forces, logistics and vital points, making it possible to reduce levels of anti-aircraft (AA) artillery in Italy, and elsewhere in the Mediterranean. This allowed regiments of heavy and light AA artillery to be disbanded, with their personnel available for re-training as infantry. A mobile heavy AA regiment, with three batteries, had an establishment of about a thousand while a light AA regiment, also with three batteries, had some 600 personnel. An AA brigade, usually of two HAA and three LAA regiments, could, therefore, provide a pool of almost 4,000 men for re-training, although not all would be suitable for infantry duties. Former gunners, and other re-assigned personnel, undertook a two-month course, reduced from the desired three months, before they could be posted to infantry units. Their initial infantry training took place at the Infantry Reinforcement Training Depot (IRTD) where the requirement for experienced instructors created the need for a training battalion, which produced another drain on manpower.[21]

As the need for AA defences reduced in early-1944, some 9,000 AA gunners were re-trained, joining infantry units prior to Operation OLIVE. Further disbandments provided another 5,000 men for re-roling; they began training in August. As more regiments were to be disbanded, there remained a pool of personnel, many of them suitable for re-training as infantry. Some heavy AA regiments re-trained as medium artillery, a role in which they excelled; others continued in their original role while many performed both roles. Since German tank numbers were also decreasing, there was a diminishing need for anti-tank guns, releasing men from infantry anti-tank platoons and Royal Artillery anti-tank regiments; they also joined the re-training scheme. In addition, the reduced need for AA defences made redundant RAF Regiment personnel manning airfield defences in Italy. They, too, re-roled as infantry, as did some Royal Navy personnel.[22]

During the winter months, pressure was eased on Eighth Army's infantry in the front line through a policy of 'dismounting' armoured regiments to perform infantry duties. Needless to say, some were critical of this policy, arguing against cavalrymen being deployed as infantry, a criticism not accepted by the commanding officer of 17th/21st Lancers in 6th Armoured Division. Lieutenant Colonel Val ffrench-Blake wrote, 'It is wasteful to use tank men as infantry, when there is tank work to be done, but it is even more wasteful *not* to use tank men as infantry when there is *no* tank work to be done'.[23] And, at that time, there was no tank work to be done. General McCreery's own regiment, 12th Lancers, took its turn in the line, forming part of Porterforce with 27th Lancers, a wartime regiment (there had been an earlier 27th Lancers in the late-eighteenth and early-nineteenth centuries) built on a cadre of 12th Lancers. Lieutenant Colonel Andrew Horsburgh-Porter of 27th Lancers commanded Porterforce – hence the name – which included some Canadian and British units as well as Popski's Private Army.[24]

The front-line routine would have been familiar to First World War veterans with battalions moving up close behind the front to rotate companies in the line. Alternatively, brigades would rotate battalions into the front line, as was the case with 1 Guards Brigade in which 2nd Coldstream and 3rd Welsh Guards relieved each other on a five-day rota throughout January. However, the five-day stint was not standard and, as the weather improved, time spent at the sharp end increased, at least according to the evidence from the war diary of 2/6th Queen's, which notes that the battalion went into the line on 26 February, remaining there until relieved by 1st Royal Irish Fusiliers of 78th Division, on 10 March.[25]

Fifth Army also adopted the policy of converting AA personnel to infantry as well as re-roling service units. The army's historian, Lieutenant Colonel Chester G. Starr, noted that:

> a large percentage of Army service units was reorganized. Here again Fifth Army and the Mediterranean Theater had to rely mainly on their own resources. The 366th Infantry had been formed by the theater from troops of other branches; on 14 January 1945 Fifth Army activated the 473rd Infantry from the personnel of the former Task Force 45, a step which forced the disbandment of the 45th Antiaircraft Artillery Brigade, the 2nd Armored Group, and the 434th, 435th, 532nd, and 900th Antiaircraft Artillery Automatic Weapons Battalions. The theater instituted a program of converting troops of other arms into infantry replacements and of sending suitable infantry and other enlisted men to local officer candidate schools so as to create more infantry officers. Together with a midwinter increase in replacements from home this program allowed the building-up of all under-strength units and even the assignment of an over-strength for the next drive.[26]

Task Force 45, created on 29 July 1944 from units of 45th Antiaircraft Artillery Brigade, with elements from other arms added, as a provisional infantry formation varying from 3,000 to 8,000 strong, was used to relieve elements of 34th and 91st Infantry Divisions on a fifteen-mile length of the Arno. On 9 January 1945 Task Force 45 was relieved by 86th Mountain Infantry Regiment north-west of Pistóia and withdrawn to reform as 473rd Infantry Regiment. For security reasons, 10th Mountain Division continued using the title Task Force 45 for some time.

The foreword to Task Force 45's history noted that:

> Task Force 45 was a polyglot task force of American and British antiaircraft gunners acting as infantry, with Italian Partisans, Brazilians and colored American troops fighting by their side. Its artillery were the antiaircraft guns pointed earthward, the guns of tanks and of tank destroyers and of captured German weapons. Its engineers were Italian civilians who were not afraid to work within the sound of guns and who built well. It did much with little. British Tommies who rode forward on American tanks, with American mortars behind and American engineers ahead, and the Yanks who stepped out of their foxholes with British artillery pounding protection behind, with Italians at their side and out ahead and with Brazilians on their flanks, learned that different peoples can fight well together.[27]

Additional artillery units were added as D Day for the offensive approached, so that Fifth Army could deploy, in addition to the artillery in the divisions, six battalions of 155mm howitzers, four of 155mm guns, two of 8-inch howitzers and one of M7 105mm self-propelled howitzers (dubbed Priests in British service). Starr noted that firepower could be increased by the deployment of six tank and five tank destroyer battalions as field artillery, while five Royal Artillery regiments continued serving with Fifth Army, deploying 240mm howitzers, 8-inch and 4.5-inch guns (in fact 178th (Lowland) Medium Regiment RA had 5.5-inch guns).[28]

(The Germans made similar conversions, although this was a more generally accepted part of German army culture. In the final winter in Italy, many servicemen who had never been soldiers were formed into army units and trained by the army, including large numbers of *Kriegsmarine* sailors who came ashore to fight in the last battles in Italy. In his *Memoirs*, Kesselring commented that Admiral Löwisch 'gladly fell in with' his [Kesselring's] suggestion that he give up sailors to the army. Whether the admiral was quite so happy at this move is debatable.)[29]

By this stage, the US Army artillery had improved beyond recognition from the arm that had entered the war in later-1941. There was much new and more effective equipment, some of which was to be found equipping British units as well, and corps artillery had been re-organized completely 'due mainly to British experience'.

Pioneered in North Africa by Brigadier General (then Colonel) Charles E. Hart and Brigadier General (then Colonel) John E. Sloan, others experimented and improved on these innovations. As a result of these experiences and the abandonment of the regiment for the group, American corps artillery became a flexible, rapid and puissant reinforcement for the division.[30]

Such developments also made close co-operation between British and American artillery much simpler, although differences remained. By 1945 gunners of both armies were working so close together as to be indistinguishable in many ways, allowing British gunners to work effectively with American armoured and infantry formations.

Artillery was important to both armies since it compensated to some extent for the reduced manpower, and as a 'means of conserving, guiding, and sustaining the heavily used infantry'.[31] British artillery was feared by the Germans more than any other arm; its power on the battlefield was devastating, its accuracy making it even more so. (In Normandy the previous summer, a planned German counter-attack by II SS Panzer Corps had been smashed before it got underway by a combination of air attack, gunfire from ships in the Channel and what SS General Paul Hausser described as 'the terrible British artillery'.)[32] Air observation by Royal Artillery officers in light aircraft ensured that the guns received almost immediate information of any movement by enemy forces and retaliation by the gunners usually followed. The US Army also used air OPs, flying in Piper Cub light aircraft. However, there was one problem for the artillery of both armies: a shortage of ammunition. It is hard to credit that, with the United States' prodigious industrial capacity, such a dearth occurred. The fault lay not so much with the munitions industry as with the military planners who had erred in calculating their requirements.

Initially, the problem was felt by Eighth Army in the winter of 1943–44 and seen as one affecting only the Mediterranean. It was dealt with through an improved system of distributing stocks in the region, salvaging from old battlefields, slight increases in shipments from Britain, and a temporary rationing scheme prior to Operation DIADEM, the final battle for the Gustav Line.[33] The British *Official History* provides an interesting insight into the use of artillery. From 1 January to 30 November 1944 Eighth Army

> used an average of 9,000,000 rounds of .303-inch ammunition per month, which was fired by all British riflemen and machine gunners. … average expenditure of 25-pdr ammunition during this same period amounted to just over 1,100,000 rounds per month. The 25-pdrs were thus firing one shell for every nine rounds fired by the infantrymen – a very high level of artillery activity.[34]

At first the problem was seen as affecting only the British. After the first winter in Italy, it had become more serious and only through careful husbanding of ammunition stocks was sufficient reserve built up for the final Cassino battles. On 21 March 1944 Alexander had ordered commanders to limit expenditure across the front to fifteen rounds of 25-pounder and ten rounds of medium shells per gun per day, except to meet enemy attacks or support offensive operations ordered or approved by him.[35] By such means, total expenditure was controlled while ammunition could be allotted as required, since not every gun would be in action every day.

Although there was sufficient ammunition for the DIADEM battles, and expenditure dropped during June, a month of considerable movement with fewer calls on artillery, it became clear with the July battles, and the preparations thereafter for the Gothic Line assault, that 'Allied ammunition expenditure had begun to exceed both British and American production' and there could be no denying that the crisis affected both armies. In fact, it was even more widespread:

> Production targets in both countries had been set too low many months before and the expenditure of 21 Army Group in Normandy had made reductions of supplies to other Theatres unavoidable.[36]

The planners' error had resulted from growing optimism in late 1943 when it seemed that ammunition stocks were so high that production could be reduced. Cutbacks in production followed in both Britain and the USA with the labour saved in Britain being transferred to the aircraft industry. By October 1944 it was clear that the estimates upon which production had been planned were too low and a decision was made to increase production. Since the effects of this would not be seen until spring 1945, the allocation of 25-pounder and medium ammunition to the corps of Eighth Army was restricted to allow the build-up of an army ammunition reserve for future operations. By the end of October allocations were reduced further, to twenty-five rounds of 25-pounder and fifteen rounds of medium ammunition per gun per day while, in mid-October, Clark's logistic staff warned that, at prevailing expenditure rates, ammunition shortages would force Fifth Army on to the defensive by 10 November.[37]

Fifth Army's G 4 staff told Clark that his ammunition supply would be exhausted by 10 November if expenditure continued at the rates then current. This meant, Clark was warned, that Fifth Army could not maintain the offensive beyond 25 October, the very date on which II Corps' offensive ground to a halt. Since Italy was low on the priority list for ammunition, allocations to Fifth Army had been reduced. In the case of 155mm ammunition, factories in the United States could not meet the demand for supplies. As a result, a careful analysis of ammunition stocks was undertaken in late November. This concluded that while sufficient supplies existed to support an offensive of thirteen days during December, such an attack would so reduce stocks that no further offensive operations could be undertaken before 28 January. After that date, delivery of planned allocations of shells would increase the army's stockpiles to the point where full artillery support for operations could be planned.[38]

With the decision to postpone the Fifth Army attack came a great reduction in allotments of ammunition to the corps, and daily restrictions of 15 rounds per 105mm howitzer, 18 rounds per 155mm howitzer, and 11 rounds per 155mm gun were imposed. Later in the winter, when the offensive was cancelled, the allocations were further reduced so as to build up ample reserves for the spring.[39]

Interestingly, McCreery commented that:

In some ways the artillery ammunition shortage was possibly a blessing in disguise, as it was impossible to mount any further big attack. Much of the artillery was limited to 5 rounds a gun a day. I do not think that the Germans attached much significance to this great reduction in our shelling. They themselves must have been only too glad of a respite.[40]

Fortunately the front-line infantrymen of Fifth and Eighth Armies were unaware of the shortage of ammunition, since they had come to place their trust in the support of the guns in both offensive and defensive situations. Such knowledge would have been a major blow to morale, already a serious problem for commanders at all levels. The greatest manifestation of that problem was in the numbers who deserted. Figures for desertions are available for Eighth Army and the British official historian is candid about the problem. In contrast, there is no mention of the problem either in the US Army's official history of the Italian campaign, or in Fifth Army's history, which, however, does refer to an 'increase in the number of courts-martial cases, which soared especially among the veteran divisions'.[41] Both sources describe efforts made in Fifth Army to maintain morale, which hints at the existence of a desertion problem without admitting that there was one.

By early-February the worst of the morale problem appeared to have passed, although it had persisted throughout the winter. However, knowing that the army groups in north-west Europe were pushing towards the Rhine, and that the Red Army was thrusting through Poland towards Germany, made it seem to the men of 15th Army Group that their war was irrelevant, that they might have no further role to play in the defeat of the Third Reich. In such circumstances, writes Sir David Fraser:

> The imminence of victory, the coming hard-to-imagine outbreak of peace, with the apparently subsidiary nature of the Italian theatre combined to depress. Desertions increased sharply. Survival looked more attractive than suffering, and the latter's value was questioned.[42]

As Fraser suggests, desertion was not a new problem but had been present for some time. Peaking in March and June 1944, the former due to the strain of service in the Anzio beachhead and the latter during the advance to Rome and beyond, it reached new heights in November and December 1944: during each month about 1,200 British soldiers were posted as 'absent without official leave' (AWOL), or as deserters. At its worst, the problem cost Eighth Army and XIII Corps, still under Fifth Army command, the equivalent of the infantry strength of a division after a sustained period in the line with 'the equivalent of a full division' required to guard captured deserters who had been sentenced to detention. Blaxland notes that the highest figure for soldiers in detention at one time was 5,150.[43]

Who were these deserters and why had they chosen to quit their posts? To answer the latter question first, it is fair to say that almost all absented themselves to avoid front-line service, although some may have had other reasons. Deserters could be classified in three general groups. First were the 'uninhibited cowards who would have been deterred only by the death penalty, which was abolished in 1939'. These men had been sent to the infantry, although, in many cases, their lack of moral fibre had been detected, but 'it had long been accepted that the infantry had to take the dregs, regardless of their moral fibre'. Among those who deserted from Eighth Army in Italy were men who had done the same in North Africa, been convicted by courts martial and returned to duty under suspended sentence. Many proved to be recidivists who often encouraged others to follow their example.[44]

The second group, rightly described by Blaxland as the 'saddest category', included men with good records, who had seen much active service but had reached the limit of their courage and endurance. This category included 'some tragic cases' in 78th Division, which had fought through Tunisia, Sicily and much of the Italian campaign. Those who deserted included men previously decorated for gallantry, or who had been wounded twice and knew that a third wound could mean repatriation, but also death. Such men were 'overwhelmed by the conviction that they could not go on escaping death or serious mutilation'.[45] In this category was a childhood neighbour of the author who, in 1993, admitted that he had lost his nerve early in the Italian campaign, but had been accepted back to his battalion and seemed to have been rehabilitated successfully; he showed the author letters from his CO of late-1944 and the former adjutant of his battalion, both of them friends of the author. He had also been recommended, unsuccessfully, for the MM in Tunisia. His experience supported Blaxland's view that the

> courage of such men might be rekindled by careful handling within units, but the wider the sheltering of the badly bruised the greater the burden on those who had not yet exhausted their store of courage – and the greater the inclination to feel it ebbing away.[46]

Against this may be balanced John Horsfall's comment on the manner in which discipline held for the majority of men whose

> spirit was now immune to whatever the fates might do – like Wellington's men in the Peninsula, or Lee's or Napoleon's, or any others long together. I think it was Stonewall Jackson who said in Virginia, 'It is fortunate that war is so horrible … otherwise we might grow to like it.' Like it? Never – but our soldiers had grown accustomed to it, and some of us had forgotten what any other life was like.[47]

Horsfall was not writing at a remove, endeavouring to produce a picture to fit a story of regimental glory, but was a fighting officer who commanded two battalions in the Italian campaign and knew intimately that of which he wrote. The comment above refers to the early winter of 1944–45 when Horsfall commanded 1st Royal Irish Fusiliers before he was wounded himself (for the second time) and removed from action. He knew the strain under which soldiers served and shared that strain with his own warriors, as he preferred to call his soldiers.

The third category of deserter included men who felt little or no sense of belonging to the unit to which they had been posted, many deserting soon after arriving at a new unit. This element of the problem could be alleviated by good management within a battalion, from CO down to junior NCOs commanding sections. Such were the exigencies of war that many fell into this category who might otherwise have never considered deserting. In part, this aspect of the desertion problem arose because the peacetime system of reinforcing units and replacing casualties, or soldiers whose time had expired, could not cope with the demands of war. Infantry training had moved from regimental depots to infantry training centres, and soldiers could be posted to a unit that needed fresh manpower rather than to one with which they had any affiliation, such as their local county infantry regiment. The Childers system, designed for a small army operating as an imperial gendarmerie, had broken down, as it had done in the previous war. This situation was exacerbated in Italy from mid-1944 by the lack of reinforcements and replacements from the United Kingdom. With men being re-roled, those sent as individual replacements could find themselves in units where they felt themselves strangers, while wounded or sick soldiers returning from convalescence might be posted to a unit other than that with which they had served before.[48] (Sometimes this latter possibility was circumvented by individuals committing what became known as 'honourable desertion', a soldier leaving his convalescence camp without permission to return to his own unit. Needless to say, if apprehended by military police en route he was liable to feel the full rigour of military law.)

The policy of converting AA gunners to infantry could have led to morale problems and an upsurge in desertions. However, where gunners from a particular regiment or battery, and it is to the battery rather than the regiment that the gunner gives his loyalty, were kept together as far as possible the problem was avoided. This could be seen especially where the gunner unit had originally been converted to the artillery role from that of infantry. An excellent example is 117th Light AA Regiment, among the first gunner units converted to infantry in Italy in 1944. Most personnel of the regiment were sent to the newly created 61 Brigade on completing their training. This brigade included three Green Jacket battalions, all from the Rifle Brigade, and 117th LAA Regiment had been converted from a rifle battalion, 8th Royal Ulster Rifles, in 1942. Thus many men still serving when 117th was disbanded in early 1944 would have been familiar with black buttons and rifle drill, and could fit easily into a Green Jacket battalion.[49]

Blaxland noted the increase in desertions after the liberation of Rome, which he connected to the landings in Normandy and a growing realization among Eighth Army soldiers that the Italian theatre was henceforth to be regarded as secondary, that the war against Germany was not going to be won in Italy. Many, he opined, found it hard to see a reason for continuing the dogged struggle up through Italy.[50] That may well be true. Whatever the truth, the feelings of those in Italy were not helped when a story gained credence, and wide circulation, that British soldiers in Italy were known as 'D Day Dodgers' in Britain. Some believed that the soubriquet originated with Nancy, Lady, Astor, MP for Plymouth, the first woman to take her seat in the House of Commons (the first woman elected, the Irish republican Constance, Countess, Markievicz refused to take her seat). However, the truth appears to be that, in December 1944, Astor had received from Italy a letter signed 'D Day Dodgers'. Imagining this to be a nickname for a unit, she responded with a letter beginning 'Dear D Day Dodgers'. This led to a furore in Italy, the reaction to which prompted the writing of a ballad, sung to the German tune 'Lili Marlene', that combined both humour and pathos and became Eighth Army's anthem. It also led the cartoonist 'Jon' (John Philpin Jones), who had created two characters, the 'Two Types', for the army newspaper in the Mediterranean theatre, to produce a cartoon showing the pair sitting in a jeep emblazoned with the names of the various D Days in which they, and many of their readers, had taken part and pondering which D Day they had 'dodged'.[51]

The Germans, whose morale seems not to have suffered to any great degree in Italy, also attempted to chip away at Allied morale with radio and loudspeaker broadcasts to soldiers in the front line. Leaflets were distributed, via shells and mortar bombs, that warned of the dangers of the river Po, a barrier bloodier than all barriers previously encountered. Other propaganda referred to wives and sweethearts at home being unfaithful with American servicemen. Such efforts, often crude in design and implementation, continued until the final offensive opened.

Blaxland had a particular reason for singling out 78th Division in his discussion on morale and desertion. The Battleaxe Division, from its divisional emblem of a golden battle-axe on a black or dark-blue ground, had been sent to the Middle East for rest and training after the battles at Lake Trasimene in June 1944 and, on its return, in October, had been diverted from V Corps to XIII Corps, then under Fifth Army command in the Apennines. It was no coincidence that XIII Corps suffered the highest desertion rate in Italy with 1,145 men making off between October and the end of January 1945; of those 600 came from 78th Division. However, the Battleaxe Division's overall morale did not break down and no ground was conceded to the enemy. This bears out the previously quoted comments of John Horsfall, who commanded 1st Royal Irish Fusiliers for much of this period. There was also good leadership at the divisional level, albeit there was 'what amounted to a palace coup' that led to the appointment of Major General Arbuthnott as GOC at the end of November. Arbuthnott proved an inspiring and popular commander whose division played an important role in the final campaign.[52]

Strangely, American official histories make no mention of desertions. This does not mean that no American soldiers deserted, only that the US authorities wanted to maintain the impression at home that all American soldiers were dedicated to their task. In contrast, Truscott's memoirs, *Command Decisions*, is more honest and includes a letter written by General Keyes for Clark shortly before Truscott assumed command of Fifth Army in which Keyes discusses the discipline problems of 34th Division:

> After an exhaustive study of the disciplinary and morale status of the 34th Infantry Division I am led to the conclusion that certain personnel of this division should be withdrawn from combat and returned to the United States, if this division is to continue in combat. The division has maintained a consistently high AWOL and Courts Martial rate for some time. An inordinately large percentage of the Courts Martial cases have been for misbehaviour before the enemy, disobedience of orders, aggravated AWOL, and related offenses. The division has a high 'exhaustion' rate. … all of these conditions are traceable, either directly or indirectly, to a common motivating influence: a deep conviction by the older, or original, officers and men of the 34th Division, that they have done their part in this war, that they should be permitted to return to the United States and the struggle left to those who have not been absent from home for two years. After periods of rest, rehabilitation, and reorganization in rear areas, the unit displays little, if any, increased efficiency when again committed to action. The attitude of the men would seem to stem, not from 'combat' weariness, but from general 'war' weariness.[53]

The story of desertions from US formations and units of Fifth Army requires more study, but it is probably safe to assume, especially from Keyes's comments on 34th Division, and the reference to the increase in courts martial, particularly among veteran formations such as 34th Division, that the problem was at least equal to that suffered by Eighth Army. Certainly, the steps taken to improve and sustain morale in Fifth Army indicate efforts to resolve a problem that included desertion.

Both armies implemented measures aimed at maintaining morale, with many common to the two forces. Following the harsh winter of 1943–44, arrangements had been made in good time for the provision of specialized winter clothing in Fifth Army:

> But in contrast to ... the previous year the Army was incomparably better prepared for the bad weather. New and improved types of clothing were on hand, this time at the beginning of the winter. The issue of shoepacs, combat trousers and jackets, and better sleeping bags and the regular exchange of clean socks issued with the rations kept the troops warmer and drier; buildings and dugouts were utilized to the utmost for shelter, though the men in extreme forward positions usually were forced to remain in foxholes.[54]

Eighth Army had also ensured that winter clothing and other equipment were issued to its soldiers. However, there was a breakdown with 78th Division, under Fifth Army command in XIII Corps. Ray, the divisional historian noted that:

> there was a shortage of socks, boots, battledress and every other kind of clothing. At one period some of the men in the front line had only one pair of socks – always wet – and cotton at that; other men were repairing roads still wearing the khaki drill trousers ... suitable only for an Egyptian summer. The men shivered in their trenches covered in wet blankets, and many, without steel helmets, were wearing balaclavas instead. Cigarettes were short – probably due to theft in the post – and the mails slow.[55]

Whatever glitch caused the breakdown had been resolved by mid-December when the front-line soldiers received at least four pairs of woollen socks each, in addition to 'Mountain Warfare' clothing, including windproof blouses and trousers, as well as thick sweaters. There were also string vests 'such as are used by Arctic explorers, sleeping bags covered with oil silk, white snow overalls, skis, snowshoes and sleighs'. Ray also commented that rations were consistently good with the men in the forward positions receiving fresh rations 'almost every day'.[56]

Brigadier F. S. Reid, CRA of 78th Division, had a slightly different perspective on the issue of winter clothing and other kit:

> The first week of January saw the arrival of the severe weather, with snow and hard frost, which was to stay for nearly four weeks. Winter clothing and equipment, including white smocks and skis, were issued with commendable rapidity and were excellent in quality. Whilst the warm clothing and smocks were vital for the foremost troops, skis were not used in a strictly operational role, but it was noticed that those who were skiers found it necessary to carry out many more reconnaissances and visits than usual.[57]

Reid's comments, when contrasted with those of Ray, might suggest that the gunners were treated better than the infantry, but 2nd Lancashire Fusiliers' war diary suggests this was not a consistent pattern:

The Battalion had by this time [5 January] been issued with snow clothing which proved most effective. Except for special boots, almost all items were issued – string vests, pullovers, jackets with hoods, waterproof trousers, gloves, scarves, cap comforters on an adequate scale, in contrast to the previous year when almost nothing had been available. In addition, white snow camouflage clothing was issued, and it was indeed essential when the snow came.[58]

In 38 (Irish) Brigade, also in 78th Division, morale was boosted by the policy of

keeping the company cooks as far forward as possible so that we were supplied with a hot meal each day ... a great boost to morale especially when we were wet and cold ... [The Americans] were very envious of our ration system of fresh food each day. They were fed on K rations, a package of dried food (biscuits, meat, cheese, etc.). Each man was issued with a package a day.

Our rations as far as I can remember originated from different countries. Biscuits (very hard) came from the UK, cheese from Canada, marmalade from South Africa. ... The cheese and marmalade went well together and helped to soften the biscuits. Very occasionally we were issued with compo rations, high quality tinned food, ... a great luxury if you could get hold of them but allegedly expensive to produce and therefore seldom seen.

The Americans were impressed by our habit of shaving daily whenever ... possible. Even if it were not possible to wash, a shave helped to freshen one up and keep alert. It could be a painful process when the only water available was in the nearest shellhole and very cold ...[59]

Reid wrote of a very positive result of the winter months spent in the Apennines by 78th Division. Having faced a 'remarkably tenacious enemy' difficult terrain and the worst that weather conditions of rain and mud, snow and ice could throw at them, he believed that:

This joint endeavour by all ranks and all arms increased the already high sense of divisional comradeship, and ... personal relationships between the infantry and their supporting gunners had a chance to become very warm and real. The respect and trust that grew up between us were to pay a big dividend in the battles of the final offensive.[60]

In 8th Indian Division the commanding officer of 1st Argyll and Sutherland Highlanders, Lieutenant Colonel F. C. C. Graham, decided to adopt a more aggressive policy in his unit and, on 29 January, established a Deep Patrol Section of ten men and two officers, Captains W. H. Griffiths and R. F. Elias,

to do nothing else in the field but attempt to get deep into the enemy lines and into his Rear HQ and Echelon areas. Issued with special equipment – boots, clothing etc. – and getting special training with a view to ambushing transport, blowing dumps etc.[61]

The section, known as the 'Zulu Scouts', remained in being until the battalion's fourth company was restored in March when its officers and men returned to their own companies.[62]

Improvisations such as the Zulu Scouts boosted morale but other measures also helped in this regard. Units that had been in the line over Christmas had been unable to celebrate the day in traditional fashion, but the opportunity to do so was taken whenever a unit was relieved. One such was 1st London Scottish, which marked the feast on 12 January with all the usual Christmas fare and the officers serving the soldiers. The war diary makes a special point of recording that the Christmas puddings enjoyed by the men were a gift from Her Majesty The Queen. Queen Elizabeth, later the Queen Mother, was Colonel of the Regiment.[63]

As the weather began improving in early February, with the onset of a thaw, the intelligence officer of 2nd Lancashire Fusiliers was prompted to make an almost poetic entry in the war diary, noting on the 2nd that 'Birds [were] heard chirping merrily for the first time in Ripiano valley'. (Other diaries record the beginning of a rapid thaw on the 3rd.) He went on to record that, on the same day, two German deserters, from a former penal battalion, surrendered to a Lancashires' patrol, although he did not connect their decision to desert with the birdsong. However, he did note that although the two 'talked willingly' they had no useful information to impart. The truth of this comment is borne out by the fact the intelligence report on their interrogation was not considered worthy of preserving.[64] While the entry on birds singing may seem strange, it hardly compares with that in the war diary of 2/7th Queen's for 2 January. The battalion IO considered worthy of note the fact that 'During the evening whilst playing Bridge the CO [Lieutenant Colonel D. C. Baynes DSO MC], Major Sutherland and the Adjutant (Captain Whitley) experience a weird hand'. That entry might also be described as 'weird'.[65]

The conditions faced by all the front-line soldiers were extremely difficult. Starr noted that 'at Cassino Fifth Army troops had fought in a mixture of cold, rain and snow; the next winter's battles occurred in much the same type of terrain and in colder weather with more snow and less rain'.[66] Eighth Army's experience was much the same with the winter months bringing harsh conditions for those on front-line duties, whether on high or low ground. A brief account in the South African history illustrates some of the difficulties faced by those in the front line:

> So cold had the weather become up in the Apennines by the end of the first week in January 1945 that weapons were liable to freeze up, as happened when the enemy attacked an ILH/KimR [Imperial Light Horse/Kimberley Regiment] platoon holding the barn and cottage at Casa Salisgastro on 10 January. It was the second night in succession that the Germans tried to overwhelm the outpost, and Lt Jeffery had to ask for assistance as Germans wearing white camouflage

suits tried to drag away Pte C. W. Hobson after he had been wounded. When the Platoon Commander and three others tried to reply to the enemy's Schmeisser machine-pistol fire, they found their own tommy-guns frozen up, but Lt Jeffery and L/Cpl McDonald grabbed rifles and drove off the Germans.[67]

Also serving in 6th South African Armoured Division, 3rd Coldstream Guards at Gardelletta suffered similar conditions but noted how their opponents celebrated the arrival of 1945:

[The] Germans started the New Year by shelling, mortaring and firing MMG tracer, which continued from 1 minute before midnight until 10 minutes past midnight. Sounds of the German celebrations were heard by a Grenadier [Guards] sentry on our left from the direction of Casa Fudelle, and also by a sentry from No. 2 Coy who was at Murazze.[68]

While the British Army had a well-established practice of providing leave centres for soldiers, this had not been the case with the US Army, which had first introduced the concept in Italy the previous winter with centres at Caserta, Sorrento and on the Isle of Capri. Truscott wrote of the centres that:

Adequate periods for rest and relaxation, facilities for entertainment and amusement, and intelligent information programs with newspapers, radio and magazines were all measures utilized to sustain and build morale. But perhaps no single activity contributed more in this respect than our rest center program.[69]

In the winter of 1944–45 the idea was extended and operated on a much greater scale in Rome, and was developed to large proportions in the Arno Valley. Hundreds of thousands of troops were rotated through the rest and leave centres set up in the railroad station at Florence and at the watering place of Montecatini. Here the men could forget the rigors and dangers of the front line, sleep in a bed, take baths, visit places of historical interest, and generally indulge in the pleasures and entertainments of civilization, if only for a short period. At Montecatini an Army-sponsored liquor warehouse, grossing an average of $300,000 per month, served a double purpose by enabling the men to purchase liquor at lower rates than in the open market and also assuring that no poisonous liquors were consumed.[70]

The official US Army history of the campaign also refers to Montecatini, 'where the troops could enjoy the therapeutic properties of sulphur springs long famed among European upper classes'. He added that 'soft beds were among the amenities that a fashionable watering place could offer, even in wartime'.[71]

That officially sponsored liquor warehouse was an acceptance by the US authorities that soldiers will seek out alcohol, a fact long acknowledged by their British counterparts. The British Army made an official issue of beer to its personnel, although that practice was not without its difficulties. In theory, the British issue was one bottle per man per week, but even this target was not always achieved, so that veterans remarked that they recalled it as 'one bottle per man per week, per haps'. Alexander was sufficiently exercised by this problem to raise it himself 'at the highest level'. The underlying difficulty was that 'supply [was] limited by shortage of worldwide production, which was itself limited by lack of malting barley'.[72] General Sir Brian Robertson, Alexander's chief administrative officer, who had travelled to London to discuss the supply problems in Italy, discussed the matter in correspondence with the chairman of NAAFI, and the possibility of increasing the ration to a bottle and a half per week was mooted, provided local production in Italy could be increased. Both General Wilson, before his promotion and departure for Washington, and the Quarter-Master General in London were approached with the latter stating that

> We shall be lucky, I think, if we ever raise it up to 2 bottles, though we will do our best to do so … The truth of the matter is that less beer is being brewed all over the world and more is being drunk.[73]

Seven decades later the importance to soldiers of that beer ration may not seem so great, but it was one element of the overall morale problem facing Eighth Army as it neared the end of its long march from North Africa to victory. The desire of commanders at the highest level to deal with the question of the beer ration indicates how well attuned they were to the needs of their soldiers. And that empathy was demonstrated in several other ways, the value of which cannot be gainsaid.

British soldiers on operations had long enjoyed the facility of leave centres where a brief spell out of the line could be enjoyed without the usual routine of military life. Sometimes, of course, there were those who found themselves in trouble for enjoying their break with a little too much enthusiasm, and there had been cases when some took advantage of the absence of many of the usual restraints of discipline to commit criminal offences for which they had to be punished. Nonetheless, the overall scheme had proved successful and was taken a step further in that final winter of war when it became possible to allow extended periods of home leave to some personnel. In this, the British soldier had the advantage over his comrade from New Zealand, South Africa or India, or his ally from the United States, since it was much easier to travel home to the United Kingdom.

For formations and units out of the line, entertainments were provided. These could be as simple as sports activities, with soccer and rugby among the most popular, although the matches played did not always conform to the usually accepted rules. This was especially so with games matching NCOs and soldiers against their officers. It would be difficult for an FA or Rugby Union referee to understand why it was necessary to use smoke grenades on the pitch, or block a goalmouth with a Bren-gun carrier or similar vehicle. As well as sports, there were less strenuous entertainments. On many occasions, these drew on talents within a unit as concert parties laid on variety shows that frequently demonstrated considerable theatrical aptitude, as well as the ability to improvise costumes and scenery from all sorts of unlikely sources and materials. In addition, shows were provided by divisional concert parties, or visiting ENSA (Entertainments National Service Association) parties. Although ENSA brought professional artists to the troops, this did not prevent military humourists claiming that the organization's initials really stood for 'Every Night Something Awful'. There were also occasions when the regimental bands of units fighting in Italy would visit the peninsula to entertain men of their own and other regiments.

In Fifth Army particular efforts were made to mark Christmas:

Wherever they were during the war, American soldiers retained their native traits and habits, and special efforts were made … to recreate the customs of Christmas. In the 15 days preceding Christmas Army post offices received 2,675 pouches and 48,383 sacks of mail for distribution by Christmas Day, and all units were issued turkey for Christmas and New Year's Day. Even the troops in the foxholes and those quartered in the old stone farmhouses near the front managed to brighten up the appearance of their surroundings for Christmas. II Corps provided the finishing touch. High on Radicosa Pass where the wind swept across the summits of the Apennines and the snow piled deep into drifts, corps engineers anchored a 40-foot tree, complete with strings of colored lights and a lighted sign reading 'Merry Xmas'. The tree was far enough behind the front to be on the friendly side of the light line, and military police stood by ready to extinguish the illumination whenever hostile planes appeared in the sky. The climax of the holiday attractions was the Spaghetti Bowl football game between … Fifth Army and Twelfth Air Force, played on New Year's Day in the municipal stadium at Florence before approximately 25,000 service men and women.[74]

We have already seen how dismounted cavalry regiments relieved infantry battalions in the front line allowing weary foot soldiers to have a rest. Rotating front-line units not only permitted those coming out of the line to rest, it also allowed them to receive replacement personnel and undergo training. Each division had established its own battle school for new personnel, now generally men converted from other arms, and those returning from convalescence or leave, to be trained under realistic conditions. Lieutenant Colin Gunner, 1st Royal Irish Fusiliers, was assigned to 78th Division's Battle School, where the chief instructor was Major Jimmy Clarke MC* of his own regiment:

The Battle School had been set up to convert sergeants and officers from anti-aircraft regiments to infantry and, with some dozen others from different regiments, I was an Instructor – not only an Instructor but a captain. Whether we were considered the dregs or cream of the fighting units I was never sure but the days lengthened, the sun shone; and Major Clarke was very tolerant about illegal visits to Florence.

The major only put his foot down once when the visits had taken such a toll that Simmons of the Buffs used to stand speechless and glazed before his class until his sergeant hissed 'Speak now' in his ear, when he would rattle off a recitation entitled *The Platoon in the Night Attack*, pick up his stick and go to bed. Still, I had tea with a Field Marshal when the Director of Infantry visited us and I actually passed him the sugar.

What those students learned I cannot say. The blind, in the hung-over sense, led the blind, but I don't think many of them ever got to the line in time to put our splendid theories into practice. If they did they were probably killed, as were two of the tutors a few weeks later.[75]

A critical factor in restoring a sense of purpose to the armies was leadership. Neither McCreery nor Truscott was lacking in that quality. With a real sense of belief at the top of both armies, it was natural that this feeling should percolate through the ranks to the soldiers on the ground. But this was not a case of personality cults such as those pursued by Clark and Montgomery, amongst others. Neither army commander had a huge ego, but both were men at the top of their profession who knew their own worth as commanders and believed that they could get the best from their commands.

McCreery's biographer notes that, during the fighting in October and November, the new Eighth Army commander 'had covered considerable distances to visit not only the commanders but also the fighting troops, often going as close to the front line as he could'. While he did not 'interfere with commanders who were doing their job properly' it was McCreery's habit 'to be as well informed on developments as possible so that he could offer advice and assistance should it become necessary'.[76] And that advice and assistance was described by one of his corps commanders, Charles Keightley, as 'clear, incisive, always helpful'.[77]

In Fifth Army Truscott also undertook a programme of visits, as his biographer notes:

> Beginning the day after his arrival, Truscott spent several days visiting various parts of the front, familiarizing himself with conditions among his troops, renewing acquaintances with many commanders and staffs, and becoming acquainted with others. Keyes had been Truscott's instructor at the training camp in Arkansas in 1917 and had been his superior as General Patton's deputy in Africa, in Sicily, and for a brief period prior to Anzio. Crittenberger had been on the faculty of the Cavalry School when Truscott was a student. Both had always been senior to him.[78]

McCreery and Truscott were making themselves known to their subordinates and getting to know those subordinates in turn. Their visits would have been known to many at all levels in each command and made the army commanders seem less distant, even to the infantryman, or dismounted tankman, in his mountainside slit trench who had not even had a glimpse of the visiting dignitary. But, in addition to boosting morale through such visits, the army commanders also sought to improve their soldiers' morale by other means, including those already noted. Of course, one important way of raising morale is showing soldiers that their efforts and sacrifices are important. There was an abiding sense that Italy was a forgotten theatre and that the armies were also forgotten at home. It was difficult to change that situation: both commanders entertained groups of politicians who visited their headquarters and met some of the soldiers on the ground. Usually, the politicians were accompanied by a retinue of pressmen, who, in Truscott's view, would otherwise not have visited northern Italy:

The problem of the 'forgotten front' was more intangible. The situation was made known to the War Department in the hope that Public Relations would be able to present a true picture to the American public which in turn would be reflected in the soldiers' mail. It was a matter of continuing concern to Public Relations officials of both the theater and the Army, and every effort was made to provide correspondents with suitable material. But many correspondents had little liking for spending uncomfortable days in the mountains seeking stories of small actions which would have limited news value. Rome not only offered more in the way of physical comforts; also, there was always the chance for an important news story in a capital city of that size under existing conditions. News of the Army front could be culled from day to day press releases by the Theater Public Relations officials.[79]

Truscott initiated a programme of sending news stories to US newspapers covering the actions of various units and the courageous exploits of individuals, the latter being sent to the home town, county or state press of the soldiers concerned. He noted that this 'produced an immediate and excellent reaction in the mail from home. And soldiers felt less forgotten when they or their units were mentioned in the home papers'.[80] Although Truscott believed that this public relations offensive achieved its aim, his biographer felt that, while a valiant effort, it had only limited success,

such as the flurry of press interest in Clare Luce Booth's visit and Bourke-White's photo spread in *Life*, [Otherwise] the rain-drenched dogfaces slogging in mud and up and down mountains in Italy remained eclipsed by the dashing of George Patton's tankers across France, which was favoured by correspondents who preferred to cover the war from the comforts of Paris.[81]

(Clare Booth Luce, wife of *Life* magazine owner, Henry Robinson Luce, was considered the most important female in the United States after Eleanor Roosevelt; she represented Connecticut in Congress.)

In addition to rest centres, entertainments and sports activities, soldiers could avail of educational programmes, although some of those could lack interest, especially if the lecturers were uninspiring. Even so, sitting in a lecture hall was preferable to shivering in a muddy slit trench. One subject on which lectures were delivered, and which featured in newssheets, was the importance of the Italian front. In Truscott's command:

Primary arguments to indicate the importance of the Italian front were the facts that Fifth Army had destroyed more than 200,000 Axis troops since the beginning of the campaign; that the Army, together with Eighth Army, was holding 24 to 28 first-class German divisions from participation in battles in eastern and western Europe; that we had captured great airfields from which heavy bombers could strike at the heart of German production; and that we had provided bases from which supplies could be shipped and flown to Yugoslavian patriots to aid them in tying up an additional 300,000 German troops.[82]

And, of course, it was essential that an army should remain efficient and effective, which required a training programme. In that final bitter winter of war every effort was made to ensure that when Fifth and Eighth Armies renewed offensive operations in the spring their men would be at their most efficient and effective. As they trained for their final operations soldiers of 15th Army Group became acquainted with new weapon systems and new operational methods, many focused on river crossing, that would more than prove their value when spring allowed the armies to launch the last assault in Italy.

Notes

1. Mead, op. cit., p.174.
2. Rottman, *US 10th Mountain Division in World War II*, p.33. Shelton (pp.160–1) notes that the formation was the last US division to enter the war in Europe.
3. Maximiano & Bonalume Neto, *Brazilian Expeditionary Force in World War II*, pp.7–8.
4. Jackson, Pt III, pp.323–5; Blaxland, pp.226, 228–9, 232 & 238.
5. Jackson, pp.163 & 196.
6. Mead, p.171.
7. Ibid.
8. See Orders of Battle (Appendix p.216).
9. Ibid; Jackson, p.236.
10. Jackson, p.409.
11. Ibid., pp.409–10.
12. Ibid.
13. Ibid., p.411; Beale at al., *Air War Italy 1944–45*, pp.182–3.
14. NA, WO170/4283, war diary, HQ XIII Corps (G), Feb '45.
15. Kesselring, *Memoirs*, p.221.
16. Blaxland, op. cit., p.245.
17. Molony, *Victory in the Mediterranean*, Pt I, pp.447–50.
18. Jackson, *Victory in the Mediterranean*, Pt II, pp.300 & 371–2.
19. Ibid., pp.371–2.
20. Anders, op. cit., p.216.
21. Molony, p.448.
22. Ibid., pp.447–50.
23. ffrench-Blake, 'Italian War Diary', p.15.
24. Blaxland, pp.230–1.
25. NA, WO170/4630, war diary, 2/6 Queen's, 1945.

26. Starr, op. cit., pp.376–7.
27. *TF 45 History*, Foreword
28. Starr, p.377.
29. Kesselring, p.220.
30. Duncan, *Royal Artillery Commemoration Book*, p.635.
31. Blaxland, p.226.
32. Ellis, *Victory in the West*, Vol. I, p.284.
33. Molony, p.444.
34. Ibid., p.447.
35. Molony, *Victory in the Mediterranean*, Vol V, pp.423–5.
36. Molony, *Victory in the Mediterranean*, Vol VI, Pt I, p.447.
37. Starr, p.368.
38. Ibid.
39. Ibid., p.369.
40. McCreery, draft memoirs, 'The Final Battle', p.1.
41. Starr, p.374.
42. Fraser, *And We Shall Shock Them*, p.357.
43. Blaxland, p.221.
44. Ibid.; NA, CAB106/453, Pt V, Desertion.
45. Blaxland, p.222.
46. Ibid.
47. Horsfall, *Fling Our Banner to the Wind*, pp.212–13.
48. Blaxland, p.222; NA, CAB106/453.
49. Doherty, *In The Ranks of Death*, pp.266 & 268.
50. Blaxland, p.222.
51. Ibid.
52. Ibid., p.223.
53. Truscott, p.461.
54. Starr, p.375.
55. Ray, *Algiers to Austria*, p.177.
56. Ibid.
57. Freeth, 'Across the Po Valley with the Americans', in Duncan, op. cit., p.327.
58. NA, WO170/5033, war diary 2 LF, 1945.
59. Trousdell, 1RIrF, to author.
60. Freeth, in Duncan, p.327.
61. NA, WO170/4987, war diary 1 A&S Hldrs, 1945.
62. Ibid.
63. NA, WO170/5041, war diary, 1 LS, 1945.
64. NA, WO170/5033.
65. NA, WO170/5061, war diary, 2/7 Queen's, 1945.
66. Starr, p.375.
67. Orpen, *Victory in Italy*, p.259.
68. NA, WO170/4978, war diary 3 Cldm Gds, 1945.
69. Truscott, p.460.
70. Starr, p.375.
71. Fisher, p.415.
72. Jackson, Pt III, pp.31–2.
73. Ibid., p.32.

74. Starr, op. cit., pp.375–6.
75. Gunner, *Front of the Line*, pp.129–30.
76. Mead, p.165.
77. Strawson papers, quoted in Mead, p.165.
78. Jeffers, p.227.
79. Truscott, p.464.
80. Ibid.
81. Jeffers, p.231.
82. Starr, p.325n.

Chapter Three

In north-west Europe Montgomery's 21st Army Group had the support of a dedicated division of specialized armour. This was Major General Sir Percy Hobart's 79th Armoured Division with its 'funnies' –Sherman Crab 'flail' tanks to create safe paths through minefields, Churchill Crocodile flame-throwers with their terrifying jets of fire, Churchill AVREs (armoured/assault vehicles, Royal Engineers) to perform a range of tasks including bridgelaying and dropping fascines in ditches to allow other tanks to cross, amphibious lightly-armoured troop-carrying LVTs (Landing Vehicles, Tracked), armoured personnel carriers (APCs) improvised from Sherman tanks with their turrets removed or de-gunned Priest self-propelled howitzers, and Duplex Drive (DD), or swimming, Sherman tanks (the latter did not come under Hobart's command but were trained by his personnel under his supervision).

That 79th Armoured Division was 21st Army Group's 'baby' did not mean that Eighth Army could not enjoy similar support. McCreery was determined that this should be so, especially as operations on the plain of Lombardy would mean crossing the Senio, Santerno, Sillaro, Reno and Idice waterways before meeting the Po. In addition, the land was criss-crossed by many small waterways and irrigation ditches with the common feature of floodbanks, some carrying tracks. In several instances, German engineers had widened canals to create even more effective anti-tank obstacles, while a large area neighbouring Lake Comácchio had been flooded. How might such obstacles be dealt with? The answer came from McCreery's new Chief Engineer, Brigadier B. T. Godfrey-Fausett, who, based on experience of the Gothic Line battles, and anticipating an 'almost endless series of water obstacles', proposed upgrading the army's existing assault engineer regiment to brigade strength, thereby creating a smaller version of 79th Armoured Division in Eighth Army. Thus 25 Tank Brigade, which included three Churchill I-tank regiments, was converted to the assault role as B Assault Brigade RAC/RE, a title changed on 6 April 1945 to 25 Armoured Engineer Brigade RE, commanded by Brigadier E. W. H. Clarke. With McCreery's support, Godfrey-Fausett's idea led to

> Armoured regiments [being] re-equipped with flame-thrower tanks, upgunned Shermans and Churchill tanks, and with tank-dozers. Some ... were fitted with widened 'Platypus' tracks to enable them to move over the soft fields of the Romagna. New armoured engineer equipment was also produced within the theatre for rapidly bridging ditches, canals and rivers. All these new equipments and devices needed specially trained crews to man them and new tactical

techniques. In the rear areas, particularly around Lake Trasimene, intensive experimental work and training went on throughout the winter.[1]

The new brigade's order of battle included 51st (Leeds Rifles) Royal Tank Regiment (51 RTR), the only unit of the original brigade, and two armoured engineer regiments, initially designated A and B Armoured Regiments RE before becoming 1st and 2nd Armoured Engineer Regiments on 6 April; the brigade was completed by C Armoured Park Squadron RE which became 631 Armoured Engineer Park Squadron.[2]

Within 25 Armoured Engineer Brigade, 51 RTR was trained and equipped with Churchill Crocodiles and Sherman Crabs, deploying two sixteen-tank squadrons of Crocodiles, and one of fifteen Crabs; both armoured engineer regiments (formed from 1st Assault Regiment and the engineers of the disbanded 1st Armoured Division) had three armoured squadrons,

each with two Armoured and two Dozer Troops. Each Armoured Troop was equipped with three Armoured Vehicles RE and three arks, each Dozer troop with three Sherman tank dozers. In addition, one of the Armoured Squadrons was equipped with mobile Bailey bridges. The equipping of the Brigade was in itself an enormous task, complete fabrication of equipment having to be carried out in some cases in Italy by already overworked RE, REME and Ordnance units.[3]

By late-1944 Churchill Mark VIIs were being delivered to Italy. This improved Churchill was 'plumbed' for flame-thrower equipment and some of the new arrivals had flame guns fitted. Although flame-gun equipment had already been used in Italy it had been mounted only in universal, or Bren-gun, carriers, the workshops not having been equipped to convert earlier Churchills to Crocodiles, as the flame-thrower version was dubbed. The Canadians used flame-throwers very effectively west of Lamone in December, prompting a decision to increase the use of these weapons. By 1 February sufficient flame-throwing equipment was available to allow the assault formations of V Corps to undertake intensive training in its use; on D Day twenty-eight Crocodiles were available to V Corps, with a squadron also supporting II Polish Corps.[4] The Wasp continued in use but the man-pack Lifebuoy flame-thrower was unpopular, although available in quantity, a factor noted in a report by the Chemical Warfare Staff of Allied Forces HQ which stated that 'Lifebuoy gave more trouble than its value as a weapon justified'.[5]

Eighth Army HQ outlined an operational doctrine for 25 Armoured Engineer Brigade: its resources were to be allotted by squadrons, each self-administering, and were not to be deployed in less than troop strength. As Jackson noted, 'An armoured troop with a dozer troop made an effective tactical group'.[6]

In addition to 25 Armoured Engineer Brigade, 9 Armoured Brigade was to operate some of McCreery's 'funnies'. The latter's commander, Brigadier R. B. B. Cooke, known as 'Cookie', was given responsibility for operating Eighth Army's two principal troop-carrying vehicles, the Kangaroo APC and the LVT Mark IV. Two armoured regiments were to operate the Kangaroos, 4th Queen's Own Hussars (Churchill's regiment; he became colonel-in-chief in 1941) and 14th/20th King's Hussars, the latter only recently arrived from the Middle East. Redundant Shermans and M7 Priests were the material from which Kangaroos were created. Reports of Canadian use of Kangaroos in north-west Europe had so impressed McCreery that, shortly after taking command of Eighth Army, he gave orders for workshops in Italy to begin local conversions. Shermans that were being replaced in service by newer models were used first, their turrets and ammunition stowage being removed to provide room for infantrymen. Later the M7 Priest was used, and its hull, being roomier than that of the Sherman, proved ideal. McCreery showed farsightedness in ordering a local conversion programme as a War Office undertaking to despatch sufficient APCs to lift an infantry battalion failed to live up to its promise. Neither 4th nor 14th/20th Hussars was entirely Kangaroo-equipped by April 1945: the former had one squadron of fifty-three Sherman Kangaroos and one of fifty-six Priest Kangaroos as well as an armoured squadron of seventeen Sherman gun tanks, while the latter had a forty-eight Priest Kangaroo squadron and an armoured squadron of twenty-eight Sherman gun tanks.[7]

Nine Armoured Brigade also included 7th Queen's Own Hussars, which trained in the use of the amphibious Duplex Drive Sherman tank. The regiment deployed three sabre squadrons, each with sixteen Sherman DDs and a single Valentine DD; in addition, it had eleven Stuart light tanks.

Cooke established a training centre on Lake Trasimene where his soldiers became familiar with the LVT. A Royal Army Service Corps (RASC) unit, 15th Transport Column, was assigned to operate the new vehicles; an additional training area on the Tiber came into use after 15 March.[8] Known in north-west Europe, where it had achieved considerable success in Canadian operations on the Scheldt, as the Buffalo, the LVT was given the codename 'Fantail' in Italy in an attempt to mislead the Germans about its presence. The LVT was an American invention, an amphibious tracked vehicle, designed by Donald Roebling, a retired engineer, for use in the Florida everglades, taken up by the US Marine Corps, which deployed it operationally in the Pacific. It was lightly armoured, carried one or two heavy-calibre machine guns and could climb muddy riverbanks. On water, its propulsion was via its tracks rather than propellers, as was the case with the DD tanks.[9] The version supplied to 15th Army Group, the LVT-4, Mark IV in British service, was improved by moving its engine forward, allowing a ramp door to be fitted at the rear of the hull and obviating the necessity for infantrymen to scramble out under fire over the sides. Some, fitted with a turreted 75mm howitzer, were effectively light amphibious tanks.[10]

Although Alexander had originally asked General Wilson for 600 LVTs to carry three assault brigades, one British and two American, this was reduced to 400 by the Combined Chiefs in February 1945 during the Argonaut conference.[11] Still sufficient for two assault brigades, the number required two regiments to operate Fantails, one of which would be 15th Transport Column; 755th Tank Battalion was assigned by Fifth Army as the second unit. Training took place on Lake Trasimene for 15th Transport Column while 755th Tank Battalion trained on the Arno, both regiments then coming together on Trasimene for further training, exercises and demonstrations. With 15th Army Group HQ allowing the loan of Fifth Army's LVTs to Eighth Army, 755th Tank Battalion came under British command in Cooke's 9 Armoured Brigade and amalgamated with 15th Transport Column as the Composite LVT Regiment, equipped with 190 LVTs, five of which were to be held in reserve.[12]

It is worth noting that many of the British specialized vehicles were produced, or modified, in Italy since adequate supplies were not available from Britain. As a result, REME workshops in the Mediterranean had to produce almost 200 specialized AFVs for 25 Tank Brigade. In spite of a shortage of local capacity, they converted fifty-nine Churchills as Ark bridge-layers, forty-seven as AVREs, a further fifty-one as fascine carriers and twenty-nine Shermans as tank-dozers. The Ark bridge-layers would see extensive use, in contrast to north-west Europe where they were hardly used at all, while the Churchill fascine carriers were supplemented by Shermans. As well as de-turreted older Shermans, each carrying two fascines, a new type of fascine called a bolster was introduced, which combined the traditional bundle with a steel lattice crib.[13] (See Figure 1)

In addition, the workshops produced four 140-foot Bailey bridge carriers and two Plymouth-bridge tanks, and modified Kangaroos from seventy-five Shermans and 102 M7 Priests. An additional contribution to the mobility of armour was the 'Grouser', an adaptation to extend a tank's track width to help it deal with muddy ground. Of several designs tested the most effective was one designed for amphibious tanks, known as 'Platypus'. Experiments by an armoured regiment with it in December 1944 'showed a remarkable improvement in … performance in soft going'. As a result some 12,000 were fabricated quickly in workshops in Naples. Possibly because they had been made so quickly, these proved defective; 3,000 'had to be re-worked' by Eighth Army's own workshops. Designed for muddy conditions, the grousers tore up paved roads and so Platypus-fitted tanks were not allowed on paved surfaces. The fittings also put additional strain on tank engines, a factor exacerbated by the introduction of the petrol-engined Sherman. In spite of the latter problem, McCreery decided that the risks involved should be accepted.[14] It is all the more ironic, therefore, that spring 1945 was very dry and Platypus extensions were unnecessary.

Another innovation for the offensive was an early infra-red aid to nocturnal tank driving, 'Tabby', which was also intended as a navigational aid. Although a crude and early example of such equipment, Tabby was used by 9 Armoured Brigade for LVT navigation in April 1945 while the sappers of 25 Armoured Engineer Brigade found it useful in bridging operations. However, gun tank commanders regarded it as inferior to half moonlight.[15]

Having specialized vehicles was of little value unless they could be used effectively. As we shall see, the plans being formulated did just that. Considerable innovation was shown that would see elements of 56th (London) Division take to the water in LVTs, while 78th Division would clear the way to and through the Argenta Gap for

6th Armoured Division with infantry racing forward in Kangaroo APCs to keep the defenders off balance; other formations were also to use Kangaroos to advantage.

In addition to the 'funnies' of 9 Armoured and 25 Armoured Engineer Brigades, improved armour was provided. In September 1944 British regiments had received some 105mm-gunned Sherman tanks, designed for close support (CS) work, which had been used in the autumn battles. Then followed Shermans fitted with the 76mm gun, a much more effective weapon than the 75mm of the earlier Shermans. Sufficient 76mm Shermans were supplied to allow this version of the American tank to become the standard AFV in both armies' armoured units. In north-west Europe, armoured regiments had also received Sherman Firefly tanks, a British adaptation fitted with the 17-pounder anti-tank gun, capable of meeting and defeating the German Mark V Panthers and Mark VI Tigers. Some Fireflies were also supplied to Eighth Army and, as spring 1945 approached, a typical British armoured regiment in Italy fielded thirty-seven 76mm Shermans, nine Fireflies and six 105mm Sherman CS tanks, with eleven Stuarts, or Honeys as they were known in British service, for reconnaissance duties.[16]

John Skellorn, a 16th/5th Lancer, recalled that his regiment first saw the 76mm and 105mm Shermans on 20 September 1944 and eventually received six CS tanks, and forty-six 76mm Shermans, although the latter figure includes the Fireflies issued to the unit; unlike north-west Europe, where each sabre troop received a Firefly, only two per squadron were provided. While 76mm Shermans and Fireflies were welcomed for their more effective firepower they had one disadvantage over those they replaced: they were petrol-engined and without 'the slogging power of the diesels'; the Shermans that were withdrawn were all diesel-engined.[17] (Another drawback of the petrol-engined Sherman was its propensity to catch fire when hit, so much so that crews dubbed it the 'Ronson' after the eponymous cigarette-lighter company's boast that its products lit 'first time'. It was estimated that a Sherman crew had only five seconds to bale out of a stricken tank to avoid being cremated; sadly, many perished in such situations.) One of the two Fireflies supplied to John Skellorn's squadron had a faulty firing pin on its 17-pounder gun and its crew were unable to practise using the weapon, thus entering battle 'without … having experienced a round being fired'.[18]

We have looked in detail at the units and equipment of the armoured engineers but the sappers had a much wider job, both in Eighth Army's front areas and behind the lines, especially in the preparations for the offensive. During the winter they were kept busy repairing roads, clearing snow off the roads across the Apennines on which the Allies depended for maintenance, repairing airfields, replacing Bailey bridges with permanent structures and clearing the harbour of Porto Corsini, the port of Ravenna. In addition, they were also developing an engineer base at Ancona, from which fuel pipelines were extended or new lines built; overhead cover and hard standings were built for stores, local towns were rehabilitated and, all the while, the sappers trained and organized for the offensive.

Engineer problems in the forthcoming battles were identified as:

The provision of large quantities of every available type of bridging and river crossing equipment; maintaining an adequate supply to formations throughout the battle.

The problem presented by the universal high floodbanks, which not only were formidable obstacles in themselves, but greatly complicated the launching of assault bridges.

The design and provision of high level maintenance bridges over wide rivers, in particular the Po, where the few civilian bridges had been wrecked by bombing, and the spans between remains of piers were far beyond the capabilities of normal Baileys.

The improvement and maintenance of congested roads behind the advance, in an area where no roadstone existed.

Training, in the limited period available, of all engineer units that were to take part in the battle.[19]

When the time came the engineers were not to be found wanting in any respect.

As with the British sappers, so with their American counterparts. Keeping roads clear during the winter, repairing their surfaces, replacing blown bridges and a myriad of other tasks kept them busy even while they prepared for the offensive. Ahead of Fifth Army were many rivers and the engineers prepared for crossings; as well as 2,000 tons of other engineer equipment they stockpiled 5,500 tons of bridging materials and prepared to extend the Highway 65 pipeline northwards to Bologna as soon as possible. With the Po presenting the greatest obstacle facing the attacking armies, careful study was made of aerial reconnaissance photographs. The projected zone of attack lay along a twenty-mile stretch from Ostiglia on Highway 12 west to Borgoforte, where the Mantova-Réggio road crossed the Po. Along this stretch sites suitable for 'assault crossings, ferries and bridges were selected' and the engineers laid their plans carefully for the provision of both floating and permanent bridges across the waterway:

Special emphasis ... was laid on the area between San Benedetto Po and Borgoforte, where the marshy ricefields about Ostiglia could be avoided; but a subsequent crossing at this latter site would be necessary to open up Highway 12 to Verona.[20]

A two–division assault crossing was provided for, with each division deploying two combat teams abreast.

Engineers were also prepared to construct a total of four floating treadways, one floating Bailey, one reinforced heavy pontoon bridge, and one semi–permanent pile bridge, the last listed to be two–way Class 50 and one–way Class 90. In addition to storm and assault boats, rafts, Quonset barges, and DUKWs, river-crossing craft included 200 LVTs ... and 60 medium tanks modified with DD equipment .... The latter two types were classified as secret equipment and were held in the rear areas, as was most of the bridging equipment to prevent the enemy from detecting our intentions. All, however, was to be brought forward on call. Since forcing the Po would be the greatest river crossing in Fifth Army experience, very careful training was given to the 39th Combat Engineer Group of II Corps, based on the probability that II Corps would make the main effort across the Po; if the effort were made by IV Corps, all or part of the engineer group would be released to support that corps. The 85th Division also received special training, and the 1st Armored Division conducted extensive work in stream and river crossings, with an eye both to crossing the Po and to overcoming the numerous small streams in the Po Valley.[21]

Artillery had played a major role since the beginning of the campaign, in spite of the ammunition supply problems, and, in early 1945, the bulk of 15th Army Group's artillery was British. In addition to the field artillery regiments of Eighth Army, the Royal Regiment of Artillery also provided medium and heavier weapons disposed in AGRAs (Army Groups, Royal Artillery), as well as AA artillery, anti-tank artillery, and specialist units to conduct artillery survey. Bofors 40mm light AA guns were available to fire tracer rounds to mark axes of advance and boundary lines in darkness or poor visibility. British artillery also supported Fifth Army with five British regiments as part of British Increment Fifth Army, while AGRAs could be deployed to support Truscott's army.

Another aspect of the artillery preparations worth noting was the use of 'artificial moonlight' for nocturnal operations. Royal Artillery searchlight regiments in Italy were redundant in their intended role but the gunners had trained to use their equipments to help infantry assemble or move during the hours of darkness. This tactic had been used in north-west Europe in 1944, preceding its introduction in Italy by days, and had proved effective, with the added bonus that the glare of the searchlights diminished opposing troops' night vision. The use of searchlights in this role soon became known as 'movement light'.[22]

The best news on the artillery front was that the shell famine was over. Judicious use of shells had allowed a substantial reserve stock to be built up, while US shipments received during March meant that Fifth Army had a sixty-day supply of ammunition; Eighth Army had 2,000,000 shells for its 1,020 guns.[23]

With such strength in guns, and with HAA regiments also acting as medium artillery, it is hardly surprising that the only significant Gunner reinforcement received by Eighth Army was 54th Super Heavy Regiment RA – actually a conversion of 54th Heavy Regiment to the super heavy role[24]– with three 8-inch guns and six 240mm howitzers disposed in three batteries, each with one gun and two howitzers; 11 Battery was placed under command of Fifth Army. Although 11 Battery was assigned to II US Corps, all other British artillery with Fifth Army was under IV Corps 'for ease of administration'.[25] Fifth Army received additional artillery – no fewer than twelve new battalions, two with 8-inch howitzers and one with 155mm guns – to increase its gunner strength so that, by mid-April, in addition to the organic artillery in the divisions, [six] battalions of 155mm howitzers, [four] battalions of 155mm guns, [two] battalions of 8-inch howitzers, and [one] battalion of self-propelled 105mm howitzers were available. In addition to five regiments … of British artillery ranging from 8-inch guns and 240mm howitzers to 4.5-inch guns, six separate tank battalions and five tank destroyer battalions could be utilized to increase the Army's fire power.[26]

With the programme of re-training gunners and other personnel continuing apace, and the desertion problem diminishing substantially, British infantry battalions were restored to four-company strength by spring 1945; this was achieved just before the opening of Operation GRAPESHOT. However, there were some reinforcement problems; due to their rates of losses, it was impossible to find sufficient reinforcements for the Guards and Rifle battalions and a battalion of each Guards brigade and one Rifle battalion were perforce disbanded.[27] (The Guards were reluctant to accept any reinforcements who had not been 'Depot trained', i.e. had not gone through the Guards' system from enlistment; otherwise it might have been possible to maintain the Guards' brigades at full strength with Guards' battalions.)

Four of Eighth Army's divisions remained at two–infantry-brigade strength: the two divisions of II Polish Corps, 56th (London) and 2nd New Zealand Divisions. While there were sufficient Polish reinforcements available – about 11,000 men – to create another two brigades, 3 Carpathian and 4 Wolwyn, many of the new personnel were very young and lacked adequate training, although there were some who had been conscripted into the German forces and had either deserted or been captured, many in Normandy. Since it was unlikely that they could achieve operational standards by April, they were assigned to supporting roles. With 6th South African Armoured Division releasing 24 Guards Brigade, Eighth Army HQ assigned the Guards to 56th Division, that formation being 'close to home' for Household troops. (The South Africans received a fresh infantry brigade, 13 Motorised, which arrived from home.) Freyberg's New Zealand Division did have three brigades, one of which was armoured, an orbat unique by that time to the New Zealanders and a result of their unhappiness with the support provided by British armour in North Africa. Raising a third infantry brigade for the division was difficult since reinforcements had to be shipped from New Zealand, and there were also many long-service men awaiting repatriation. Nonetheless, an additional infantry brigade, 9 Brigade, was formed to take part in Operation BUCKLAND. The New Zealanders re-roled existing units, the Divisional Cavalry Regiment, 22nd Motor Battalion of 4 Armoured Brigade and the divisional Machine Gun Battalion (27th), to form 9 Brigade. Reinforcements from New Zealand included men who had served with 3rd New Zealand Division in the Pacific before that formation had been repatriated in 1944.[28] We have already noted that 43 Gurkha Brigade was included in Eighth Army's orbat, as were 2 Parachute and the Jewish Hebron Brigades.

In Fifth Army 'several reinforcements arrived in preparation for the final spring offensive' and, late in March, 442nd Infantry Regiment with attached units returned from France, while Gruppo Legnano, was assigned to Fifth Army. It was possible not only to train divisions but to rest them, so that by 1 April three divisions of Fifth Army were resting. Overall, 'All divisions were over strength, close to 7,000 men and officers over and above tables of organization having been assigned to combat units.'[29]

Both armies benefited from the addition of new Italian formations, although Eighth Army was more enthusiastic about this reinforcement than Fifth. These new formations, *Gruppi di Combattimento*, or Combat Groups, were formed from the restructuring of the Italian co-belligerent forces, i.e. the forces of Marshal Badoglio's new government, which had negotiated an armistice with the Allies in September 1943, becoming a co-belligerent partner a month later. The first element of the Italian co-belligerent forces had been formed in late-September 1943 from soldiers of the *Regio Esercito*, or Royal Army. These 295 officers and 5,387 men, formerly members of two Regio Esercito divisions, had been encamped near Lecce in Puglia awaiting re-organization and, having escaped capture by the Germans, were formed into *1° Raggruppamento Motorizzato*, or 1st Motorized Combat Group.[30] According to Italian historian Piero Crociani, the group was outfitted with Regio Esercito tropical uniforms, it being considered impolitic to provide them with the grey-green heavy uniforms normally worn in Italy.[31] Thus they entered combat wearing uniforms entirely unsuited to an Italian winter and shivered through that bitter winter of 1943–44 in the Apennines in Campania. Their part in the fighting at Monte Lungo, which they captured, helped remove the scepticism felt by many of the Allies about their erstwhile foe.

The Raggruppamento Motorizzato was renamed the *Corpo Italiano di Liberazione* (Italian Liberation Corps), or CIL, on 17 April 1944 as the numbers of volunteers for the co-belligerent forces increased. With even more volunteers came the need for major re-organization and thus the creation of the Gruppi di Combattimento. General Alexander, then commanding the Army Group, was keen to include more Italians in his command to increase his strength, especially with the planned departure for southern France of the French Expeditionary Corps and VI US Corps. However, he met opposition from the Americans who refused to provide equipment or help train an expanded Italian force. Churchill took a different attitude and agreed to arm, equip and train four new 'divisions', each 12,000 strong, although US permission was needed to allocate Lease-Lend matériel to the Italians.[32]

Six combat groups were formed eventually: Cremona, Friuli, Folgore, Legnano, Mantova and Piceno. In addition, auxiliary divisions for support duties were created. Of the six combat groups, four were ready for operational deployment by April 1945, three being assigned to Eighth Army and one to Fifth; Mantova was ready to join Eighth Army as the war was ending while the sixth, Piceno, was still in training when the Germans surrendered. Cremona, Friuli and Folgore joined Eighth Army and Legnano went to Fifth.[33] Each group equated to a light British division, being at two-brigade strength. Fifth Army's historian described them as being 'about two thirds of the size of an American division'.[34] Based on divisions of the Italian Royal Army, each gruppo included two regiments (brigades), each of three infantry battalions, with artillery, engineer and other support and service elements. Only one artillery regiment, including field, anti-tank and anti-aircraft guns, was included in a gruppo.[35]

We have noted that both Polish divisions had only two brigades and that reinforcements had been received, allowing additional brigades to be formed, but a crisis developed around II Polish Corps, effectively the Polish national army, that threatened to upset all Eighth Army's careful planning. That crisis was born in the Crimean resort city of Yalta, where the Argonaut Conference of Churchill, Roosevelt and Stalin was held in February 1945. One result of this was to redefine Poland's eastern border, so that parts of the country east of the Curzon Line would be ceded to the Soviet Union, effectively becoming part of Russia. Moreover, the entire country was to come into the USSR's sphere of influence. When news of this arrangement reached Polish soldiers in Italy during March, it led to outrage and a sense of bewilderment and betrayal. General Wladyslaw Anders, commanding II Polish Corps, was affected so badly by the news that he threatened to withdraw the Poles from active service. Although due to go home on leave, General McCreery made a point of meeting Anders but the Pole was so disheartened that he would not listen, even suggesting that his men be made prisoners.[36]

While McCreery was home, and attending his mother's funeral, both Field Marshal Alexander and General Clark met with Anders and made personal appeals, but to little avail. On his return to Italy, Sir Richard met Anders again. Of this meeting, he wrote later:

> When I visited him he said 'how can I ask my soldiers to go on fighting. I must withdraw them from the line.' I replied that there were no troops to replace them, and that a 10-mile gap would be opened up! Anders remained silent for a moment and then said 'you can count on 2nd Polish Corps for this coming battle, we must defeat Hitler first.'[37]

That simple statement, describing Eighth Army's predicament should the Poles withdraw, touched Anders. He admitted subsequently that he had expected Eighth Army's commander to try to make excuses for the Yalta decisions and to argue with him. However, McCreery's straightforwardly honest comment about a ten-mile gap in Eighth Army's front had more influence than a parliament of carefully structured arguments.

> All my pent up emotions and anxieties, all the complexities, all the many pressures and arguments and counter-arguments had been reduced by one single sentence to one single physical consideration, the crux of a ten-mile gap. ... I knew in my heart what I had to do. If we who were fighting for a free Poland did not fight in this battle not only would we ruin the Allied victory in Italy, but we would forfeit the chance of our continuing to fight for our independence ... I told McCreery that we would fight on.[38]

And so II Polish Corps remained in Eighth Army's order of battle. As a demonstration of his confidence, McCreery placed 7 Armoured and 43 Gurkha Brigades under command of the Polish Corps. As his biographer notes, 'This [episode] was a fine example of Dick's deep understanding of his fellow man'.[39]

Although the Allied armies did not possess a massive superiority in manpower, they held many advantages, and their morale was now high, although there was the inevitable awareness that the war was almost over, which must have had an effect on many minds. However, they could see that the Allied air forces ruled the skies, that German and pro-Mussolini aircraft made few appearances, that their own equipment and levels of training were better than ever before, and that it would be possible to destroy the Axis forces on Italy's northern plains.

Notes

1. Jackson, *The Battle for Italy*, pp.293–4.
2. NA, WO170/4452, war diary, 25 Armd Engr Bde, 1945; Jackson, *Victory in the Mediterranean*, Pt III, pp.208–9; Bailey, *Engineers in the Italian Campaign*, pp.49 & 96.
3. Bailey, p.49.
4. Jackson, *Victory in the Mediterranean*, Pt III, p.407.
5. Ibid., p.406.
6. Ibid., p.403.
7. Ibid., pp.403–6.
8. NA, WO170/4422, war diary, 9 Armd Bde, 1945.
9. Hogg & Weeks, *Illustrated Encyclopaedia of Military Vehicles*, p.311.
10. Ibid.
11. Jackson, *Victory in the Mediterranean*, Pt III, pp.148–9.
12. Ibid., pp.405–6.
13. Ibid, pp.402–3; information about bolsters and cribs from WO170/4634, war diary, 2 RTR, 1945.
14. Jackson, pp.405–7.
15. Ibid., p.407.
16. NA, WO170/4456, war diary, 26 Armd Bde.
17. Skellorn, 'What Did You Do in the War, Grandpa?', p.19.
18. Ibid.
19. Bailey, p.48.
20. Starr, op. cit., p.393.
21. Ibid., pp.393–4.
22. Routledge, *Anti-Aircraft Artillery*, p.317.
23. Doherty, *A Noble Crusade*, p.284; Jackson, p.214.
24. Frederick, *Lineage Book of British Land Forces*, Vol. II, p.561.
25. Jackson, p.214.
26. Starr, p.377.
27. Jackson, p.207.
28. Ibid., pp.207–8.
29. Starr, p.385.
30. Blackwell, *Fifth Army in Italy*, pp.158–61; Doherty, *Eighth Army in Italy*, pp.177–8; *I Gruppi di Combattimento*, passim.
31. Prof Piero Crociani to author, 19 Nov 2013.

32. Jackson, *Victory in the Mediterranean*, Pt II, pp.55–6.
33. *I Gruppi di Combattimento*, passim.
34. Starr, p.377.
35. Archivio dell'Uffizio Storico dello Stato Maggiore Esercito. War diaries of Gruppi Cremona and Folgore.
36. Mead, pp.173–4; Anders, op. cit., pp.247–54; Harpur, pp.134–6; Blaxland, pp.257–8.
37. McCreery, op. cit., p.8.
38. Harpur, *The Impossible Victory*, p.135.
39. Mead, p.174.

Chapter Four

Other than the limited offensives already described, the winter of 1944–45 was one of static warfare. On Eighth Army's front, that warfare resembled closely the fighting on the Western Front of the Great War – and there were senior officers who could recall those days, including Sir Bernard Freyberg VC, GOC of 2nd New Zealand Division, who had fought on the Western Front, earning the VC, and Gallipoli. According to the New Zealand official historian:

> The line where the German armies stood in the winter of 1944–45 was largely gratuitous; it had no particular strategic significance; it was where the Allied offensive had come to a halt because of the troops' exhaustion, the bad weather, the lack of ammunition, and the need for regrouping. Between the Adriatic and the Apennines it crossed the Romagna on the line of the Senio River; it continued along the last northern ridge of the mountains south of Bologna and to the coastal plain where the Germans still held, in front of Massa, a remnant of the Gothic Line.[1]

Although there had been little activity since December, other than the pinching out of those German lodgements south of the Senio, the enemy had fortified his positions in his usual diligent fashion, creating a series of lines that began with the Irmgard along the Senio itself, backed up by the Laura on the Santerno, Paula on the Sillaro and Genghis Khan along the Idice, its left resting on the flooded land west of Lake Comácchio, an area the Germans considered impassable for an attacker. This system of defences was intended to protect Bologna from the south-east while, at their northern end, a further line, based on the Reno river, into which the others flowed, added depth to the defence of the Po, particularly closer to the coast. Strategically, the German intention was that this eastern sector of the line would hold firm, allowing the western sector to hinge back towards the line of the Adige and the mountain passes into Germany.[2]

The Germans had also been busy constructing the Venetian Line, behind the Adige on the high ground between the Adriatic at Chióggia and Lake Garda, backed up by the *Voralpenstellung*, the Pre-Alpine Defence Position, and the Alps themselves. General Buelowius, Inspector of Land Fortifications South-West, oversaw these works, built by thousands of Italian and foreign labourers forced into the Todt Organization; no fewer than 5,340 German specialist engineer and construction troops were also involved.[3] All this effort was in vain due to Hitler's obsession with holding ground. Had Army Group C withdrawn behind the Po before spring 1945, the Venetian Line and the *Voralpenstellung* might have proved effective obstacles. However, Hitler had forbidden any move that involved ceding ground and thus Army Group C's *Herbstnebel* – autumn fog – plan, drawn up in autumn 1944, for a strategic withdrawal to stronger positions, was vetoed.[4]

Because of Hitler's direct interference at both operational and tactical levels, the opposing army groups settled into a war of attrition, especially along the Senio. (Although Allied accounts refer to the Senio as a river, it is only a stream – *torrente* – and shown as such on Italian maps.) However, its waters rise after heavy rain in the mountains, or when winter snows melt, and it is, therefore, bounded by high floodbanks. The Senio would have presented an obstacle to any attacker, but its effectiveness was multiplied many times by those floodbanks.

It was not possible to apply a simple description to the floodbanks since no two were alike. They rose across the plain wherever there was a waterway and could be up to thirty feet high and about ten feet wide at the top, although the river or stream might be less than twenty feet wide and, usually, only a few feet deep:

> Each one had its own character. They were all too steep to drive a tank straight up them. In places there were cart tracks traversing the side and sometimes ramps that a tank could go up. The rivers between these banks varied too in width, depth and speed of current. They had all been spanned by high level bridges – that is from the top of one floodbank to the other. I do not think any of [the bridges] had been left intact. …
>
> Any visibility that there was in this flat country was either from a floodbank or some high house, and neither of these enables you to get a close view over the floodbank on the other side.
>
> There was one good thing about this part of the world. Owing to its agricultural richness there were plenty of houses, and owing to the nature of the vegetation it was very difficult for the Germans to see many of them. The [enemy] had no Air OP like we had.[5]

The winter stalemate allowed the Germans to fortify the floodbanks, tunnelling through them in places and creating strongpoints (see Figure 2). On its way from the Apennines to the Reno, the Senio meanders across the flat landscape of the Romagna, forming numerous loops that often allowed one side or the other the tactical advantage of being able to see behind the opposition's front line. On some stretches the Germans held positions on the reverse side of the British, or near, floodbank; in such cases they built bridges or rafts to reach their forward positions.

In early March 78th Division began relieving 56th Division along the Senio with 38 (Irish) Brigade taking over from 169 (Queen's) Brigade. Facing them, 98th Volksgrenadier Division deployed two battalions from each of its three grenadier regiments with orders to oppose any small-scale attacks and exploit any opportunity for small gains. As well as holding the entire western bank in this sector, with its floodbanks some two feet higher than those on the eastern side, 98th Division had several posts on the western side of the eastern floodbank, and a strong line of machine-gun positions. For this deployment, the Irish Brigade included its two fusilier battalions, 2nd Inniskillings and 1st Irish, and 56th Reconnaissance Regiment; its other infantry battalion, 2nd London Irish Rifles, was in reserve. Additional support was provided by a squadron of the Bays (who fired armour-piercing rounds through the floodbanks to hit enemy positions), an anti-tank battery, a field company of sappers and a company of the divisional support battalion with medium machine guns and 4.2-inch mortars. The troopers of 56 Recce relieved 44 Recce who had been holding only two positions on the floodbank, although both were held in depth. Since the town of Cotignola was opposite the reconnoitrers, and the Germans there could see behind the opposing floodbank, daylight movement was impossible.[6]

This was a throwback to the trench warfare of an earlier conflict, with a distance between the front lines often less than that experienced generally in the First World War. Both sides learned quickly the lessons of trench warfare, including the importance of keeping heads below parapets during daylight hours. Peering over a parapet invited a sniper's attention; periscopes were used instead. With both sides so close, it was possible to hurl grenades across the gap, a tactic refined by bundling grenades in a bag before throwing the bag across, reducing the possibility of bombs rolling out of the target area.[7] Where the Germans held the reverse side of an Allied floodbank it was impossible to call down artillery fire on the bridges or rafts and so the infantry improvised with their PIATs, using them as mortars to rain fire on the bridges. Elsewhere, PIATs were used simply as mortars, firing into the enemy lines, especially at night, as Lieutenant Jim Trousdell, of 1st Royal Irish Fusiliers in 38 (Irish) Brigade, recalled:

> The main activity took place after dark when we kept up a continuous fusillade of small arms, grenades, 2-in mortars and a new use for the PIAT – fired as a mortar. The bomb made quite a noise falling and must have proved unnerving to the opposition.[8]

G Branch 78th Division's war diary records that a single PIAT fired 600 bombs as mortars in one day, such was the enthusiasm for this hitherto unloved weapon.[9] Company Sergeant Major Robbie Robinson, also of the Irish Fusiliers, described how both the 2-inch mortar and PIAT were employed:

> Amongst platoon weapons in constant use … was the 2″ mortar. … In order to reduce the range … and bring targets 40–75 yards away into effective range, half the propellant charge from the cartridge … was removed. Mortar crews became very proficient at hitting close-range targets on the opposite bank. … On the Senio [the PIAT] was used as a mortar and fired at high angle. PIAT bombs exploding on the roof of a dugout could cause damage and severe shock waves underneath and its blast effect was quite considerable.[10]

Brigadier Scott summed up the experience of the Senio for his own and other Eighth Army soldiers when he noted that darkness was the signal for increased activity along the floodbanks:

Grenade duels, machine-gun fire and mortar stonks were continually going on from both sides. Most of the roads on our side were swept by spandaus in the forward company areas. This racket used to go on most of the night. There was very little shelling. The real characteristic of this fighting was that the infantry were in very close contact – sometimes only about 8 to 10 yards apart – and that it was the infantryman's war almost entirely. There was now an enemy our soldiers could get to grips with, relying on their own skill and their own weapons entirely. There was someone they could vent their spleen on.

Cautiously at first, but getting ever bolder, the battalions started about making life unpleasant for the Germans on their side. Patrolling, in the ordinary sense, was inappropriate. The technique was to locate and gain full details of some position, and then, next night, send a section along the floodbanks to deal with it. Mines were the biggest curse and over uncharted floodbanks it was necessary for mine prodders to lead the way.[11]

Another echo from the Great War was trench raiding, which both sides practised; this could include tunnelling through the floodbank where only that earthen construction separated the foes. No sooner had 56 Recce taken over its sector on 10 March than one of its positions was attacked by enemy troops using grenades and sub-machine guns, while the centre troop position was subjected to intense mortaring. Three days later heavy shelling and mortaring was directed on A Squadron, although only one soldier was wounded slightly. An AGRA shoot was called for and the German guns fell silent. However, on the 19th there was a more serious attack by up to thirty Germans in which one man was killed, six were wounded and a troop HQ collapsed. In re-establishing contact with squadron HQ, Sergeant Patrick Cronin earned the Military Medal while Lance Corporal George Duffy received the same decoration for rescuing wounded in full sight of the enemy. (Sergeant Cronin was killed in action on 29 April and is buried in Argenta Gap War Cemetery.)[12]

Brigadier Pat Scott's comment that enemy positions were identified and, the next night, dealt with by a section of soldiers is the background to a patrol from 2nd Royal Inniskilling Fusiliers on the night of 12 March. Lance Sergeant Patrick Joseph 'Rex' Doherty led the patrol to 'destroy a Spandau position which had been harassing and inflicting casualties on a forward platoon':

L/Sgt Doherty led his men along the floodbank to within 15 yards of the emplacement when Schu mines were encountered. The patrol moved cautiously on, removing the mines as they advanced. At this point the patrol was heard, and the enemy threw grenades at them, but the patrol kept on advancing and retaliated with their own grenades, whereupon the enemy sent up three white Very lights and threw over a large number of grenades, slightly wounding L/Sgt Doherty and one other member of the patrol. L/Sgt Doherty withdrew his patrol, reformed, and attacked again. This time he was met with Spandau fire as well as another shower of grenades. The Spandau position was rushed and silenced, and has not opened up since, but the patrol suffered three casualties in doing so, one of them falling just in front of the gun. L/Sgt Doherty immediately went to his aid, although he was not sure then that the gun had been silenced, and helped him to get clear, and then withdrew his patrol intact.[13]

For his outstanding courage and leadership, which led to the success of the operation, Sergeant Doherty was awarded the Military Medal.

Seventy-eighth Division was withdrawn from the line after four weeks of trench warfare. However, individual units spent shorter spells in the front line; the Irish Brigade battalions were withdrawn on 26 March, although the Inniskillings were then in brigade reserve and had taken part in Exercise HOSANNAH, training for the forthcoming offensive, on the 25th. Since they had been in the line on St Patrick's Day, the Irishmen had not been able to celebrate the Saint's day, but rectified this situation with a large-scale celebration in Forlí on the 29th. Following Divine Service, and a parade at which shamrock was distributed by V Corps' commander, General Keightley, there followed an outburst of celebration that included a football match (one of several) during which a German tank made an appearance on the pitch, and the consumption of large quantities of alcohol, including gin from a water tanker that had been filled at a nearby distillery, but which had been emptied by evening. For Lieutenant Colonel M. J. F. 'Murphy' Palmer, commanding 1st Royal Irish Fusiliers, the 'Faughs', there was an unexpected sequel to the celebrations. When he and his driver went to visit wounded Faughs in the nearby general hospital he was intercepted by the matron who delivered such a tirade about the number of drunken Irishmen occupying beds in her hospital that would be needed for casualties from the offensive that Colonel Palmer decided that a tactical withdrawal was advisable. He told the author that he would have preferred to face a panzer division than meet the matron again.[14]

We have already noted 2nd Royal Inniskilling Fusiliers' participation in a training exercise for the offensive. By now, the training programme was reaching its peak. On the day after their St Patrick's Day celebrations, the Inniskillings were involved in another exercise, a river crossing on the Ronco, which 2nd London Irish repeated later. On 31 March the Irish Rifles and C Squadron Bays took part in Exercise MASSA, designed to test co-operation between infantry and tanks, especially in wireless procedure. Both Inniskilling and Irish Fusiliers also undertook MASSA with their assigned Bays' squadrons.[15] Brigadier Scott also learned that his brigade was to use heavy armoured vehicles, Kangaroos, to transport one of his battalions for the breakthrough.

The Irish Brigade had operated with armour many times in the past but ... further training could only help to improve the quality of such preparation. And there was a different aspect to the use of armour in the forthcoming advance for the men of the Rifles would be riding into battle in converted tanks. They were to become the Kangaroo Army.[16]

The Black Cats of 56th (London) Division were getting to know another new form of riding into battle. Although a battalion of the division had used Kangaroos during Operation CYGNET in January, the men of Major General Whitfield's division were now to become acquainted with another innovation, the American LVT, or Fantail. The Queen's Brigade battalions (2/5th, 2/6th and 2/7th Queen's Royal Regiment) moved to Lake Trasimene to train in amphibious operations with LVTs, as part of what the divisional historian described as secret

> preparations ... for amphibious operations on Lake Comácchio and across the swamps to the south of it. These were to form part of the Spring offensive and at the outset to help further the Eighth Army plan to turn the line of the Santerno at its extreme end.[17]

Those preparations included using LVTs not only to carry infantry but also to transport 25-pounders that could fire from the vehicles when afloat. Lieutenant Colonel Spicer, CO of 113th Field Regiment, conducted a series of experiments to determine the best and safest ways to carry his guns in the LVTs so that they could provide covering fire for the infantry and lay down a smokescreen for the Fantails during the assault. Spicer's estimates for smoke-laying proved accurate and played a major role in 169 Brigade's success. The other original brigade of 56th Division, 167 (9th Royal Fusiliers, 1st London Scottish and 1st London Irish Rifles), was to assault enemy positions along the Senio while 24 Guards Brigade, recently joined from 6th South African Armoured Division and replacing 43 Gurkha Brigade, was also to have an amphibious role. More use might have been made of LVTs had more been available when the offensive began, but there were sufficient only to lift one brigade, which required a modification of the plans for their use.[18]

The training and preparation phase involved everyone in both armies as its aims included enhancing all-arms co-operation, as well as familiarizing personnel with new equipment and weapons. Co-operation between arms was essential and had been improving greatly throughout the Italian campaign. Even so, there were still shadows of the distrust that had soured relations between armour and infantry especially. By training intensively with each other, these arms would increase the level of mutual trust and come to see themselves not as discrete elements but as parts of the same team. Operation GRAPESHOT would demonstrate levels of all-arms co-operation hitherto not seen.

Engineers especially were kept busy during this phase, as they would be in great demand in the assault phase. Nor would the pressure on them relent in the subsequent advance. The engineers were now at the top of their game, having 'trained' in the most demanding engineering academy of them all – the campaign through Italy. This was particularly true of the British, Commonwealth and Imperial sappers, of whom those of 2nd New Zealand Division are a perfect example. The New Zealanders' CRE, Colonel Hanson, devised a highly successful crossing technique. Hanson believed that the type of river and canal crossing between the Senio and the Po was suited to low-level Bailey bridges 'built in situ at the bottom of the riverbanks, only a few feet above water' and that such bridges were 'by far the speediest means of getting tanks and Divisional transport forward'. Moreover, it was possible to construct such bridges in half the time demanded by the orthodox method of building and launching a 100 to 150-feet Bailey at the natural bank height above water and, due to the greatly reduced span at the bottom of the banks, much less bridging would be needed. This latter was a critical factor 'when supplies are short and replenishment difficult'.[19] Access was created by blasting gaps in the floodbanks, obviating the need to build ramps for high-level bridges. Hanson, aware that bridging was critical, ensured that equipment was brought as far forward as possible to enable bridges to be built on site and rafted across, and developed a technique of assembling the girders, launching them on a raft and building the bridge as the raft was pushed across the river. It proved possible to assemble forty-to-fifty-foot-long bridges in times from thirty-five minutes to an hour.[20] The value of Hanson's ideas and training would be demonstrated when Freyberg's men crossed the Senio and Santerno. Strangely, although Hanson organized demonstrations of these techniques for engineers from other formations, none employed them in action. Hanson's sappers were supported by a specialist assault squadron formed within the division: 28 Assault Squadron had a range of 'funnies' including four Sherman dozers, four Sherman Arks, four Sherman fascine carriers, two Sherman Kangaroos, four Valentine bridge-layers and three Stuart/Honey recce tanks.[21] As noted in Chapter Three, p.46, Fifth Army's engineers were also well prepared to tackle the river crossings, especially that of the Po.

On Fifth Army's left was a three-mile-wide coastal plain, cut by many water courses, each fortified by the enemy. On the right of that plain was a 'mass of sharp peaks, tremendous gorges, and sheer rocky cliffs called the Apuan Alps, absolutely impassable to large forces'. Farther to the right came the high ground of the northern Apennines, out of which the main body of Fifth Army would attack; a preliminary operation into the coastal plain would precede that attack.[22]

Before moving on in the next chapter to consider the plans for the offensive, a brief summary of the ground facing both armies and the problems it posed would be useful. Map 1 shows the dispositions of the opposing armies in spring 1945, with inter-army boundaries marked. In 1947 General McCreery wrote that 'The difficulties of ground confronting both armies were great'.[23] Even on a small-scale map, those difficulties may be appreciated. Studying a larger-scale map, those difficulties are even plainer. Looking from the west coast to the east, we can see the topographical features the Allied planners had to consider: that strip of western coastal plain, for example, left Fifth Army's flank open to attack, and hence the need to secure it before the offensive proper began. To the right centre, Bologna beckoned Mark Clark's attention, as it had the previous autumn, but was not to provide such a distraction for Lucian Truscott. Although the bulk of his army would debouch from the Apennines close to the city, Truscott would not allow it to become a magnet. Army Group C's inter-army boundary ran north-south to the west of Bologna with the bulk of Fourteenth Army facing Fifth Army, which also faced the Army of Liguria; the bulk of Tenth Army faced Eighth Army. Fifteenth Army Group's inter-army boundary was about four miles to the west of its German equivalent.

What is apparent about this region above all else is that, having left the mountains behind, the fighting was to be done on flat land. Once the Allied armies had launched their assaults, they would be striking into the great northern plain of Italy. Covering much of Lombardy and the area known as the plain of the Po, this includes the regions of Lombardy and Emilia-Romagna, and parts of Piemonte and Venetia. (Since the term 'Lombardy' once included all northern and central Italy, the home of the Germanic tribe called the Lombards, the description 'plain of Lombardy' is used in this book for the northern plain.) Much of Italy is mountainous with only a small proportion of flat land, the largest element of such land being in the area over which 15th Army Group was preparing to fight in those final weeks of war.

Flat land may be more attractive for fighting, especially for armour, than mountainous terrain. However, the flat land onto which the Allies were about to strike was far from attractive for either infantry or armour. This is one of Italy's most important agricultural areas, where crops include much of the country's rice, and was once marshy land due to the regular flooding of the many rivers and streams cutting across it. Such floods occur in springtime, as melt water from the winter snow rushes down from the mountains, and in the autumn, as the rains come down, swelling the waterways. Over the centuries, the area has been criss-crossed by irrigation and drainage ditches, some of the drainage system having been designed by Leonardo da Vinci. As a protective measure against flooding, high banks line either side of rivers and streams. To the casual visitor, especially in summer, these banks may appear extravagant since, in many cases, they dwarf the watercourses they protect. Those along the Senio are a case in point; it is hard to imagine this gentle stream needing to be checked by such powerful guards. So it must have appeared to those soldiers with the task of garrisoning its floodbanks in that final winter of war, or assaulting them in April 1945.

Difficult as the floodbanks were for the infantry, they posed a greater problem for armour. In most places, the 'friendly' bank was so steep that it defied all but the Churchills; and even Churchills would have had problems at times. Even if a tank could climb the bank, its belly would have been exposed to enemy anti-tank fire as it crawled over the top. That problem, of course, related to the assault phase. What of the subsequent phase, the pursuit? In that case, the armour would again have to cross floodbanks presenting similar difficulties. Even the smallest stream created problems. The historian of 17th/21st Lancers, who was the regiment's commanding officer in 1945, Lieutenant Colonel Val ffrench-Blake, noted a problem peculiar to the Sherman Firefly, with its long-barrelled 17-pounder gun, 'a long unwieldy weapon, which projected so far beyond the tank, that it frequently hit the ground, breaking off the elevating gear'.[24] This comment referred to the propensity for the 17-pounder's long barrel to dig in to the far bank of a narrow stream as the Sherman dropped into the water. It created yet another caveat for tank crews as D Day approached, but was a problem to which creative thinking was applied, and Sherman Fireflies were adapted to carry fascines, or cribs and baulks (see Figure 3).[25]

The need to get armour across the many water obstacles placed a heavy burden on the engineers, both those with the attacking divisions and the specialized engineers of 25 Armoured Engineer Brigade. So that momentum could be maintained, it was essential that tanks and other armoured vehicles, including Kangaroos, should not lose time crossing streams and rivers. Thus, as we have seen, large quantities of bridging equipment were brought forward and 25 Armoured Engineer Brigade included specialist bridging tanks, based on the highly adaptable Churchill. Other brigades employed Sherman Arks and Twabies, while war-weary Shermans were de-turreted and adapted as fascine carriers, an improvisation also used in II Polish Corps.

Those many watercourses provided the Germans with further opportunities to demonstrate their defensive skills. The Senio provided a formidable obstacle and was backed up, as noted on p.53, by further lines along the Santerno, Sillaro and Idice. In order to prevent the Germans making orderly withdrawals to their next defensive line, speed in the advance was essential. The major advantage that 15th Army Group had in this respect was Allied control of the air.

Both Fifth and Eighth Armies were supported by tactical air forces that had matured in experience and operational capability throughout the campaign. This was especially true of the British 1st Tactical Air Force, the Desert Air Force, which had served alongside Eighth Army and its predecessors since the campaign in North Africa and which had 'written the book' on close air support. Although Montgomery claimed to have initiated close co-operation between ground and air forces, such co-operation had already been in existence when he arrived in the desert in August 1942, and had been encouraged by General Sir Claude Auchinleck, Commander-in-Chief, Middle East, and Air Marshal Sir Arthur Tedder, Air Officer Commanding-in-Chief, Middle East. Even before Auchinleck arrived in Cairo in mid-1941, Tedder had been advocating much closer co-operation between the RAF and ground forces, a policy with which Auchinleck agreed wholeheartedly, as shown by his inclusion of an RAF element in the expanded Staff College at Haifa.[26]

By spring 1945 Allied tactical air arms had developed their operational art to the point where immediate close air support was available to ground troops whenever weather conditions permitted. This support came from squadrons of the Desert Air Force for Eighth Army and of XXII Tactical Air Command for Fifth Army, although there was sufficient flexibility for either air force to support either field army. In the stripping out of Allied forces in Italy to reinforce those in north-west Europe, both air forces had suffered as well as their armies. This was especially true for XXII Tactical Air Command whose parent formation, Twelfth Air Force, on the proposal of General Marshall, was to send five fighter groups, a light bomber group, a reconnaissance unit and two night-fighter units to north-west Europe. However, Alexander protested that 'it was all the more desirable to keep as much air power as possible in the theatre' if he was to lose ground formations. Alexander was especially worried about the possible loss of American light or medium bombers because British air forces in Italy were strong in heavy bombers and tactical support aircraft but weak in light and medium bombers. Eventually, a compromise was agreed: two fighter groups would move at once, but 'Alexander was instructed to negotiate with Eisenhower for release of as much of the rest of US Twelfth Air Force to France as would not endanger the security of the Italian front'.[27] Although deep cuts were not inflicted on the Desert Air Force, its squadrons had to make do without the latest aircraft that were available to 2nd Tactical Air Force in north-west Europe. No Typhoons, Tempests, or later-mark Spitfires joined the Desert Air Force's squadrons, although P-51D Mustangs (Mustang Mk IVs in RAF service) were in use. However, since the Luftwaffe had all but disappeared from the skies in northern Italy, the RAF squadrons could perform their tasks with the older machines they possessed. In spite of this equipment situation, as General McCreery commented to Brian Harpur,

> we had some things going for us. We had aerial supremacy. The support we had there was derived from the Desert Air Force, which I believe to be the most skilled tactical air power in the world. It was the key to our survival and to our attack.[28]

In February McCreery asked that Eighth Army be given the greatest possible air support for its offensive 'in view of the fact that the over-all striking power of my Army has been materially curtailed by recent decisions'[29] that removed formations from Eighth Army.

Although close support of ground forces was the task of the tactical air forces, these formations were themselves constituent parts of much larger organizations that played critical roles in the campaign generally, and in the final offensive. Under the overall umbrella of Mediterranean Allied Air Forces (MAAF) came the Mediterranean Allied Strategic Air Force (MASAF), the Mediterranean Allied Tactical Air Force (MATAF) and the Mediterranean Allied Coastal Air Force (MACAF).

MASAF included the strategic bomber element of the Allied air forces, including the US Fifteenth Air Force, with five heavy bombardment wings, and No. 205 Group RAF with a 'pathfinder' and four heavy bomber wings. The US XV Fighter Command also came under command of Fifteenth Air Force, its units having the task of escorting heavy bombers on daylight missions.

Originally, Twelfth Air Force had included strategic bombers but was re-organized as a tactical formation and, on 19 October 1944, its XII Tactical Air Command became XXII Tactical Air Command. Alongside the Desert Air Force, its aircraft provided close air support for Fifth and Eighth Armies, as well as carrying out interdiction against enemy ground communications and logistics.

MAAF also included transport, maritime patrol and strike aircraft, tactical bombers and communications planes. Its aircraft ranged from tiny Austers and Cessnas, employed as air observation posts for the artillery, through single-engined fighters, fighter-bombers and reconnaissance machines, to twin-engined light and medium tactical bombers, night-fighters, target-finders and C-47 Dakota, or Skytrain, transports and the four-engined heavies, including the American B-17 Flying Fortress, B-24 Liberator and British Halifax bombers, and the Sunderland maritime patrol flying boats.[30]

As well as the close support for ground troops by the Desert Air Force and XXII TAC, other elements of the Allied air forces played an important role in the campaign, including the final offensive. Clark had long asked for the heavy bombers to be deployed in support of the ground forces, but this had not been possible when those bombers were needed to attack strategic targets such as oil refineries in German-occupied territory. However, as the Germans were forced back on the Eastern Front, and in Yugoslavia, the number of such targets was decreasing and it became possible to assign the heavies to assist the Allied armies.[31]

Of course, there is little doubt that many missions flown by strategic bombers from Italian bases against targets outside Italy had an effect on ground operations in the peninsula. This was especially true of raids on oilfields and oil refineries, as well as those against railway marshalling yards and ports. Such was the success of these raids, combined with those of RAF Bomber Command and US Eighth Air Force from Britain that, on 21 February 1945, General Koller, the Luftwaffe Chief of Staff, cut the issue of aviation fuel to the Luftwaffe in Italy to nine tons per day. That contrasts with 407 tons daily for the Eastern Front and 403 for the Reich and the Western Front. This restricted severely Luftwaffe operations in Italy. However, there were few aircraft left in the theatre; an assessment of 10 January put Luftwaffe strength in Italy at no more than sixteen long-range reconnaissance aircraft, of which thirteen were serviceable; twenty-nine tactical reconnaissance aircraft with twenty-three serviceable; and twenty-three night ground-attack aircraft, only fourteen of which were serviceable.[32] The ANR was estimated to have about forty Messerschmitt Bf109s, a figure later increased to fifty-five, and a small force of Savoia-Marchetti SM.79 bombers. By the end of February it was estimated that the Luftwaffe and ANR had no more than 551 tons of fuel available in Italy.[33] The fuel shortage also limited the mobility of German and Italian ground forces. Nor had the German offensive in the Ardennes in December, which had consumed large quantities of fuel for aircraft and vehicles, helped the overall fuel situation.

As well as attacks on fuel facilities, strategic bomber raids on transport centres, such as railway marshalling yards and lines of communication between Italy and Germany and Austria, had a material effect. Not only was the supply of equipment and matériel to Army Group C reduced to a trickle, but the flow of industrial goods and foodstuffs out of Italy to Germany was much reduced. This latter factor is important since it underlines one of the main reasons the Germans continued to hold northern Italy. The British official historian notes that, on 4 March, Field Marshal Wilhelm Keitel, head of OKW (*Oberkommando der Wehrmacht*), the chief of the German armed forces and, effectively, Hitler's war minister, wrote to Albert Speer, Minister of Armaments and War Production, telling him that Hitler had 'recently and repeatedly' stated that, following the loss of the eastern territories, 'it was all the more important to retain this area, whose industrial and agricultural resources supplied not only the fighting troops in the theatre but "also, in part, the Home Zone"'.[34] While this was no longer the case in early 1945, thanks to disruption of rail and road links, it illustrates Hitler's mentality, which was becoming more divorced from reality.

While strategic bombers had contributed to cutting the links with Germany and Austria, the main burden of that task had fallen on the tactical air forces' light and medium bombers. Such attacks had caused severe damage to roads, bridges and railways in northern Italy and the Brenner Pass railway. The last-named was targeted heavily by MATAF units and headed a list of priority targets issued by its commander, Major General John K. Cannon, on 3 November 1944. MATAF's intelligence staff had realized that the Germans were dealing effectively with interdiction of the river lines and that it would be more effective to deny them the Alpine passes, since finding alternative routes would prove difficult. Although MATAF retained an overall priority for direct support of Fifth and Eighth Armies, and counter-air operations, its primary task was to destroy and disrupt the German Lines of Communication with the three-fold object of

a. Denying all movement by rail to and from Italy (isolation of Italy).
b. Reducing the flow of supplies by rail and road from existing dumps in Italy to enemy forces on the Italian front.
c. Destroying the enemy's means of transport, including fuel supplies, wherever possible.[35]

Flowing from this directive, the medium bomber force was to interdict routes and destroy specialized means of supply and transport in this order of priority:

a. Brenner Pass
b. North-eastern Italian lines

1. Piave river line
2. Brenta river line
3. Tagliamento river line

c. Po and Adda rivers
d. Fuel, motor transport and locomotives, including repair and maintenance depots.[36]

Operations against the Brenner Pass proved particularly dangerous, due to high concentrations of anti-aircraft, or flak, defences. The success of earlier Allied operations in decreasing the area of Italian territory under German control had increased the density of AA defences. By November 1944 it was estimated that the Germans had about 2,500 AA guns in Italy. As Allied attention to the Brenner Pass increased so, too, did the flak defences, from 274 heavy and 130 light AA guns in October 1944 to 454 heavy and 498 light AA guns in March 1945. By now the German AA gunners were highly proficient and were claiming significant numbers of Allied aircraft* so that counter-measures had been developed. Those counter-

---

* A study of MATAF losses in 1944 indicated that 91 per cent of all bombers and 90 per cent of all fighters and fighter-bombers lost had fallen victim to flak.[37]

measures included using 'Window' to confuse the gun-laying radars, smoke canisters to obscure the gunners' optical sighting systems and deploying fighter-bombers to suppress flak. This latter tactic involved eight or more fighter-bombers for every dozen bombers in the strike force.[38]

As late as autumn 1944 the Allied high command was concerned as much about the material being exported from Italy to aid the German war effort as about that being brought in to maintain Army Group C. One method of reducing traffic in both directions was to cripple the railway's electrical power supply. Thus was Operation BINGO born, a plan to reduce the 24,000 tons daily, in each direction, that the railway could handle using electric locomotives, to 6,750 tons, the limit with steam engines. BINGO demanded that Allied airmen destroy the transformer stations along the route – damaged cables could be repaired easily. Preferably, this had to be done in pairs of stations or more, since the loss of a single station could be compensated for by drawing surplus power from one of its neighbours, whereas the loss of three neighbouring stations would lead to disruption along a lengthy section of line, causing a reversion to steam locomotives.[39]

MATAF planned to cut the railway line in as many places as possible and then knock out the transformers. A mix of Desert Air Force and XXII TAC fighter-bombers, US medium bombers and MASAF heavy daylight bombers was deployed, with the heavies striking at the line on the northern side of the pass. BINGO began on 6 November and, before long, traffic on the railway was reduced 'to an intermittent trickle', a situation that prevailed until the Brenner campaign ended in April 1945: MATAF and MASAF kept up attacks on the line and transformer stations were knocked out on a regular basis whenever weather conditions permitted. During Hitler's conference on 6 November, General Alfred Jodl, Keitel's deputy in OKW, reported that:

> OB Südwest 'had no railway' into Italy, the Brenner line having been cut in eleven places and alternative routes also wrecked. von Vietinghoff had begged for a surprise intervention by a 'few hundred' fighters, to deter the Allied bombers, which, for lack of opposition, were flying (in the words of his Evening Report) 'as if at a sporting event'. However his plea was rejected by Hitler, and presumably with reference to the concentration of forces for the Ardennes offensive Jodl agreed that 'at the moment nothing more could be transferred to Italy'.[40]

Because of Hitler's attitude, von Vietinghoff and General Ritter von Pohl, Luftwaffe commander in Italy, devised a plan to protect vital centres such as Bolzano, Innsbruck and Verona with strong concentrations of AA guns, even if this meant reducing levels of such defences on the front and at vulnerable points in the Po valley. Pohl was to write after the war of the efforts made by the railway engineers and AA gunners, 'whose services could be compared to the defence of the Messina Straits in 1943':

> A special Engineer Task Force was set up to do nothing else but to keep some traffic flowing. We do not know the extent of the trickle they succeeded in

maintaining, but can illustrate the resourcefulness of *OB Südwest*'s railway engineers in another context. By 13 November they had repaired the rail bridge over the Po at Ferrara, and although it was again badly damaged by bombing on the 22nd, in the intervening period it carried 115 trains with 2,450 wagons, loaded with produce from the Po Valley.[41]

Yet, in spite of the damage sustained by the Brenner Pass railway, the Germans achieved the remarkable feat of removing two complete divisions – 356th Infantry and 16th SS Panzer Grenadier – out of Italy through the Brenner by rail, relieving them with 278th and 710th Infantry Divisions. These moves were made with all four divisions remaining almost intact, although carried out slowly with many delays. In the Germans' favour was the fact that the moves occurred in January in weather conditions so bad that XXII TAC aircraft could fly an average of only two missions per day.[42]

Soldiers on the ground are inclined to criticize their comrades in the air unless they can see the work being done by those airmen. Naturally, the soldier in his slit trench or gunpit along the Senio or looking down on Bologna had little or no idea of what the bombers were achieving to the north, although they would frequently have seen the planes passing overhead. Nor would they have been aware of the levels of danger faced by the flyers. However, there were few 'doubting Thomases' when it came to the work of the tactical air forces. By late 1944 the infantryman and tankman had come to repose considerable confidence and trust in those 'among the clouds above'.

The solid foundation for that confidence was the doctrine developed by the Desert Air Force and adopted by the USAAF for close support. Born in the deserts of North Africa and nurtured in the hothouse of conflict, the doctrine had grown to maturity before being translated to Sicily and Italy. It was a doctrine that harnessed closely airpower and ground power, airmen supporting the armour and the infantry, and adding their strength to the artillery to produce a team that outmatched the Germans by bringing all-arms co-operation to a level not before experienced. In one sense, that doctrine was simplicity itself; in another, it was a complex equation. However, it may be summed up in one word: Rover.

'Rover' was both a description and a radio call sign. It described what those with the call sign did – they roved on the ground with the soldiers; army liaison officers and RAF ground control officers worked together. Using the call sign 'Rover David', these teams operated with the ground forces ('embedded' in modern military parlance), travelling in an armoured vehicle close to the front and with a brigade HQ. Not only were these officers in close contact with the Army Air Support Control (AASC) units, they could also communicate by VHF radio with the fighter-bomber pilots patrolling the sky above in what had already become known as a 'cab rank'. And, just as someone could hail a cab on the street, these men could hail a fighter-bomber, or more, from the cab rank. To reduce the possibility of misunderstandings between pilots and ground personnel, both used identical large-scale maps of the operational area, the maps marked with number- and letter-coded grids. Aerial photographs were also used when available. It was thus possible for the Rover David team to call down numbers of fighter-bombers to deal with any target for which the army asked for air support. The target could be bombed, strafed with machine guns or cannon, or struck with rocket projectiles. Should the original target have moved or ceased to be a concern, or should a more urgent target have materialized, the Rover David team could direct the overhead aircraft to the fresh target, using the gridded maps, pointing out prominent local features, or by asking artillery to mark the target area with smoke shells.[43]

Fifth Army adopted this procedure during the Gothic Line battles in 1944. Known as 'Rover Joe', it 'was borrowed from Eighth Army ... to deal with targets needing immediate neutralization'. Forward observation posts, Rover Joe, manned by experienced air and ground personnel, were established with front-line formations and directed the fighter-bombers onto their targets. 'By this system air attacks could be made well within the bomb safety line and in some instances within twenty minutes of the call for air support by the infantry.'[44]

Co-ordinating artillery fire and ground attack aircraft, as well as that of other weapons, made the system complex, but it had been refined through constant practice in the advance through Italy and, by spring 1945, had evolved to a fine art. Today the system is known as 'joint fires', a term encapsulating the complexity of the task. It was a task taken in their stride by those who executed it in 1945.

Much information for artillery and tactical air forces came from aerial reconnaissance, which was carried out in a number of disciplines: tactical reconnaissance (Tac/R), photographic reconnaissance (PR), strategic reconnaissance (SR) and photographic survey. The first roles were normally performed by single-engined aircraft adapted for the purpose with Tac/R being conducted at low level, although aircraft could fly at up to 7,000 feet, with the pilot observing or photographing, using vertical or oblique cameras; both visual observation and photography could be combined. PR was carried out normally at heights of about 25,000 feet or more with vertical cameras. Both Tac/R and PR were performed over the forward battle area and the enemy's rear areas to a distance of about seventy miles. Strategic reconnaissance was conducted by single-engined or twin-engined machines at greater distances behind the enemy's front lines; missions were flown at 25,000 feet or more using vertical cameras. Finally, survey photography was a medium-altitude activity using vertical cameras, carried out to support production of maps.[45] In the Desert Air Force, the principal single-engined reconnaissance aircraft was the Supermarine Spitfire with the de Havilland Mosquito the twin-engined plane used for strategic reconnaissance. By early 1945 the Desert Air Force deployed No. 2 Photographic Reconnaissance Unit and No. 208 Tac/R Squadron RAF as well as Nos. 40 Tac/R and 60 PR Squadrons of the South African Air Force and 1437 SR Flight.[46] The principal USAAF aerial reconnaissance machine was the Lockheed F-5 Lightning, a dedicated PR version of the twin-engined P-38 long-range fighter. Both Mosquito and Lightning, being capable of very long-range flights, carried out missions over Germany and the Balkans.

In contrast, the Germans had very little opportunity to obtain information by aerial reconnaissance. Most Luftwaffe aircraft in northern Italy could not survive over Allied lines, due to Allied air superiority. There was one exception. A handful of jet-engined Arado Ar234 Blitz bombers was assigned to the theatre and used for aerial reconnaissance.[47] With a speed of 461mph and operational ceiling of 32,800 feet, the Blitz, the world's first jet reconnaissance aircraft, was immune from interception by Allied fighters and flew above the effective height of the AA guns in Italy. Many sightings of the Ar234 were mis-identified as the Messerschmitt Me262, and such was the concern caused by its appearance over Allied lines that the USAAF deployed two Lockheed YP-80A Shooting Star jet fighters to Italy as a deterrent. However, there were no interceptions of Blitzes by Shooting Stars. The war diary of 12 AA Brigade notes the presence of jet-propelled aircraft at 32,000 feet (on 17 April one is identified as an Me262)[48] while, on 3 April, the war diary of 2nd Royal Inniskilling Fusiliers notes 'high-flying aircraft' having been spotted over the Eighth Army area during the past two days, as a result of which camouflage measures were to be improved.[49] Twelve AA Brigade history records:

2 Apr 45 was notable as being the day on which the first jet-propelled aircraft, an Me262, was observed over the Eighth Army area. No early warning was received and its vapour trail, seen by guns in the Forlí area, alone showed its presence. It was flying at 35,000 ft at an estimated speed of 430mph and carried out an extensive recce of the Army area. It was not engaged by AA. There was a similar raid on 5 Apr, also by an Me262; there was again no early warning as it had been identified over Ancona as friendly, but it was engaged by guns in the Ravenna area.[50]

Two other aspects of Allied air power deserve mention. One has already been alluded to in the quotation from Brigadier Pat Scott at the beginning of this chapter: 'The [enemy] had no Air OP like we had.' This was a reference to the air observation posts of the Royal Artillery, small Taylorcraft Auster light, high-winged monoplanes, flown by Gunner officers who provided direction for the guns from their cockpits. First used in Tunisia, the AOP system had been perfected by the closing stages of the Italian campaign, by which time four squadrons of Austers, one manned by Poles to support II Polish Corps' artillery, were operational in the peninsula. (A flight of No. 651 Squadron that flew in to Réggio on 6 September 1943 had been the first Allied aircraft based in mainland Europe since the collapse of Greece in 1941.) Although the aircraft and ground crews were RAF, and bore RAF squadron designations (later to be transferred to the Army Air Corps), the pilots were officers of the Royal Artillery, trained as forward observation officers and as pilots.[51]

The introduction of Air OPs demanded a new system for controlling gunfire from the air. Ever since the First World War gunners had used a clock code system, referring to the hands of the clock, with twelve o'clock directly in front of the gun positions. This was replaced by the Air OP pilot giving his orders to the guns by referring to the line of fire and the distance between guns and targets. Another innovation was the Merton photograph, a gridded print that was the brainchild of Captain Merton RA, a Royal Artillery officer involved in the trials to establish the value of aircraft as OPs.

Merton came up with the idea of a gridded print that eventually became standard not only for Air OPs but also for the artillery on the ground and the Rover David officers, since it allowed identification and fixing of targets from photographs.[52]

The slow, unarmed Austers faced many dangers and, although the Allies had air supremacy, there remained the risks of enemy AA fire, small-arms fire, and even friendly artillery. Since the Austers flew so low, shells in flight could hit them; some came back to base with fuselages bearing the scars of such encounters. Others not so fortunate were blown out of the sky by shells en route to their intended targets.

In Fifth Army's area, Air OPs were carried out in Piper L-4 light aircraft, similar to the Auster. Known officially as Grasshoppers – a name also applied confusingly to other light aircraft – they were more commonly known by their civilian designation of Cub.

The other aspect of Allied air power worthy of mention was the support given to the Italian partisans through supply drops. Since supply-dropping aircraft had to fly over northern Italy, MAAF HQ had decided, in summer 1944, that unarmed C-47 Dakotas or Skytrains (the latter name used in US service) could not survive, and decreed that long-range combat machines such as the RAF's Halifax and Liberator bombers would be used instead. Added to the instruction of the Combined Chiefs of Staff that 'additional forces of heavy bombers and troop carriers were not to be diverted from their primary operational tasks except in an emergency',[53] this contributed to 'a remarkably poor response to the Italian Resistance's need for supplies compared with Tito's Partisans'.[54] Between May and the end of October 1944, Italian partisans received only 1,072.42 tons, with a mere 73.15 tons dropped in October, when Alexander had called for 600 tons.[55]

After much debate, with Air Marshal Slessor arguing that such operations in northern Italy were wasted effort, Alexander won the day. With new dropping techniques and the diversion of the USAAF's 51st Troop Carrier Wing, with its C-47 Skytrains, from operations in Yugoslavia to northern Italy (the wing was based in Tuscany) the situation changed. November saw 289.72 tons dropped, a figure that rose to 737.33 in December. Bad weather in January caused a drop to 437.82 tons, but over 1,000 tons were dropped in February and 1,100-plus in March. Between January and the end of the war, no less than 3,030 tons were dropped.[56]

In December 1944 the partisan leadership and the Allies signed a military agreement under which the former agreed to obey the orders of the Allied Commander-in-Chief during operations, and after the German withdrawal to do its utmost to preserve law and order and to safeguard economic resources until the arrival of Allied Military Government. In return the Allies agreed to pay the Committee a monthly subsidy which would be allotted to regions by the Supreme Allied Commander.[57]

In a linked political agreement, the Italian government agreed to recognize the Committee as the representative body of the anti-Fascist parties in Italian territory still occupied by the Germans.[58]

As the Allies prepared for the offensive partisan groups were active in northern Italy and ready to play their part in the liberation of their homeland. They would play a significant part in that liberation.

Notes

1. Kay, *From Cassino to Trieste*, pp.370–1.
2. Jackson, Pt III, p.233.
3. Kay, p.372.
4. Jackson, pp.273–5.
5. Scott, *Account of the Irish Brigade*.
6. Ibid.; NA Kew, WO170/4464, war diary, 38 (Ir) Bde, Jan–Mar '45; Doherty, *Clear The Way!* (*CTW!*), pp.220–4.
7. Doherty, p.224.
8. Trousdell to author.
9. NA Kew, WO170/4386, war diary, HQ 78 Div (G), Mar '45.
10. Robinson to author.
11. Scott, op. cit.
12. NA Kew, WO170/, war diary, 56 Recce, 1945; Doherty, *Only the Enemy in Front*, p.227.
13. NA Kew, WO373/13, citation for MM to L/Sgt Doherty.
14. NA Kew, WO170/5018, war diary, 2 Inniskns, 1945; Doherty, *CTW!*, p.229–31; Doherty, interview with Lt Col Palmer, October 1989.
15. NA Kew, WO170/4621, war diary, Bays, 1945; WO170/5019, war diary, 1 RIrF, 1945; WO170/5045, war diary, 2 LIR, 1945.
16. Doherty, *CTW!*, p.231.
17. Williams, *The Black Cats at War*, p.111.
18. Ibid.
19. Kay, p.420.
20. Doherty, *Eighth Army in Italy*, p.200.
21. Belogi & Guglielmo, *Spring 1945 on the Italian Front*, p.360.
22. Truscott, pp.470 & 480; Fisher, pp.459–60; Starr, p.391.
23. McCreery, *RUSI Journal*, Vol XCII, No.565, February 1947, p.3.
24. ffrench-Blake, *The 17th/21st Lancers*, p.110.
25. NA Kew, WO170/4634, war diary 2 RTR, 1945.
26. Evans, *Decisive Campaigns of the Desert Air Force*, pp.199–202; Doherty, *A Noble Crusade*, p.66n; NA Kew, CAB44/97, p.10.
27. Jackson, *Victory in Italy*, Pt III, pp.148–9.
28. Harpur, op. cit., p.125.
29. NA Kew, CAB106/441: The Campaign in Lombardy 1945.
30. Jackson, Pt III, App 3, pp.381–4.
31. Ibid.
32. Ibid, p.187.
33. Ibid.
34. Ibid., p.155.
35. Ibid., p.59.
36. Ibid.

37. Ibid, p.57
38. Ibid.
39. Ibid.
40. Ibid., p.61.
41. Ibid.
42. Bernstein, *P-47 Thunderbolt Units of the Twelfth Air Force*, p.70.
43. Jackson, pp.45–6; Evans, pp.126–7.
44. Starr, pp.341 & 364n.
45. Owens, *How influential was aerial intelligence on the battles of El Alamein*, p.6.
46. Ibid.; Evans, p.185.
47. Kesselring, p.220. Almost all Allied sources mis-identify the aircraft as Messerschmitt Me262s.
48. NA Kew, WO170/4857, war diary HQ 12 AA Bde, 1945.
49. NA Kew, WO170/5018, war diary, 2 Innisks, 1945.
50. *History HQ 12 AA Bde*, p.17.
51. Doherty, *Ubique*, pp.61–2 & 179–81.
52. Ibid., p.61.
53. Jackson, p.411.
54. Ibid.
55. Ibid., p.412.
56. Ibid., pp.411–12.
57. Ibid., p.413.
58. Ibid.

Chapter Five

Planning for the spring offensive began in January 1945 during the period in which Alexander chose to maintain an offensive-defensive stance in northern Italy. With the pressures of events outside Italy, especially in Greece and Yugoslavia, bearing on him, Alexander was happy to allow the planning to be the prerogative of 15th Army Group HQ.[1] In fact, in November, he had told Churchill that 'We must be careful not to interfere in American domestic affairs',[2] a comment that sums up his sensitivity; with an American general at the helm of the army group, he was aware that it could be seen as an American interest.

The rationalization of the armies in January, with XIII Corps returning to Eighth Army, was part of the planning process. This left Eighth Army with a line from east of Point 602, Monte Grande, to the Adriatic, giving McCreery operational, as well as administrative, responsibility for all that sector. (On 4 February, Clark amended the boundary to include Monte Grande in Eighth Army's sector, thus narrowing Fifth Army's front.) While most British-equipped formations were now under command of Eighth Army, it had not been possible to release 6th South African Armoured Division from Fifth Army's front and many British artillery units remained in Fifth's order of battle; Gruppo Legnano was also British equipped.

With the armies halted until the offensive, and the rest and re-training programme underway, and scheduled to be complete by 31 March, it was time for the army HQs and that of the Army Group to focus on planning. Clark issued a general plan to both McCreery's and Truscott's HQs on 24 January:

> The instructions contained in this letter are issued at this time … to enable you to plan your rest and reorganization period so that your troops will be in the best possible condition to resume extensive offensive operations in the spring. While it is not practicable now to determine the date for launching this offensive, you will plan your reliefs, reorganization and training so that they can be concluded by 31 March 1945.
>
> There are no indications that the enemy intends to withdraw forces from Italy for employment elsewhere. We know from experience that it is contrary to his habit to give up valuable terrain until forced to do so. It is possible, however, that he may be obliged to execute a major withdrawal from Italy as a result of developments on other fronts. In such an event, 15th Army Group would attack as soon as possible following the basic plan contained in this directive. Army commanders must be prepared to launch such an attack on short notice. The present strength and disposition of enemy forces south of the Po River are

such that a hostile offensive is a capability. It is considered that the two most probable areas are in the Po valley against Eighth Army on Rimini, or against Fifth Army's left directed against Leghorn. Both armies will prepare and keep current plans rapidly to meet such attacks.[3]

As Fifth Army's historian notes, no full-scale attack would be launched 'until after 1 April, unless the enemy appeared to be withdrawing from Italy'.[4] That meant that operations would take place in weather conditions suitable for campaigning in the mountains, while ammunition reserves would have been built up and both armies would have received fresh formations.[5]

The Army Group plan assumed that the Germans would hold their line in northern Italy as long as possible, but contingency plans were made for other eventualities, as indicated in Clark's order. It was known, for example, that, by 1 February, the Germans had completed plans for a withdrawal to the line of the Adige river, although there was no indication about when, or if, these would be put into action. At its simplest, the overall Army Group plan was to smash enemy forces in Italy. Clark was concerned about a sudden German withdrawal into the Alps, the Americans giving more credence to the supposed Nazi 'National Redoubt', but Alexander believed that Italian partisans and wide-ranging Allied reconnaissance aircraft would ensure early warning of any such move.[6]

Some of the frictions of a coalition persisted. Clark saw Fifth Army as 'the dominant partner in the Italian enterprise and ... [viewed] the Fifth Army's role in the forthcoming offensive as essentially a continuation of that played during the long quiescent Bologna offensive'.[7] In his memoirs Clark reveals little of his thinking at this stage, nor of the strategy he wished to pursue. His biographer is more enlightening, noting that Clark's elevation to command 15th Army Group 'did little to allay his private suspicions of the British', before going on to record:

> When the Canadian Corps was pulled out of the Eighth Army in Italy and sent to join the Canadian army in Holland, McCreery asked to regain control of two British divisions still in the Fifth Army so that he could make the main effort in the next Allied attack. Clark 'heartedly' disagreed with the idea. 'If there is one thing I am sure of,' he wrote in his diary, 'the principal "carrying of the ball" will be done by the American infantry divisions, as they have always done in the past'. Transferring the two British divisions to the Eighth Army would weaken the Fifth, expose the port of Leghorn, and make impossible a strong thrust through the mountains to Bologna, the city on the Po River Plain.[8]

Writing to his wife, Clark commented:

> I certainly have a hodge-podge outfit – every nationality in the world. It is not like having all Americans like the other commanders in France have. The transportation and all the weapons and ammunition of the British are entirely different from the American. They can't be switched around. The German

divisions opposite me are all the same – all German with the same equipment. ... I cannot put a British division or an Indian division on a snow-capped mountain like I can the Americans. [Inflexibility was] inherent in an inter-allied command. There has never been one so complex as my Army Group. I am not complaining.[9]

In fact, Clark *had* placed a British division on a snow-capped mountain, and an Indian division had stabilized Fifth Army's front during the Serchio fighting in December, nor was the opposition homogenous. His army commanders held a different view of the situation and of what was possible. Alexander's clearly expressed objective was to destroy Army Group C south of the Po and on this, at least, Clark came to agree with his supreme commander, and with McCreery and Truscott. 'Came to agree' since, in his operational instruction of 12 February, Clark outlined three phases for the offensive: 'to break through and establish a firm base around Bologna; close up to the Po; and then cross the Po with the aim of securing Verona, sealing the Brenner Pass and closing up to the Adige'.[10] Destroying Army Group C south of the Po received no mention. Jackson goes on to describe how a meeting with General Gruenther, Clark's Chief of Staff, on 18 February failed to clarify outstanding British concerns, and quotes the British record as saying:

15 Army Group felt unable to state clearly the task of Eighth Army in Phase I of the offensive. It was quite evident, however, that the Army Group Command considers Fifth Army as the predominating partner, and that Eighth Army's task is accordingly to prepare the way for Fifth Army by attracting enemy reserves on to itself.[11]

A detailed strategic appreciation was sent from Allied Forces HQ by Alexander's Chief of Staff, Lieutenant General Sir John Harding, to Clark for 'information' on 3 March. AFHQ stressed the necessity of destroying Army Group C south of the Po, while agreeing with Clark that Fifth Army should make the main effort, since it seemed to have more room for decisive operations. It was also felt that weather conditions might not favour an offensive before early May.

It seems to have been this appreciation that brought Clark round to agreeing with Alexander, McCreery and Truscott on the imperative of destroying Army Group C. However, disagreement continued when it came to discussing the means of so doing. Clark still wanted Fifth Army to make the main offensive, striking out to take Bologna, whereas Truscott wanted his thrust line left of Bologna, using the higher, less-heavily-defended ground to advantage; he realized that Clark maintained his fixation with the city.

Truscott pointed out to Clark that Fifth Army would make better progress with a main effort west of Highway 65, avoiding the 'greatly increased' enemy defences immediately south of Bologna. Because of those defences, between Highways 64 and 65, Truscott considered that in developing the operation, we should clear the area up to the general line Pianoro–Pradura–Mt Mantino and establish a firm base for subsequent operations. Since prepared defences west of Highway 64 are a great deal thinner than to the east of that road, we should be prepared in attacking from that line to make our main effort west of Highway 64, isolating Bologna from the north and northwest, preparatory to the final stage.[12]

Clark responded that he was pleased that Truscott was 'in accord with the general plan he had outlined and he agreed with my comments on preliminary operations'[13] but went on to state that he could not agree to the main attack being along 'the high ground west of Highway 64'.[14] Nonetheless, Truscott 'was determined to retain this concept in our final plans, and I did not want Clark, because of his predilection for PIANORO, to interpose a restriction which would make it impossible'.[15] Clark's change of direction in the breakout from Anzio, which had allowed a German army to escape destruction, had not been forgotten.

Clark told McCreery that Eighth Army would play only a supporting role to Fifth Army, which, said Clark, would have 'Bologna as its primary goal',[16] while Eighth would contain the enemy along the Senio by attacking first and drawing off German reserves. This displayed Clark's belief that Eighth Army was worn out, and that the British would not 'carry the ball'. In McCreery's words, 'Clark did not expect a very big dividend' from Eighth Army, which he thought might be battle-weary.[17] McCreery was not prepared to tolerate this. He spoke to Alexander and Truscott. The result was a decision to obey Clark's orders in principle, but to fulfil his own objective by destroying those enemy formations facing Eighth Army before they could withdraw across the Po.

> Having cleared his lines with Alexander first, he began to formulate a plan which would deliver much more than expected by Clark, who continued to believe that Eighth Army was worn out. Dick conferred closely with Truscott, who agreed with him that between the two armies they could achieve a much better result, and they found a ready ally in Al Gruenther. [Clark's Chief of Staff][18]

Thus the final army group plan combined the work of both army commanders. Following a conference at Clark's headquarters in Florence on 18 March, the plan was issued six days later as Operations Instruction No. 4, calling for what the Germans called *Keil und Kessel*, or 'wedge and trap', a double encirclement with both armies trapping and destroying the enemy army group. 'The final plan was not a compromise, a course invariably fatal, but contained the inputs of two highly professional army commanders.'[19] McCreery commented:

> General Clark's plan was to destroy the German armies South of the River Po by a pincers movement, the Eighth Army advancing on the general axis of Route 16 to Ferrara and Bondeno and the US Fifth Army attacking North through Bologna to the Po about Ostiglia. The Fifth Army was then to exploit to Verona–

Lake Garda to cut off the whole of the Axis forces in North-West Italy, and the Eighth Army was to cross the Po and drive north-eastward towards Venice and Trieste.[20]

However, McCreery was annoyed to see that Fifth Army's effort was still considered the 'main effort' since the plan noted that Truscott's command would 'Launch the *main effort* [author's italics] of 15th Army Group and attack with the mission of debouching into the PO Valley with secondary mission of capturing or isolating the city of BOLOGNA'. Truscott must have been equally annoyed to see the importance still accorded to Bologna although, earlier in the Instruction, in what would have been described as the 'Intention' in a British plan, Clark stated that '15th Army Group will launch an all-out attack [on] 10 April 1945 to destroy maximum number enemy forces south of the PO, force crossings of the PO River and capture VERONA.'[21] Both army commanders had discussed the plans in detail, and were confident of achieving their objectives, while the inclusion of the intention of destroying enemy forces south of the Po gave Truscott scope to assign that objective a greater priority than Bologna. Eighth Army's plan was codenamed Operation BUCKLAND, Fifth Army's CRAFTSMAN, and the overall offensive GRAPESHOT.[22]

The weather in northern Italy had taken a turn for the better during that final winter of the war. Less snow had fallen than in the previous year, reducing the volumes of melt water in rivers and streams, and the possibility of flash floods, and February had been exceptionally dry. (War diaries record poor ground conditions, especially early in the month due to the rapid thaw but, with little rainfall to add to the melting snow, the ground began drying out.) Combined with the reduction in melt water, this meant much more chance of the ground in the Po valley being firm enough for wheeled and tracked vehicles by mid-April. As a result, Clark announced at his conference on 18 March that D Day would be 10 April. With the intention noting that the attack was 'to destroy maximum number of enemy forces south of the Po', it seemed that the message had finally got through to the army group commander.

At that conference, Clark also stated that 15th Army Group's D Day would be the day on which Eighth Army made its attack across the Senio. However, both armies would launch supporting operations before D Day, Fifth to protect its left flank from attack from the coastal plain beyond the Apuan Alps, and Eighth to protect its right by Lake Comácchio. Other than these subsidiary operations, there was also a deception plan, with several fictional formations posing as an Eighth Army strategic reserve.

On D Day Eighth Army was to execute Phase I of the overall plan. In Operation BUCKLAND, it was to:

1. Breach the SENIO and SANTERNO Rivers.
2. Attack immediately after a bridgehead is established over the SANTERNO:

   a. In the direction BASTIA. [*Author's note*: Highway 16, Via Adriatica, crosses the Reno south of Argenta at Bastia.]
   b. In the direction of BUDRIO.

3. If the situation is favourable, launch an amphibious operation, combined with a parachute drop, to assist the ground forces to break through the ARGENTA Gap. (Note: Depending on the success of operations to secure the ARGENTA Gap, the Commanding General, 15th Army Group, in consultation with the General Officer Commanding, Eighth Army, will make the decision that an attack on FERRARA is to be the main effort of Eighth Army with a secondary attack on BUDRIO.)[23]

With Clark still considering that Fifth Army's would be the main effort, he was allowing Truscott more freedom than McCreery, even backing down on the assignment of the capture or isolation of Bologna as the main objective. This is clear in his instruction that:

Fifth Army will:

1. Launch the main effort of 15th Army Group and attack with the mission of debouching into the PO Valley with a secondary mission of capturing or isolating the city of BOLOGNA. Fifth Army will be prepared to launch the first phase of its main attack on 24 hours' notice after D + 2.[24]

Although Bologna remained as 'a secondary objective', Truscott had more flexibility than before since Clark did not prescribe his axis of advance. Fifth Army's commander intended to do a McCreery by using 10th Mountain Division's specialist skills to take advantage of the higher ground west of Highway 64, just as his counterpart had used Indian soldiers' mountain-fighting skills in the final phase of the OLIVE battles.

Mention has been made of the subsidiary 'setting up' operations, but only that of Fifth Army was mentioned in Operations Instruction 4, which indicated that the army would:

2. Launch a preliminary attack to capture MASSA (P 9101) on D – 5. Be prepared on capture of MASSA to exploit toward LA SPEZIA.[25]

Eighth Army's preliminary operations, codenamed ROAST and FRY, involved 2 Commando Brigade and M Squadron Special Boat Service. The former included four commandos, Nos. 2 and 9 (Army) and 40 and 43 (Royal Marine). By eliminating German positions on the spit between Lake Comácchio and the Adriatic, Operation ROAST was intended to deny the enemy the opportunity to observe Eighth Army's right flank; FRY was the seizure of the islands in the lake.

In Phase I the priority for air support would go to Eighth Army until Fifth Army's attack began, at which point the mass of air power would switch to the latter. HQ MATAF was to issue the plans for air support for Operations BUCKLAND and CRAFTSMAN.

In Phase II of Operation GRAPESHOT Eighth Army was to:

1. Prevent enemy forces escaping northwards by seizing and holding key road -------- which dominates the main ---------- over the river RENO, and the PO crossing areas at FERRARA and BONDENO.
2. Make earliest possible contact with exploiting columns of Fifth Army in the BONDENO-FERRARA area.
3. Send strong mobile columns of armor and infantry for this purpose directed on FERRARA and BONDENO with intermediate objectives PORTOMAGGIORE (M 2669) and S. NICOLO FERRARESE (M 1871), by way of the ARGENTA Gap.[26]

Fifth Army's tasks in Phase II were to:

1. Exploit with armor and infantry in the corridor between the RENO and PANARO Rivers, with a view of joining Eighth Army at the earliest possible time in the BONDENO or FERRARA area, thereby completing the encirclement of enemy forces south of the PO River.
2. Seize S. GIOVANNI (L 7765). Thence direct the main effort on CENTO (L 8574)–S. AGOSTINO (L 9381)–BONDENO, denying to the enemy crossings of the RENO River.
3. Launch a secondary effort northwest from the S. GIOVANNI area to seize crossings of the PANARO River near BOMPORTO and CAMPOSANTO, thence to turn northward in the corridor between the PANARO and SECCHIA River, moving on OSTIGLIA.[27]

Clark also laid down a third phase in which both armies should be prepared to seize 'any opportunity to capture existing bridging and ferrying equipment' that would be useful for a crossing of the Po. However, the first two phases were so successful that Phase III became redundant.

Deception plans were also laid as part of GRAPESHOT. By far the most successful were diversions laid on by the Royal Navy off the Adriatic coast. Earlier in the campaign the Germans, with neither doctrine for nor experience in amphibious warfare, had proved susceptible to any apparent preparations for seaborne landings. That they had been caught wrong-footed on previous occasions made them no less susceptible this time. After all, they had the experience of the Anzio landings to provide a very real precedent for the Allies using a seaborne hook, and so prepared to defend against a possible seaborne right hook on this occasion. Thus the Royal Navy's simulation of 'the preparation of an amphibious operation in the area of Porto Garibaldi' was taken seriously. This operation was to be 'a demonstration by landing craft and supporting units' off Porto Garibaldi; a small commando raid was to be made north of Porto Garibaldi if practicable. On the west coast a naval bombardment would support Fifth Army's attack along the coastal plain while a further demonstration by light naval craft off Chiavari would simulate a landing 'at a time to be selected by 15th Army Group'.[28]

Other elements of the deception plans included the 'creation' of a Headquarters XIV Corps with, under its command, 42nd and 57th Divisions as well as 5th Airborne Division, to which the real 2 Parachute Brigade was assigned. A further make-believe British division, 34th, was supposed to be in the Middle East, preparing to move to Italy in March.[29]

To what extent did the Germans accept this subterfuge? The existence of XIV Corps and the impending disembarkation of the fictitious 34th Division at Bari were accepted as genuine. Moreover, from summer 1944 until mid-January 1945, German Intelligence also believed in the existence of 42nd and 57th Divisions. After the latter date both divisions were re-classified as training formations, subsequently disappearing from OKW's situation maps for Italy. However, those maps continued showing three British parachute brigades in Italy, including 2 Parachute Brigade, which was marked as positioned forward. Therefore, the pretence of a British airborne division seems to have been accepted.[30]

Since Clark was still committed to Fifth Army making the main effort, he also gave that army priority in planning deception, agreeing to a scheme showing II US Corps, with two divisions, and the fictional XIV Corps in Eighth Army's sector, leaving IV US Corps holding all Fifth Army's front. McCreery was concerned that the difficult task of crossing the Senio and breaching the Argenta Gap would be even more difficult if German reserves were drawn to Eighth Army's front by such deception measures. To alleviate this, he proposed a threat to the German Adriatic flank by short, wide amphibious hooks, aimed at the coast between Lake Comácchio and the Po, combined with wider hooks towards Istria. However, the latter would have to be authorized and handled at a higher level and, because the concept did not fit Clark's strategic deception policy, it was not accepted.[31]

As outlined earlier, the simulated short hooks were executed; some LCTs, LCAs and minesweepers deployed to create the illusion of an amphibious force assembling at Porto Corsini, the port of Ravenna, and at Ancona. Air support for the simulated operation was to be provided by the Desert Air Force while signals traffic and camouflage would also play their part.[32]

The Germans did move reserves to cover the possibility of amphibious operations on the Adriatic coast but the deception measures outlined above played little or no part in that, since they were implemented too late for the Germans to appreciate and react to them. Instead, the move of reserves to meet an imagined threat owed much more to Berlin and to Hitler and Dönitz, commander of the Kriegsmarine:

From OKW records, it is clear that during March there was a division of opinion about Allied intentions in Italy. Foreign Armies West suspected, but could not confirm, the Canadian moves, suggesting that the theatre had become a sideshow as far as the Allies were concerned. They found no evidence of planning for operations on a strategic scale. On 2 March the Admiral attached to OKW's Operations Branch reckoned that there was enough amphibious shipping in the Mediterranean to lift five or six divisions. Hitler at a conference with Dönitz gave it as his view, on 4 March, that Allied landings on the Italian Adriatic coast 'aimed at outflanking us' might well occur, and that the situation on this coast needed watching. 10th US Mountain Division's operations in the Mt Belvedere area were at that time attracting attention and led to the despatch of 29th Panzer Grenadier Division to check the American offensive.[33]

The German high command was nothing if not confused. Less than two weeks after Hitler's appraisal, and before von Vietinghoff returned to Italy as OB Südwest, OKW received a report from Army Group C's chief of staff which suggested that, even without 1st and 46th Divisions, there were still as many as twelve divisions behind the Allied front line, and that the relief of Eighth Army's veteran formations by others of less proven quality indicated preparations for an offensive rather than a lack of interest in the theatre.[34] This was a clear case of an intelligence analysis obtaining the right answer from the wrong information, although the answer probably owed as much to the instinct of the German intelligence officers as it did to any analysis.

On the eve of its final offensive, Eighth Army had an effective strength of 632,980 men[35] in an order of battle (see Appendix, p.216) including formations and units of many nationalities. Two formations were effectively national armies – II Polish Corps and 2nd New Zealand Division – while the Jewish Brigade represented the army of a nation in waiting, and the Italian *gruppi di combattimento* were the army of a democratic Italy fighting for its liberation from fascism, and German occupation. Eighth Army, arguably the finest field army that Britain has ever put into the field, had been written off by Clark but, inspired by its new commander, found a renewed vigour and sense of purpose. Brian Harpur described its revival from the tired army of late 1944 to the battle-winning force of April 1945 as the 'most unlikely miracle in military history since David slew Goliath'.[36]

General McCreery issued the final orders for Eighth Army's main offensive on 3 April. In Operation BUCKLAND, V Corps and II Polish Corps would cross the Senio along a ten-mile stretch between Fusignano southwards to Felisio, continuing their attack across the Santerno between Massa Lombarda and Mordano. Thereafter, V Corps would strike rapidly northwards for Bastia and Argenta while the Poles continued north-westward on two axes, towards Budrio on their right and Castel San Pietro on Highway 9 on their left. Should the Polish advance be stalled, 2nd New Zealand Division could strengthen the thrust.

In the early days of March, Lieutenant General Hawkesworth's X Corps HQ, having returned from Greece, took over the southern half of XIII Corps' sector. Both X and XIII Corps were, with aggressive patrolling and minor operations, to pin down those German divisions positioned in Eighth Army's sector of the Apennines. XIII Corps had the additional task of holding Monte Grande while ensuring that much of 10th Indian Division remained in reserve so that it might deploy to strengthen the drive towards Bologna or execute limited offensive operations from its Apennine positions.

On the evening of 3 April, General McCreery gave a dinner for Allied soldiers at the Grand Hotel in Riccione.[37] This Army Commander's dinner, attended by men from the many formations and nationalities represented in Eighth Army, was a clear example of McCreery's care for his soldiers. Next day he addressed his commanding officers down to the rank of lieutenant colonel, from V and X Corps, at Forlí to outline his plans. Later that day he addressed those of his own Main and Rear HQs, as well as those of 6th Armoured Division, in the cinema at Cesena. On the 5th he spoke to II Polish Corps at Castrocaro and XIII Corps in the mountains south of Imola. Among those present at Cesena, Lieutenant Colonel Val ffrench-Blake, of 17th/21st Lancers, recalled how:

> In his quiet, almost apologetic, voice, [the Army Commander] said that the theatre had been stripped of troops for France; the army was like an old steeplechaser, full of running, but rather careful; that it was his intention to destroy the Germans south of the Po, rather than to allow them to withdraw to further defence lines to the north, on the Adige, and finally within the 'fortress' of the Austrian Alps. The plan was then outlined.[38]

Truscott had issued his final orders for Operation CRAFTSMAN on 1 April, the day on which British commandos began operations on Lake Comácchio. On D Day for CRAFTSMAN, IV US Corps was to strike west of Highway 64 to seize positions level with II Corps' left flank, an attack Truscott hoped would pull enemy forces away from Highway 65 towards Bologna, thereby easing II Corps' initial attack. Once IV Corps had captured Praduro, Fifth Army's main effort would shift westwards with the two corps advancing alongside each other, but skirting Bologna. IV Corps was to be ready to attack on 12 April while II Corps would remain on twenty-four hours notice to join the attack when Truscott considered the time opportune.[39]

On 6 April General McCreery issued a directive on exploitation in the event of a quick break-through at the Argenta Gap. (By this stage, the initial elements of Eighth Army's offensive, amphibious operations on Lake Comácchio, had been completed or were underway.) Since the Argenta Gap has been mentioned several times, and it played a critical part in Eighth Army's plans, an explanation of its significance is appropriate. McCreery himself had identified the 'Gap' and its importance to Eighth Army: the Gap was a product of German efforts to impede any advance by Eighth Army in the immediate area of Argenta and so no 'gap' will be found on modern maps. The Germans had flooded 'large areas on each side of the Argenta Gap', which was only 4,000 yards wide, astride Highway 16 for some miles north of Bastia; in this gap was constructed 'a strong defensive system … of minefields, entrenchments and defended villages'.[40] Argenta town lies close to the western shore of Lake Comácchio, which the Germans considered sufficient barrier to any British attack in that area. Believing that so much water was such an impediment, it seemed logical to extend its expanse by flooding the low land close to Comácchio. Floodgates were opened, allowing a considerable volume of water to cover much of the ground to the west, increasing greatly the barrier to any British movement and permitting local defences to be thinned out.

However, the Germans reckoned without McCreery's eye for ground.

Several times I went up in an Auster aircraft to look at the ground 'the other side of the hill' at a height of about 5,000 ft. The Germans had flooded considerable areas of ground on each side of the R. Reno so that, between the floods and Lake Comácchio, there was only a narrow defile astride the main road Ravenna-Ferrara which became known to the troops as the Argenta Gap. Argenta was a small village on the main road alongside the Reno.[41]

He saw that narrow gap at Argenta as something to be exploited. Nor did he see Lake Comácchio and its associated inundations as obstacles, but as another opportunity for exploitation. And he had ensured that Eighth Army had the tools to exploit that opportunity. (McCreery made considerable use of the Auster; he also had a small communications aircraft, a Beech C-45 Expeditor, which could carry six passengers and a crew of two, provided by the AOC Desert Air Force. Leese, his predecessor, had had the use of a USAAF C-47, but Cannon had decided that this was too large an aircraft for an army commander.) [42]

And so back to the directive of 6 April. Should V Corps be successful, it would wheel north-west to smash the enemy forces south of the Po with a secondary role of pushing north to Ferrara to reconnoitre the best sites for crossing the Po west of the city. So that V Corps could concentrate on its primary task, HQ X Corps would be brought forward on the right to take responsibility for crossing the Po, assuming command of all the forces around Lake Comácchio, as well as a special bridging force that Eighth Army's Chief Engineer had assembled at Ravenna. The forces around Lake Comácchio that would come under command of X Corps included a division from V Corps, and most amphibious elements deployed in the area.[43]

The alternative to this plan, should the Argenta Gap prove hard to breach, would be to concentrate on the north-westerly thrust to Budrio, in which case 2nd New Zealand Division would be strengthened by 10th Indian, with both formations under command of XIII Corps. This would leave V Corps responsible for the remainder of the front to the Adriatic, while X Corps would assume XIII Corps' role in the Apennines.

McCreery believed this development to be the more likely because there were so many hazards connected with the Lake Comácchio operations. He directed General Harding to send a small skeleton headquarters to the main front ready to take over at short notice.[44]

Also considered for exploitation purposes, if not deployed at the Argenta Gap, was 2 Parachute Brigade. This did not happen although, by mid-April, no fewer than twenty-five detailed plans had been made for the brigade. Another use of airborne forces was Operation HERRING, the dropping, on the night of 20/21 April, of small parties of Italian paratroopers behind German lines to harass their withdrawal. The plan called for 600 men, but only 250 adequately-trained troops were available from the Italian F Reconnaissance Squadron of the SAS and Nembo Regiment of Gruppo Folgore. Thirteen C-47s of 64th Troop Carrier Group carried the paratroopers, although one did not drop its soldiers. Although most drops were wide of their targets, the groups carried out their tasks and reported taking and handing over 700 German prisoners.[45] Airborne operations were not looked on keenly by the Desert Air Force who considered that the density of enemy anti-aircraft fire would increase as the Germans withdrew, thereby increasing the risk of casualties to airmen and machines, a critical factor since the Desert Air Force was not receiving adequate replacement aircraft.[46]

As planning had gathered pace so too had the training, which had to fit in with keeping the front line manned fully in case of attack. Nonetheless, a programme was established and units withdrawn from the line found that they could enjoy a spell of rest and re-organization, as well as taking part in a variety of exercises. By this stage, the shape of the attacking forces had been decided and specific roles allocated to formations and their constituent units.

Not every unit had concentrated entirely on training for the forthcoming operations. While 1st King's Royal Rifle Corps had trained in its role as a motor battalion in an armoured division, there had also been an emphasis on peacetime soldiering during the time out of the line. This was aimed undoubtedly at sharpening discipline and *esprit de corps* within the unit.[47] However, it seems to have been peculiar to this particular Green Jacket battalion. More typical of the training being undertaken was that of 8th Argyll and Sutherland Highlanders, in 36 Brigade of 78th Division. Since 78th Division was to be one of the two formations striking towards the Argenta Gap, the Argylls' training programme included co-operation with tanks, use of Kangaroo APCs and practising river crossings. At Bagnola, on 26 March, the Argylls took part in Exercise HOSSANAH, which each unit of the division undertook in turn; this included an element of co-operation with the tactical air forces through the Rover David system. There were also signals exercises.[48]

Another battalion to train with Kangaroos, in Exercise BOUNDER, was 2nd Lancashire Fusiliers. On 5 March this battalion also had 'the doubtful honour of a visit by the Army Inspector of Surplus Equipment', but the diarist noted that 'Forewarned is forearmed, and suitable measures were taken'.[49] It seems as if that diarist did not anticipate the possibility of someone in 'higher authority' reading his entry. Training with the Kangaroo could be dangerous, as on 20 March when a Kangaroo of 4th Hussars, carrying Coldstreamers, 'exploded on [a] dump of mines causing the complete wreckage of the Kangaroo and killed 3 Guardsmen and wounding 5. The comd was killed and the driver was seriously wounded'.[50]

As well as learning about the Kangaroo APC, troops made the acquaintance of the Wasp, flame-thrower equipment on a Universal carrier. The Intelligence Officer of 2nd Royal Inniskilling Fusiliers noted that his battalion was given a demonstration of the Wasp at Forlí on 17 February; four days later, it had, for most soldiers, the first sight of a Kangaroo, described as 'a Sherman tank with the turret off, and the unnecessary fitments taken off, making it capable of carrying 9 men'. Two days later the Skins' companies exercised with Kangaroos. At the same time, two Inniskillings' junior officers started a four-day attachment to the Desert Air Force 'to study their method of working etc. and a pilot of the DAF was attached to the Battalion for [the] same period and purpose'. A Canadian company commander lectured on 'the peculiarities of fighting in this type of country' including rivers and 'methods used in crossing them', as well as German tactics for holding river lines.[51]

In 6th Armoured Division 1 Guards Brigade's battalions trained to form battlegroups with the regiments of 26 Armoured Brigade. Lieutenant Colonel P. T. Cliften's 3rd Grenadiers were at Fermo where the battalion was training and exercising with Lieutenant Colonel Val ffrench-Blake's 17th/21st Lancers. As well as a rafting course at Pesaro for the guardsmen, Exercise IVY saw lancers and grenadiers preparing for 'the new conditions which would be found in the Po plain' where they would find board-flat countryside, cut across by many watercourses, and orchards with their trees coming into leaf.[52] Eighth Army's commander wrote of it:

> The Po Plain is an extremely fertile area filled with vines, most of them growing up tall poles, and therefore making visibility over any distance very difficult. The Plain also grew heavy crops of vegetables, maize and fruits. One of the big difficulties facing us was the crossing of another series of rivers running out of the mountains in a northerly direction to join the great river Po.[53]

It was terrain where 'an infantryman lying down could see a hundred yards, under the trees, [while] a tank commander, with his head among the branches, could see for only twenty'. Such conditions added a sharp incentive to the imperative for close co-operation in the battlegroups.[54] Ironically, having trained together, 26 Armoured and 1 Guards Brigades were not to fight together, the Green Jackets of 61 Brigade being teamed with the armour instead.

Infantry units were also given demonstrations of the Churchill Crocodile flame-thrower while those of the Queen's Brigade in 56th (London) Division trained with the Fantails, or Buffalo LVTs. All three Queen's battalions, 2/5th, 2/6th and 2/7th, moved to Lake Trasimene for training and a series of exercises with Fantails.[55] A modified organization for a Fantail-borne infantry platoon was devised.[56] Although demonstrations of the Lifebuoy flame-thrower,[57] carried by an individual soldier, were given, this equipment was not popular with the infantry. Also demonstrated was Viper equipment for clearing safe paths through minefields[58] and Kapok foot bridging equipment. Units also trained for house-to-house fighting.[59]

Armoured units that were to support the infantry, or carry them into battle in Kangaroos, were involved heavily in training. Among them 12th Royal Tank Regiment's war diary noted that the 'Battalion [was] to carry out mass flaming of Senio floodbanks'.[60] This was one of the units converted to the specialist armour role. Among other armoured units taking part in the offensive, 27th Lancers had a dual role with one squadron operating Kangaroos while the remaining two took on the armoured reconnaissance role and thus the regiment trained for both. Both the Queen's Bays (2nd Dragoon Guards) and 7th Queen's Own Hussars were assigned specialist roles. The Bays came under command of 38 (Irish) Brigade as part of 78th Division's force designed to open the Argenta Gap while 7th Hussars were to trade in their Shermans for swimming Shermans, the DD, or duplex drive, amphibious version of the tank, which they were to use to cross the Po. The Hussars were not enamoured of the idea of converting to the DD role,[61] but the Bays, who had already supported the Irish Brigade in the Senio Line, were happy with their intended task.

On 24 March Bays' officers, down to troop leaders, attended a planning conference at HQ 38 (Irish) Brigade at which the discussions were 'directed jointly by Commanders 38 Brigade and 2 Armoured Brigade', the latter being the Bays' parent formation. Next day the regiment took part in Exercise HOSANNAH and, on the 26th, moved on to bridging training, including the use of fascines and cribs, explosives and Shermandozers. The Bays also learned about local resources for crossings, the working of such crossings by day and night, siting of Ark crossings, and repair and demolition of bridges and culverts. Two officers and two NCOs were selected as bridge advisers.[62]

Meanwhile, 2nd Royal Tanks trained to support 43 Gurkha Brigade in II Polish Corps, having previously trained with 56th (London) Division with whom the Gurkhas had been serving. Earlier 2 RTR, in common with other Sherman-equipped armoured units, had re-equipped with the 76mm-gunned Sherman, although some 75mm Shermans were retained and there were also six 105mm Shermans for close support work, plus seven Sherman Fireflies, which, with their 17-pounder guns, could engage both Panthers and Tigers. In addition, the battalion's reconnaissance troop had ten Stuart, or Honey, tanks. During March, the war diary notes the fitting of Platypus tracks to unit tanks.[63]

And so the training programme rose to its crescendo with exercises such as LOMBARDY, PO and MOONSHINE marking the score. Morale was high, as was confidence in equipment and the armies' ability to smash decisively the German forces in northern Italy. Not only had both armies trained to a high level of efficiency, but it had also been possible for soldiers to rest and, for many in Eighth Army to go home to the UK on leave. For those remaining in Italy there were leave centres and an interesting recreation programme; the war diary of 5th Northamptonshire Regiment notes that 'recreational facilities include Battleaxe Cinema'; the Northamptons were in 78th Division, the Battleaxe Division.[64]

While all this was going on, Allied Intelligence staffs were building up their picture of the opposing forces. As Eighth Army's commander was later to tell Brian Harpur:

> normally one could with the help of a good Intelligence staff make a reasonably accurate guess about where to concentrate one's attack upon the enemy without having to mount an expensive assault all along his defensive positions to find a weak spot.
>
> Just look at some of the many ways intelligence was gathered which in the end gave one the precious picture. Our aerial photographs, patrolling, interrogation of prisoners, interception of wireless messages, and even civilians straying between the lines all contributed vital information. We had dozens of sources for the clues we wanted. ...we even located the enemy mortars and guns by taking compass bearings on their flashes at night time from different positions, so that

by a simple process of triangulation we could work out where they were sited. But that is all self evident. It's the interpretation and use of the evidence which is important. To do that one has to have an awareness of the enemy. One has to ask oneself constantly what is he in the habit of doing? This thing 'habit' is very important because it enabled me in the final battle for the River Po to predict largely how he would react to certain of my moves. Equally, his knowledge of our habit enabled me to lull him into the conviction that he could predict ours when in fact I was planning something spectacularly different.[65]

Across the two armies plans were being discussed and finalized. Artillery and engineers prepared their plans, supply and transport commanders did likewise, medical plans were studied, and assaulting force commanders refined theirs. Ammunition dumps held more than adequate supplies of shells, Eighth Army having some two million rounds while Fifth Army held sufficient for sixty days' fighting; artillery commanders preparing their fire-plans did not have to worry about rationing shells. Likewise, the engineers had large parks of bridging equipment with the AGREs (Army Groups Royal Engineers) of Eighth Army. Assigned to V Corps was 22 AGRE, formed from Eighth Army Troops and the South African Corps Troops, SAEC; II Polish Corps had 16 AGRE, although this would switch later to XIII Corps, to deal with the many bridging tasks that lay ahead. Twenty-two AGRE would revive the Po Task Force, created the previous autumn but disbanded when the advance had halted, to build two pontoon and one high-level Bailey heavy bridges over the river.[66]

In the initial assault, Operation BUCKLAND, the full weight of the tactical air forces – Desert Air Force and XXII TAC – was to be available, but the strategic air forces would also play a major part. In all, 825 heavy bombers, 242 B-17s and 583 B-24s, were to help open BUCKLAND, dropping over 1,500 tons of fragmentation and general-purpose bombs on enemy positions. Since such tactical use of heavy bombers on previous occasions had caused casualties in Allied forces, every effort was made to ensure that the bombs would fall where they were intended, and not on friendly troops. To this end, the heavy anti-aircraft guns of 12 AA Brigade were to mark a 'bomb line' in the sky. The brigade's war diary includes the operation order for the task:

> The hy bomber programme for ... [BUCKLAND] involves the bombing of areas APRICOT from 1350 to 1420 and APPLE from 1420 to 1520 hrs on D day and area CHARLIE from 1100 to 1145 hrs and BAKER from 1145 to 1230 hrs on D + 1.
> Approx 42 groups each of 18 planes are to take part.
> Groups are to fly at 2 mins interval and are to carry 100% AP [anti-personnel] bombs.
> Groups are to approach the coast at CESENATICO and fly by means of ground markers, smoke, etc., astride a line joining CESENATICO and COTIGNOLA which will be used as the axis of approach. Bombing will be from 18,000 to 20,000 ft, speed 240mph.[67]

Eight troops – thirty-two guns – from 55th (Kent) and 57th (Wessex) HAA Regiments were to deploy for the task, firing 2,380 rounds on D Day and the same number on D + 1. The troops were to fire four rounds, one per gun, 300 yards apart, at intervals of thirty seconds to burst at 15,000 feet with the lines of burst 'in prolongation of each other'. In addition, 2nd Polish HAA Regiment was to be prepared, should the operation on D + 1 be cancelled, to participate in a fire plan over Cesenatico to warn off the bombers. This was to take the form of firing to produce a cross of bursts.[68]

By 1945 co-operation between the tactical air forces and armies had developed to a state where teamwork was at a level rarely seen before, and not excelled anywhere else. From difficult beginnings in the early days of the desert war through the work done by Auchinleck and Tedder and the subsequent co-location of Eighth Army's tactical HQ with that of the Desert Air Force, levels of trust had increased, as had the level of co-operation. However, in late 1944, when Sir Richard McCreery took over command of Eighth Army, and as Air Vice Marshal William Dickson handed over Desert Air Force to Air Vice Marshal Robert 'Pussy' Foster, there were some problems in the relationship. These

> came to a head at a meeting on 19 December when Dick was highly critical of the Desert Air Force's allocation of priorities and its commitment to attacks in support of his troops. Foster pointed out that he had certain responsibilities outside Eighth Army, was short of equipment to a point at which he was considering disbanding squadrons and was as concerned as Dick about losses of personnel, whom he found difficult to replace. What was at times a difficult discussion cleared the air and from then on the relationship developed into a very close one, and the Desert Air Force played an increasingly important role in future operations. Dick demonstrated his own commitment to the relationship by dining in the RAF mess on Christmas Day.[69]

The plans for the offensive were for Eighth Army to step off first, smashing the German line along the Senio and then the Santerno. Since Eighth Army did not enjoy great numerical superiority – conventional wisdom suggested a three-to-one advantage – it was to have considerable assistance on the Senio. Not only would the artillery play its usual effective role, but, as noted, the four-engined bombers of the strategic air forces would also be employed, in addition to the tactical air forces whose role in the initial assault would be co-ordinated closely with the artillery.

Fifteenth Army Group's task had been to: Find – Fix – Finish – Strike – Exploit. It remained only to strike and exploit. These were to be masterly strokes, highlighting the genius of Sir Richard McCreery and providing perhaps the best example of manoeuvre warfare by the western Allies in Europe.

Sir Richard told Brian Harpur that 'the key to everything in battle is simple really', before outlining four key factors. The first was good intelligence, which Fifth and Eighth Armies had in abundance. Next came good organization; neither army was lacking: their soldiers were well trained, well supplied and well motivated. The third factor was 'an enormous element of surprise because this can fox the enemy, give you the initiative, save lives, and provide an unforeseen bonus which it is to you to identify and exploit before it disappears'. Finally, it was essential to allow the enemy no rest:

> Never let him rest. Always be doing something to which he has to react. If you don't then he'll be doing something to which you have to react and you have lost the initiative. No, never let him rest. And I mean that literally as well. ... A soldier who gets little or no sleep becomes demoralized and useless. No, never let them rest. Keep their High Command twitching about your next move and don't let even one of their soldiers have a good night's sleep.[70]

From 9 April onwards Eighth Army and Fifth Army would ensure that Army Group C's soldiers would be denied any rest at all.

Notes

1. Jackson, op. cit., p.195.
2. Ibid., p.196.
3. Quoted in Truscott, op. cit., p.476.
4. Starr, op. cit., p.387.
5. Ibid.
6. Fisher, op. cit., p.446.
7. Ibid., pp.444–5.
8. Blumenson, op. cit., pp.238–9.
9. Quoted in ibid., p.239.
10. Jackson, p.202.
11. Quoted in ibid., p.202.
12. Truscott, p.478.
13. Ibid.
14. Ibid.
15. Ibid., pp.478–9.
16. Mead, op. cit., p.175.
17. McCreery, op. cit., p.5.
18. Mead, p.175.
19. Bidwell & Graham, *Tug of War*, p.390.
20. McCreery, *RUSI Journal*, op. cit., p.3.
21. NA, WO170/4178, war diary HQ Eighth Army (G, main), Mar 1945; Harpur, op. cit., p.155.
22. Jackson, p.204; Harpur, p.155.
23. Harpur, p.178; WO170/4178, op. cit.
24. Harpur, p.178.
25. Ibid.
26. Ibid., p.179.
27. Ibid.
28. Ibid., pp.180–1; Jackson, p.206.
29. Jackson, pp.204–8.

30. Ibid.
31. Ibid.
32. Ibid.
33. Ibid., pp.230–1.
34. Ibid., p.231.
35. Ibid., p.223.
36. Harpur, p.101.
37. NA, WO170/5040, war diary, 1 LS, 1945.
38. ffrench-Blake, *A History of the 17th/21st Lancers 1922–1959*, p.209.
38. Jackson, pp.228–9; Truscott, p.481.
40. McCreery, *RUSI Journal*, op. cit., p.3.
41. McCreery, draft memoir, p.4.
42. Mead, p.173.
43. Jackson, p.227.
44. Ibid.
45. Ibid., p.295.
46. Evans, op. cit., p.189.
47. NA, WO170/5026, war diary, 1 KRRC, 1945.
48. NA, WO170/4988, war diary, 8 A&S Hldrs, 1945.
49. NA, WO170/5033, war diary, 2 LF, 1945.
50. NA, WO170/4622, war diary, 4H, 1945.
51. NA, WO170/5018, war diary, 2 Innisks, 1945.
52. NA, WO170/4979, war diary, 3 Gren Gds, 1945; WO170/4629, war diary, 17/21 L, 1945.
53. McCreery, draft memoir, p.3.
54. NA, WO170/4979, op. cit.; ffrench-Blake, *The 17th/21st Lancers 1759–1993*, p.11.
55. NA, WO170/5059, 5060, 5061, war diaries, 2/5, 2/6 & 2/7 Queen's, 1945.
56. NA, WO170/5060, op. cit.
57. NA, WO170/4992, war diary, 1 Buffs, 1945.
58. Ibid.
59. NA, WO170/5051, war diary, 5 Northants, 1945.
60. NA, WO170/4638, war diary, 12 RTR, 1945.
61. NA, WO170/4623, war diary, 7 H, 1945.
62. NA, WO170/4621, Bays, 1945.
63. NA, WO170/4634, war diary, 2 RTR, op. cit.
64. NA, WO170/5051, war diary, 5 Northants, op. cit.
65. Harpur, pp.123–4.
66. Jackson, p.316.
67. NA, WO170/4857, war diary, HQ 12 AA Bde.
68. Ibid.
69. Mead, pp.165–6.
70. Harpur, p.123.

Chapter Six

By the end of March 1945 the Germans had done all they could to ensure strong defences in northern Italy. Army Group C expected an Allied offensive at the beginning of April[1] and had prepared for it, taking

> full advantage of the lull to retrain, refresher courses being run at a large number of battle schools north of the Po. … the outlook as regards supplies was very sombre, but such stocks as were in the theatre were conserved by rigorous economies and expedients such as the use of methane and wood-gas in MT, and the substitution of horses and even oxen for towing equipment. Most divisions were tolerably up to the strength levels of the time, and when von Vietinghoff returned in mid-March he was not perturbed by their morale. The troops were deeply concerned for their homeland, but they still had faith in the Führer and were constantly reminded by Goebbels' propaganda machine that the 'miracle weapons' would soon be in action. Moreover, the Italian front, alone of all the fighting fronts, was still unbroken.[2]

That unbroken front consisted, as previously noted, of the Irmgard, Laura, Paula, Anna and Genghis Khan lines – respectively the Senio, Santerno, Sillaro, Gaiana and Idice – providing defence in depth as these tied into the Reno line, itself running east-to-west about twenty miles south of the Po, to which it ran parallel. Around Argenta, isolated by inundations, the Germans had created an island of defences, a 'fortress' with depth provided by several lines of strongpoints. Having breached all these, the Allies would then have to cross the Po and face the Venetian Line, or Red Line to the Germans, from the southern end of Lake Garda along the Alpine foothills to the Adriatic coast via Verona and the line of the Adige. Beyond the Adige lay the Blue Line, or *Voralpenstellung*, in the Alpine foothills. Layered with the Blue Line, further defensive lines were being prepared along four rivers, Brenta, Piave, Tagliamento and Isonzo, with those on the Tagliamento and Isonzo closer to completion. Once again, German engineers were doing their best to stop the Allies. The story of the Italian campaign, one of river assaults, would be repeated in the spring offensive.

Facing Eighth Army along the Irmgard, or Senio, Line was General Traugott Herr's Tenth Army with LXXVI Panzer Corps, commanded by General Gerhard Graf von Schwerin, and I Fallschirmjäger Corps, under Lieutenant General Richard Heidrich, from the Adriatic to beyond the Eighth Army/Fifth Army boundary. As Map 1 shows, on 9 April, when Eighth Army launched Operation BUCKLAND, the formations of these two corps opposed Eighth Army formations as follows: 42nd Jäger

Division faced 56th (London) in the Argenta area; 362nd Infantry faced 8th Indian and 78th, and 98th Volksgrenadier faced 2nd New Zealand. The Lake Comácchio area was covered by 162nd (Turkoman) Division. Heidrich's Fallschirmjäger were deployed with 26th Panzer Division facing II Polish Corps, 4th Fallschirmjäger Division against X Corps and 278th Volksgrenadier Division opposing XIII Corps. The final formation of I Fallschirmjäger Corps, 305th Infantry Division, faced Fifth Army's area and opposed Gruppo Legnano in II US Corps. (The *Volksgrenadier* title was awarded to three divisions, 98th, 278th and 334th, on 6 April. All three were proud of their new titles, bestowed to mark distinguished service.) Against Eighth Army's area were two further German corps: LXXIII under General Anton Dostler, overseeing minor units deployed on defence and coast-watching duties between the Po and Venice; and General Ludwig Kübler's XCVII Corps, which included 237th Infantry in Istria and 188th Gebirgs Division, north of Trieste. Kübler's command was transferred to Army Group E on 10 April. In Tenth Army reserve were 155th Training and 29th Panzer Grenadier Divisions, both in Venetia, although 15th Panzer Grenadier Regiment of the latter was in reserve east of Ferrara by 7 April.

General Joachim Lemelsen's Fourteenth Army, of two corps, opposed Fifth Army. General Fridolin von Senger und Etterlin's XIV Panzer Corps included three divisions: 65th Infantry faced 34th and 91st US Divisions; 8th (formerly 157th) Gebirgs stood in the way of 6th South African Armoured; and 94th Infantry was also up against an armoured formation – 1st US Armored. LI Mountain Corps, commanded by General Friedrich-Wilhelm Hauck, included 334th Volksgrenadier, 114th Jäger, 232nd Infantry, Italia, and 148th Infantry. The first two were arrayed, respectively, against 10th Mountain and 1st Brazilian Divisions while 232nd Infantry was deployed in the centre of the Northern Approach, Italia Division (an Italian Fascist formation) in the Serchio Valley, and 148th Infantry against 92nd US Infantry on the west coast. Lemelsen had no significant reserve.

The Italian Army of Liguria (General Alfredo Guzzoni) included the Italian Corps Lombardia, commanded by Lieutenant General Kurt Jahn, and LXXV Corps under Lieutenant General Richard Schlemmer. Corps Lombardia deployed San Marco Marine Infantry Division in the Genoa area, where also was deployed *Kampfgruppe* Meinhold, which included Fortress Brigade 135 and parts of the Italian Monte Rosa Division. Schlemmer's corps, including 34th Infantry, 5th Gebirgs, Littorio Divisions, and the larger part of Monte Rosa, was deployed in the western Alps to protect the Italo-French frontier.

Vietinghoff's army group's sole reserve was 90th Panzer Grenadier Division, located in the Modena area, with the flexibility to strike towards Bologna should Fifth Army forces threaten that city, or interdict any movement west of Highway 64 by 10th Mountain Division. Fourteenth Army's 29th Panzer Grenadier Division had been relieved in the line by 334th Infantry on 22 March, after which it was to refit near Modena. However, on the evening of the 22nd, a battlegroup from the division was detached to cover the coast between the Piave and Po rivers; by 5 April the entire division had been redeployed to Venetia. Although it has been claimed that this move was in reaction to Allied deception plans, evidence suggests that those plans were implemented too late for such a reaction. As Jackson posits, the move 'was no more than a basic military precaution, to be expected of *OB Südwest* in view of the length of his Adriatic flank and its vulnerability to amphibious operations'.[3] Thus, as suggested on p.79, it was the experience of previous Allied amphibious operations in Italy, combined with German lack of experience of such operations, that prompted this move. Jackson also notes that the first battlegroup to arrive in Venetia had, by 7 April, been redeployed south, to positions east of Ferrara, where it remained in reserve.

Vietinghoff commanded some 394,000 German and Italian troops in his three armies with another 91,000 Germans protecting lines of communication, or manning anti-aircraft defences, while SS General Karl Wolff had about 100,000 men under his command in the northern provinces. In all, Army Group C had 1,436 field artillery pieces, about 400 medium anti-tank guns and some 450 self-propelled artillery pieces (assault guns in German parlance). No German tanks faced Fifth Army's front but 261 serviceable tanks opposed Eighth on 9 April. That was little more than the strength of 6th British Armoured Division, Eighth Army's main armoured formation, while Fifth Army had two armoured divisions and several armoured brigades were available to 15th Army Group. The German heavy anti-aircraft gunners were mostly deployed on lines of communication or coastal installations and only forty-one troops, about 200 guns, were with front-line formations; another 179 troops guarded lines of communication. Fifth Army's Intelligence officers assessed enemy strength facing the army as including 789 guns, of which forty-seven were tanks employed as artillery, while it was considered that two German divisions from north-west Italy and another two from north-east Italy might be moved to oppose the army's advance. However, their estimate added:

> Due to the increasing shortage of motor fuel and to the interdiction of road and rail by our Air Force, movements of reserve forces are expected to be somewhat slower than in the past. Examples of this are the approximately 8 days travel time required to move the 114th Division from the Lake [Comácchio] area to the Mt Belvedere area. Other indications of enemy transport difficulties are the recent reports of the practice of one truck pulling two others, oxen being employed to move artillery pieces, and the extensive use of hand carts for supply. However, during the attack adequate fuel may be initially available to make tactical moves, fuel being saved by the economy indicated.[4]

In terms of fighting soldiers in front-line divisions, the Allies had little advantage, with the well-constructed enemy defensive lines making their tasks even more difficult. However, Vietinghoff suffered two major disadvantages. He lacked air support, with surviving Axis aircraft restricted to only nine tons of fuel per day, and supplies, especially, as indicated in that Fifth Army Intelligence assessment, that most critical commodity for a modern army – petrol. On 6 April he warned OKW that his supply situation was 'below tolerable' levels, but there was little that either he or OKW could do about that: the rail lines into northern Italy were now beyond the engineers' capacity to repair. Indeed, the fuel situation could only get worse; the western Allies had overrun the Ruhr, reducing drastically the supply of coal, and the Hungarian oilfields were about to fall into Soviet hands. The admiral commanding the Kriegsmarine in the Mediterranean told OKM (*Oberkommando der Marine*) on 22 March that his ships could not go to sea unless more fuel became available.[5]

In spite of all this, the Germans were determined to fight on in Italy, which von Vietinghoff's Order of the Day for 30 March described as 'an important outpost for the overall conduct of the war'. He told his soldiers that, no matter what happened, they must do their duty, trust in themselves and their commanders and finished by telling them that 'the hour of decision must find us all of one mind, and ready with iron determination to fight every superiority with all means in our power'. As Jackson comments, 'It is greatly to the credit of his troops that they obeyed almost to the letter.'[6]

Vietinghoff was not alone in issuing Special Orders to his troops. Alexander issued one that told his soldiers: 'Final victory is near. The German Forces are now very groggy and only need one mighty punch to knock them out for good'. But he qualified that by stating that 'It will not be a walkover; a mortally wounded beast can still be very dangerous. You must be prepared for a hard and bitter fight; but the end is quite certain.'[7] Clark's Special Order was much more loquacious. He wrote that with the enemy now weakened 'by recent blows on other fronts the shock of a severe attack here will do much to speed his defeat' and that:

It is therefore of extreme importance that every individual should devote himself completely to the success of this new offensive. Each man, whatever his job, must give himself up utterly to the execution of these operations in order that every possible advantage will be denied the enemy and every opportunity taken to crush him completely. All must make full use of past training, of ingenuity, of material, and finally, of that courage which is needed to drive the battle home to the enemy in spite of every discouragement which may lie in the path that leads to complete victory.[8]

In contrast McCreery's message to Eighth Army was to the point, telling his soldiers that 'the army which started the great tide of Allied victory at El Alamein, is about to strike a knock-out blow against the Germans in Italy'. Declaring that the enemy 'must not be allowed to use his Armies in Italy to form a garrison for a Southern German stronghold', he emphasized that 'We will destroy or capture the enemy south of the Po'. He noted the 'powerful air' of the Desert Air Force and that Fifth Army would be assaulting 'at our side' with the American Air Forces in Italy bringing their 'full weight to bear in support of our attack'. The longstanding contribution of the 'brave soldiers of Poland' was also praised, with the comment that 'it is a matter of especial pride to our Empire Army that in this battle our gallant Polish Allies will be striking a decisive blow'. Nor were the Italian combat groups and partisan army forgotten: 'Eighth Army recognises and appreciates the part that gallant Italian forces are taking in the struggle.' Finally, McCreery wrote, 'Together we will all go forward to final victory.'[9] McCreery's message was distributed to Italian and Polish troops in their own languages.

As the protagonists prepared for battle, elements of Eighth and Fifth Armies were ready to strike the first blows of the final offensive in Italy. These formations would execute 'shaping' operations on either flank: on Eighth Army's right units of 2 Commando Brigade (2 and 9 Army Commandos and 40 and 43 Royal Marine Commandos) deployed to strike in the Lake Comácchio area, and on Fifth Army's left 92nd Division, with 442nd Regimental Combat Team and 473rd Infantry; 370th Infantry was also to play a brief part in the operation. Both operations were intended 'further to confuse the enemy and to pin down his troops'.[10] Those operations were successful, resulting in gains that helped secure both flanks before the main assaults began. In addition, they also saw the awards of five of the highest gallantry decorations to participating soldiers. In Eighth Army two posthumous Victoria Crosses were awarded, one to a junior NCO of 43 (RM) Commando, Corporal Thomas Peck Hunter, and one to a Danish officer of the Special Air Service, Major Anders Lassen. Three Medals of Honor, two posthumous, were awarded to soldiers of Fifth Army, Private First Class Sadao S. Munemori, Second Lieutenant Vernon Baker and Technical Sergeant Yukio Okutso.

Operation ROAST aimed to eliminate German positions on the spit between Lake Comácchio and the Adriatic, eliminating a threat to Eighth Army's right flank.

> We hoped to make use of Buffaloes on Lake Comácchio and the flooded country South of the lake to help outflank the position, but it was necessary first to turn the enemy off the long spit of land between the lake and the sea. The risk of losing some degree of surprise for the main attack had to be taken; in any case this preliminary operation helped the cover plan of drawing attention to the Adriatic Sea flank.[11]

Launched on the evening of 1 April, Easter Day, both 2 and 9 (Army) Commandos were to cross Comácchio in LVTs, but fell foul of the drier conditions that the region enjoyed that spring. Lake Comácchio, not deep at the best of times, was shallower than usual. The Fantails wallowed in slime and could not move off. Fortunately, it was possible to change to storm-boats and the commandos got underway. Carrying twenty men each, the plywood, flat-bottomed storm-boats, each towing two assault boats, made good speed across the lake, following navigation lights laid down by M Squadron SBS. To cover the noise of the boats' engines, considerable sound diversions were deployed. Aircraft circled above, tanks drove up and down the lateral road behind the British front line, 43 (RM) Commando played Wagnerian music over loudspeakers from the base of the spit and the gunners bombarded the German positions.[12]

Since an artillery bombardment was a known signature to a British advance, the Germans ought to have expected an attack. However, they did not, and were caught off balance when the commandos attacked at 3.00am on the Monday. Off balance they may have been, but they fought stoutly for two days before the spit was cleared. One account noted that 'despite rifle, machine-gun, mortar and artillery fire, and many mines, the whole spit was in our hands, along with nearly 1,000 prisoners. Small enemy outposts in the lake were also wiped out.'[13] Two troops of 9 Commando captured the enemy strongpoint codenamed 'Leviticus' in a typically vicious action in which the attackers crossed 150 yards of open ground in the face of machine-gun fire, to the accompaniment of a piper playing 'The Road to the Isles', taking the strongpoint and nearly a hundred prisoners.

As the army commandos fought their battle, the Royal Marines of 43 Commando secured the east side of the spit, an action in which the Royals went into battle in Kangaroos of 4th Hussars. The APCs proved a great boon in tackling well-fortified enemy positions. On Easter Tuesday the brigade advance continued with 2 and 43 Commandos leaving their start line at 2.00pm, the commandos advancing with armour support. Although 2 Commando had to take cover from heavy artillery and mortar fire after a thousand yards, 43 Commando pushed on, taking Scaglioca and advancing towards the Valetta canal. Approaching the canal, C Troop met heavy fire, but pressed on. During this action Corporal Thomas Peck Hunter, who was in charge of a Bren-gun section, earned a posthumous Victoria Cross, the citation for which notes that:

> Having advanced to within 400 yards of the canal, he observed [that] the enemy were holding a group of houses south of the canal. Realizing that his Troop behind him were in the open, as the country there was completely devoid of cover, and that the enemy would cause heavy casualties as soon as they opened fire, Corporal Hunter seized the Bren gun and charged alone across two hundred yards of open ground. Three Spandaus from the houses, and at least six from the North bank of the canal opened fire and at the same time the enemy mortars started to fire at the Troop.[14]

Corporal Hunter attracted most of the enemy fire as he charged, firing his Bren from the hip. With 'complete disregard for the intense enemy fire' he ran through houses, changing magazines on his Bren. Alone he cleared the houses of enemy, six of whom surrendered to him; the remainder fled to safety across a footbridge.

As C Troop came up behind Hunter it became the target for all the machine guns on the north bank. At this stage, Hunter again offered himself as a target, lying in full view on a heap of rubble while engaging concrete pillboxes across the canal. Drawing most of the enemy fire, he allowed the bulk of the troop to reach the safety of the houses as he shouted encouragement to them. 'Firing with great accuracy up to the last, Corporal Hunter was finally hit in the head by a burst of Spandau fire and killed instantly.'[15] Only his speed and agility had saved him from being hit earlier. His actions demoralized his foes and saved the lives of many of his comrades.

Two nights later, in Operation FRY, the small islands in Lake Comácchio were liberated in a joint effort by the SBS and Italian partisans of 28 Garibaldi Brigade. Both 2 and 43 Commandos had also reached the Valetta canal, securing the spit.[16]

As these British preliminary operations continued, Fifth Army launched its operations to secure its left flank. For this task, 92nd Division was deployed but with a much revised order of battle. Of the formation's three regiments, only Colonel Sherman's 370th Infantry played any part, and then only a brief one, while 365th and 371st were assigned to guard IV Corps' left flank. Under command of 92nd Division, instead of its regular formations, Major General Edward Almond had 442nd Regimental Combat Team and 473rd Infantry, the latter composed of re-roled anti-aircraft gunners.[17]

On 5 April Almond's men moved off towards Massa, five miles from Fifth Army's front lines, and then La Spezia. As well as a bombing attack by US aircraft, the division was supported by tanks and gunfire from Royal Navy ships. It was difficult country with a three-mile-wide coastal plain to the left, cut across by many well-fortified water courses, and the mass of the Apuan Alps to the right. The latter being impassable to large forces, the divisional advance was funneled into the strip of hills and lower peaks between the plain and the mountains. The plan of attack was for the 442nd to strike into the mountains overlooking the plain while 370th Infantry advanced through the lower hills to hook in behind enemy strongpoints on the plain. However, although 370th made good progress initially, a German counter-attack forced them back. The poor morale that plagued the formation forced Almond to commit 473rd in its place on the 8th.

Meanwhile, 442 RCT

had passed through the 371st on Monte Cauala and made an encircling attack on Mt Fragolita, which fell together with several other hills by dark. Materially aided by our fighter-bombers, the 442nd Infantry then continued north and in hard fighting during the rain and fog of the 7th cleared the summit of its first major objective, Mt Belvedere, overlooking Massa.[18]

In the course of this hard fighting one of 442nd's soldiers earned a posthumous Medal of Honor. Private First Class Sadao S. Munemori was a Japanese-American, or Nisei, soldier in A Company 100th Infantry Battalion. On 5 April, in mountains near Seravezza, his unit was pinned down by heavy enemy fire and his squad leader wounded. Command of the squad fell on Munemori who

made frontal, one-man attacks through direct fire and knocked out two machine guns with grenades. Withdrawing under murderous fire and showers of grenades from other enemy emplacements, he had nearly reached a shell crater occupied by two of his men when an unexploded grenade bounced on his helmet and rolled towards his helpless comrades.[19]

Aware of the danger to the other men, Munemori rose from cover into the enemy fire, dived towards the grenade and threw himself on it, taking the full force of the blast as the device exploded. By this swift, heroic act Pfc Munemori saved the two men 'at the cost of his own life and did much to clear the path for his company's victorious advance'.[20]

Although 370th Regiment's advance stalled, it had made good initial progress, during which one of its black officers, Second Lieutenant Vernon Joseph Baker, from Cheyenne, Wyoming, earned the Medal of Honor. Lieutenant Baker's unit assaulted a German strongpoint at Castle Aghinolfi with Baker leading his heavy weapons platoon through the enemy defences to within sight of the castle. En route, he destroyed a machine-gun position, two observation posts and two bunkers, not to mention a network of German telephone lines. Baker was awarded the Distinguished Service Cross, but this was upgraded to the Medal of Honor following a US Army study, commissioned in 1993, that discovered widespread racial discrimination in the award of the Medal, with no black soldiers receiving it.[21] In 1997 Vernon Baker was the only surviving black soldier to receive a Second World War Medal of Honor from President Clinton:

> Second Lieutenant Vernon J. Baker demonstrated outstanding courage and leadership in destroying enemy installations, personnel and equipment during his company's attack against a strongly entrenched enemy in mountainous terrain. When his company was stopped by the concentration of fire from several machine-gun emplacements, he crawled to one position and destroyed it, killing three Germans. Continuing forward, he attacked an enemy observation post and killed two occupants. With the aid of one of his men, Lieutenant Baker attacked two more machine-gun nests, killing or wounding the four enemy soldiers occupying these positions. He then covered the evacuation of the wounded personnel of his company by occupying an exposed position and drawing the enemy's fire.[22]

On the night of 6 April, Baker volunteered to lead his battalion's advance through minefields and heavy enemy fire. The citation concluded by stating that his 'fighting spirit and daring leadership were an inspiration to his men'.[23]

Also awarded the DSC in 1945 but upgraded to the Medal of Honor fifty years later was Technical Sergeant Yukio Okutsu. Another Nisei soldier, born in Hawaii, he too served in 100th Battalion and earned the Medal of Honor on Monte Belvedere on 7 April when he 'distinguished himself by extraordinary heroism'. Three enemy machine guns had bracketed his platoon and pinned it down. In spite of this,

> Technical Sergeant Okutsu boldly crawled to within 30 yards of the nearest enemy emplacement through heavy fire. He destroyed the position with two accurately placed hand grenades, killing three machine gunners. Crawling and dashing from cover to cover, he threw another grenade, silencing a second machine gun, wounding two enemy soldiers, and forcing two others to surrender. Seeing a third machine gun, which obstructed his platoon's advance, he moved forward through heavy small arms fire and was stunned momentarily by rifle fire, which glanced off his helmet. Recovering, he bravely charged several enemy riflemen with his submachine gun, forcing them to withdraw from their positions. Then, rushing the machine-gun nest, he captured the weapon and its … crew of four.

By these single-handed actions he enabled his platoon to resume its assault on a vital objective.[24]

The citation concludes by noting that 'the courageous performance of Technical Sergeant Okutsu against formidable odds was an inspiration to all'. His decoration was upgraded following a review of the service records of Asian-Americans awarded the DSC. On 21 June 2000 Yukio Okutsu was one of twenty-two Asian-Americans awarded the Medal of Honor by President Clinton; only six had survived to receive the Medal.

The advance on Fifth Army's left flank continued with 473rd Infantry, with tank support, reaching Massa on the 9th. Next day the town, a relic of the Gothic Line, was liberated by 92nd Division. Carrara followed on the 11th and then the attackers ran up against a strong German line and determined opposition along the Carrione river. Fighting continued on the left flank but, although progress was slow, 92nd Division had achieved its primary objectives, inflicting heavy losses on the enemy and forcing him to put all available reserves into the line, including a battalion of 90th Panzer Grenadier Division, which was committed on the 14th, the day on which Operation CRAFTSMAN was launched.[25]

On Eighth Army's front, 56th (London) Division was to launch Operation LEVER on the night of 5/6 April. Mindful of the problems of 2 and 9 Commandos, plans were amended to ensure no repetition. This involved 167 Brigade, led by 1st London Irish Rifles, crossing the Reno westwards from San Alberto to create a wedge between the Reno floodbank and the inundated area west of the lake, thereby establishing a secure, slime-free LVT launching point.

The first infantry to cross met no opposition and two troops of 10th Hussars' Shermans were also rafted across. However, the Germans reacted later, soldiers of 42nd Jäger Division opening fire from pillboxes. Although many casualties occurred in 167 Brigade, especially amongst the sappers, the brigade consolidated and repelled attacks. With a wedge now firmly in place, and dubbed such, 167 Brigade's positions along the Fossa di Navigazione secured V Corps' left flank. (As well as 1st London Irish, the brigade included 9th Royal Fusiliers and 1st London Scottish.) The success of Operation LEVER also provided a base for the next attack, against Menate and Longastrino, to secure the road between the villages from where further advance would be made to Bastia bridge. The war diary of HQ V Corps (A&Q) notes that:

> Field Marshal Alexander accompanied by the Army Commander and the Corps Commander watched the progress of the battle and in the afternoon decorated personnel of Cremona Gruppo in Ravenna for the part they had played in March while advancing up to Lake Comácchio.[26]

All seemed to be going well with the overall plan. Then, on the night of 6/7 April, German artillery began bombarding Allied positions. This worried the Allied commanders who had been concerned that von Vietinghoff might withdraw to the

Genghis Khan Line, shortening his front and making easier a retreat to the Po. It was believed that the artillery programme was intended to cover just such a withdrawal. In this the Allied commanders were correct, but withdrawal had been forbidden by OKW; the guns had fired simply because orders for the programme had not been rescinded. Vietinghoff had wanted to pull Tenth Army and the left wing of Fourteenth Army north to the Genghis Khan Line, based on the Idice and Reno rivers, thereby abandoning the salient south-east of Bologna. OKW had overruled him and also refused permission for Herr to thin out Tenth Army's front by withdrawing elements of his command to the Santerno. As events turned out, parts of Herr's plan were executed, to the detriment of his soldiers. Allied commanders could breathe a sigh of relief when it was realized that the Germans were staying put – although units of 26th Panzer Division were positioned along the Santerno by the 8th and both 98th Volksgrenadier and 362nd Divisions were ordered, on Herr's initiative, to withdraw during the night of 9/10 April, a move that meant they were caught in the open by the Allied bombardment and bombing.[27]

With Eighth Army due to launch Operation BUCKLAND on 9 April, a small operation was mounted on the night of the 8th/9th. This 'fighting reconnaissance' was to Comácchio town, on the north shore of Lake Comácchio, to cause confusion and casualties while giving the impression of a major raid; prisoners were also to be taken. (The *Official History* quotes an unidentified source as describing such actions as 'Noisy diversions'.)[28] Leading the reconnaissance patrol was Major Anders Lassen MC**, a Dane, commanding M Squadron SBS. Since no previous reconnaissance had been possible, the raiders were on unfamiliar ground as they approached the town on a narrow road flanked by water on both sides. Sending two scouts ahead, Lassen led the remainder of his patrol, fewer than twenty men, towards Comácchio town.

Having covered about 500 yards, the patrol was challenged from a position alongside the road. Responding that they were fishermen, the raiders tried to move forward again to overcome the enemy post, but the ruse had failed and they came under machine-gun fire from the position, and from two strongpoints to the rear. Lassen attacked the first position, manned by four men with two machine guns, with grenades, knocking it out before charging forward to tackle the second position under covering fire from his men. Once again he silenced it, using grenades. The patrol then advanced; two Germans had been killed, two captured, and another two machine guns were out of action. However, Lassen's patrol had also suffered casualties.[29]

Although enemy fire was still intense, Lassen rallied and re-organized his men, bringing fire to bear on the third German position. Once again he went forward himself, throwing grenades and closing to within yards of the position when he heard a cry of 'Kamerad'. He then ordered the defenders to come out and made ready to accept their surrender.

Whilst shouting to them to come out he was hit by a burst of Spandau fire from the left of the position and he fell mortally wounded, but even whilst falling he flung a grenade, wounding some of the occupants, and enabling his patrol to dash in and capture this final position. Major Lassen refused to be evacuated as he said it would impede the withdrawal and endanger further lives, and as ammunition was nearly exhausted the force had to withdraw. By his magnificent leadership and complete disregard for his personal safety, Major Lassen had, in the face of overwhelming superiority, achieved his objects.[30]

Even while dying, Lassen gave his men covering fire. The Dane, a merchant seaman at the outbreak of war, was awarded a posthumous Victoria Cross which, the *Official History* states, was for 'consistently brave leadership' as much as for his actions at Comácchio. He is buried at Argenta Gap war cemetery, as is Corporal Tom Hunter VC.

With 167 Brigade firm along the Navigazione canal and Lassen's operation complete, final preparations were underway for Operation BUCKLAND. Far to the south, at Foggia, MASAF heavy bombers were being prepared for their mission on the 9th. So, too, were medium bombers of the Tactical Air Forces and fighter-bombers of the Desert Air Force and XXII TAC. Closer to the front, engineers were making ready to gap the Senio floodbanks and bridge the stream, while the specialist armour of 25 Armoured Engineer Brigade took up positions for the assault. Gunners manned their equipments in their new positions, each gun having a ready supply of some 600 rounds. Many vehicles moving equipment and supplies to the front did so along newly-built roads, another task completed by the engineers. The front-line infantry along the Senio, who would make the assault at H Hour, were withdrawn a safe distance, over 400 yards, from the waterway to give the artillery and air support a clear run. Patrols on the night of 8/9 April confirmed that the enemy continued to hold the Senio in strength. Detachments of 55th (Kent), 57th (Wessex) and 2nd Polish HAA Regiments took post to fire their 3.7s to mark the bomb-line for the strategic bombers.[31]

In the early afternoon those gunners received the order to fire as the drone of heavy bombers approached. A total of 825 B-17 Fortresses and B-24 Liberators dropped 1,511 tons of bombs on a sector of ground some two miles square across the front of II Polish Corps, codenamed 'Apricot' and an L-shaped area beyond Lugo of about nine miles square on V Corps' front, codenamed 'Apple'. Both lay between the Senio and Santerno. (See Map 3.) Most bombs were 20lb devices, but 100lb general-purpose bombs were also dropped. Although great efforts had been taken to ensure accuracy, with navigational aids and markers on the ground as well as the exploding anti-aircraft shells marking the bomb line, errors occurred. Both Polish and New Zealand troops were hit by Allied bombs, the more serious of two incidents seeing a squadron of eighteen bombers target the concentration area of 3rd Carpathian Division's assault brigades, killing thirty-eight officers and men and wounding 188. One aircraft emptied its bomb bay on the New Zealand Division's area but, in this case, no serious damage was caused. Next day there were two further incidents as the bombers targeted the Santerno. As many as thirty New Zealanders were killed on the

Canale di Lugo while 8th Indian Division's bridges across the Senio were hit heavily, causing many casualties and serious damage to vehicles.[32]

Two Polish battalions were struck by bombs intended for 'Apricot' and there was concern that they might not be able to take part in the assault. However, General Anders visited the stricken units and both were re-organized in time for the assault that evening. Anders had been with Mark Clark when the tragedy occurred and went immediately to visit the stricken battalions. He commented that 'Commanding officers took energetic action to replace the losses at once, and, thanks to the speed with which this was done, the attack was not delayed'.[33]

In the German lines the main effect of the bombing was to sever all telephone communications in the forward area. The non–availability of telephones would have a detrimental effect on the control of German artillery when Eighth Army's attack began. However, there were few casualties, although Jackson notes that this may have been the psychological 'starting point from which desertions were to grow, but it did not in itself have a decisive effect on morale'. He quotes a German artillery officer of 4th Fallschirmjäger Division who wrote in his diary:

> There were no losses in men or material, but all signals communications were completely destroyed. Thank goodness they were only fragmentation bombs, against which you only need to get into a hole to have adequate cover.[34]

Jackson's comment about a psychological starting point is apt also for the combined air and artillery assault that was unleashed, something he describes as 'inspiring' for Eighth Army's soldiers but having 'a numbing effect on the Germans'. The 'inspiring' effect for Eighth Army soldiers was such that many believed that the Germans must have suffered heavy losses. What followed the bombing confirmed them in that belief.[35]

There was to be no let-up for the Germans. True to his word, McCreery was denying them rest. An hour after the carpet-bombing began, medium bombers struck at enemy artillery positions. Twin-engined B-25 Mitchell bombers attacked target areas 'Tom', 'Dick' and 'Harry' on the Poles' front over a thirty-minute period. A quarter of an hour after that strike ended, Mitchells also hit the 'Stalk' area in front of V Corps: in total, 234 Mitchells dropped 24,000 fragmentation bombs. While all this was happening, Desert Air Force and XXII TAC fighter-bombers had been attacking communications until 2.00pm, after which XXII TAC switched its attention to enemy HQs, as well as armed reconnaissance of all roads leading to the battle area. After 2.00pm Desert Air Force aircraft were on call to the officer commanding No. 1 Mobile Operations Room Unit.[36] Both tactical air forces turned their attention to targets in the forward area from 3.20pm. The Army Group account of the campaign summed up these and subsequent events:

> The blows that knocked out the Germans in Italy began as slow, deliberate punches with heavy fists. Within two weeks the enemy was staggering; the fists

became wide-stretched hands, with fingers probing, then grasping vast numbers of Germans and all of Italy's north.[37]

Some 720 machines struck at command posts, strongpoints, gun and mortar positions. This lasted until 7.30pm, the time at which it was believed that fading light would make operations too dangerous. Blaxland, a veteran of the campaign, comments that the fighters swooped 'upon such German guns, tanks or even motor cyclists as became visible beneath the huge clouds of yellow dust thrown up by the fragmentation bombs'.[38]

At 3.20pm the guns opened up. Each assaulting division had about 380 guns in support, including its own divisional artillery, and the Germans were subjected to a blizzard of fire from almost 1,200 guns, ranging from 25-pounder to 240mm weapons and with heavy mortars firing on the floodbanks' reverse slopes. As the bombardment lifted from the river line on to the ground beyond, enemy soldiers emerged from their dug-outs, ready to man their weapons for the expected assault, only to be caught in the artillery fire as the guns shortened their range and brought their fire back on to the river line.[39] The AGRAs involved were demonstrating just how effective the British artillery was. The fire-plan, Operation FESTA, included twelve Air OPs directing fire on twenty-four enemy batteries simultaneously, an aspect of the plan suggested by Major H. V. Kahn.[40]

A New Zealand account of the bombing and the artillery bombardment describes the scene along one section of floodbank:

We prepared our ears for the guns, but before we heard them the patch of the [floodbank] ahead seemed to be lifted in the air. Black earth, grey smoke, yellow dust, red and ochre flames suddenly rose along its edge. Then, and then only, came the sound of the guns, roaring and baying and clamouring one after another, until the whole eastern horizon was solid sound.[41]

There were to be four more such bombardments in Operation FESTA, each lasting between twenty and thirty minutes. At the end of each, fighter-bombers would swoop again, strafing the German line with bombs, rockets, machine guns and cannon. This 'layer cake' of fire from artillery and aircraft lasted until 7.10pm, by which time the Germans had endured over five hours of bombing and shellfire. The fifth bombardment ended at 7.10, as the day's light waned and, once again, fighter-bombers swooped. This time, however, they dropped no bombs, nor did they fire rockets, machine guns or cannon. Their final attack was a feint, to divert enemy attention from the next phase of the operation. As the guns had fired their fifth bombardment of the day, the 'funnies' of 25 Armoured Engineer Brigade were trundling up to the Senio.[42]

As the Germans watched the aircraft climb away and wondered if the guns were about to open fire again, their questions were answered as spurts of fire streaked towards them from Eighth Army's lines. Churchill Crocodile flame-throwers were in action, together with the smaller Wasp weapons. (The author was told by a former

Fallschirmjäger who served in Italy that he and his comrades considered the flame-thrower such an 'unfair' weapon that they would have shot any captured flame-thrower crews.)[43] The Wasps were not as effective as had been hoped, partially due to the work of the bombers, which had destroyed some of the ramps built by the sappers for the smaller flame-throwers. This meant that many Wasp flame guns had to fire at a high angle and failed to reach their targets.[44]

The terror inspired by the flame-throwers also diverted German attention from the next phase of Operation BUCKLAND. While the guns had fallen silent, they remained so for only two minutes before beginning a protective barrage on the far side of the Senio. The infantry assault was going in.

On V Corps' front the assaulting divisions were 2nd New Zealand and 8th Indian, each attacking with four battalions. Ahead of the infantry were the flame-throwers, Crocodiles and Wasps, the latter drawn from across all V Corps' divisions.

The forward floodbank had already been made uninhabitable, and it was with a certain lurid relish that the crews of their vehicles came to a halt at its edge and belched forth their flames, as with the multiple swoosh of mighty bellows. An enormous blaze rapidly turned into black smoke. Spectacular and heartening in its impact on the assault troops, it may have inflicted little material damage on the enemy, and it penetrated the far bank only in places, but its addition to the demon concoction already absorbed undoubtedly completed the collapse of willpower in many German breasts.[45]

Of the infantry assault that followed Jackson commented that in those areas where the near floodbank had been in British hands before D Day 'things went better than elsewhere as the leaders of the assaulting troops and the Sappers, who were to bridge behind them, had been able to reconnoitre the obstacles before the attack'.[46] Plans for those sectors were thus 'more complete and practicable' and he cites as evidence the success of Freyberg's New Zealanders and 19 Brigade of 8th Indian Division.

The New Zealanders had moved into the line on 1 April, relieving 78th Division which then set about final training for its role in BUCKLAND. On the Senio the Battleaxe Division had begun clearing the near floodbank but this task was still underway when Freyberg's men took over. Over the next few days the New Zealanders completed the task, evicting Germans with bayonet and bomb, tunnelling through the bank and dropping sacks of grenades over the crest into the German positions. Thus the forward New Zealand brigades held both sides of the near bank and could reconnoitre in detail. Among other information, they knew the depth of the Senio in their sector. Although 15th Army Group's Chief Engineer had earlier produced a report on anticipated water levels in the rivers,[47] this had been based on historical averages but 1945 proved an exception, with very low levels following recent dry months. As a result, the leading battalions of 5 and 6 Brigades simply stormed the far bank of the Senio and advanced under cover of the artillery barrage, suffering little loss. The New Zealanders were on V Corps' left and, with 8th Indian, attacked, separated by five miles of the Senio between their respective inner flanks. In the initial assault, 5 Brigade attacked with 21st and 28th Battalions, the latter a Maori unit, while 6 Brigade, on the right, deployed 25th and 24th Battalions (battalions are listed from the right).[48] Freyberg's division had the unique orbat of three infantry and one armoured brigades; in Operation BUCKLAND an armoured regiment was assigned to each infantry brigade so that the latter fought as brigade battlegroups.

Eighth Indian Division also deployed two brigades, 19 and 21, each with two battalions forward also. In 19 Brigade the leaders were 1st Argyll and Sutherland Highlanders and 6/13th Royal Frontier Force Rifles; 21 Brigade's attack was made by 1/5th Mahratta Light Infantry and 3/15th Punjab Regiment (units are again listed from the right).[49] The leading companies of 19 Brigade were across the Senio in fifteen minutes – the division had held some posts on the near bank before the assault – but follow-up companies faced more difficulties. So, too, did both battalions of 21 Brigade. The Argylls' war diary recorded:

1920: A Coy assaulted the near bank. There was no opposition. The enemy PW stated that our assault was so quick that they had no time to get from their bunkers to their slits.

1925: B & C Coys assaulted the far bank successfully and pushed on to a depth of 200 yards. Again opposition was light owing to the speed of our assault.

1938: A Coy took up posn area 376431. Tac Bn HQ moved to near bank of river at 375427 and 5 mins later over river to 374431. Meantime B Coy had pressed on and consolidated successfully at Crossroads 373434 by about 2000 hours. C Coy were also on their 2nd objective at the road between 372434 and 368427. They secured the houses on both sides of the road.[50]

Opposition in the centre of the line was much more stubborn than on the flanks. While 19 Brigade's leading companies passed over the floodbank when most defenders were still shocked and under cover, as the Argylls' prisoners reported, as the follow-up companies started to cross, many soldiers of 362nd Division had recovered their senses, at least partially, crawled from their concrete bunkers and manned their weapons. The toughest opposition faced the Mahrattas and Frontiersmen but, in each instance, an individual soldier's courage and initiative carried the day. The two *jawans* who took centre stage in this drama earned the Victoria Cross, and survived to receive their awards.

In the Mahrattas' sector, north of San Polito, the leading company had captured the near floodbank, allowing another company to pass through three minutes later to assault the far bank. Since the Senio at that point is quite narrow and shallow, the company waded across. Sepoy Namdeo Jadhao, a company runner, crossed with his company commander, close behind a leading section. While the party waded towards the far bank, at least three German posts opened fire, wounding the company commander and two other men, and killing the others except Namdeo Jadhao. In spite of heavy machine-gun and mortar fire, Namdeo Jadhao carried a wounded comrade through the water, up the steep slope of the near bank through the mine

Field Marshal Sir Harold Alexander, Supreme Allied Commander Mediterranean, who had commanded the Allied Army Group in Italy until his promotion in November 1944. *(9th HAA Regiment Archive)*

General Mark Clark, commander 15th Army Group. Alexander's successor as Army Group commander, Clark had previously commanded the US Fifth Army. *(NARA)*

Lieutenant General Sir Richard McCreery, commander of Eighth Army and the finest British field commander in Europe. Previously commander of X Corps, McCreery was appointed to command Eighth Army when Sir Oliver Leese was promoted and transferred to South-East Asia. *(McCreery Family)*

Lieutenant General Lucian King Truscott Jr. Clark's successor as commander of Fifth Army, the only US general to command at regiment (brigade), divisional, corps and army levels during the Second World War, Truscott was the most outstanding US field commander in the European theatre. *(NARA)*

An Italian mule train carrying supplies to troops in the front line in the mountains. Note the six-wheeled US Army lorry that has fallen off the mountain track. *(NARA)*

Italian troops played an active part in Operation GRAPESHOT with four combat groups serving in the Army Group and another two preparing for operations when the war ended. These soldiers of Gruppo Cremona are pictured during the winter when the Gruppo was holding part of the Allied line. *(UK Government official / Public Domain)*

Among the many innovations available to support the attacking forces were Churchill bridgelaying tanks. This photograph was taken in March when B Assault Brigade, which became 25 Armoured Engineer Brigade on 6 April, laid on a demonstration of the tank's capabilities at Mezzano. *(UK Government official/ Public Domain)*

Lance Sergeant Patrick Joseph 'Rex' Doherty, 2nd Royal Inniskilling Fusiliers. On the night of 12 March, L/Sgt Doherty led a patrol along the Senio floodbank during which he saved the life of one of his soldiers while attacking a German machine-gun position that had been harassing a forward platoon position. *(Mrs Barbara Downey)*

Corporal Thomas Peck Hunter VC lost his life during an attack on German positions on 3 April while 43 (RM) Commando was advancing towards the Valetta canal. Drawing enemy fire on himself, Corporal Hunter saved the lives of several men of his troop by sacrificing his own. *(Author's photo)*

Major Anders Lassen VC MC**, M Squadron SBS, was killed leading a reconnaissance patrol on Comácchio town on the night of 8/9 April. Lassen was killed as he covered the fighting withdrawal of his soldiers. *(Author's photo)*

Private Joe Hayashi, 442 RCT, was killed in action at Tèndola on 22 April as he led an attack on strongly-held enemy positions. Two days earlier, Hayashi had led a similar operation in which he had subdued enemy positions, saved the lives of wounded comrades and allowed his divisional advance to continue. *(NARA)*

An Auster AOP of the RAF flies low over flooded land west of Lake Comácchio. It was from one of these Austers, popularly known as 'Whizzers', that General McCreery identified the Argenta Gap. The Auster is flying over the pumping station at Menate, which was still standing in 2013 but scheduled for demolition. *(9th HAA Regiment Archive)*

Facing Eighth Army was the German-held Senio Line, which used the floodbanks of the Torrente Senio to provide cover and defensive positions. The two forces were often only yards apart and, in places, occupied opposing sides of the floodbank on the Allied side of the Senio. This is a section of the British sector of the line. *(Author's collection)*

A determined-looking soldier of 78th Division in the Senio Line during March. He is armed with an American M3 sub-machine gun, known as the 'Grease Gun' due to its similarity to that tool. *(Author's collection)*

The Senio today. Although it looks unimpressive, this small waterway was a major obstacle to the advance of armoured forces. It was near this location that Rex Doherty earned his MM in March. This is also in the area where 2nd New Zealand Division crossed in Operation BUCKLAND. *(Author's photo)*

Mortarmen of 92nd Division in action near Massa on Fifth Army's front. This was part of Fifth Army's preliminary operations to secure the left flank before launching Operation CRAFTSMAN. *(NARA via Ken Ford)*

A Consolidated B-24 Liberator of the US Fifteenth Air Force dropping its bombs during a raid on railway yards north-west of Vienna on 2 April. Over 800 B-24s and Boeing B-17 Flying Fortresses took part in the bombing of enemy positions along the front before Operations BUCKLAND and CRAFTSMAN. *(NARA)*

Although there were few enemy fighter aircraft still in Italy, there were strong anti-aircraft artillery defences and this Liberator, 'Stevanovitch II' of the 464th Bomb Group, fell victim to flak over Lugo on 10 April, while supporting New Zealand and Indian attacks. Only one of the crew of ten survived. *(NARA)*

New Zealanders with bridging equipment moving up to the Senio on 9 April. The New Zealanders' plans for crossing the waterway were detailed and had been well rehearsed, contributing to their success and rapid advance. *(9th HAA Regiment Archive)*

With the Senio in the lower foreground and Cotignola in the middle ground, this photograph gives a good impression of how the battleground appeared on 9 April as Operation BUCKLAND got underway. *(Author's collection)*

The Sappers planned to put low-level bridges across the Senio where possible. To do so, they had to blow breaches in the floodbanks. This is one such breach with vehicles queuing to cross the bridge. *(Author's collection)*

A jeep convoy moving up to the Senio on 10 April. By then the New Zealanders were attacking the Santerno, several miles farther on. *(Author's collection)*

The terrain in northern Italy features many narrow waterways that presented major obstacles to tanks, especially the Sherman Fireflies with their long-barrelled 17-pounder guns. Older 75mm Shermans, withdrawn from service, were stripped of their turrets and adapted to carry fascines to aid in crossing such obstacles. These fascine-carrying Shermans belonged to 2nd New Zealand Division's 28 Assault Squadron. *(Author's collection)*

Other redundant Shermans, and M7 Priest self-propelled howitzers, were modified to act as armoured personnel carriers, dubbed Kangaroos. Infantry of the New Zealand 9 Brigade wait for the order to advance in their Kangaroos. *(Author's collection)*

Another indication of the enormity of the engineers' bridging tasks is given by this photograph of a Churchill of the North Irish Horse crossing the Senio over two Churchill Ark bridging tanks. *(Author's collection)*

Not long after Operation CRAFTSMAN began, soldiers of 10th Mountain Division were sending back their first German prisoners. Hays' mountaineers had begun operations with a pace that they were to maintain to the Po and beyond. *(NARA)*

A Churchill Crocodile of 25 Armoured Engineer Brigade firing its flame gun in support of troops of 2nd New Zealand Division. In Eighth Army, 25 Armoured Engineer Brigade was the equivalent of Hobart's Funnies in 21st Army Group. *(UK Government official/Public Domain)*

Spitfire fighter-bombers – Spit-bombers – of a South African Air Force squadron of the Desert Air Force prepare to take off for a mission in support of Eighth Army. *(UK Government official/Public Domain)*

Republic P-47D Thunderbolt of the Brazilian Air Force, operating as part of the USAAF 350th Fighter Group of the US XXII Tactical Air Command, on the ground between missions. The Brazilian *1º Grupo de Caça* (1st Fighter Group) carried out many close support missions, as the bomb symbols under the cockpit canopy of this Thunderbolt indicate. *(NARA)*

Bailey bridges were essential to operations in Italy and especially so during Operation GRAPESHOT. This example of a section of the highly-adaptable bridging equipment is on permanent display outside the Senio Line Museum in Alfonsine. *(Author's photo)*

A heavily-camouflaged Sherman Firefly crossing a Bailey bridge over the Santerno near Imola. Since the Fireflies were prime targets for enemy anti-tank gunners and *panzerfaust*-armed infantry, efforts have been made to make the 17-pounder appear shorter. *(Author's collection)*

Soldiers of 5th Battalion Northamptonshire Regiment fighting their way through the ruins of the town of Argenta on 17/18 April. The Northamptons were counter-attacked by the Germans but that assault was repelled and the Argenta Gap had been opened. *(UK Government official/Public Domain)*

An aerial reconnaissance photo of intact bridges over the Panaro river at Bomporto. The photograph shows clearly the difficulties facing armoured units operating in this terrain. *(NARA)*

A Panzer Mk V, Panther, uses the ruins of a house near the Sillaro river as cover on 16 April. By this stage of the campaign the Germans were forced to use their tanks in small groups, or even individually, in defensive actions. *(Author's collection)*

Italian partisans played a vital role as the campaign developed, often taking control of villages, towns and cities before Allied forces arrived. The partisans were supplied with British battledress, as shown in this photograph, while the man in the foreground is operating a Browning .50-inch machine gun. *(NARA)*

Tanks of 6th South African Armoured Division preparing to move towards Bologna. The division had stopped to allow a US infantry division to pass. *(NARA)*

A Sherman crew from 2 Warsaw Armoured Brigade of II Polish Corps. As well as its own 2 Armoured Brigade, II Polish Corps had the British 7 Armoured Brigade under its command during the early phase of Operation BUCKLAND. Two Warsaw Armoured Brigade was upgraded to divisional status, but too late to see action as such. *(Polish Institute & Sikorski Museum)*

A Fantail carrying US troops enters the Po on 26 April. These amphibious vehicles had played a major role in operations at Lake Comácchio, taking the Germans by surprise when 56th (London) Division deployed them to cross the inundated ground bordering the lake. *(NARA)*

A German divisional commander surrenders to Brazilian troops at Fornovo on 29 April. *(NARA via Ken Ford)*

Near San Benedetto, US troops cross a treadway pontoon bridge over the Po. This was the first bridge over the river to be completed and it was opened on 25 April, two days after the first assault crossing of the Po. *(NARA)*

Allied troops examine a German mobile ten-barrelled *Nebelwerfer* mounted on a half-track vehicle. *(NARA via Ken Ford)*

The detritus of an army: wrecked and abandoned equipment of LXXVI Panzer Corps lying south of the Po. *(Author's collection)*

belt to safety. Returning for the other injured soldier, he took him to safety as well, ignoring fire from enemy posts on both sides of the Senio.[51]

Such courage in the face of mortal danger for the sake of one's comrades might have been deemed sufficient by most individuals, but that was not Namdeo Jadhao's attitude. Seeking to avenge his dead comrades, he took up a Thompson sub-machine gun and attacked the enemy positions on the reverse of the near bank. Dashing at the closest German post, he knocked it out with his SMG but a wound to the hand left him unable to fire his weapon again. Throwing away the Thompson, he used grenades to continue his one-man assault, wiping out two more posts. At one stage, he even crawled to the top of the floodbank to obtain more grenades from his comrades on the reverse slope.

Having silenced all machine-gun fire from the east [near] bank, he then climbed on to the top of it and, in spite of heavy mortar fire, stood in the open shouting the Mahratta war cry and waving the remainder of the companies across the river.

This Sepoy not only saved the lives of his comrades, but his outstanding gallantry and personal bravery enabled two companies to hold the river banks firmly, and eventually the battalion to secure a deeper bridgehead, which in turn ultimately led to the collapse of all German resistance in the area.[52]

While Namdeo Jadhao stood on that floodbank urging on his comrades with cries of 'Shivaji Maharaj Ki Jai!', the Mahratta war cry, German mortar rounds fell around him and bullets from enemy rifles and machine guns laced through the air.

Three company commanders had fallen, but the Mahrattas, responding to such dauntless leadership, swarmed back across the river and ferreted the maze of boltholes, terrier fashion. With both banks clean they pushed on into the night, to deal with the obstinate garrisons of a number of houses in the flat fields adjoining the river.[53]

Twenty-year-old Namdeo Jadheo's courage was paralleled in 6/13th Frontier Force Rifles by that of Sepoy Ali Haidar. Ali Haidar's company, his battalion's follow-up company, was ordered to attack well-dug-in German positions on the far bank, near Fusignano; his platoon was on the company's left and his section on the platoon's left. No sooner had they waded into the water than machine guns opened fire from two posts some sixty yards away. Accurate and heavy fire took a serious toll of the left platoon, only three of whom reached the far bank; the remainder of the company was stalled.[54]

Among the survivors was Ali Haidar. With his two comrades giving him cover, on his own initiative he

charged the nearest post which was about [thirty] yards away. He threw a grenade and almost at the same time the enemy threw one at him, wounding him severely in the back. In spite of this he kept on and the enemy post was destroyed and four of the enemy surrendered. With utter disregard of his own wounds he ... charged the next post in which the enemy had one Spandau and three automatics, which were still very active and preventing movement on both banks. He was again wounded, this time in the right leg and right arm. Although weakened by loss of blood, Sepoy Ali Haidar crawled closer and in a final effort raised himself from the ground, threw a grenade, and charged into the second enemy post. Two enemy were wounded and the remaining two surrendered. Taking advantage of the outstanding success of Sepoy Ali Haidar's dauntless attacks, the rest of the Company charged across the river and carried out their task of making a bridgehead.[55]

The wounded Ali Haidar was carried back to safety from the second enemy position. His inspiring actions had prevented many casualties in the battalion, and ensured that the crossing went ahead on time, allowing a bridge to be built over the Senio. Blaxland summed up the battalion's progress after Ali Haidar's actions:

There was little left now to stop the remaining assault troops, and in fast-falling darkness, thickened by persisting pyres of smoke, they chivvied the enemy from hides on both sides of the far bank.[56]

In the subsequent rapid advance, the Frontiersmen captured 220 Germans and took their objectives. By dawn 8th Indian Division had advanced a mile and a half from the Senio. Fighting lasted all night at some points but, as the division's sappers had also bridged the river, Churchills of 21 Tank Brigade were available as support. That tank support continued throughout the 10th as did that of tactical aircraft.[57] The Argylls' war diary noted that they had linked up with 6/13 RFFR along the far bank of the Canale di Lugo by 4.00am on the 10th and that, fifteen minutes later, A Squadron North Irish Horse, under Major Robin Griffiths MC, crossed the just-completed Selkirk Bridge.[58] A further tank-bearing Bailey bridge, Stirling, came into operation an hour before noon.[59]

Although the sappers completed their bridging tasks on schedule on 19 Brigade's front, allowing tanks to move up, the fighting on 21 Brigade's front was so intense that no bridges could be built but, just before daylight, an Ark was driven into the waterway, permitting 'three squadrons of tanks to scramble into the bridgehead'. By 9.00am, a trestle bridge for wheeled vehicles was in place.[60]

With the aid of tanks and fighter-bombers, 19 and 21 Brigades closed up to the Santerno, some four miles from the Senio, by daylight on the 11th, the day Lugo was liberated by 1st Jaipur Infantry. Lugo's mayor greeted his town's liberators with a white flag and a bottle of wine. At this stage 17 Brigade came forward for the Santerno crossing. Russell, the GOC, had stressed the need to keep the brigade for this operation:

The Division must fight with one policy in mind. Keep 17 Infantry Brigade fresh for the Santerno. Only if there is a danger that the Division will not be able to carry out its task will 17 Brigade be committed previously. All must plan to give the maximum support to 17 Brigade and to render the difficult tasks allotted to that brigade easier. Remember always that the Division's task is to secure a bridgehead over the Santerno river and that all our efforts must be directed to this end.[61]

The advance of 17 Brigade was led by 3/15th Punjabis and 5th Royal West Kents. The West Kents' war diary notes that 'at first light [on the 10th] isolated enemy pockets gave themselves up'. By early afternoon the battalion had taken 127 prisoners.[62]

The Indians had made good progress, but V Corps' pace was set by 2nd New Zealand Division. Jackson commented that 'The New Zealanders gained a lead during the first night's crossing of the Senio which they never lost.'[63] Much of their success was due to detailed planning and training, not least by the divisional engineers. Colonel Hanson, commander of the divisional engineers, had worked his men hard but had prepared well for the operation, his decision to bring bridging equipment as far forward as possible paying rich dividends for infantry and armour. Not surprisingly, 2nd New Zealand Division had five tank bridges over the Senio by 6.30am on the 10th. Eighth Indian had only one tank bridge, Selkirk, of the three bridges their sappers had built, while II Polish Corps had none.

As already noted, the assaulting New Zealand battalions were 21st and 28th of 5 Brigade and 25th and 24th of 6 Brigade. In most places crossing the Senio was remarkably easy, the *New Zealand Official History* noting that:

In the first stage – the assault crossing of the Senio and mopping up of resistance as far as the start line for the set-piece advance, 300–600 yards beyond the river – 21st Battalion had three companies forward, while the fourth company and also the Surreys of 78th Division gave covering fire; the other battalions had two companies forward, covered by men on the near stopbank.[64]

On 21st's right flank, D Company encountered one of the few German posts to survive both shelling and flaming, but its opposition ended when Second Lieutenant D. G. Boys attacked it with a PIAT, knocking it out at point-blank range. In the centre of the advance, B Company had a platoon commander and the company commander, Major V. C. Butler, wounded at a surviving German footbridge over the Senio. A Company, on the left, lost contact with the advance but cleared enemy troops from buildings and a strongpoint beyond the floodbank. Meanwhile, the other companies – A and B of both 28th and 25th Battalions and C and D of 24th – also crossed quickly, a platoon of the 24th finding another intact footbridge, met little resistance, took many prisoners and suffered few casualties.[65]

The speed of the New Zealanders' advance may be gauged from the fact that they were on the start line for the advance to their next objective by 8.05pm. At that point, the artillery lifted their bombardment, which was falling 600–900 yards beyond the start line, in the first of a series of lifts at intervals of five minutes and distances of a hundred yards. With eight field regiments involved, a 25-pounder for every fifteen yards, and concentrations also being put down by five medium and one heavy regiment, it was an effective bombardment. (Also on hand were an additional 25-pounder regiment for counter-mortar tasks, a regiment of M7 Priest self-propelled 105mm howitzers and two troops – eight guns – of 3.7-inch anti-aircraft guns.) An hour after it began the bombardment paused for thirty-five minutes 300 yards in front of the objective before lifting at the same pace for another fifty minutes and then standing for twenty-five minutes, until 10.55pm, 300 yards beyond the objective on a line some 3,000 yards from the Senio.[66]

Although artificial moonlight, provided by searchlights, was in use, augmented by tracer from Bofors guns to mark boundaries in the advance, there was so much dust and smoke that the infantry found direction-keeping difficult, even with constant use of compasses. This problem was exacerbated by the axis of advance being diagonally across roads and vineyards. In spite of such problems, with companies losing contact, and progress 'depressingly slow', the objective was taken, with many prisoners. Opposition was light, although two 88mm SPGs and a Tiger tank were encountered on the Barbiano-Lugo road. One NCO, Lance Corporal R. J. Parker, attempted to engage the Tiger from behind with a PIAT but his weapon misfired twice. When Parker realized that the PIAT's safety catch was still engaged, he picked it up, ran down the road in pursuit of the tank, hit it from behind and put it out of action.[67] (Many such accounts refer to Tigers when the opposition was really Mark IVs, particularly Mark IV Specials, but it is likely that Parker engaged a Tiger as 504th Heavy Panzer Battalion Tigers were in this area at the time.)

The advance continued, although 6 Brigade's commander was concerned that the Poles might not be able to catch up with his brigade, thus leaving his left flank open; he ordered 26th Battalion to be ready to deploy companies to the left flank. Not long after midnight, 26th Battalion was assigned to the flank protection role; A and B Companies took positions facing west between the river and Barbiano.

By daylight on the 10th the New Zealanders were well on their way to the Santerno. However, their newest brigade, 9, formed from the Divisional Cavalry Regiment, the armoured brigade's Motor Battalion and the Machine-Gun Battalion, had been denied its first opportunity for action that morning when it had been assigned the task of liberating the small town of Cotignola in the pocket between the assaulting divisions. Twenty-seventh Battalion, with the Shermans of A Squadron 19th Armoured Regiment, Kangaroos of C Squadron 4th Hussars and a detachment of E Assault Squadron, RAC/RE, was delayed crossing the Senio as the support weapons of 21st and 28th Battalions had prior claim on Felix, the bridge close to Cotignola. By the time the battlegroup assembled on the other side its task had been overtaken by events as 78th Division, between the New Zealanders and Indians, having reported white flags in the town, moved into what remained of the town.[68]

Although the New Zealanders were en route to the Santerno on the 10th, a pause was necessary for a second heavy bombing programme in the late morning. This time the targets for MASAF's B-17s and B-24s were along the Santerno, including enemy troop and artillery positions facing V Corps and II Polish Corps, codenamed respectively 'Baker' and 'Charlie'. Targets along the Santerno had already been hit by the heavies during the previous night. 'Charlie' was bombed from 11.00am on the 10th with bombers switching to 'Baker' fifteen minutes later; 848 heavy bombers took part in the raid, dropping 1,600 tons of 20lb bombs. Once again, the 3.7s of 12 AA Brigade and the Polish Corps marked the bomb line.[69] And, once again, there had been some Allied casualties from bombs falling outside the target areas, a number of New Zealanders suffering as a result. McCreery, who had watched the previous day's bombing from an OP, was

> in an Auster at about 5,000 ft when suddenly almost below me – of course I was about 2,000 yds our side of the front line – a number of explosive spurts from the small fragmentation bombs went up, and I thought that another whole group of the heavies had made the same mistake as the day before. Luckily this time it was only three aircraft which bombed short, but even so these three caused some seventy casualties on the crowded roads behind the front.[70]

Having resumed their advance, Freyberg's leading units were at the Santerno by nightfall. Since assaulting the Senio the division had covered some five miles, crossing four canals or floodbank-protected streams en route. In theory, the Santerno should have been a tougher obstacle than the Senio, but the Germans, harried and chivvied as they fell back, were unable to consolidate effectively on the Laura Line. Their resistance, while sharp in places, was unable to repel the New Zealanders whose leading brigades, and supporting tanks, breached the line on the 11th. At the cost of fewer than 200 casualties, 5 and 6 Brigades broke the line, took over 700 prisoners and destroyed three battalions of 98th Volksgrenadier Division. In spite of the deployment of Tigers of 504th Heavy Panzer Battalion, as well as tank destroyers, the impetus of the New Zealanders' advance, supported by intense artillery fire and close air support, forced the defenders to loosen their grip on Laura and begin another withdrawal. Three divisions, 42nd Jäger, 362nd and 98th Volksgrenadier had lost many men, including over 2,200 made prisoner by the attacking Eighth Army formations.[71]

In spite of his division's progress or, perhaps, because of it, Freyberg still had worries about the integrity of his flanks since 8th Indian Division was not yet conforming with his right flank and the Poles were even farther behind on the left. Anders had assigned the Senio crossing to 3rd Carpathian Division, which deployed its two veteran brigades and 6 Lwow Brigade, on loan from 5th Kresowa Division. Although both Polish divisions had been brought up to three-brigade strength, the new brigades were not fully trained and could not be committed to battle – hence the 'borrowing' of 6 Lwow Brigade. Nonetheless, both fresh brigades were given a role: as Rud Force they were to hold the line astride Highway 9.

The Carpathians had not had a favourable start, having suffered the loss of men, mostly among their specialist assault troops, when USAAF bombers had bombed short on the 9th. When it came time to assault the Senio in the Felisio sector that evening, the distance between the Polish positions and the near floodbank, almost a half mile, was greater than that to be covered by the other divisions. Moreover, the ground had been seeded heavily with mines and the division had to call on Sherman Crabs to flail paths to the Senio, as well as using hand-clearing techniques. Even with these efforts, the leading troops suffered casualties from mines while moving up to the near floodbank. However, as Blaxland comments, 'guts and determination prevailed' and the division had two brigades across and beyond the Senio by the morning of the 10th. It had been a difficult task since the assault had to be made by three battalions, 1 Brigade on the left having to attack with a single battalion because the brigade had to be prepared to provide protection for the exposed southern flank. On the right, 2 Brigade, its right battalion working closely with its neighbouring New Zealand battalion, seized the far floodbank by 8.45pm, the best progress made by II Polish Corps. The left-flank battalion of 2 Brigade, with 1 Brigade's leading battalion, was assigned to mine-clearing, which took about three hours. Those two battalions then had to fight hard battles with 9th Panzer Grenadier Regiment for both floodbanks and buildings beyond the far bank.[72]

When dawn broke on the 10th the Poles had not established a firm bridgehead. What they held suffered two strong and determined counter-attacks by 26th Panzer Division, which had recovered from the previous evening's shock. Equally determined resistance by Polish soldiers, who had no intention of being bested by Germans, supported by defensive fire from the corps artillery, rocket-firing fighter-bombers, and tanks firing from the near floodbank, broke both attacks, allowing 3rd Carpathian Division to consolidate its positions, including Solarolo. The Polish attack, directed at the boundary between LXXVI Panzer Corps and I Fallschirmjäger Corps, and specifically between 98th Division of the former and 26th Panzer Division of the latter, forced the German corps commanders to adjust their front: Heidrich of I Fallschirmjäger had to take the brunt of the Poles' pressure, while von Schwerin tried to reform what remained of 98th and 362nd Divisions. So it was that II Polish Corps did not close up to the Santerno until the night of 11 April, a day after 2nd New Zealand Division had reached the Laura Line.[73] By then the New Zealanders were across the Santerno and preparing for the next phase of operations.

Let us return briefly to 10 April when the Germans began withdrawing to the Laura Line, following the loss of the Lugo-Cotignola salient and the mauling of 98th Division. On that date Gruppo Cremona launched Operation SONIA. With the gruppo's artillery providing supporting fire, 3rd Battalion 22nd Regiment (3/22nd Regiment) liberated Fusignano, defended by 1 Company 504th Heavy Panzer Battalion with Tigers. With Fusignano secure, an assault force of 2/22nd and 2/21st Regiments advanced northwards to encircle Alfonsine. However, 1/21st Regiment launched a frontal attack from a start line farther along the main road and took the town, unopposed, at 1.00pm.[74]

Another Italian combat group, Friuli, had also been in action, working with the Jewish Hebron Brigade and Polish Rud Force. In Operation PASQUA, 1/88th Regiment of Friuli moved to encircle Riolo dei Bagni from the west while an assault force of 2/87th and 2/88th Regiments crossed the Senio and attacked the Badia-Cuffiano area at 4.30am. Meanwhile, 2nd Battalion Palestine Regiment of the Jewish Brigade launched an attack against Tebano as Rud Force advanced along Highway 9. Although the German 1st and 4th Fallschirmjäger Divisions had begun falling back, two Fallschirmjäger regiments, 11th and 12th, deployed as rearguard.[75]

Elsewhere on the 10th, 56th (London) Division was preparing for Operation IMPACT PLAIN, an amphibious operation on the south-west shore of Lake Comácchio. This began at 9.15pm with 40 (RM) Commando – 2 Commando Brigade was under command of 56th Division – moving off on foot from the northern end of the 'Wedge' to advance on Casale della Fossa, north of Menate, which it was intended to reach before dawn the following day. At much the same time, 2/5th and 2/6th Queen's of 169 (Queen's) Brigade embussed at Mandriole in eighty LVTs crewed by 27th Lancers and 755th US Tank Battalion. Their destination was Canaletta Umana, but they were delayed significantly by traffic congestion at Sant'Alberto.[76]

Of the three divisions that had crossed the Senio the New Zealanders had made best progress. On an axis parallel to Highway 9, the Via Emilia, and with their spearhead fourteen miles due south of Argenta, their advance threatened Bologna, which suited McCreery's strategic purpose. Moreover, that advance had won ground from which an outflanking attack on Argenta could be launched, or from which a diversion from Argenta could be created. And should the advance towards Argenta fail, the diversion could become the main effort. To that end, with the possibility of 2nd New Zealand Division transferring to XIII Corps to operate alongside 10th Indian Division, Lieutenant General Sir John Harding, commanding XIII Corps, had been warned of the possible switch. Such a switch could hardly be described as weakening V Corps, which, on 1 April, had had 'the largest force ever under the command of one Corps' with a ration strength of some 160,000.[77]

Operation BUCKLAND was well underway. As the New Zealanders crossed the Santerno at dawn on the 11th and 8th Indian Division fought its way up to the river, Major General Whitfield's 56th (London) Division was about to spring yet another surprise on the Germans while Major General Arbuthnott's 78th Division prepared to unleash its 'Kangaroo Army'.

Notes

1. Jackson, op. cit., pp.232–3.
2. Ibid., p.233.
3. Ibid.,
4. Quoted in Truscott, p.480.
5. Jackson, p.236.
6. Ibid., p.237.

7. Harpur, pp.155–6; NA, WO170/ 4178, war diary HQ Eighth Army (G, main), Mar 1945.

8. NA, WO170/4178, war diary HQ Eighth Army (G, main), Mar '45.

9. Ibid.

10. Starr, op. cit., p.394.

11. McCreery, *RUSI Journal*, p.5

12. Blaxland, op. cit., pp.251–2; Messenger, *The Commandos*, pp.370–1; Doherty, *A Noble Crusade*, p.287.

13. *Finito*, p.12.

14. *London Gazette (LG)*, 12 Jun '45.

15. Ibid.; Messenger, pp.373–4.

16. Jackson, p.259.

17. Starr, p.394; Fisher, op. cit., pp.460–1.

18. Starr, p.395.

19. US Army Center of Military History, http://www.history.army.mil/medalofhonor 23 Nov '13.

20. Ibid.

21. Ibid.

22. Ibid.

23. Ibid.

24. Ibid.

25. Starr, pp.395–6.

26. NA, WO170/4242, war diary, HQ V Corps (A&Q), 1945. No mention of this occasion is made in Cremona's war diary.

27. Jackson, pp.260–1.

28. Ibid.

29. Messenger, pp.374–5.

30. *LG*, 7 Sep '45.

31. Jackson, pp.261–3; Routledge, op. cit., p.284; NA, WO170/4857, war diary HQ 12 AA Bde, 1945.

32. Jackson, pp.262–3.

33. Anders, op. cit., p.266.

34. Jackson, p.262.

35. Lt Col B. D. H. Clark MC GM, and other 78 Div veterans to author.

36. Jackson, pp.262–3; Blaxland, pp.255–6; Evans, pp.189–90.

37. *Finito*, p.13.

38. Blaxland, p.256.

39. Ibid.

40. Duncan, op. cit., p.614.

41. Cox, *The Road to Trieste*, pp.79–80.

42. Jackson, p.263.

43. During an interview in Germany for a BBC Radio Ulster programme in 1991.

44. Kay, op. cit., p.415.

45. Blaxland, p.256.

46. Jackson, p.263.

47. NA, WO170/4148, war diary, 15 AG Chief Engineer, 1945.

48. Kay, p.415.

49. Jackson, pp.263–5; *The Tiger Triumphs*, pp.187–8.

50. NA, WO170/4987, war diary, 1 A&S Hldrs, 1945.
51. Jackson, p.265; Blaxland, op. cit., p.257; *The Tiger Triumphs*, p.189.
52. *LG*, 19 Jun '45.
53. *The Tiger Triumphs*, p.189.
54. Ibid., p.188.
55. *LG*, 3 Jly '45.
56. Blaxland, p.257.
57. Ibid.; Jackson, p.265.
58. NA, WO170/4987, war diary, 1 A&S Hldrs, 1945.
59. Jackson, p.265; *The Tiger Triumphs*, p.190; NA, WO170/4633, war diary, North Irish Horse, 1945.
60. Jackson, p.265.
61. *The Tiger Triumphs*, p.187.
62. NA, WO170/5021, war diary, 5 RWK, 1945.
63. Jackson, p.263.
64. Kay, p.415.
65. Ibid, pp.415–16.
66. Ibid, p.416.
67. Ibid., pp.417–18.
68. Ibid., p.422; Ray, op. cit., p.201.
69. NA, WO170/4857, war diary, HQ 12 AA Bde.
70. McCreery, draft memoir, p.12.
71. Jackson, pp. 266–7; Belogi & Guglielmi, p.137.
72. Ibid., p.266; Blaxland, op. cit., p.259; Belogi & Guglielmi, pp.146–7.
73. Belogi & Guglielmi, pp.146–7; Blaxland, p.259.
74. Belogi & Guglielmi, pp.132–3; *Diario storico militare (DSM) del Gruppo Cremona*, pp.109–11.
75. Belogi & Guglielmi, p.137; *I Gruppi di Combattimento*, pp.190–5.
76. NA, ADM202/87, war diary 40 Cdo, 1945; WO170/4630, war diary, 27 L, 1945; WO170/5059, war diary, 2/5 Queen's, 1945; WO170/5060, war diary, 2/6 Queen's, 1945; Belogi & Guglielmi, p.132.
77. NA, WO170/4240, war diary, HQ V Corps (G), Mar-Apr '45.

Chapter Seven

Although Lake Comácchio had earlier proved unsuitable for the LVTs, the inundated land to its west was useable, being firm enough for the tracks of the amphibians to gain purchase while making their way back onto dry land. Thus eighty Fantails closed on Menate and Longastrino as dawn broke, their engine noises being the first clue the enemy had of their deployment, as well as the first indication of what Eighth Army was setting out to achieve. With the launching of the Fantails at Idrovora Umana delayed until 8.45am, they would make landfall in daylight. Although this was not desirable, they had the element of surprise and had been preceded by large-scale bombing of the area between the two villages.[1]

While the Germans could hear the LVT engines, they could not see them. A single German plane spotted the Fantails, but by the time this information reached the troops of 42nd Jäger Division on the ground it was too late. As an additional precaution, a smokescreen laid by guns carried in the vehicles, shrouded their final approach. Thinking the floodwaters formed an impassable barrier, the Germans were amazed to see the huge vehicles emerge from the water. Although 42nd Jäger Division knew that the Allies 'had some form of amphibian on the lake [they] thought it was a three to four man machine' and the LVTs were a major shock:

> Few shots were fired at them as their great square hulks gradually rose out of the water and trundled through the slush to emit their loads. Each of the leading ones carried a small platoon,[*2] and its men leapt out with a machine gun blazing from the Fantail's forward turret.[3]

The war diary of 2/6th Queen's records that:

> the coys make for their objectives. The battle patrol is immediately detached to capture a house 400 yds to our left and they get 12 PW. The ground is completely flat and there is very little cover so the 700 yds to our first objectives is a difficult time. The Boche are dropping mortars 150 yds to the right. No mines encountered so far, and enemy resistance is only from MG fire coming from the houses in front. In the initial stages Fantails gave useful support from their Brownings.[4]

---

* A smaller platoon of twenty-seven men was introduced for those units using LVTs.

With the reserve companies ashore, the battalion made steady progress with Tactical HQ established in Longastrino by 2.00pm. In the course of the operation, civilians were evacuated from nearby houses by 755th Tank Battalion crews. However, as the Fantails sailed off with the evacuees, a German SPG, firing from the western end of the flooded area, hit one, killing many of its passengers.[5]

Later in the afternoon an Air OP, spotting two tanks south-west of A Company's area, called down fire from 'a regiment of guns' to neutralize them. Then the battalion was told to move further south to support 167 Brigade, which was 'encountering some opposition'.[6]

The brigade achieved its objectives, liberating Menate and taking prisoner 300 of 42nd Jäger Division at little loss to the two Queen's Royal Regiment battalions. Blaxland notes that:

> None were more ardent for the fray than the Queen's. They owed it to their GOC and regimental colleague, Maj Gen Whitfield, that they had retained their integrity as a Queen's Brigade, and their officers were ready to respond to his exhortation that they should enter battle in a spirit of self-sacrifice, even at this late stage of the war.[7]

While 169 (Queen's) Brigade was taking the Germans off balance and pushing on to their objectives, 40 (RM) Commando, also under command of 56th Division, was advancing along a ditch to a bridge north of Menate and the nearby pumping station; the marines were also to protect the divisional right flank. Opposition was stiff and many casualties were sustained, some from mines but most from the defenders at Menate bridge, but the Royals prevailed to take their objective with the aid of fighter-bombers that broke the resistance. Another of Whitfield's brigades, 167, also encountered determined opposition as 1st Royal Fusiliers and 1st London Scottish advanced westward along the Reno. Much of that opposition came from I/25th Regiment of 42nd Jäger Division and 129th Armoured Reconnaissance Battalion, the latter deployed from the Argenta area. However, with support from 169 Brigade, the Fusiliers and London Scots were able to win through and, by the end of the day, a bridgehead had been established between Menate and Longastrino; most of 129th Armoured Reconnaissance Battalion had been captured. With the Menate-Longastrino bridgehead secure, all was set for the next phase of the operation – exploitation towards Filo on the Bastia road, and to the confluence of the Reno and Santerno.[8]

South of the Reno, Gruppo Cremona's assault force of 2/21st and 2/22nd Regiments was advancing on the axis of Highway 16 but ran up against II/40th Regiment of 42nd Jäger Division at Taglio Corelli where the advance was brought to a halt. Eighth Indian Division had also encountered doughty opposition along the Santerno but, by evening, the Jaipur Infantry were up to the river and two battalions of 1059th Regiment of 362nd Division had been destroyed, although hard fighting continued. The New Zealanders were still setting the pace and, with support from their own armour, Desert Air Force fighter-bombers and artillery, they strengthened

6 Brigade's small bridgehead. Opposition was tough in pockets but was overcome after some sharp fighting. In one instance, three Tigers of 504th Heavy Panzer Battalion, holding a gap between 5 and 6 Brigades, were struck by a heavy artillery bombardment. The Massa Lombarda area was hammered by fighter-bombers throughout the day and by nightfall a Bailey bridge had been put across the Santerno, some tanks having already crossed over an Ark to clear the way for the engineers to emplace the Bailey.[9]

Massa Lombarda was bypassed and 9 Brigade took over from 5 Brigade to continue the advance, parallel to the railway, to the Sillaro, the Paula Line. By now the gap between New Zealanders and Poles was narrowing, allowing 26th Battalion to lay down its flank protection role and link up with 28th in the van of 6 Brigade. II Polish Corps included the British 7 Armoured Brigade and the Gurkhas of 43 Brigade; the former formation included three battalions – 2nd, 6th and 8th – of the Royal Tanks, and the latter 2/6th, 2/8th and 2/10th Gurkha Rifles. These brigades, with 6th and 8th Royal Tanks on the right and left flanks respectively, and 2nd in the centre, with their Gurkha battalions, crossed the Santerno; elsewhere elements of II Polish Corps were subjected to a fifteen-minute artillery bombardment and lost contact with the enemy north of Highway 9. However, the Poles occupied Bagnara without opposition and, that evening, 1 Carpathian Brigade closed up to the Santerno west of the town against a doughty and renewed resistance. Meanwhile, Rud Force, which had crossed the Senio on the 10th, extended its bridgehead along Highway 9 towards Castel Bolognese.[10]

Elsewhere, 3rd Palestine Regiment of the Jewish Hebron Brigade had crossed the Senio in X Corps' sector at 6.00am, liberating Cuffiano four and a half hours later. The battalion then linked up with Gruppo Friuli to advance on Monte Ghebbio, where only mortar fire was met. Having crossed the Senio on a front of almost four miles to a depth of over 1,000 yards, 2/87th and 2/88th Regiments of Friuli liberated Riolo dei Bagni en route to Cuffiano. Gruppo Folgore was also in action on 11 April with the 3rd Battalion Nembo Regiment, taking Tossignano against light opposition. Gruppo Friuli was under command of X Corps while Folgore was in XIII Corps.[11]

The impetus of Eighth Army's advance led to the withdrawal of 1st Fallschirmjäger Division, which began with a pivot from Monte Grande before swinging back across the Santerno and into 4th Fallschirmjäger Division's sector. That move squeezed out 278th Volksgrenadier Division, which withdrew out of contact with V Corps.[12]

The original plan for the offensive set D Day for Operation CRAFTSMAN as two days after the opening of BUCKLAND and Fifth Army had prepared accordingly, only to be thwarted by weather conditions. Heavy rain and low cloud in north-western Italy meant that close air support would not be possible, and the assaulting formations had to wait patiently for favourable flying conditions. That would not be until the 14th, but Eighth Army was not suffering as a result of the absence of the second punch. Far from it. As Thursday, 12 April, dawned, the day on which President Franklin Roosevelt died suddenly, Operation BUCKLAND was moving up a gear.

Operation IMPACT PLAIN continued with, south of the Reno, 167 Brigade's 1st London Irish moving off just after midnight from Longastrino towards Filo, advancing towards the confluence of the Santerno and Reno at Palazzo Tamba. On the north side of the Reno, 169 (Queen's) Brigade began its westward expansion of the bridgehead at Menate at noon, with 2/7th Queen's advancing on the right along the Strada della Pioppa and 2/5th Queen's on the axis of the Bastia road. Both battalions advanced with armour support, artillery and fighter-bombers on call. Although stiff opposition was met, especially from 15th Panzer Grenadier Regiment of 29th Panzer Grenadier Division, progress was made and a junction effected with 169 Brigade's bridgehead. Among the defenders along the way, 167 Brigade had engaged the Italian Barbarigo Battalion of the Decima MAS Division, which endured a hard pounding. Elements of Gruppo Cremona also closed up along Highway 16, the assault force of 2/22nd Regiment, followed by 1/22nd having attacked towards the Santerno at 5.45am. In the face of heavy opposition, the river line was reached at 6.00pm and Cremona linked up with 56th Division.[13]

German reaction to 56th Division's operations had not been limited to the opposition to the division's advance. On 11 April von Vietinghoff ordered the move of all of 29th Panzer Grenadier Division from Venetia to oppose V Corps. Fifteenth Panzer Grenadier Regiment, already in the area of operations, was ordered to deploy to the Argenta Gap where, next day, it took up position on the eastern side of the Gap, under command of 42nd Jäger Division. However, the remainder of 29th Panzer Grenadier Division had a difficult journey from north of the Po, being held up by shortage of fuel and Allied air attacks, and was not complete in the Argenta area until the 14th. Its orders there were to defend the Gap; it would absorb what was left of 42nd Jäger Division. General Herr also intended that 26th Panzer Division should leave I Fallschirmjäger Corps and reinforce the Argenta defences, but it would not arrive in time to execute this role.[14]

Eighth Indian Division was also across the Santerno on the 12th. The assault crossing by 17 Brigade had begun the previous evening when 1/5th Gurkhas and 1/12th Frontier Force Rifles gained the far bank at some cost, after fighting that, at times, seemed to flow in the defenders' favour. The brigade was supported by tanks from 6th Duke of Connaught's Own Lancers and the North Irish Horse, while Kangaroos of 4th Hussars ferried infantrymen, although these were unable to cross until an Ark bridge was in place thirty minutes before noon on 12 April. Before that, 1st Royal Fusiliers had linked the Gurkha and Frontier Force lodgements by clearing a street in the ruined village of Mondaniga, the Fusiliers also repelling a German dawn counter-attack. Assisting in the operation by attacking the San Bernardino bridge were the armoured cars of 12th Royal Lancers, which was under corps command, and fighter-bombers. With 8th Indian and 2nd New Zealand Divisions now firm in their bridgeheads it was time for the next elements of McCreery's plan, the launch into action of the Kangaroo Army and the switch to XIII Corps of 2nd New Zealand Division.[15]

The Kangaroo Army, formed from the Irish Brigade of 78th Division and 2 Armoured Brigade, was under overall command of 78th Division. Keightley, V Corps' commander, and previously GOC of 78th Division, now passed the division through 8th Indian to take up the chase, break out through the German defences and begin its exploitation role. Although 78th Division was an infantry formation, it had been extemporized into an all-arms grouping with an armoured battlegroup, the Kangaroo Army, within the division. This armoured battlegroup included a 'Break-out Force' of two battlegroups, a 'Mobile Force' – the Kangaroo Army – under command of HQ 2 Armoured Brigade and a 'Reserve Force'.

BREAK-OUT FORCE

1st Royal Irish Fusiliers	2nd Royal Inniskilling Fusiliers
A Squadron The Queen's Bays	B Squadron The Queen's Bays
MMG Platoon, D Support Group	MMG Platoon, D Support Group
Scissors Bridge	C Squadron 51 RTR (Crocodiles)
Recce Party Royal Engineers	Recce Party Royal Engineers

In immediate support of the Break-out Force were two regiments of field artillery: 17th Field Regiment, which usually supported the Irish Brigade, and 11th (HAC) Regiment Royal Horse Artillery.

MOBILE FORCE (KANGAROO ARMY)	RESERVE FORCE FOR SPECIAL ROLES
HQ 2 Armoured Brigade	C Squadron The Queen's Bays
9th Lancers	254 Anti-Tank Battery
4th Hussars (Kangaroos)	SP Troop, 254 Anti-Tank Battery
Z Troop 209 SP Anti-Tank Battery	Armoured Troop Royal Engineers
Assault Detachment Royal Engineers	Mortar Platoon, D Support Group
2nd London Irish Rifles	

(D Support Group was from 1st Princess Louise's Kensington Regiment, 78th Division's support battalion. D Support Group usually supported 38 (Irish) Brigade; 'support group' was the term used to describe a company of a support battalion.)

The Kangaroo Army disposed over a hundred main tracked vehicles from 4th Hussars and 9th Lancers. Since the Hussars had operated with the Irish Brigade before, they knew the idiosyncrasies of the brigade and had trained with them to ensure that all went as smoothly as possible in this operation. The London Irish, known as the Irish Rifles within the Irish Brigade, were mounted in the Kangaroos of 4th Hussars with each rifle company assigned eight Priest Kangaroos; Battalion HQ had a further eight, two for reserve ammunition; another two were for medical purposes. Each Kangaroo section had sufficient food and ammunition for forty-eight hours' independent operating.[16]

The Irish Rifles' companies were each 'married' to a squadron of 4th Hussars, thus creating battlegroups within the battlegroup; all operated under command of HQ 2 Armoured Brigade. Flexibility was built into the organization; as well as the self-propelled anti-tank guns, Sherman Crabs for mine clearance, Sherman dozers and Arks, elements of the Reserve Force could also be attached, as could Crocodiles, some of which deployed with the Inniskillings' battlegroup.

The rationale behind the Kangaroo Army was that the armour could lead until anti-tank opposition was encountered, at which stage the infantry would 'debus' to deal with the problem. It was never intended that the Kangaroos should take on enemy tanks or guns: they were to carry the Rifles across fire-zones with a high degree of protection against small-arms fire or grenades. And, of course, they would also allow infantry to move at the speed of armour.[17] In north-west Europe, where their use had been pioneered by the Canadians, and earlier in Italy, APCs had proved their worth, but their part in 78th Division's breakout operation was arguably the most systematic application of the doctrine to date.

On 10 April the Irish Brigade Group left Forlí, less its armour, concentrating south of Bagnacavallo. Two assembly areas had been established east of the Senio, one for infantry and one for armour, but the marrying of infantry and armour was to take place west of the Senio, near Lugo. At 6.00am on the 11th the move to the marrying area began. A co-ordinating conference was held at 9.00pm to check the plans, the tying-up of the entire group and arrange a provisional order of march. By then the New Zealanders were across the Santerno and, with the Indians up to the river, it was expected that a firm bridgehead would be available next day.

In fact, the Santerno bridgehead was secure by noon the following day with bridges to carry the Kangaroo Army expected to be across that afternoon, but then came a change of plan. H Hour for the Irish Brigade was delayed when it was appreciated that there was little organized resistance east of the Santerno. The original plan for 36 Brigade to sweep northwards along the Santerno's east bank and on the right flank of the Irish Brigade was changed so that 36 Brigade switched to the left flank, with elements of 56th Reconnaissance Regiment on the east bank. Thirty-six Brigade was to strike to the west, towards San Patrizio and Conselice, thereby giving the Irish Brigade more manoeuvre room as it moved off; it would also cover its flank thereafter. As a result, 36 Brigade would have to move first, which it did without problems during the evening. However, since congestion of tracks and bridges and shelling of their assigned bridge prevented the Irish Brigade moving forward that evening, its attack was postponed until dawn. In the interim the Irish Fusiliers, the 'Faughs', maintained contact by patrolling, while soldiers of 17 Indian Brigade performed the same task in front of the Inniskillings.[18]

Having passed through 17 Indian Brigade, 36 Brigade moved rapidly towards San Patrizio where it encountered 525th Heavy Tank Destroyer Battalion, equipped with Nashorn 88mm anti-tank guns, and captured intact two bridges over the Canale dei Molini en route to Conselice which they prepared to attack.[19]

Meanwhile, the New Zealanders were preparing for an attack on the Sillaro river, the Paula Line, having hustled the Germans back to that position where 278th Volksgrenadier Division was digging in. Massa Lombarda was entered by 21st Battalion, which met no opposition and found partisans in charge of the town; the battalion moved on towards the Scolo Zaniolo. Freyberg planned a night attack on the Sillaro and the Scolo Correcchio, which lay beyond, and parallel to, the river.[20]

At Mordano, II Polish Corps had crossed the Santerno with 16th and 17th Battalions of 6 Lwowska Brigade, 5th Kresowa Division, in the lead, supported by 1st Armoured Cavalry Regiment of 2 Warsaw Armoured Brigade. However, a series of spirited counter-attacks by 4th Fallschirmjäger blocked the brigade's advance towards the Scolo Gambellara. To the south, Castelnuovo had been taken by 5 Wilenska Brigade, also of Kresowa, but the meandering nature of the Santerno proved a defensive asset for German troops north of the village, compelling the 3rd Battalion of 1 Carpathian Brigade to deploy in readiness for a co-ordinated attack. Along Highway 9, Rud Force had taken Castel Bolognese, the village having been liberated in the early hours by the 12th Battalion of 4 Wolynska Brigade, one of the recently-formed Polish brigades.[21]

Elsewhere along the front, the Hebron Brigade continued its advance, as did 3/88th Regiment of Gruppo Friuli while 3/188th Nembo Regiment of Folgore lost contact with the Germans and advanced to occupy Codrignano. In the early afternoon of the 12th, the Grado Battalion of the San Marco Regiment, which had liberated Ronco, ran up against 3rd Fallschirmjäger Regiment from 1st Fallschirmjäger Division, who were holding the pivot of the German withdrawal and who also halted the Bafile Battalion at Monte dei Mercati. This was part of the withdrawal manoeuvre that saw 278th Volksgrenadier Division squeezed out between the two Fallschirmjäger divisions and redeployed to Sesto Imolese to cover the inter-corps boundary and prepare to relieve 98th Volksgrenadier Division. Acting as rearguard for 278th Division's withdrawal was the Italian Fascist Forlí Battalion, regarded as an élite unit by its German allies.[22]

That German withdrawal was in direct contravention of OKW's order that no sector of the front line could be given up unless it had been penetrated by the enemy. It would seem that Herr chose to disregard this order so that he could straighten out I Fallschirmjäger Corps' Apennine salient. Now, as 26th Panzer and 4th Fallschirmjäger Divisions pulled back to the Sillaro, 1st Fallschirmjäger Division straightened its own line in the high ground on the corps' western wing.[23]

Further changes on Eighth Army's front that day saw XIII Corps ordered to leave its existing sector in the Apennines, handing it over to X Corps, and take command of 2nd New Zealand Division so that the advance along the Sesto Imolese-Medicina-Budrio axis might be reinforced and better co-ordinated. X Corps' sector was extended westward to include Gruppo Folgore and Mac Force, an extemporized grouping of several battalions holding the Monte Grande area, the pivot point of Eighth Army's manoeuvre. (Mac Force included the Lovat Scouts, 2nd Loyals, 2nd Highland Light Infantry, 3/1st Punjab Regiment, 4/11th Sikhs, Jodhpur Sadar and Nabha Akal battalions, the last two being Indian State Forces units.)[24]

Those who are superstitious dread Friday the 13th, supposedly an unlucky day. In April 1945 the 13th was a Friday, D + 4 of Operation BUCKLAND. And it would prove an unlucky day for many – although no more so than any average day in war. It was also the day on which Eighth Army's operations divided into two distinct but co-ordinated advances. As Jackson comments, these 'were pressed with equal vigour' by V Corps on one axis and by II Polish Corps and XIII British Corps on the other. V Corps now included 56th and 78th Divisions; both would be in action on this 'Black Friday', the Black Cats of the former continuing their exploitation and the Battleaxe men of the latter for the first time in this operation.[25]

While 56th Division had been fighting for several days, the burden of their effort had fallen on 167 and 169 Brigades. It was now the turn of 24 Guards Brigade, the newcomers to the division, to make the next move. Blaxland describes this as 'an ambitious descent from the north, relying on the Fantails to make another outflanking movement across lake and flood, whereby 24 Guards Brigade ... were to seize Argenta, with right flank protected by 2 Para Brigade'.[26] Keightley intended this to be one arm of a pincer movement, the other being 78th Division's advance from the south. The 'descent from the north', Operation IMPACT ROYAL, was to be made by 1st Buffs, who had succeeded the disbanded 5th Grenadiers in 24 Guards Brigade. The Buffs were to make a waterborne attack on the Fossa Marina, two miles in front of the forward positions of 169 (Queen's) Brigade, seizing the fossa's banks, while 9 Commando came in from their right, also waterborne and under command of 24 Guards Brigade. A drop by 2 Parachute Brigade near Bando, about a mile from the Fossa Marina, was to take the Bando bridge, from which the Buffs and 9 Commando would advance on Argenta.[27]

The old axiom that 'no plan survives first contact' would have been in most minds but, on this occasion, the plan began unravelling even before first contact. More accurately, it began to unravel when intelligence on the paras' drop zone was studied. Reports that elements of 26th Panzer Division had deployed to the Fossa Marina, and aerial reconnaissance that showed increased AA defences in the area, indicated much higher levels of risk for an airborne operation than had been assumed earlier. It might have been possible to deal with the problem by using fighter-bombers but the tactical air forces, preparing for Operation CRAFTSMAN, could not divert sufficient fighter-bombers to the area, prompting McCreery to call off the airborne element of IMPACT ROYAL. This was setback enough, but worse was to come when it was discovered that 9 Commando's route was blocked by a high bank. Reconnaissance indicated no suitable diversion and 9 Commando's part in the operation was also cancelled. The Buffs were on their own.[28]

Following hectic nocturnal preparations, the Buffs embarked on their LVTs, accompanied by their padre, the Reverend G. Tyson, at Idiovora Umana at 5.45am. Artillery support was arranged, but this, from 'static, overstrained' gunners, was not enough for the task, a rare event in Eighth Army at this time, and the Buffs suffered; C Company's four Fantails were all targeted by enemy tanks:

No opposition was met until the leading LVT was less than 100 yds from the landing point, when it became evident that the enemy was prepared, and determined, to contest the landing. What had appeared to be a house revealed itself as a Mk IV, opening up on the leading LVT at point-blank range, and at the same time the remaining [vehicles] were engaged by at least two more [tanks] on the flank. All LVTs were hit, and, with one exception, all ramps jammed, men coming down under heavy enfilade fire from MGs sited on the Left and Right as they tried to leave the damaged vehicles.[29]

The company had made landfall next to the bank of the Fossa Marina close to some houses. Blaxland, a Buffs officer (he was serving with 5th Buffs), agrees that three tanks opened fire and wrought havoc in the company 'catching some men inside their tin cages with ramps jammed and felling others in large quantities as they jumped out'.[30] Of those who got ashore, thirty-five were hit crossing the top of the bank at the water's edge. Major W. S. Riley, the company commander, re-organized his company as a platoon and continued the attack until ordered to abandon the effort and consolidate. Subsequently, the Germans offered medical aid for the badly wounded, while Riley, with about twenty men left, withdrew after dark. Another thirteen soldiers, with two American crewmen and a German prisoner, reached their own lines that night.[31]

Some 600 yards away a second attacking company also met enemy fire but this was less effective and the company continued its attack. Lieutenant Aylett's No. 2 Platoon cleared houses to the flank, capturing nine Germans, while Sergeant Whitbread, with No. 3 Platoon, seized a canal bridge. A third company made landfall in less hostile territory, its LVTs' American crews having been given authority to decide where to land. This company also met opposition and was unable to move to support the other two but it did capture a farm and some hundred German and Turkoman troops. After dawn next day a junction was effected with the surviving forward company, although Whitbread's platoon at the bridge had to endure all of Saturday in their positions before 2nd Coldstream, with tanks of 10th Hussars, came to their relief in the evening. The Coldstream found that Whitbread, an AA gunner turned infantryman, had held on to thirty-four prisoners as well as the bridge.[32]

The defence that met the Buffs had come from two battalions of 15th Panzer Grenadier Regiment, still under tactical command of 42nd Jäger Division, with some Mk IV tanks of 129th Panzer Battalion. It was clear that the Germans' spirit was still strong and that yet more effort was needed to smash their lines completely. Further proof of this was given by the rebuff of an attack by 169 Brigade near Filo at noon on the 13th. In this clash 2/7th Queen's were stopped by elements of the same panzer grenadier regiment that had inflicted such hurt on the Buffs. To their left, 2/5th Queen's, with 10th Hussar tanks, had closed up on Filo during the morning. That afternoon an attack by 167 Brigade, with elements of 1st London Irish advancing on either side of the Reno, was stopped by I/40th Regiment of 42nd Jäger Division. There was some better news on Gruppo Cremona's front where, although 1/21st Regiment's attack north of Highway 16 in the morning met strong resistance, 2/22nd crossed the Santerno by the railway bridge farther south. Although the Germans had prepared the bridge for demolition, their intentions were thwarted by partisans who removed the charges. That afternoon Gruppo Cremona crossed and took up positions less than a mile to the north-west on Highway 16. But the best news of the day came from 78th Division and the Kangaroo Army. Although it now looked as if Argenta could not be taken from the north, 56th Division was approaching via Bastia and 78th from the south, both presenting effective threats to the defenders.[33]

In spite of the setbacks encountered on the 13th, Eighth Army had gained the objectives set thus far, with 56th Division having eaten into the Argenta defences. General McCreery had now to choose how to continue his advance. Although there were no reports of German reserves moving towards his front, there were signs that Tenth Army was wilting; indications first noted on the 11th that Herr's command might be falling back in the upper Santerno valley were getting stronger. As Jackson notes, by the 12th Tenth Army's withdrawal extended across all of XIII Corps' front and on V Corps' front Tac/R reported 'unusually large traffic movement ("MT, tanks, guns and horse-drawn vehicles"), moving north-westward out of Massa Lombarda'.[34] When a report was received early on the 13th from II Polish Corps of 'No ground contact' with the enemy, McCreery decided to maintain pressure on Argenta as well as continuing the thrust north-west towards Budrio. Although no written order has survived, this was when he decided to move XIII Corps into the battle, with 10th Indian Division under command. XIII Corps, under Lieutenant General Harding, would take over the north-westward advance from V Corps on the Saturday, as well as taking command of 2nd New Zealand Division on Saturday evening, leaving V Corps to concentrate on the Argenta battle.[35] Still in Eighth Army Reserve was the British 6th Armoured Division under Major General Horatius 'Nap' Murray.

The New Zealanders pushed up to the Sillaro on Friday, overcoming rearguard forces along the way. Although they found two bridges intact across the Zaniolo Canal, a temporary halt was called since the tactical air forces had permission to bomb beyond the canal and the risk of casualties from Allied fighter-bombers was too high to risk an advance. The Germans covered their withdrawal to the Sillaro with small fighting groups of infantry supported by Nebelwerfer fire, some tanks and SPGs. Those tanks included Panthers of I/26th Panzer Regiment, 26th Panzer Division, which took cover inside houses and discharged a few rounds before beating a retreat to the Correcchio canal, parallel to the Sillaro. By the end of the day the New Zealanders had fought their way up to the river line, with 22nd and 26th Battalions and 19th and 20th Armoured Regiments leading the advance under cover of a creeping artillery bombardment. Kangaroos of 4th Hussars were also deployed, but the Panthers on the Correcchio canal forced the infantry to dismount. Infantry opposition came from 9th Panzer Grenadier Regiment of 26th Panzer Division, which was withdrawing to the Sillaro. However, the defences along the Sillaro were not as strong as those along the Senio, Santerno or Idice. Although a Panther knocked out a Sherman of C Squadron 19th Armoured Regiment, it was then engaged and knocked out by a Firefly; the Panther caught fire. Two Tigers were also destroyed by medium artillery, with a third possibly damaged.[36]

At 2.30am on the 14th, a fifty-minute artillery bombardment of the area between the Correcchio canal and the Sillaro was begun by five field regiments and two medium regiments. Two and a half hours later, half the Divisional Cavalry Regiment, now officially the Divisional Cavalry Battalion (although its sub-units were still styled squadrons), of 9 Brigade, had crossed, but 22nd Battalion took casualties from Allied fire and had to stop on the near bank of the river. On the northern flank, two other battalions, 24th and 26th, had created a small bridgehead but their tank support,

20th Armoured Regiment, was unable to cross the river. With daylight, the Germans counter-attacked the bridgehead, deploying Tigers, mortars and Nebelwerfers, but the New Zealanders called down artillery support and fire from tanks on the other side of the Sillaro. The line was held. Later in the day, a ford suitable for tanks was found in 24th Battalion's sector but this was counter-attacked also. Again, the Germans were beaten off, and an Ark deployed to allow armour to cross. When the engineers opened routes for tanks, the leading infantry were joined by 19th and 20th Armoured Regiments. A further German counter-attack, in the early evening, forced the Divisional Cavalry Battalion and 19th Armoured Regiment to withdraw across the river until an artillery bombardment assisted them in regaining their bridgehead. The New Zealanders were now seven miles beyond the Santerno. Although a set-piece attack was planned for later that evening it had to be postponed as the additional artillery regiments required were not available. The operation was delayed by twenty-four hours, but that did not prevent 22nd Battalion, with a thirty-minute artillery programme, wading the Sillaro to dig in on the far side under harassing fire from the foe. Blaxland describes the 24th Battalion as 'inexhaustible', a description that might equally be applied to the entire New Zealand division. During the day they had almost lost both their GOC, Freyberg, Churchill's 'Salamander', and the corps commander, Keightley, when the latter was visiting Freyberg's headquarters and both had to dive for cover 'as a clutch of shells landed around them'.[37] (A divisional tactical headquarters would not have been in a building but in a group of vehicles, or the open.)

Returning to 56th Division's operations, 24 Guards Brigade was still in action seeking to gain crossings over the Fossa Marina-Canaletta di Bando canals and facing stiff resistance from 29th Panzer Grenadier Division which, by the Saturday, had its headquarters established at Masi Torello and had re-assumed command of 15th Panzer Grenadier Regiment in the Argenta area. Both I and II Battalions of that regiment were battling 24 Guards Brigade and not until 4.30pm did 2nd Coldstream, advancing north-west towards Fiorana, reach the Buffs. At 7.30 on Saturday morning 169 (Queen's) Brigade launched an attack on Filo, which was defended by 42nd Jäger Division, following, first, a heavy artillery bombardment and, then, a bombing attack that reduced the town to rubble. The defending Jägers should have had support from 504th Heavy Panzer Battalion, but the battalion's ability to provide support and its operational flexibility had been debilitated by the move of its repair workshops to Argenta and the loss of its recovery vehicles. While 2/7th Queen's spearheaded the attack, it was 2/6th Queen's who took the ruins of Filo at 9.30am. However, the brigade's third battalion, 2/5th Queen's, found their way obstructed at Bivio Palazzuola for most of the day by Panzer IVs of 129th Panzer Battalion and Nashorns of 525th Heavy Tank Destroyer Battalion. Fifty minutes before midnight, the tanks and tank destroyers had been knocked out by British artillery. At the Bastia bridge, 9th Royal Fusiliers and 1st London Irish launched an attack at 5.00pm but failed to take their objectives.[38]

II Polish Corps' advance continued against opposition from both Fallschirmjäger divisions, which were fighting sharp rearguard skirmishes while withdrawing to new positions behind the Sillaro. The Fallschirmjäger were still comparatively fresh and had certainly not had their morale and fighting spirit eroded. Elsewhere on the corps' front, 43 Gurkha Brigade deployed 2/10th Gurkhas with tanks of 14th/20th King's Hussars in an attempt to cross the Sillaro at Castel Guelfo, but a determined counter-attack by 9th Panzer Grenadier Regiment and what remained of 26th Armoured Reconnaissance Battalion put paid to their efforts. However, west of the Santerno, 18th Battalion of 6 Lwowska Brigade was hustling the Germans while 4 Wolynska Brigade attacked Imola from the north-east in the afternoon. By 7.00pm 7th and 8th Battalions of 3 Carpathian Rifle Brigade were entering Imola, the former along Highway 9 and the latter from the north-east. On the flank, armoured car patrols of 12th Royal Lancers kept contact with both 2nd New Zealand and 10th Indian Divisions. Italian troops were also active with the Maiella Partisan Brigade, numbering about 1,500 men, supporting Polish troops in pursuing the Germans at San Prospero and Castel San Pietro. In X Corps' area, 1/88th Regiment of Gruppo Friuli, in line with the Polish advance, crossed the Santerno to approach Imola from the south and south-west. While the Bafile and Grado Battalions of the San Marco Regiment of Gruppo Folgore attacked Monte dei Mercati at 8.00am they made little headway against the defence put up by 3rd Fallschirmjäger Regiment.[39]

We left 78th Division with 36 Brigade deploying on the evening of the 12th to advance to the San Patrizio-Conselice line and with the Kangaroo Army having to delay its H Hour until the morning of 13 April. Ahead of them 36 Brigade had captured intact two bridges over the Canale dei Molini, close to Conselice, but 6th Royal West Kents' advance was stopped by the resistance of 1059th Regiment of 362nd Division. By 6.30am on Friday the Irish Brigade Group's Break-out Force had passed through 19 Indian Division's Santerno bridgehead and swung north to take the bridge over the Reno at Bastia. This involved an advance of almost seven miles, much too deep a penetration to execute without changing the leading units as German resistance was expected to be fierce. As the Irish battlegroups moved off, they knew that 36 Brigade had not only given them manoeuvre room but had also upset the enemy's equilibrium. The line of advance was due north along a 1,000-yard-wide corridor between the Santerno, on the right, and the Fossatone canal over terrain typical of the northern plain, completely flat, dotted with orchards, vineyards and farmhouses and with the occasional hamlet. Only canals, streams and small rivers of differing widths provided variety.[40]

It fell to 2nd Inniskillings to lead the advance, with C Company under Major John Duane MC as the spearhead. As the company passed over a canal bridge and awaited support from behind, Duane tried to identify the enemy defensive positions, noting two tanks and at least two anti-tank guns about 700 yards away. He had two close shaves while observing the enemy as anti-tank shells passed close to him. Support was called for, but the three Shermans of the Bays that arrived were knocked out almost immediately by the anti-tank guns. Artillery support was arranged, including smoke rounds, and the company was to attack the German strongpoint. The Inniskillings moved forward under cover of some trees but were soon in an open area some 200 yards short of the strongpoint.

By the time we reached the open space the smoke bombs had been put in place to hide our attack. With two platoons up under George and Michael Murray … [we] went in at the double. This was a dangerous situation, difficult to identify the enemy. The Bren guns, fired from the hip, were in the foreground. The German position was very quickly overrun. We captured the anti-tank gun. The two tanks got away with some German soldiers. We took fourteen prisoners. … We had six wounded casualties of our own.[41]

B Company came forward to join C. Both were caught in a German bombardment that caused some casualties in B Company but did not prevent them renewing their advance when the guns fell silent. Minor pockets of resistance were overcome and, on the right, the Faughs came through to continue the advance, their first objective being to cross the Fossatone canal, with armour support, to secure the flank. With the aid of their assault engineers, the crossing was made and the advance resumed.[42] At much the same time, the Kangaroo Army crossed the Santerno and started preparations to pass through the Break-out Force. An Irish Fusiliers' officer recalled the Fossatone crossing:

The only memory I have of this action was taking quite a number of prisoners when we reached our objective and having only one casualty … . The Germans as usual were very well dug in along [the] canal and their weapon pits so well camouflaged as to be almost impossible to see until you were right up to them. … they were well armed with Spandau machine guns which fortunately they seemed unwilling to use. In fact they surrendered quickly and appeared happy to do so. I threw most of the Spandaus into the canal to make sure they would not be used again but fired one in the direction of the enemy. They were belt fed and had a high rate of fire. My platoon did not approve as they feared it might attract retaliatory fire on us.[43]

Both fusilier battalions pressed on with their advance, the Inniskillings overcoming German strongpoints at San Bernardino where, supported by a tank, B Company fought from house to house until opposition had been quelled. For the loss of one man dead and four wounded, the company had secured the position, killed eight Germans and taken fifty-six prisoners. By midday, the Break-out Force was approaching La Giovecca where less than a thousand yards separated Santerno and Fossatone and where there was determined opposition. Once again a company-strength attack was launched, this time using C Company. After a bitter battle the Inniskillings had suffered eight dead and four wounded but had taken their objective and over a hundred prisoners.

By the time the battle at La Giovecca ended, the Mobile Force had arrived, from which the Kangaroo-borne Irish Rifles, with 9th Lancers gun tanks in support, pushed on to take the crossings at Conselice from where they were to advance to the Reno. G Company led and resistance was light, mainly from Panzerfaust-armed Germans:

At first little resistance was encountered. The Skins and the Faughs had given the enemy a good shaking and he was on the move back. Scattered enemy Bazooka men were met and one tank was lost through the fire of an anti-tank gun, but a number of prisoners were taken by G Company.[44]

Closer to the canal the rivers flanking the Mobile Force opened out allowing H Company, with C Squadron 9th Lancers, to come up on G Company's left. Some Germans in La Frascata village were by-passed by the Lancers who made for Cavamento, some two miles from Bastia. However, the bridge over the canal at Cavamento was blown as the leading tanks approached. By 6.30pm, G, H and E Companies, the last having moved up to clear La Frascata, had secured a bridgehead.

The enemy had been surprised by the speed and weight of the attack. Few of them, not more than ten, had been killed, but all three forward companies had taken numbers of prisoners. By 1830 hours the total was eighty.

The bridgehead was firmly established by 2200 hours and Companies were dug in for the night. Sappers were building a bridge over the canal, the armour was in leaguer and plans for the following day were being made. A large increase in the number of wrist watches possessed by H Company was noticed.[45]

Before dawn on Saturday, Irish Fusilier patrols were checking to the west while Irish Rifles patrols did likewise on the road to Lavezzola and the Reno. Two columns of armour followed the Rifles at first light, one making due north on the axis of the main road and the second skirting to the right to avoid minefields near Lavezzola. The whole area was mined heavily and houses were booby-trapped, but, since the Germans had failed to remove their warning notices, no one was injured. The Sherman Crabs had a field day flailing the minefields.

Eight Germans who were busy laying mines were captured by the Rifles as they made their way to the Reno, which was reached at 9.40am; the minelayers were then forced to lift their own mines. The road and rail bridges across the river some six miles short of Bastia had been destroyed, but there was rubble enough for the infantry to cross without getting their feet wet.

Reconnaissance was carried out and a plan evolved for two platoons of E Company to cross and form a small bridgehead. This took place at 1130 hours without resistance and under cover of smoke, but while the platoons were advancing North from the river they were heavily counter-attacked and most of them overrun. No assistance could be given by the tanks owing to the high floodbanks and the absence of a bridge.[46]

The two platoons had fallen for a surrender ruse, being 'suddenly overwhelmed by Germans who sprang up all round them after an initial, pacific approach'. Although a reconnaissance was carried out for a deliberate crossing, it was then decided to remain on the southern bank overnight as launching such an assault across a wide river required more preparation time than was available. Orders were subsequently received for the battalion to hold its positions for the next two days.[47]

And so the first bound of the Kangaroo Army had been made. The setback at the Reno meant that Keightley's plans to pinch out the Argenta Gap from both north and south had been thwarted. He now had to look anew at V Corps' situation and decide how to get through the Gap.

Keightley was not the only commander looking anew at his situation. With pressure from Eighth Army increasing and Fifth Army launching its punch, von Vietinghoff reviewed the situation of Army Group C with his staff and made a further appeal to Hitler for permission to withdraw. But, as Jackson notes, Hitler was now removed from reality:

> the Führer was concerned only with mirages, political as well as military. Although Eisenhower's armies were deep into Germany and Soviet forces were poised for the drive to Berlin, two developments had refuelled Hitler's belief that his enemies would fall out at the eleventh hour. On 10 April the War Diary of OKW's Operations Staff noted the capture of the Allies' plan for the post-war division and administration of Germany – Operation ECLIPSE. Made thus aware that the Americans' advance to the Elbe would bring them into the Russian Zone, Hitler's hopes of inter-Allied friction were given a further boost by the death of President Roosevelt. This news was hailed by himself and Goebbels on 13 April as marking a turning point in their country's history, and in a proclamation, issued to his troops on the Eastern Front two days later, the Führer announced that 'Fate had already removed from this earth the greatest war criminal of all time'. He also declared that 'the break in of our enemy in the West, despite everything, will fail in the end' and that the 'last onslaught from Asia' would also be broken if the troops did their duty and held their positions.[48]

Thus Army Group C was doomed by its supreme commander to stand and fight, and await destruction. Not that von Vietinghoff could have saved his forces from defeat, but he may have been able to make a fighting withdrawal into the Alps and perhaps end the war with many fewer casualties than was actually the case.

Eighth Army had already inflicted heavy loss on the German armies, forcing them to withdraw from their original lines, yielding ground and blood. Now that Fifth Army had launched its offensive, it was clear that Tenth and Fourteenth Armies could not hope to check the Allied advance and, with supplies of fuel and ammunition sufficient only for fourteen days, would soon be forced to surrender. Even then, Hitler's attitude remained unchanged. No further supplies could be provided for Army Group C and Jodl warned that there would be 'serious consequences' for commanders who adopted defeatist attitudes and failed to obey to the letter their Führer's orders.

Notes

1. Belogi & Guglielmi, op. cit., p.142; Jackson, op. cit., pp.267–8; Blaxland, op. cit., pp.259–60.
2. NA, WO170/5059, war diary 2/5 Queen's.
3. Blaxland, p.259.
4. NA, WO170/5060, war diary, 2/6 Queen's.
5. Ibid.
6. Ibid.
7. Blaxland, p.260.
8. Jackson, p.; NA, WO170/4483, war diary HQ 167 Bde.
9. Jackson, pp.268–70; Belogi & Guglielmi, pp.142–4; *DSM*, Gruppo Cremona, pp.112–13.
10. Belogi & Guglielmi, pp.143–7; NA, WO170/4240, war diary, HQ V Corps (G), op. cit.
11. Belogi & Guglielmi, pp.146–7; *I Gruppi di Combattimento*, p.271.
12. Jackson, pp.268–9; Belogi & Guglielmi, p.146; *I Gruppi di Combattimento*, pp.198–203.
13. NA, WO170/4367, war diary, 56 Div, Mar-Apr '45; Belogi & Guglielmi, p.152; Jackson, pp.267–8.
14. Jackson, p.269.
15. Belogi & Guglielmi, pp.152–3; *The Tiger Triumphs*, pp.191–3.
16. Jackson, p.272; Doherty, *CTW!*, pp.234–6; Ray, pp.201–3.
17. Bredin, 'Account of the Kangaroo Army.'
18. Jackson, pp.272–3; NA, WO170/4387, war diary, HQ 78 Div (G), Apr '45; Ray, pp.203–4; Doherty, *CTW!*, p.236.
19. Belogi & Guglielmi, p.154.
20. Kay, op. cit., p.447; Belogi & Guglielmi, pp.155–6.
21. Belogi & Guglielmi, pp.156–7.
22. Jackson, p.268; *I Gruppi di Combattimento*, p.274.
23. Belogi & Guglielmi, p.157.
24. Jackson, p.268; *I Gruppi di Combattimento*, pp.274–5.
25. Belogi & Guglielmi, p.157.
26. Jackson, p.269; NA, WO170/4240, war diary, HQ V Corps (G), Mar-Apr '45; WO170/4285, war diary, HQ XIII Corps (G), Apr '45.
27. Blaxland, p.260.
28. Ibid., pp.260–1; Jackson, p.271.
29. Jackson, p.272.
30. NA, WO170/4992, war diary, 1 Buffs, 1945.
31. Blaxland, p.261.
32. Ibid., Doherty, *A Noble Crusade*, p.294, NA, WO170/4992, war diary, 1 Buffs, 1945.
33. NA, WO170/4992, war diary, 1 Buffs, 1945; Blaxland, p.261; Doherty, *A Noble Crusade*, p.294; *DSM*, Gruppo Cremona, pp.115–16.
34. Jackson, p.272; Belogi & Guglielmi, pp.164–5.
35. Jackson, p.268.
36. Belogi & Guglielmi, pp.167–8; Mead, p.181; Blaxland, p.263.
37. Kay, p. 447; Jackson, p.269.
38. Kay, pp.448–55; Jackson, pp.278–9; Blaxland, p.262; Belogi & Guglielmi, 178–80; *DSM*, Gruppo Cremona, pp.121–2; *I Gruppi di Combattimento*, pp.279–81.
39. Jackson, p.273; Belogi & Guglielmi, pp.176–7.
40. Belogi & Guglielmi, pp.180–1.

41. Jackson, pp.272–3; Ray, pp.203–4; Doherty, *CTW!*, pp.236–9.
42. Duane, notes to author.
43. Ibid.
44. Trousdell, notes to author.
45. Bredin, 'Account of the Kangaroo Army'.
46. Ibid.
47. Ibid.
48. Jackson, p.274.

Chapter Eight

As so often before in the Italian campaign, weather forced change or postponement on even the best laid plans. In the case of Fifth Army's Operation CRAFTSMAN, for which D Day, when IV Corps would launch its offensive, had been set as 12 April, low cloud over the Apennines and morning fog over Allied airfields led to a twenty-four-hour delay. Conditions were no better for the 13th and another twenty-four-hour delay had to be accepted. However, with a more encouraging forecast for the 14th, Truscott set this date as the new D Day, with H Hour at 6.00am. Although meteorological reports that afternoon indicated yet more unfavourable weather on the 14th, Truscott decided to wait until the morning before making yet another postponement:

Time: 0500, the morning of April 14th. Place: My small mess tent at Army Command Post at Traversa. Present: General Darcy and I, Carleton and Wilson, my aide; Sergeant Hong serving coffee. Other equipment: A battery of telephones. One rings. Darcy answers. 'Grosseto fogged in, visibility zero.' One after another, each fighter base reports 'Fogged in. Visibility zero.' The attack is set for 0800. I telephone Crittenberger and give him the bad news. He is to hold troops in readiness to attack on one hour's notice, and I will keep him informed. More coffee. Darcy with a telephone in each hand, frequently talking into both, checks the bases. Still fogged in. More coffee. A telephone to Crittenberger. Darcy again checks the bases. Still fogged in. Airplanes are waiting with engines warmed up and pilots in the cockpits. More coffee. Another report to Darcy – a glimmer of hope – 'Grosseto – fog may be thinning – visibility now nearly one quarter mile.' Telephone to Crittenberger. More coffee. Darcy again checks bases. An interruption: Grosseto. 'Can see end of runway. They're taking off.' Minutes pass as flight after flight is reported airborne. We can almost hear the motors seventy-five miles away. We cheer. Telephone Crittenberger. 'The attack is on 0900.' It had been a strenuous three hours, for the fighter group from Grosseto which was airborne at 0800.[1]

Not only Grosseto but other airfields were clear of fog and the fighter-bombers' support was assured, at least for the first day of CRAFTSMAN. But first came the heavy bombers of MASAF, striking at German positions from 8.30am. For the next forty minutes hundreds of B-17s and B-24s, followed by fighter-bombers and medium bombers, cascaded thousands of tons of fragmentation, high-explosive and napalm bombs on the enemy positions. (Over the next four days, MASAF heavies flew 2,052 sorties in support of, first, IV Corps and, then, II Corps.) Then came fighter-bombers, including USAAF P-47s Thunderbolts and RAF Spitfires and Kittyhawks, all under command of XXII TAC, hitting the Germans' main line of resistance. In 459 sorties, mostly in flights of four machines, they struck at 'gun positions, strongpoints, troop areas, and other defensive works immediately opposite the IV Corps front',[2] as well as the crossing between the Porrettana and Vergato-Zocca roads. Once again napalm was used, many of the sorties targeting Monte Pigna, 10th Mountain Division's first objective, some four miles north-west of Vergato. When the last planes flew off, the artillery took over, firing a thirty-five-minute bombardment, using guns ranging from the 75mm howitzers of 10th Mountain's artillery units to the massive 8-inch and 240mm howitzers of the army artillery:

> The smoke and dust raised by the massive aerial and artillery bombardment turned the morning into a gray twilight, whereupon the mountain division's infantrymen began moving to a [start line] on the forward slopes of Monte della Spe, just north-east of Castel d'Aiano, overlooking the northernmost of two lateral roads connecting Vergato with Castel d'Aiano and a secondary road that was to be the axis of advance for the division in 'carrying the brunt of the attack to the Po Valley – and beyond'.[3]

By early afternoon, Truscott was in the air with Wilson in his L-5 to visit the IV Corps front where, from an OP on Monte Castellana, they watched Major General Hays' 10th Mountain Division scale and capture Monte Rocca di Roffeno:

> Fighting was heavy, opposition was intense in spite of the bombing and artillery barrages, with high explosives and fire bombs. But we watched the Mountaineers reach and clear the top. The 10th Mountain Division were forging ahead and the drive of the 1st Armored Division soon got under way.[4]

Although Fifth Army's D Day was delayed, Truscott's attack still gained the advantage of surprise. The Germans had been waiting for the Allied left hook, but when it had not opened at dawn, or shortly thereafter, it was not expected until either that night or the next dawn.

Tenth Mountain Division attacked with two regiments (equivalent to British brigades) on a front extending eastward from Castel d'Aiano. On the right was Colonel David Fowler's 87th Mountain Infantry Regiment and on the left Colonel Raymond Barlow's 85th. Colonel Clarence Tomlinson's 86th Regiment would come in later, behind the 87th. The first objectives were the German defences across the Pra del Bianco basin, as far east as Rocca di Roffeno. Having taken these positions, the division was to swing north-eastward and advance down the hills that marked Truscott's Green and Brown Lines. In the mountain soldiers' path were the men of 334th Volksgrenadier Division while, in front of 1st Armored Division, 94th Grenadier Division held the ridges down which the mountaineers would advance in their drive to the north-east. The thrust of 10th Mountain Division's attack had been very well chosen, since it hit the boundary between the two German divisions. More than that, the interdivisional boundary was also the boundary between LI Mountain Corps, on the German right, and XIV Panzer Corps on their left. The American attack was intended to clear 'the high watershed between the Samoggia stream on the left and the Reno valley on the right'.[5]

First Armored Division (its soubriquet was, and is, Old Ironsides; its men are known as Iron Soldiers), the first US Army armoured formation to see action in the Second World War, was on the western side of the Reno valley while 1st Brazilian Division was on 10th Mountain's other flank, west of the Samoggia. Once the mountaineers had cleared the 'high watershed', the Iron Soldiers could operate in the Samoggia valley.

The resistance encountered by the mountain troops was ferocious and the next three days were to prove the bloodiest in their wartime experience. The 85th was on the first hills north of the Pra del Bianco basin early in the afternoon but was stopped later on; the regiment's objectives were Hills 913, 909 and 915. It seemed that, despite the ferocity of the bombing and shellfire, the Germans had survived with relatively few casualties. While they had been in well-prepared positions, and were able to take advantage of those, a critical factor in the ferocity of their resistance was a belief that the mountain troops would take no prisoners. This story was discovered in a captured diary, and, as a field report stated, 'undoubtedly accounted for the fanatical resistance that our troops encountered, which often meant digging the Germans out of their well-prepared bunkers'.[6]

Against such a background, 10th Mountain Division gained its sole Medal of Honor of the war. The posthumous award was earned by Pfc John D. Magrath, a radioman in G Company of the 2nd Battalion of Barlow's 85th Regiment. As the company made its way down the slope of Monte della Spe and then up the heavily-mined Hill 909 the GIs came under heavy fire:

> Men were dropping all over from small-arms fire, mortars, and artillery fire. Above them, the hill's summit was in chaos. Pulling up in front of a stone farmhouse, [Edward] Nickerson was astonished to see a German machine gunner firing away at troops on a far-off flank; the noise from the bombing was so loud the German didn't even see G Company on his front lawn, thirty yards away.[7]

Although the remainder of G Company dug in on the slopes, seeking cover from the fire, Magrath dashed forward, ignoring that fire, and making for a machine-gun post close to the top of Hill 909. Seemingly immune to bullets and mortar bombs, he killed two enemy soldiers, wounded others and, in under a minute, had seized the machine gun, which he turned on its previous owners. However, the weapon jammed as soon as he pulled the trigger. Undeterred, Magrath changed the barrel and soon had it working.

Now more heavily armed, Magrath continued his rampage, killing or wounding five more Germans and capturing several more. In his frenzy, Magrath almost seemed to burst with power. When a German soldier came upon him from the window of the shattered house, Magrath whirled on him and yelled 'Surrender!' The German spontaneously dropped his weapon and raised his hands. Magrath moved out again, well in front of the rest of his company.[8]

When Magrath's skills were required for radio work, Edward Nickerson was sent forward to bring him back as G Company needed to regroup. Some seventy-five yards forward, Nickerson found Magrath lying on the ground, firing the German machine gun, almost certainly an MG42, although one source suggests an MG34. As his friend approached, Magrath called to him, 'I've been having fun!'

Magrath obeyed the order to return after giving Nickerson brief instructions on how to operate the MG42 and leaving him with the weapon. Nickerson was relieved some time later and ordered some prisoners to carry a wounded GI down the hill. The injured man, Richard Condo, died en route, and so intense was the German shelling that 'at least twenty German prisoners and one American guard were killed' on the descent. By the time Nickerson returned to the summit of Hill 909, Magrath had just been killed by one of the many mortar and artillery bombardments that reduced G Company to a third of its strength.[9] The citation for Magrath's Medal of Honor relates that:

> his company was pinned down by heavy artillery, mortar, and small arms fire, near Castel d'Aiano, Italy. Volunteering to act as a scout, armed with only a rifle, he charged headlong into withering fire, killing two Germans and wounding three in order to capture a machine gun. Carrying this weapon across an open field through heavy fire, he neutralized two more machine-gun nests; he then circled behind four other Germans, killing them with a burst as they were firing on his company. Spotting another dangerous enemy position to his right, he knelt with the machine gun in his arms and exchanged fire with the Germans until he had killed two and wounded three. The enemy now poured increased mortar and artillery fire on the company's newly won position. Pfc Magrath volunteered again to brave the shelling in order to collect a report of casualties. Heroically carrying out this task, he made the supreme sacrifice – a climax to the valor and courage that are in keeping with highest traditions of the military service.[10]

Pfc Magrath had been born on Independence Day 1924 in East Norwalk, Connecticut. His body was returned to his native town after the war, and is buried in a Revolutionary War cemetery.

In spite of the weight of Allied artillery fire brought down on the German mortar and artillery positions, it was the mountain infantrymen themselves, 'stubbornly fighting their way forward despite the fire' who deserve the credit for silencing the devastating fire of the enemy machine guns. Many of Magrath's comrades also displayed great courage that day and would do so over the following days.[11] Magrath was one of 286 members of the division killed in the first three days of Operation CRAFTSMAN; another 1,047 were wounded. Of those casualties, 553 were killed, wounded or missing on the first day.[12]

Nor had machine guns, mortars and artillery been the only weapons with which the Germans fought back. Minefields had prevented 751st Tank and 701st Tank Destroyer Battalions providing armoured support to the infantry whilst also inflicting many casualties on the engineers whose task was to clear paths through them. Another casualty of the 14th, on Hill 913, was a junior officer of I Company of the 85th who had joined as a replacement. Second Lieutenant Robert J. Dole 'was leading a patrol when machine-gun fire killed two scouts and ripped into Dole's neck and arm. He spent the next forty months in army hospitals.'[13] No fewer than ninety-eight men died in the assault, according to Dole.[14] So badly hit was I Company that K Company 'came alongside and finally ascended the heights'.[15]

Only after Hill 913 was securely occupied by Allied forces were the medical teams permitted to retrieve the killed and wounded. That's when the medics found me. One of the guys peeled my shirt back and pulled out my bloodstained dog tags …. (I still have my stained tags to this day.) Lifting my left arm slightly, he tied a six-inch label around my bloodied forearm, on which he wrote my name and serial number. On the tag were some preprinted boxes to describe my condition: the soldier checked WOUNDED; SEVERE; LYING (as opposed to 'walking case,' or a 'sitting case').[16]

On the divisional right flank, 87th Regiment advanced as far as the hamlet of Torre Iussi during the afternoon, fighting its way through the houses by nightfall. Meanwhile, the 86th, following the right rear of the 87th, suffered some delay due to the battle in Torre Iussi but pushed on to Rocca di Roffeno, a rocky outcrop amidst a mass of hill ground, by mid-afternoon. The advance was stopped across the entire front before nightfall and a defensive stance adopted for the night. Although the Americans expected the usual German counter-attack, none came.

To the left of 10th Mountain Division in IV Corps was the Brazilian Expeditionary Force (*Força Expedicionária Brasileira*, or FEB), which had already been blooded in combat and had shown its mettle as a capable infantry division. However some Americans, including Crittenberger, persisted in doubting their capabilities, due to the failure of Brazilian troops to capture Monte Castello in December, although they subsequently took it in February. In Operation CRAFTSMAN, the task assigned to General Mascarenhas de Moraes (the oldest Allied divisional commander in the Mediterranean, if not the oldest in any theatre; he was older than the army, army group and theatre commanders)[17] and his troops had been a diversionary one, reconnoitring the enemy facing them and pursuit of the Germans should they withdraw. However, the commander of 10th Mountain, Major General Hays, was concerned that elements of XIV Panzer Corps could present a threat to his left flank in the Montese-Montelle area. Hays raised his concerns with Crittenberger at a IV Corps conference on 8

April and Mascarenhas proposed that his division could protect the left flank of the advance by attacking such elements. Crittenberger agreed and, at 12.15pm on 14 April, told the FEB commander that he could begin the attack when he wished. Crittenberger allocated 760th Tank and 849th Tank Destroyer Battalions to support the Brazilians.[18]

In the centre of the FEB's attack was the 3rd Battalion 11th Infantry Regiment (as the Brazilians adopted American practice, this equated to a British brigade), or III/11th Infantry. The battalion, supported by some American armour, advanced via Serreto, Paravento and Montello, with I/11th to its left, passing through Montaurigola and Montese while, to the right, II/1st Infantry provided the link with the left flank of the American advance. Before the attack, an 11th Infantry reconnaissance patrol was engaged by the enemy and Sergeant Max Wolff Filho was killed by machine-gun fire. Sergeant Filho's gallantry, described as 'almost suicidal bravery',[19] had been marked just days before by the award of the Bronze Star. He had been a member of a close combat platoon (*pelotão de choque*).

The FEB attack began at 1.30pm and senior commanders observed the advance of their troops from positions in Sassomolare that allowed a clear view of Montese. Of course, such a view was denied to those making the advance, but their move was aided by information gathered by a night-time reconnaissance patrol two days earlier. That patrol had been led by Lieutenant Iporan Nunes de Oliveira, who commanded 3 Platoon of 2 Company, the first platoon to enter Montese. His patrol had reconnoitred Montaurigola and cleared a lane through a minefield, although one of its number had been killed by a burst of machine-gun fire from a nearby house. Nonetheless, de Oliveira felt that the patrol had provided valuable information for the advance, by identifying the locations of the minefield and machine-gun post.

The attack on Montese was led by two platoons of 2 Company, the other being 3 Platoon under Lieutenant Ary Rauen, who was killed by gunfire when his platoon was pinned down in front of a minefield on the right flank of the advance. Two Platoon's commander had intended to attack Montese from Montaurigola but had to change his plans as 1 Platoon had not taken that village, instead following an overgrown gully seeded with booby traps before scaling the slopes to Montese. Both leading squads came under fire when they reached the top of the slopes, which de Oliveira described as resembling 'big staircases'. Since the ground between his and the German positions was open, he decided to sidestep his third squad to the left to attack from there, supported by fire from the other two squads. The tactic worked, although the attack impetus slowed as the squad approached the houses in which the Germans were located, and Lieutenant de Oliveira decided to take direct command of the attacking squad.

His timing could hardly have been more fortuitous. As the squad prepared for the final assault, it was bracketed by an Allied artillery bombardment. But the shelling also bracketed the Germans, allowing de Oliveira to order his men to race forward to the houses. The Brazilians reached their objective and were on the enemy positions before the dust and smoke had cleared. However, the Germans had taken shelter below ground, which proved their undoing as they were overcome quickly while trying to react. The platoon had penetrated the German defences but there was still much resistance to overcome. When Lieutenant de Oliveira tried to reconnoitre the ground beyond his new positions he come under machine-gun fire from the side windows of a large house in which the enemy were still ensconced firmly.

All three squads of 3 Platoon attacked enemy positions. That evening the other platoons of 2 Company arrived and, next morning, under the company commander, Captain Alvares, a systematic house-to-house clearance of Montese began, during which de Oliveira captured two German artillery observers in the town's medieval watchtower. It took until the 16th before Montese was cleared, and required the support of 8 Company from 6th Infantry. Over the three days of battle the FEB lost 453 men killed or wounded, and took prisoner the same number of Germans.[20] Montese was devastated and has the unwanted distinction of being the worst affected town in Modena province with 833 of its 1,121 houses destroyed; of its population, 189 were killed and over 700 injured, many of them suffering life-changing injuries. Starr notes that:

> Throughout the period of the main IV Corps push on the right very heavy artillery concentrations from enemy guns on the upper Panaro fell in the Brazilian zone, especially about Montese; during the first twenty-four hours of the IV Corps attack this area received over 1,800 of the 2,800 rounds of enemy shell fire reported in the entire corps zone.[21]

The FEB had secured the left flank of 10th Mountain Division while, on the latter's right, 1st Armored Division had also made good progress. General Mascarenhas later wrote that Major Lisboa's 11th Infantry 'with singular offensive spirit, penetrated the town of Montese, enveloping and breaking up the enemy's defenses'.[22] However, III/6th, knocked back by 741st Jäger Regiment at Monte Buffone on the morning of 16 April, had to be relieved by II/6th. On that morning also, the FEB's 1st Regiment began relieving 85th US Mountain Infantry Regiment.

As the Brazilians fought their way into Montese, 10th Mountain Division continued its advance, with its left flank covered by 85th Regiment while 86th pushed towards Monte Mantino and 87th towards Monte Pigna. Once the FEB had secured Montese it was intended that it should relieve 85th of the flank protection role. Both Monte Pigna and Monte Mantino were taken on the 15th, Pigna in the morning and Mantino that evening; south of Monte Mantino 1st Armored had taken Suzzano and reached the slopes of Monte Pero, the last peak in the Green Line. During the afternoon the hills north of Monte Pigna were secured by 3/87th in readiness for a thrust over the final ridge into the village of Tolé.

The hardest opposition had been encountered by 85th Regiment on the left. As it left its start line the regiment had been hit by heavy artillery and mortar fire, and brought to a standstill. Only very slowly did the GIs in this sector inch forward, against determined resistance. At noon Hays ordered the 85th to organize for defence as he deployed 10th Anti-Tank Battalion to 'tie the left flank in with the Brazilians'.[23] Crittenberger, meanwhile, ordered the weight of 10th Mountain to be shifted to the north-east.[24]

On the other side, General Bernhard Steinmetz, commander of 94th Division, realizing that his front was in danger of collapse, sought permission from HQ XIV Panzer Corps to withdraw his left-flank regiments. When that permission was not forthcoming, Steinmetz acted on his own authority on the 16th and ordered the units on his left and centre to withdraw to new positions, the Monte San Michele line or *Michelstellung*, during the night.

> But he had waited dangerously long, for the Americans had already cut the few roads leading from that sector. Steinmetz's troops had to withdraw cross-country in the darkness over mountainous terrain, abandoning much of their heavy equipment along the way and falling prey to harassing American artillery fire. So cut up was the division's left flank battalion as to become virtually useless.[25]

The day that Steinmetz decided to withdraw much of his division, other evacuations were in hand. A smokescreen was laid along the northbound road through Tolé to cover the withdrawal of artillery and other elements from the Monte Mantino–Monte Mosca area. Such was the pressure from the American offensive that 756th Regiment of 334th Division had cracked, while the rear areas of Steinmetz's division were in danger of being overrun. Although the GIs of 10th Mountain did not know it, they had broken the cohesion of the enemy front, cracking the line between 334th and 94th Divisions. Now, in typical German fashion, a sharp delaying action was begun to cover a withdrawal to positions along the Panaro.

But that delaying action could not curb the onward rush of 10th Mountain, which was on the cusp of breaking through the enemy's front between the Samoggia and Lavino rivers. On 16 April 2/87th Regiment took the hills north of Monte Mantino, allowing 3/87th to pass through in its drive to Monte Mosca, the final high point of the eastern ridge line. That drive was not easy as the Germans defended doughtily with mortar and artillery fire directed on the advancing troops. Although 3/87th assaulted Monte Mosca at 2.15 that afternoon, the fight to clear the crest, and mopping up, took almost two hours. And that was not the end of the struggle: the Germans launched no fewer than ten counter-attacks on the GIs who fought off each one and held the summit. Even while 3/87th fought for Monte Mosca 2/87th was attacking down towards Tolé. The village was a mass of rubble from shelling and bombing and opposition was light, allowing the battalion to occupy and secure it quickly. By then 86th Regiment, supported by 751st Tank Battalion, which had cut north behind the Monte Mosca attack, was advancing into better ground north of Tolé. That evening the regiment and its supporting tanks stopped for the night at Monzuno.[26]

The other element of IV Corps' attack was 1st Armored Division, under General Vernon Pritchard, which crossed its start line at 5.00pm on D Day, the last of the assaulting divisions to move off. 'Old Ironsides' launched a two-pronged attack immediately above Highway 64, aimed north–eastward along the Reno valley and against the nearby heights. Suzzano was the objective for one prong of the attack, carried out by 14th Armored Infantry and 13th Tank Battalions, with 11th Armored

Infantry following. Suzzano was taken the next afternoon, following which 14th Armored Infantry struck east towards Monte Pero, which it captured on the morning of the 16th. On that day 6th and 11th Armored Infantry struck out from Suzzano to Monte Mosca, which was in the hands of 10th Mountain Division troops, and turned to the north-east with 6th Armored Infantry on the left. Both battalions advanced quickly on 17 April, 6th Armored reaching Monte d'Avigo and 11th Monte Milano.

The other prong of the advance was along Highway 64 itself where 81st Cavalry Reconnaissance Squadron (Mechanized), equipped with the new M24 Chaffee light tank, had the task of advancing on the critically-situated town of Vergato. At 5.50pm the squadron attacked Vergato but its assault was brought to a stop by concentrated mortar and machine-gun fire from the defenders, I/267th Regiment of 94th Division. But the dismounted GIs persevered with their efforts and, by 8.00pm, had taken half the town, fighting through the southern outskirts to seize what remained of the railway station. This attack so distracted the Germans that they offered almost no opposition to 14th Armored Infantry coming up on the left en route to take Suzzano. At 11.15pm, 27th Armored Artillery Battalion hammered the German-held part of Vergato with a number of salvoes from their M7 105mm howitzers. House-to-house fighting continued until daylight, by which time Vergato was in American hands. Reconnaissance elements then pushed along the Reno valley for almost five miles into positions below the armored infantry on Monte Milano. Thus far, 1st Armored Division had encountered only 'light to moderate opposition, consisting largely of mortar and artillery fire and minefields; the sharpest infantry action had occurred at Vergato'.[27]

Truscott had intended II Corps to go into action when IV Corps reached the Green Line, which had been achieved on D Day plus one. Now II Corps was to join IV Corps for the next phase, both advancing abreast towards the Brown Line. The subsequent phase was to the Black Line, at the beginning of which 85th Division was to move from Army Reserve to pass through 1st Armored and join II Corps. At that stage 1st US and 6th South African Armoured Divisions would form an exploitation force. However, the plan was flexible enough to be modified in the light of circumstances, as was to happen.

Before II Corps launched its attack across its fifteen-mile front, the heavy bombers and tactical air forces made their contributions. On 15 April 765 B-17s and B-24s bombed targets along both main roads between the enemy front line and Bologna. The heavies were followed by medium bombers striking at troop assembly areas near Praduro, and at vital installations. Then came the fighter-bombers, 120 in all, in flights of four or eight, which attacked enemy positions in the Monte Sole sector. Just before darkness the fighter-bombers switched their targets, hitting strongpoints along the German front facing II Corps, 'dropping tons of flaming napalm on known enemy emplacements and illuminating the darkening landscape with pillars of fire'.[28] The heavies attacked again next morning, as did the mediums, which changed their targets to the German lines of communication in the Bologna area. Fifth Army's artillery added to the punishment being meted out to the Germans with 548 pieces firing against artillery positions and anti-personnel bombardments as II Corps forces counted down to their H Hour.

The first formations of II Corps to attack were 6th South African Armoured and 88th Infantry Divisions, on the corps left, who moved off just after darkness fell on the 15th. The South Africans faced Monte Sole, across the high ground twixt the Reno and the Setto stream while 88th Division, the Blue Devils, faced Monterumici. Smoke and dust still hung in the air and drifted into the valleys as both divisions went forth to battle. On the corps' right wing, 91st and 34th Divisions began their attacks at 3.00am on the 16th. The latter pair had the more difficult task as German resistance, aided by terrain and minefields, was tougher on their front; 91st Division, straddling Highway 65, faced Monte Adone and 34th Division's objectives were two ridges north-east of Monte Belmonte, Savizzano and Gorgognano. Once again, the attackers found that enemy reaction was fast, in spite of pummelling from air and artillery. The Germans had simply taken shelter in deep bunkers, emerging swiftly to man their positions as the attack was launched and the guns and aircraft fell silent. All three infantry divisions were limited to 'slow, costly advances, so familiar to the veterans of the previous autumn's operations'.[29] Also under Keyes' command in II Corps was Gruppo Legnano, the only Italian formation in Fifth Army, but its role was to be restricted, as Blaxland puts it, to 'further extending the menace by making offensive gestures on the right flank'.[30] Keyes had decided that the group would 'demonstrate but not attack when the II Corps' phase of the operation began'.[31]

Much of the reason for the tough resistance encountered by II Corps' formations was that they were attacking the strongest enemy defences. Truscott was well aware of this, knowing that the Germans had been preparing to meet an American attack on Bologna. Attuned to Clark's obsession with the city, the Germans had built their defensive positions on the sector south of the city around four features that, as Allied reconnaissance had shown, were mutually supporting. Those were Monte Sole, the most important since Truscott intended to make his main effort in the Reno valley; Monterumici and Monte Adone, overlooking Highway 65 from the west, and a line of hills north of Monte Belmonte that overlooked the same length of Highway 65 from the east, represented the second and third features. The fourth was the town of Pianoro, which had obsessed Clark, on Highway 65, only eight miles from Bologna. Clearing the high ground would permit an advance to Pianoro, while the capture of Monte Sole, combined with IV Corps' operations west of the Reno valley, would open the way for an attack towards the Praduro road junction on Highway 64, where the Setto flows into the Reno.[32]

Since capturing one of these features would not lead to a successful breakthrough, Keyes realized that he would have to attack simultaneously across his entire front to prevent the Germans moving local reserves from one threatened point to another. Fixing the enemy in place would allow II Corps to exploit its manpower and matériel superiority by concentrating enough strength at a chosen point to crack open the enemy front. The German defence south of Bologna was more than four divisions strong: 65th Infantry and 8th Gebirgs Divisions were deployed between the Reno and Highway 65 on II Corps' left, dominating the main route through the sector while 1st Fallschirmjäger and 305th Infantry faced II Corps' right; some of 94th Division also faced Keyes' left. However, II Corps had more manpower and artillery firepower, and the Allies enjoyed air supremacy.[33]

While the three infantry divisions were making slow progress, on the South African front Keyes could report better news as the Springboks, through a series of spirited assaults, supported by artillery – 35,000 rounds were fired – captured Monte Sole on the morning of the 16th. The Witwatersrand Rifles/Regiment de la Rey (WR/DLR) had a firm hold on Monte Caprara by 7.30am, whence they advanced to clear the saddle between there and Monte Sole, aided by tanks from Prince Alfred's Guard (PAG). Later in the day, from 5.30 to 7.00pm, the South Africans holding Monte Sole fought off a determined counter-attack by I/296th Regiment of 8th Gebirgs Division. Also in the South African sector, Monte Abelle was taken by First City Regiment/Cape Town Highlanders (FC/CTH), who advanced to their objective along the mountain ridge. Later that afternoon the WR/DLR pushed on to Sperticano and linked up with 81st Cavalry Reconnaissance Squadron. Meanwhile, 6th Armored Infantry Battalion had secured Suzzano and Cereglio and, in conjunction with 14th Armored Infantry, advanced to take Monte Pero. By now 85th (Custer) Division was preparing to relieve 1st Armored.[34]

Also in action was the 88th Division, the Blue Devils, whose 1/349th Regiment had occupied Furcoli before dawn and endured fire from German positions in caves, while 2/ and 3/350th fought to wrest Monterumici from the Germans. At much the same time as 1/349th occupied Furcoli, 2/ and 3/361st were attacking the village of Brento, which sits on a crossroads, and Monte Adone; at 8.00am the Americans were counter-attacked by a battalion from 65th Division but repelled the German onslaught. At 2.00pm that day 3/350th were ambushed by 8th Gebirgs Division's 297th Regiment and had a five-hour-long struggle to free themselves.[35]

On the IV Corps front, 10th Mountain Division's 3/87th, with elements of 1st Armored, was firm on Monte Mosca, as we have seen, where they fought off several counter-attacks while 86th Regiment had advanced as far as Montepastore, which was occupied that evening in spite of resistance from elements of 94th Division. That day the German defences west of Highway 65 began to crumble, but those astride the road remained firm. Next day, the 17th, came indications that those positions also were under extreme pressure as 91st (Powder River) and 34th (Red Bull) Divisions swept the enemy from the heights flanking the highway. West of the Reno and Highway 64, IV Corps' penetration was widening while II Polish Corps of Eighth Army threatened Bologna from the south-east. For the Germans south of Bologna time was running out very quickly.[36]

Keyes now began sidestepping his divisions westward, in anticipation of a decision by Truscott to shift the balance of Fifth Army and move the inter-corps boundary to the west, a move that would make II Corps the engine of the army's advance to the Po. Such a shift of balance would place the road junction at Praduro in II Corps' area, and Highway 64 and the Reno would become part of Keyes' area. His prescience and clear understanding of his commander's intent allowed Keyes to shape II Corps for the next phase of operations. First, he moved 88th Division to his left, placing it between the South Africans and the Reno. This would put the 88th alongside 85th Division, which, originally intended to join II Corps, was now allocated to IV Corps and was about to relieve 1st Armored on IV Corps' right flank. Over the opening days of CRAFTSMAN Truscott had perceived 'an important enemy weakness' on 10th Mountain Division's right flank and was determined to exploit it. He had also appreciated that the efforts of the South Africans and their success

> was as much to the advantage of [IV Corps] as to the remainder of [II Corps], and quickly sensing that the left flank was the place for exploitation, Truscott allotted his reserve, the 85th Custer Division, to Crittenberger, contrary to the expectations of the man under whom it had served with such distinction, Keyes.[37]

Following its relief by 85th Division, 1st Armored redeployed some ten miles to the west, to assume positions along the Panaro, where the ground was better suited to armour and where the division could also protect the extended left flank of Hays' division. Tenth Mountain was to become the vanguard of Fifth Army's attack in the next phase of operations. Both 91st and 34th Divisions were also sidestepped to the west, thereby closing the gap resulting from moving 88th Division to the left. Since that move widened the sector held by Gruppo Legnano, which was fairly quiet, it set Highway 65 as the boundary between the group and 34th Division. The regrouping complete, Truscott expected that the next two days would produce a break-out from the mountains onto the Lombardy (Po) plain.[38]

By now Fifth Army had hammered a deep wedge between Fourteenth Army's two corps and the advance of 10th Mountain had severed the few roads leading northward from the enemy lines, forcing the Germans to abandon much of their heavy equipment in the mountains. Steinmetz of 94th Division had already recognized that the front facing the American IV Corps was crumbling, and the situation compelled von Vietinghoff to deploy 90th Panzer Grenadier Division on the western flank of the gap created by 10th Mountain Division. Vietinghoff ordered that deployment on the 17th, for which he 'was criticized by von Senger in that it left [Fourteenth Army] with no reserve for a future fight in the Po valley'.[39]

On Eighth Army's front, the battle for the Argenta Gap had absorbed the energies of 56th and 78th Divisions, but it was drawing to its conclusion as Truscott's men prepared for their next phase of operations. The plans drawn up by McCreery and Truscott had been sound and were coming to fruition as their soldiers, sensing that the end was not far away, dug deep into their reserves of energy and courage for the break-out onto the Lombardy plain and exploitation to the Po and beyond.

Notes

1. Truscott, op. cit., p.486.
2. Fisher, op. cit., p.471.
3. Ibid.; Truscott, p.487.
4. Truscott, p.487.
5. Jackson, op. cit., p.276.
6. Jenkins, *The Last Ridge*, p.215.
7. Ibid., p.218.
8. Ibid.
9. Ibid., p.219.
10. US Army Center of Military History, http://www.history.army.mil/medalofhonor 23 Nov '13.
11. Fisher, p.72.
12. Rottman, *US 10th Mountain Division in World War II*, p.37; Starr, op. cit., p.400.
13. Shelton, *Climb to Conquer*, p.240.
14. Dole, *One Soldier's Story*, p.148.
15. Ibid.
16. Ibid.
17. Maximiano & Bonalume Neto, *Brazilian Expeditionary Force in World War II*, p.9.
18. Ibid., p.19.
19. Ibid., p.20.
20. Ibid., pp.19–22.
21. Starr, op. cit., p.401.
22. Mascarenhas, *The BEF by its Commander*, p.267.
23. Starr, p.401.
24. Fisher, p.474.
25. Ibid.
26. Starr, p.402.
27. Ibid., p.403.
28. Fisher, p.478.
29. Ibid., p.479.
30. Blaxland, op. cit., p.274.
31. Fisher, p.478.
32. Ibid., p.477.
33. Ibid., pp.477–8.
34. Orpen, *Victory in Italy*, pp.278–9.
35. Fisher, pp.478–9; Belogi & Guglielmi, p.211.
36. Belogi & Guglielmi, p.211.
37. Fisher, pp.474–6; Belogi & Guglielmi, pp.210–11 & 224.
38. Blaxland, p.264.
39. Fisher, p.479.

Chapter Nine

We left 78th Division's Kangaroo Army with the Mobile Force stopped at the Reno and Keightley having to revise his breakthrough plans for Argenta. Vietinghoff had deployed 29th Panzer Grenadier Division to defend Argenta while Herr had moved 278th Division from the mountains to meet the New Zealanders who, at 6.00pm on 14 April, switched from V Corps to Harding's XIII Corps. The mountain sector hitherto held by XIII Corps was handed over to Hawkesworth's X Corps and Harding sent 10th Indian Division on a meandering journey through the rear areas of X and II Polish Corps to deploy in reserve behind the New Zealanders.[1]

Meanwhile, Keightley had decided against an assault crossing of the Reno, into which flowed most of the other waterways already traversed and which was, therefore, much wider. Instead, he resolved to bring 11 Brigade, now 78th Division's leading formation, across the river on a Bailey about three miles east of Bastia on ground held firmly by Gruppo Cremona, which had advanced up to the river alongside 56th Division, whose 167 Brigade continued its advance on Bastia as 169 Brigade maintained pressure on the right flank.[2]

These two brigades of 56th Division had already reduced 42nd Jäger Division to a shadow of what it had been, cracking its morale and leaving it with so little fighting cohesion that its remnants had to be taken under command of other formations. So it was that the principal obstacles in the path of 167 Brigade were not presented by the jägers.[3] Leading the brigade's advance on Bastia were 9th Royal Fusiliers, supported by Shermans from 10th Hussars, but a railway embankment proved a major impediment to the armour's advance. The infantry were able to cross the embankment with care, W Company being first to reach it. It took some time before a 10th Hussars' Sherman was manoeuvred over the obstruction but, when it did, it joined X Company in an attack on a factory at San Biágio on the outskirts of Bastia. As it happened, the enemy had abandoned Bastia, or at least that part of it, and so there was no fighting. Perhaps that was a Godsend. The factory produced treacle and much of its product had spilled from containers ruptured by shellfire or bombs, and the fusiliers found themselves trying to wade through treacle reaching over their boots. A warrant officer all but disappeared from view when he stepped into a treacle-filled bomb crater. The sight was too much for the Sherman crew who burst into laughter at the sergeant major's plight but they soon found themselves in the same predicament as their tank also fell into a hole full of treacle. Had the Germans not abandoned Bastia, this situation could have proved exceptionally difficult for X Company. An Army photographer captured the 'sunken' Sherman on film, preserving its plight for posterity.[4] The pit into which the tank plunged was a cistern full of treacle rather than a bomb or shell crater.[5]

With Bastia in British hands, the next stage was to break through the Argenta Gap. That had to be done quickly so that, once through, the attackers could sever the line of retreat of the greater part of the enemy forces. The need for speed was emphasized by the knowledge that the Germans had inserted a regiment of 29th Panzer Grenadier Division between Argenta and Bando; the newly-arrived troops were ensconced in the high-banked Fossa Marina, which was well fortified. Eighth Army did not have the luxury of the time needed to call up MASAF's heavy bombers to pound the defences. The soldiers on the ground, the men of 56th and 78th Divisions, would have to break the line themselves, with support from fighter-bombers.[6]

The divisional commanders, Whitfield of 56th and Arbuthnott of 78th, were experienced soldiers who had faced similar problems before. Between them, they decided that the main breach of the fossa should be made by 11 Brigade of the Battleaxe Division, to the north-east of Argenta. And so, as dawn was about to break on the 16th, 11 Brigade passed through the Queen's Brigade to traverse three miles of flat, wet countryside. In the lead were 1st East Surreys, on the right, with 5th Northamptons on the left and 2nd Lancashire Fusiliers in reserve; supporting 11 Brigade were tanks of the Bays and 'funnies' of 51 RTR. Resistance was light and those pockets that did exist were dealt with by infantry attacks following air strikes. Mines proved a greater problem, but partisans were able to advise on the locations of many of the minefields, although these thickened closer to the Fossa Marina. As the brigade reached the outskirts of Argenta and the defensive line along the fossa, resistance was much tougher. It became clear that a full-scale assault was necessary.

Arbuthnott's plan was for the Surreys to move forward on the right after dark and secure a firm base for the Lancashire Fusiliers to assault the fossa and outflank Argenta. Next day 38 (Irish) Brigade would pass through the 11 Brigade bridgehead and create manoeuvre room for the Kangaroos.

The preliminary advance was successful, the Fusiliers began their assault, and within twenty minutes were fighting hand-to-hand. As their first company forced their way across the canal the waters were streaked and laced with blood, and ugly with corpses. By midnight, however, the battalion had succeeded in gaining a bridgehead on the far bank of the canal, two companies strong and 200 yards deep. Thanks to the fortitude of the sappers, working steadily under shellfire, there was an Ark bridge behind them and three of the Bays' tanks across it.[7]

The fighting for the bridgehead was desperate. The Germans needed to hang on to their line to ensure the safe withdrawal of their forces to and across the Po, and were determined to wipe out the Lancashires' lodgement. Heavy shellfire and mortars pounded the fusiliers, who also had to repel three counter-attacks. At no time did the Lancashires allow the enemy even the smallest gain. Their commanding officer, Lieutenant Colonel Pulford MC, was wounded and *hors de combat* but his second-in-command, Major J. A. H. Saunders, took command, earning the DSO for his sure and steady handling of the battalion. In spite of all that the Germans threw at the fusiliers, 'as dawn broke our salient still pointed at the enemy's inner defences, and the German troops on its flanks were wavering'.[8]

Part of the reason for that wavering was that the British artillery, supplemented by the Kensingtons' 4.2-inch mortars, had been putting down intensive supporting fire. The beginning of this fire-plan had caught 29th Panzer Grenadier Division's regiment in the process of relieving the earlier defenders of the Fossa Marina. Many Germans were caught in the open and suffered accordingly:

> Only later, as the bridgehead began to expand, did the remarkable results of the fire become apparent. Both from the barrage and from defensive fire the enemy's casualties were exceptionally heavy, and this at a time when he could ill afford to lose a single man.[9]

Although the artillery had played a significant part in the success of the attack, the main burden had fallen on the infantry. Ray describes it as 'chiefly a plain infantry slogging match', an achievement such as could be gained only by foot soldiers, 'a bitter, painful struggle; and a solid valuable prize, though small when measured in yards'.[10]

A Surreys' company was ordered forward at first light on the 17th to protect the Lancashires' left flank and, having ousted some very determined Germans and taken thirty-three prisoners at a cost of twenty-two casualties, established itself in Argenta's north-eastern outskirts.[11] Small though the 11 Brigade bridgehead may have been it represented a crack in the enemy's defences and Major General Arbuthnott knew that the crack could be widened by using the full strength of 78th Division. As he prepared to wield the battleaxe, 5th Northamptons held a line on the edge of Argenta, providing a pivot for the main divisional assault. Supported by flail tanks and M10s, B and D Companies of the Northamptons began probing the German defences south of Argenta as a distractor for the main attack, due to be made from the east.[12] It was time to pass the Irish Brigade through the bridgehead to create elbow room for the Kangaroo Army's next bound.

Arbuthnott ordered Pat Scott's Irish Brigade to pass through the Lancashires' 'tiny bridgehead in order to widen the gap so as to allow the armour and the Kangaroos to pass through'.[13] Such an operation was neither easy to plan nor execute since there was but one track and a single bridge over the Fossa Marina available for the move, which meant that each brigade had to pass through the one in front. Moreover, the timing of the move of the Kangaroo Army was critical: send 2 Armoured Brigade forward too soon and its tanks and APCs would create a traffic jam on the approach to the fossa, blocking the only track and robbing the advance of its momentum. But Eighth Army had come a long way from the days of Montgomery's traffic jam at El Alamein and Leese's in the Liri valley, and good planning, co-operation and execution were second nature to the commanders of the brigades involved. Ray wrote succinctly that 'it all went like clockwork'.[14]

The Irish Brigade passed through, Irish Fusiliers to the right and Inniskillings to the left, and were on their objectives by late afternoon, while the East Surreys came up on the Lancashire Fusiliers' left on the near side of the Fossa Marina and the Northamptons began clearing Argenta. 'Clearing' is both an understatement and a euphemism. 'The few civilians remaining in the town stated that the Germans had withdrawn ... shortly after our troops had entered the Eastern end.'[15] Argenta had been reduced to a mess of rubble, with islands of corpses piled upon each other, and German soldiers held out in cellars and in fortified strongpoints. Throughout the day, C Company of the Northamptons, with Crocodiles of 51 RTR, worked to winkle out the last Germans. By 6.20pm C Company had reached the railway station and, twenty minutes later, the first phase of the operation was complete when the company reached a central crossroads. As darkness came down the gruesome task had been completed, battalion HQ was established and all four rifle companies were in the town.[16] But the Germans had not given up. During the early hours of 18 April a counter-attack, supported by a tank, was launched from the north. Although Ray describes this as a company-strength effort 'with tank support' the Northamptons' war diary notes:

[at 0245] A German tank followed by about 30 men and a further 20 on the flanks came down route 16 and over-ran C Coy's FDLs at [map reference] 274609. Defensive fire was brought down on the road by our arty and a period of confused fighting followed. Other tanks were thought to be in the vicinity but only one was definitely active.[17]

The Northamptons not only beat off the counter-attack, but pushed the attackers into the path of 2nd Inniskillings, who were fighting their way round to the north of Argenta.

The Inniskillings were embroiled in very hard fighting in and around Argenta, a battle that lasted for two days and a night and which saw the first two of the Skins' supporting Shermans of the Bays knocked out by a German self-propelled anti-tank gun while Tigers pinned down the leading infantry sections. Between noon on the 17th and midnight the following day, D Company accounted for a Tiger, took sixty-six prisoners and killed eleven Germans.[18] At one stage the company was also shelled by British guns, which the war diary attributed to supporting fire for an attack by the Faughs, but which Ray believed was for an attack by 2 Commando Brigade.[19]

With Argenta secure it was time for the next phase of 78th Division's operation. This involved by-passing those Germans still fighting just north of the town, as well as leap-frogging both 11 Brigade, the soldiers of which were now quite tired, and the Irish Brigade's two fusilier battle-groups. The baton was to be taken up by 36 Brigade with 2 Armoured Brigade's Kangaroo Army. Arbuthnott intended 36 Brigade to advance at the earliest opportunity to Boccaleone, two miles from Argenta on the road through the Gap, and Consandolo, after which the Kangaroos would advance north-north-west towards the two canals twixt San Nicolo and Portomaggiore.

At 2.00am on the 18th the Royal West Kents left their start line for Boccaleone, striking across country since the Germans were then counter-attacking the Northamptons in Argenta and it was thought that there might be tanks on the road north. Then the Argylls moved off for Consandolo: 'two spearheads were driven in on the rear flank of the enemy whilst he was concentrating on an attempt to take Argenta.'[20] When dawn broke the West Kents were entering Boccaleone from the east and the Argylls closing on Consandolo. There were still pockets of resistance, with small groups of Germans determined to fight it out.

A more significant pocket, however, was located in Sant'Antonio, west of Argenta on Highway 16. Faced by Allied troops on three sides, and with the river on the west, these men had no intention of giving up, and their chances of being able to withdraw were almost non-existent. Although 78th Division's reconnaissance regiment, 56 Recce, was deployed to clear Sant'Antonio it proved impossible for the regiment to make significant progress, so many were the demolitions and so poor the going for vehicles.[21] (The regiment was equipped with American Greyhound armoured cars and some Humber light recce cars.)

Boccaleone was in the hands of 6th Royal West Kents by 9.30am, as were thirty-eight Germans and a self-propelled gun. But the Argylls had encountered the fiercest resistance they had met thus far in the offensive, with four of their supporting tanks out of action in rapid succession, while German infantry had closed with their attackers and bayonets were used. In addition, the Argylls were subjected to heavy mortar and artillery fire, but the fighting was so close that British guns could not be brought into play due to the great risk to the Argylls. Still the battle continued and, even when the Argylls called for air support, shortly after noon, the Germans persisted with their resistance. Consandolo was all but destroyed but the defenders refused to be cowed. Not until a heavy bombardment supporting an infantry assault at about 4.00pm did the remains of the village fall. The defenders had taken literally their führer's order not to yield any ground.[22]

While the Argylls were engaged in their grim struggle, the Kangaroo Army was again on the move, to the right of the Argylls, having passed the Irish Fusiliers, and was in the open, the tanks of the armoured units engaging enemy tanks and SPGs. In the words of Bala Bredin, CO of the Irish Rifles, 'This was an unforgettable move'. The Kangaroos and tanks passed through the orchards north of Argenta, moving through the narrow gap between lake and canal, and passing over the single bridge that had been built across the main water obstacle. All around lay the wrecks of enemy vehicles and equipment, and the bodies of dead German soldiers:[23]

By mid-morning the whole front was ablaze. The Armoured Brigade, aiming at the twin canals Fossa di Porto and Scolo Bolognese, was forcing its way out into the open with the railway on the right and the unprotected flank on the left. Further west the Argylls were held up just short of Consandolo by determined enemy in strong points, and to the left again was an open flank down Route 16, until the Royal West Kents were met in Boccaleone, mopping up some difficult enemy pockets. Further south the RAF, at the request of 36 Brigade, was attacking [Sant'Antonio] and shortly afterwards 56 Recce made a little progress up Route 16 towards this troublesome block.[24]

That evening the Kangaroo Army had made solid progress. As the advance continued, the weight of armour made itself felt and the result was counted in the increasing number of prisoners. At about 5.00pm the tanks had found an intact crossing of the Fossa Benvignante, and both AFVs and infantry were soon making for the next obstacle:

> As it was now late in the evening, this took the enemy completely by surprise and an officers' mess, a battery of 15cm guns, a battery of 88mm guns and numerous smaller AA and A.Tk pieces together with approx. 200 prisoners were overrun. This all in spite of the enemy's attempts to hold us by close range firing over open sights. By the light of numerous burning houses and with a sense of complete victory, the battalion moved to its final area for the night in the vicinity of Palazzo and Coltra, having already three intact bridges over the next canal in its hands.[25]

This penetration, made by three squadrons of 9th Lancers and Irish Rifles, had reached the gun lines of 42nd Jäger Division. Jackson comments that 'the number of prisoners became embarrassing', putting their number at 'over 450', more than twice the figure quoted by Bredin.[26] Blaxland's comments on the success of the Kangaroo Army are interesting:

> Arbuthnott had been wise to keep this team intact, and by dash and fine co-operation they gleaned a tremendous haul, which included two bridges over the wide Fossa Benvignante, four tanks, twenty guns ranging in calibre from 150mm to 88mm, and 455 prisoners. It was a great achievement, far from lightly won, gained under the command of two officers who had fought the Germans in 1940 and had suffered wound and won decoration at regular intervals, ever since, Price of the 9th Lancers and 'Bala' Bredin of the London Irish Rifles.[27]

By now the Germans were in considerable confusion. The doughty resistance of 29th Panzer Grenadier Division had not been enough to stop 78th Division and the shattered remnants of 42nd Jäger were busy trying to surrender; even 17th and 132nd Field Regiments were accepting jäger prisoners. However, there were still some pockets holding out along Highway 16, which was to be the axis of advance for 6th Armoured Division as it struck towards Ferrara. South of Boccaleone a furious battle developed, involving most units in the vicinity. Under a heavy bombardment, 2 Commando Brigade attacked from the south, followed by 2nd Inniskillings who cleared houses and floodbanks until dawn when the West Kents arrived from the north, closing the noose around the enemy and bringing that particular fight to an end. Meanwhile 5th Buffs had marched, literally, across country under cover of darkness to reach Benvignante and had pushed farther than any of the armour. Theirs had been the longest foot march of Operation BUCKLAND and brought 78th Division into the open and through the Argenta Gap. In some sixty hours of operations that involved every battalion and armoured unit in the division, Arbuthnott's command had driven 29th Panzer Grenadier Division, and elements of 26th Panzer, 42nd Jäger, 98th and 362nd Infantry Divisions, from their defensive positions and into retreat on the plain of the Po.[28]

> The Division was out in the open, and 6th Armoured Division was about to pass through, striking north-west for Ferrara along Route 16; the Argenta Gap was broken and the enemy lay, straggled out along the southern bank of the Po, vulnerable at a hundred points.[29]

Some indication of the scale of the defeat that the Germans had suffered may be gleaned from a look at the wider scale of operations on 17 April. This was the day when 24 Guards Brigade crossed the Fossa Marina-Canaletta di Bando, both east and west of Fiorana, an advance made by 2nd Coldstream over a Bailey at 4.00pm, exploiting an earlier crossing of the Fossa Marina by the Scots Guards. Having made the crossing, the Coldstream advanced over open, mined and flooded countryside for more than a mile. To those difficulties was added the surprise of a strafing attack by a lone German or ANR fighter-bomber.[30]

The 17th was also the day on which 2 Commando Brigade, still under command of 56th Division, ousted some of the survivors of 42nd Jäger Division from Idrovora Saiarino. No. 2 Commando had earlier passed through No. 43 Commando to launch the attack, Operation WOODBINE, at 9.00am, following an air and artillery bombardment. After ninety minutes, the commandos had the bridge area which they held against several counter-attacks over the next five hours. With 2 Commando Brigade advancing along the Reno and 169 (Queen's) Brigade arriving, the pressure on the defenders of Argenta was building. When the sappers had a Bailey across the Fossa Marina less than a mile north of Argenta, 2/6th Queen's received permission to cross the canal. Meanwhile, a road was being built farther to the east. During the previous night I/29th Panzer Grenadier Regiment and 29th Artillery Regiment, both of 29th Panzer Grenadier Division, had arrived at Portomaggiore from Treviso, but it proved impossible to commit them in time to halt the British advance.[31]

V Corps' task had been made even more difficult by the Germans extending their programme of creating yet more obstacles. Their engineers had increased the flooding programme, sabotaging vital pumping stations, and had cratered roads running on embankments.[32] As ever in Italy, German engineers played a critical part in defensive schemes, but now the front was widening as they lost the protection of Lake Comácchio on their left flank and the Reno on the right. That V Corps had succeeded in the task set it, however, was proved at noon on 18 April when McCreery released 6th Armoured Division to V Corps. The Argenta Gap had been breached.

When V Corps had begun its operations on 9 April it had done so with a view to developing attacks on two axes, the northern directed on the Argenta Gap and the north-western towards Bologna. On 14 April 2nd New Zealand Division had been switched from V Corps to XIII Corps, which was being brought into the battle to take over the north-westerly advance, leaving V Corps to concentrate on the Argenta Gap. In addition to the New Zealanders, Harding's XIII Corps included 10th Indian Division. On the New Zealand left, II Polish Corps was also pushing north-westward.

As before, the New Zealanders had hustled the Germans as they pushed their way forward, the advance of XIII Corps tying in with that of Fifth Army's IV Corps to outflank the enemy from east and west. XIII Corps had begun its operations on the Sunday, 15 April, when 10th Indian Division established a fresh, if shallow, bridgehead over the Sillaro near Villa Serraglio. The New Zealanders' crossing of the Sillaro, postponed for a day to allow the development of the artillery fire-plan, opened with 6 Brigade on the right and 9 on the left, the attack being made by 24th and 26th Battalions of 6 Brigade and 22nd and the Divisional Cavalry Battalions of 9. The artillery massed to cover the assault included seven field regiments, four medium regiments (including one from II Polish Corps), a battery of 155mm guns, a battery of 55th HAA Regiment and C Squadron 18th Armoured Regiment, using its tanks in the artillery role.[33] At 2.00am on the 14th the artillery opened fire; the guns were to bombard the opening line, the Scolo Correcchio, for thirty minutes before advancing at the rate of 100 yards in five minutes for 2,500 yards, and dwelling for the final fifteen minutes 'on a straight line 300 yards beyond the farthest bend in the Sillaro just north of the railway'.[34]

Almost no effective opposition was presented to the attack. Six Brigade had occupied positions on the far bank by dawn and taken prisoners from 278th Volksgrenadier Division, which had arrived to relieve the exhausted and battered 98th Division. By midnight, the brigade was almost at Fantuzza, with many more prisoners, and had knocked out two Panther tanks. In the 9 Brigade sector, four Panthers fell victims to PIATs or phosphorous grenades and 27th Battalion penetrated as far as Sesto Imolese. The Germans were forced to pull back more than a mile, losing some of their Hetzer SP 75mm (or Jagdpanzer 38s) anti-tank guns.[35]

Meanwhile the Poles were also making good progress. Rak Group, elements of 2 Warsaw Armoured Brigade with engineers and artillery, crossed the Sillaro at 6.00pm under heavy enemy fire on the corps left flank, allowing 16th Battalion of 6 Lwowska Brigade to advance on Castel Guelfo from the south-east. At much the same time 4 Wołynska Brigade, of Rud Force, supported by 8 RTR, reached the Sillaro in front of Castel San Pietro. On the right flank, 2/10th Gurkhas of 43 Brigade, still under Polish command, advanced on Medicina, carried in Kangaroos of 14th/20th Hussars. And in the south, in X Corps' area, Friuli Group's 3/87th and 2/88th, with 1/184th Nembo, had converged on Dozza at 9.30am while the remaining battalions of Nembo deployed to the Sillaro valley in the west. Fallschirmjäger at Monte del Re, desperate to hold the southern pivot on the Laura Line, fought off an attack by the Bafile and Grado Battalions of San Marco Regiment.[36]

All of this action, it will be remembered, took place as IV US Corps was making its own steady progress and had occupied much of Vergato and taken Monte Sole, inflicting heavy casualties on the enemy.

In XIII Corps' area Medicina fell on the 16th, the day on which 10 Indian Brigade came into action with 4/10th Baluch Regiment and 2/4th Gurkhas forcing the Scolo Sillaro, a wide canal running north-by-north-east, although the liberators of Medicina were actually men of 43 Gurkha Brigade, still under command of II Polish Corps, which had enveloped Imola and crossed the Sillaro on the night of the 15th/16th, with Gurkhas on the right and 5th Kresowa Division on the left. Supported by 2 RTR, 2/6th Gurkhas in Kangaroos of 14th/20th Hussars took Medicina to give the Hussars one of their three Second World War battle honours. In spite of the presence of troops of 10th Fallschirmjäger Regiment, and Italian 105mm self-propelled guns manned by a Luftwaffe unit, Medicina fell to the Gurkhas and the Hussars after a brief but intense fight.[37]

Harding had decreed that his policy was to maintain progress on the New Zealand Division's axis and feed 10th Indian in 'on the right or left of the ... Division depending on how things went'.[38] That policy was now being put into effect as Freyberg's division extended its bridgehead over the Sillaro.

Both to the north and south the bridgehead was expanding, with fascines being laid south of Sesto Imolese an hour after midnight; the building of a Bailey north of the railway followed about three hours later. While engaged on their bridging task the sappers were subjected to enemy artillery fire but persevered with their work, and by 7.00am two armoured regiments, 20th and 19th, had crossed the river and the division was advancing, under cover of heavy mist, towards the Medicina canal. In that advance, 6 Brigade led with 25th Battalion to the right and 26th to the left and tanks of 20th Armoured Regiment in support. By noon the brigade and its tanks were at the Scolo Sillaro where a halt was called until sappers constructed a fascine crossing of this wide waterway for the tanks in 25th Battalion's sector. With the crossing complete, the advance resumed and both battalions had reached the Scolo Montanara by 7.00pm. Ahead lay the Gaiana river, the next significant barrier, which the Germans had planned to defend. And 2nd New Zealand Division had gained another brigade with the transfer of 43 Gurkha Brigade to Freyberg's command, another marker of Harding's determination to maintain progress on the New Zealand axis. The Gurkha brigade was already operating in XIII Corps' area as a stretch of front over a mile long was transferred from the Poles to the New Zealanders; on the other flank the New Zealanders handed over a similar stretch of front to 10th Indian.[39]

Although the Polish Corps had suffered a series of counter-attacks, it had consolidated its bridgehead over the Sillaro. Having taken Castel Guelfo, with the support of Rak Group, 5 Wilenska and 6 Lwowska Brigades followed the New Zealand advance as 3 Carpathian Rifle and 4 Wolynska Brigades of Rud Force advanced on Castel San Pietro along Highway 9. Gruppo Friuli, in the X Corps area, pushed 88th Regiment as far as the Sillaro banks where, at Medazzuoli, an hour before midnight, the regiment was counter-attacked by 3rd Fallschirmjäger Regiment.[40]

The Gaiana was one of several small watercourses between Medicina and Budrio, the others being the Acquarolo, Quaderna, Fossatone (a tributary of the Quaderna) and the Centonara Vecchia, while beyond Budrio was the larger Idice river, into which these other streams and canals flow. The Idice, 'yet another formidable, high-banked river'[41] was also the defensive line that the Germans had dubbed the Genghis Khan Line. This was to be manned by I Fallschirmjäger Corps, but that formation was now facing threat from the south-east instead of, as expected, the east and was having to swing to face that threat. Before moving into the Genghis Khan Line, the Fallschirmjäger Corps deployed into an intermediate line on the Quaderna canal, manned by 278th Volksgrenadier Division, and on the Gaiana river, manned by 1st and 4th Fallschirmjäger Divisions. Both fallschirmjäger divisions were in positions dug into the floodbanks, which were about eighteen feet high. Five fallschirmjäger battalions, supported by ten Panthers, faced the New Zealanders, while the weakened 278th Division with ten Tigers faced 10th Indian Division, and four fallschirmjäger battalions, reinforced by the hurriedly deployed reconnaissance battalion of 305th Division, faced II Polish Corps. Behind the fallschirmjäger line was 26th Panzer Division, with about fifty Mark IVs and two weak panzer grenadier regiments, which was moving northward via Malalbergo.[42]

The Gaiana proved a formidable obstacle for XIII Corps, although it had been expected to be otherwise. In the New Zealand sector, 9 Brigade's advance was led by 22nd and 27th Battalions, which had differing fortunes. Although 22nd Battalion reached its objective beyond the Quaderna, clearing pockets of opposition en route, 27th was engaged by German self-propelled artillery when it moved forward to attack the floodbanks. While SPGs engaged the New Zealanders' tanks from the flanks, the fallschirmjäger opened fire with machine guns and heavy mortars. Counter-attacks were directed at both battalions, the 22nd being struck at 6.00pm and 27th two hours later. The former was relieved by the Divisional Cavalry Battalion by midnight, while the 27th was digging in and consolidating. Forming the second prong of the New Zealand attack was 43 Gurkha Brigade, whose supporting tanks of 2 RTR reported that the Germans still held the river line on that front. That the Germans were determined to hold the line was proved when, at about noon, the Kangaroo-borne 2/6th Gurkhas crossed the river on a wide front along the Medicina-Bologna road only to suffer heavy losses, forcing withdrawal in a disorganized state.[43] This setback, described by Blaxland as 'a smarting repulse', left the brigade with only one fresh battalion for the operations to follow.[44]

A fresh plan was devised. It seems that Freyberg, concentrating too much on the Idice, had been lulled into a sense of false security about the Gaiana. Considerable thought and preparation went into the next attack on the Gaiana. Freyberg discussed harassing fire with his Commander Royal Artillery (CRA):

> The Germans opposing the Division were 'fresh from the mountains and haven't been shelled for some time. We will have to educate them.' He obtained an assurance from Gentry [commanding 9 Brigade] that the enemy had not gone, and told him, 'Do not fight tonight. It is no good having a little bridgehead.' He advised 5 and 6 Brigades to be sure to get plenty of rest, and he assured Barker [commanding 43 Brigade] that it was 'going to be tough, but OK, we will put

some solid harassing [fire] in front of you tomorrow.' Barker said the enemy had panicked in Medicina the previous night, 'but the para boys fought like hell against us today. We gave them everything we had – fought them hard and they still came back on us. We killed a lot of them today because of their sheer bravado. They are really fanatical.' The General replied, 'After we have finished with them they will be in a ripe state to yield us plenty of PW!'[45]

It was decided that the new attack would not be made that night but the following night, allowing more time for preparation. As well as 2nd New Zealand Division, 10th Indian and II Polish Corps troops would also be involved. The Germans were not only waiting for a renewed onslaught, but were also aggressive, sending a counter-attack force into the New Zealand positions on the afternoon of the 18th.[46] It was known that the Germans had not got many men but were very strong in weapons and were dug in on the reverse side of the near floodbank as well as the far bank. Brigadier Gentry suggested that the situation suited 'another SENIO technique'. Thus flame-throwers were to be included in the plan.[47]

The artillery fireplan for the attack included all three regiments of the New Zealand divisional artillery, another three field regiments, two batteries of a fourth field regiment, four medium regiments, two heavy batteries, a battery of 3.7-inch HAA guns and a battery of LAA guns.[48] Even with such firepower on hand, Freyberg was still concerned about the operation, worrying that the enemy might have slipped away from the banks of the Gaiana:

He had to justify this tremendous expenditure of shells. He had to show results, German casualties in dead, wounded and prisoners on the morrow. Above all he was gravely worried about our own casualties. Even with the Gurkhas to help this must be our last attack, or at the best our last but one. Yet he knew the Division was desperately anxious to be in the open warfare which must come soon, and which had been promised to the Eighth Army all the way up Italy. He knew too that we were better fitted, from our desert days, for open warfare than anyone else in Italy.[49]

Although it was not appreciated at the time, the assault on the Gaiana river was to be the last major attack of the Italian campaign. It began at 9.30 that evening when the guns opened fire, tearing the sky like a series of electrical storms. Almost 72,500 rounds were fired with the field and medium guns shooting on a 3,600-yard frontage along the Gaiana, which then lifted 500 yards and, an hour after the first shots had been fired, began moving forward at 100 yards in five minutes to a depth of over 3,000 yards, dwelling for thirty minutes en route. While the fields and mediums were thus engaged, the heavies and mediums, heavy anti-aircraft guns and mortars fired in the counter-battery and counter-mortar roles as well as putting down timed concentrations. The Bofors light anti-aircraft guns were used to mark brigade – and dummy – boundaries on both flanks.[50]

The Crocodile and Wasp flame-throwers, deployed one every fifty yards, joined in at 10.00pm:

The fearful molten streams curved through the air and slobbered all over the river. Soon the levees were outlined in sizzling, licking fire and looked like walls of hot lava. At every fresh spout of the flaming fluid, the glare would light up the pillaring clouds of smoke giving the sky the appearance of a display of the southern aurora.[51]

The infantry, who had been pulled back 500 yards before the bombardment, moved off as the flame-throwers finished and were quickly across the Gaiana. Blaxland writes that 'Great slaughter was inflicted on the men of 4th Para, and there were signs that even their morale was beginning to wither, most of all under the flame cast upon them by Crocodiles and Wasps'.[52] Slaughter there truly was: those fallschirmjäger deployed on the near stopbank suffered the full weight of the artillery bombardment and the flames of Crocodiles and Wasps. Thus 9 Brigade, with the Divisional Cavalry Battalion and 22nd Battalion leading, crossed almost without hindrance and found many burnt corpses. Both battalions pushed on for over 3,000 yards to the limit of the bombarded area before they met significant opposition as machine guns, mortars and Nebelwerfers opened up on them. On the right flank of 43 Brigade 2/8th Gurkhas met only light opposition as they made for the Fossatone canal and despatched two companies towards the Quaderna river. It was a different story on the left flank, however, where 2/10th Gurkhas ran into determined resistance and were unable to keep pace with 2/8th. The fallschirmjäger in 9 Brigade's area were concentrating their machine-gun, mortar and Nebelwerfer fire on the river to prevent the sappers building bridges, but it proved possible to bulldoze a crossing in 22nd Battalion's sector; this would be used to pass the armour through for the advance to Budrio. A Bailey was built on the Medicina-Castanaso road in 43 Brigade's area and 19th Armoured Regiment's Shermans were able to cross at 6.15am. A German counter-attack was mounted on the Divisional Cavalry Battalion half an hour later, and it was not until late afternoon that resistance ended, allowing the advance to resume with support from 19th Regiment tanks. Harassing fire continued from mortars and concealed SPGs but some bridges were found intact, another sign that the Germans were losing cohesion, and 28 Assault Squadron bridged the Quaderna with a scissors bridge. So swift was the advance that the leading troop of 19th Armoured had gone beyond the bomb line and been set upon by Desert Air Force Spitfire fighter-bombers.[53]

In II Polish Corps' sector, 5 Wilenska Brigade had suffered a night of unending counter-attacks, but had been able to launch an attack at 8.00am. Preceded by an artillery bombardment, 13th, 14th and 15th Battalions of 5 Brigade had pushed forward and were over the Gaiana by 11.00am. Rud Force also attacked, at 10.00am, but met fierce resistance from I/1st Fallschirmjäger Regiment at the heavily-bombed Palazzo Coccapane. Also involved in that battle, although they were in X Corps' area, were 88th Regiment and 2/ and 3/184th Regiment of Gruppo Folgore, which, also at 10 o'clock, attacked Casalecchio de'Conti and Casa Grinzane.[54]

As the New Zealanders set off for Budrio and the Genghis Khan Line along the Idice, there was little doubt that the Germans were soon to lose Bologna for the Americans were irrupting onto the flat lands from the mountains to the west and New Zealanders, Poles and Italians were threatening to complete the encirclement from the east. Vietinghoff defied the orders from OKW and Hitler and decided that withdrawal was essential. On the 19th he instructed the Army of Liguria to execute *Herbstnebel*; next day he ordered a general withdrawal from the Bologna area, reporting his decision to Hitler in a signal which also asked the dictator for his approval, which was, of course, refused.[55]

Notes

1. Blaxland, op. cit., p.264; Jackson, op. cit., pp.275–9; Ray, op. cit., pp.206–8; NA, WO170/4240, HQV Corps (G), 1945.
2. Jackson, pp.282–3; Ray, pp.209–10.
3. Williams, op. cit., pp.116–17; Belogi & Guglielmi, op. cit., pp.218–19.
4. Blaxland, p.264.
5. Belogi & Guglielmi, p.205
6. Blaxland, pp.264–5.
7. Ibid.; Ray, p.208.
8. Ibid.
9. Ibid., p.209.
10. Ibid.
11. Jackson, p.282; Blaxland, pp.265–6.
12. NA, WO170/5051, war diary, 5 Northants, 1945.
13. Ray, p.210.
14. Ibid.
15. NA, WO170/5051, op. cit.
16. Ibid.; Blaxland, p.266.
17. NA, WO170/5051, op. cit.; Ray, p.210.
18. NA, WO170/5018, war diary, 2 Innisks, 1945.
19. Ibid.; Ray, p.210.
20. Ray, p.211.
21. Ibid.; Belogi & Guglielmi, pp.232–3.
22. Belogi & Guglielmi, p.233; Ray, p.211.
23. Bredin, 'Account of the Kangaroo Army'.
24. Ray, p.212.
25. Bredin.
26. Jackson, p.283.
27. Blaxland, pp.266–7.
28. Ray, pp.211–13; Blaxland, pp.267–8; Belogi & Guglielmi, pp.233–4.
29. Ray, p.213.
30. Belogi & Guglielmi, pp.218–25.
31. Ibid.

32. NA, WO170/4192; war diary Eighth Army and British Troops Austria, Jan-Jly '45, Intelligence Summaries 903, 904 & 905, 15, 16 & 17 Apr '45
33. Kay, p.456.
34. Ibid., p.449.
35. Ibid.; Belogi & Guglielmi, pp.191–4.
36. Belogi & Guglielmi, p.194; *I Gruppi di Combattimento*, pp.209–12.
37. Ibid.
38. Kay, p.452.
39. Ibid., pp.456–60.
40. Belogi & Guglielmi, p.209; *I Gruppi di Combattimento*, pp.209–12.
41. Blaxland, p.271.
42. Jackson, pp.278–80; Belogi & Guglielmi, pp.219–22; Kay, pp.465–7.
43. Kay, pp.465–70; Belogi & Guglielmi, pp.219–22.
44. Blaxland, p.271.
45. Kay, pp.470–1.
46. Ibid., p.471.
47. Ibid., pp.472–3.
48. Ibid., p.473.
49. Quoted in Kay, p.474.
50. Kay, p.475.
51. Quoted in ibid.
52. Blaxland, p.271.
53. Kay, pp.475–80; Belogi & Guglielmi, pp.221–2; NA, WO170/4634, war diary, 2 RTR, 1945.
54. Belogi & Guglielmi, pp.222–3.
55. Jackson, p.284.

Chapter Ten

As Freyberg's men overcame the German defences along the Gaiana and pushed towards the Genghis Khan Line, Crittenberger's IV Corps was about to strike onto the plain from the mountains. Regrouping of the corps placed 1st Armored Division east of the Panaro river, strengthening 10th Mountain Division's exposed left flank. On the mountaineers' right, 85th Division had moved into place. IV Corps' advance did not slow down as these changes were effected, and '10th Mountain Division continued to serve as the spearhead in [IV Corps'] drive down the last rolling hills toward the Po Valley'.[1]

At midnight on the 17th the 85th, 87th and 86th Mountain Infantry were in line from left to right; eleven miles ahead of our most advanced elements lay Highway 9, the main east-west artery behind the German lines. On the 18th the 86th Mountain Infantry advanced swiftly to the hamlet of Sulmonte, two and one-half miles north of Montepastore; then in the afternoon resistance stiffened as the men attempted to move north-east about 1,000 yards from Sulmonte to Mongiorgio. A heavy battle developed, and by 1900 the enemy was resisting with artillery, mortar, machine-gun and small-arms fire. The leading elements of the battalion pulled back toward Sulmonte and held for the night. On the right the 2nd Battalion moved to the north-east from Montepastore toward the village of San Chierlo against considerable machine-gun and small-arms fire. Despite this resistance the enemy was withdrawing as rapidly as possible, harassed though he was by our many air attacks on his horse-drawn columns. By evening the 10th Mountain Division had captured 2,917 prisoners, and small scattered groups all along the front were still surrendering.[2]

On the 18th the Brazilians also completed the relief of 85th Mountain Infantry, which then moved to San Chierlo and, next morning, passed through the 86th to lead the divisional, and corps, advance. This was the day on which von Vietinghoff ordered the Army of Luguria to begin its withdrawal. It was also the day on which, notes Fifth Army's historian, 'the enemy withdrawal broke into a rout'.[3] By 4.30pm 1/85th Mountain Infantry held a road junction three miles north-east of Monte San Michele, pausing there to allow its supporting elements and reserves to come up. On the left, 87th, having taken over the battle at Mongiorgio that morning, gained control of the village by mid-morning after some sharp fighting before pushing forward on 85th's left; the resistance at the village had been a screen to cover the continuing German withdrawal. No organized opposition met the advance of 86th

Regiment on the division's right flank. By the evening of 19 April all three regiments 'could look northward over the last few rolling hills into the Po Valley'.[4] Next day they debouched from the foothills onto the plain, spreading out on the valley floor with Ponte Samoggia, where, as its name suggests, Highway 9 crosses the Samoggia on a bridge ten miles north of Bologna, as their objective. By 3.00pm 1/86th, on the centre line of the advance, had crossed Highway 9. Five hours later 3/86th had secured Ponte Samoggia. The other two regiments were not far behind, 85th on the right and 87th on the left.[5]

Tenth Mountain had only a small complement of artillery, in the form of 75mm pack howitzers, light guns that could be moved easily in difficult terrain and could fire in the upper register to clear crests. However, the division also had a British medium artillery regiment supporting it. This was 178th (Lowland) Medium Regiment, a Scottish TA unit, equipped with sixteen 5.5-inch medium guns in two batteries. The commanding officer of 178th Medium Regiment later wrote of his unit's time with the mountaineers, for whom he had great respect.

> Since April 14th the Division, with the sixteen 5.5 guns of 178th (Lowland) Medium Regiment as its sole medium artillery support, had been fighting its way down from the mountains, and had covered some twenty miles over difficult tracks repeatedly blocked by enemy demolitions.[6]

In the seven days since CRAFTSMAN began, 10th Mountain had smashed through the defences in the Apennines to advance the sixteen miles from Castel d'Aiano to Highway 9. The division had been in the van of IV Corps since the beginning and, on the 20th, continued to lead, with 1st Armored behind and to their left, and 85th Division behind and to the right.

East of the Samoggia the Germans were so disorganized they could offer no real resistance to the Americans pressing towards the plain. However, west of the Samoggia, 1st Armored Division was still meeting resistance. 'Old Ironsides' had sidestepped across the rear of 10th Mountain and its left flank defence efforts had assisted greatly Hays' advance. Meanwhile, 85th Division, the Custermen, which, with 10th Mountain, had led off the renewed IV Corps advance was advancing on the right:

> From the first the 85th Division … experienced no contest. Trying to withdraw, the Germans had become so disorganized that they found it difficult to make a stand anywhere. By nightfall of the first day the two leading regiments of the 85th Division had advanced five miles to hills north of the village of Piano di Venola, halfway between Vergato and Praduro.[7]

The Custer Division had led, with 338th Regiment on the right and 337th on the left, on a broad front almost four miles wide. It was on the left that 'occasional spotty resistance'[8] was encountered beyond Monte Luminasio; 2/337th and 3/338th had attacked and passed Monte Luminasio, taking Monte Torrenara 'without much difficulty' before meeting much stiffer defence on the Laguno ridge. While the two battalions closed on the enemy on Laguno ridge, just before dawn, the division was ordered to change its boundaries.[9] A westward shift was called for: 88th Division of II Corps had encroached on the Custermen's ground in a parallel shift of II Corps that resulted from the 'eagerness [of the 88th] to reach the flat country of the Lombardy plain beckoning ahead'.[10] However, the Blue Devils' sidestep caused confusion with the division becoming 'the bottom of a gigantic T trying to punch through a top which was the 10th and 85th Divisions'. A speedy and simple resolution was implemented by having 88th Division units 'relieve in place all 85th Division units as they were overtaken'.[11]

As a result of this redrawing of boundaries, 338th Regiment, advancing along Highway 64, was ordered into reserve and relieved by 6th South African Armoured Division. In reality, this was more a case of its being pinched out, since the South Africans, 'crossing the Reno to get on Highway 64, encountered 88th Division elements north of the 85th Division and moved on from there'.[12] Only 1/337th Regiment of 85th Division was not affected by the boundary change; it remained far out on the left flank and was directed to continue pushing northwards. Although held up near Rasiglio for most of the 19th, the battalion renewed its advance next day, making for Gesso, six miles west of Bologna, which was taken at 8.25am on the 20th. The next objective was Casalecchio, on the outskirts of Bologna. In Casalecchio a bridge had been important to the enemy in maintaining a supply route into the city; it was now important to them for evacuating the city.[13]

At this point the Po Valley was not quite a level plain. But passing down through the hedges bordering the gently swelling fields the troops had begun the great advance through the Po Valley, meeting almost the last stiff resistance they were to encounter in the European war. The tanks moved slowly ahead, the jeeps following, the riflemen in files on either side of the road went slowly, not knowing what they were to meet in the way of resistance. From the hills to the rear and sides sniper fire and a few artillery and mortar rounds drove them occasionally into the ditches beside the hedges. But when this sporadic fire ceased the advance along the road was taken up again.[14]

There was also resistance in the hills to the right where 1/ and 3/337th were advancing at a slower pace as they engaged small German groups who fought tenaciously before surrendering. While this hill fighting was still underway, Truscott ordered 85th Division to deploy forces to its right in a broad sweep across the front of both 88th Infantry and 6th South African Armoured Divisions. These elements from the Custer Division were to make for Casalecchio and establish outposts along the road leading north-west from there to cut off the Germans' line of retreat along Highway 64. The task was assigned to a reinforced 2/337th, which established its outpost line by midnight, having had a tough fight, during which five artillery battalions bombarded Casalecchio. With the outpost line extending westward from the high ground above Casalecchio to the Communale bridge over the Lavino, the exit into the

Po valley was secure. In the meantime, troops of 6th South African Armoured had entered Casalecchio:[15]

> Many Germans were cut off by the quick thrust around from the left, and fighting and movement continued throughout the evening. After midnight the 351st Infantry on the right and the 338th Infantry on the left passed through to continue without let-up the drive to smash the German forces before us. Casualties in the 85th Division for the period 18–20 April had totalled only 88 in all.[16]

By Wednesday 18 April 1st Armored Division's combat commands had been re-organized: Combat Command A (CCA) included 1st Tank, 14th Armored Infantry and 19th Armored Field Artillery Battalions, part of 81st Cavalry Reconnaissance Squadron (Mechanized) and part of 16th Armored Engineer Battalion; CCB included 4th Tank, 11th Armored Infantry and 27th Armored Field Artillery Battalions with the remainder of 81st Cavalry Reconnaissance Squadron; CCC comprised 13th Tank and 6th Armored Infantry Battalions. These organizations could be adapted to suit circumstances, the basic intention of the system being flexible formations. Each new grouping, each further divided into three columns, had been established by 6.00am on the 18th.[17]

Combat Command A made for the Samoggia, encountering intense fire from some German SPGs en route but the centre column had taken Savigno by 6.30pm and, by dusk, was some four miles beyond on the west side of the river. However, counterattacks forced it to pull back two miles during the night. The left column of CCA was stopped east of Montombraro, or Monte Ombraro, a hilltop road junction and a strongpoint guarding the German withdrawal route through Zocca. CCB, having passed Chiesa Nuova, took Monte Termine and then attacked Montombraro, which was defended by what remained of 754th Regiment of 334th Volksgrenadier Division. Meanwhile CCC had advanced to Savigno, reaching there at 6.30pm, before the bulk of the command joined forces with CCB in the fighting at Montombraro. The defenders fought tenaciously, and some Shermans were destroyed by mines, SP anti-tank guns or *Panzerfäuste*.[18]

Substantial progress had been made during the day; 1st Armored's thrust down the left was bearing the brunt of enemy efforts to strike into the flank of 10th Mountain's spearhead probing for the Po valley. On the 18th the chief source of opposition had been infantry and anti-tank weapons. Late in the day the Germans brought up the armor of 90th Panzer Grenadier Division, and on the 19th tank fought tank as the enemy made desperate efforts to stop or slow the breakthrough, which by then was assuming disastrous proportions.[19]

The 19th was a decisive day. First Armored was protecting the flank of IV Corps so effectively that the pressure on 10th Mountain and 85th Divisions reduced considerably. As Fisher comments, 'With the 1st Armored Division obviously capable of handling the nuisance on the flank, the 10th Mountain and 85th Divisions had no cause for concern.'[20] The 19th was also the day on which von Vietinghoff ordered the

Army of Liguria to begin its withdrawal, and on which he also informed Hitler that Army Group C could survive only through a 'mobile strategy':

> His dutiful assurance that he 'awaited the Führer's orders' evoked a reply briefly summarized in OKW's log for 20 April: he was informed that 'local break throughs' were not to occasion continued retractions of his front, and that any commander who 'entertained thoughts of defeat' must be dealt with most severely.[21]

Over the days that followed OKW continued to issue unrealistic – even fantastic – orders. With Hitler obsessed with Berlin and his own fate, which he regarded as intertwined, and Dönitz authorized, from 20 April, to act on Hitler's behalf in controlling forces in the northern sector of the Reich, OKW had a free hand with what was happening on the southern fronts. Some sense of realism began to emerge with, for example, Jodl authorizing a withdrawal by Army Group C to the Ticino-Po line on the 23rd although there was still something delusional about his thinking. The withdrawal was intended to ensure sufficient troops to man the Voralpen Line in the foothills of the Alps, thus preserving Army Group C for the 'fight against Bolshevism'. Next day, Jodl informed the southern army groups that the struggle against Bolshevism 'must be waged to the last consequence'. Hitler intervened on the 24th with an order to construct an 'inner fortress' in the Alps as the final 'bulwark of fanatical resistance'. A stronger sense of realism evolved on 25 April when Kesselring was appointed OB Süd with control of Army Groups C and E, as well as G in southern Germany; he was to consult OKW on 'basic questions of strategy'. All of this came much too late. The Voralpen Line could not be manned; the 'inner fortress' could not be supplied; and only those German forces opposing the Russians and Yugoslavs could be expected to fight to the end. By the end of the month Kesselring was calculating that troops in the Alpine massif, but not the 'inner fortress', might be able to hold out long enough to allow the German armies in Austria, Czechoslovakia and Yugoslavia to retreat into Anglo-American occupation zones. Although this was not to be either, it did play a part in the secret negotiations for the German surrender then taking place.[22]

No Allied troops fighting in northern Italy had any idea of what was happening in the upper echelons of the rapidly crumbling Third Reich, nor of any surrender negotiations. Their eyes were still focused on the immediate task: defeating the German armies in the field.

Three rivers dominated the tactical equation of the German retreat: the Panaro in XIV Panzer Corps' area to the west, the Reno in I Fallschirmjäger Corps' area in the centre and the Po di Volano in LXXVI Corps' sector to the east. Only the last named served any delaying function as the speed of the Allied advance shredded all the carefully prepared plans for withdrawal to the Po. The intention had been that each division would fall back through intermediate lines until, approaching the Po, 'it would find its route clearly marked and would receive its orders from an assigned Command Post, which itself would be in line communication with the main Crossing Command'.[23] A senior officer, General Baumgartner, had been appointed Commander Po Crossings.[24]

However, after 20 April, the speed of the Allied advance would pick up so much that the Germans would find it impossible to hold the delaying lines. Such was the harassment from the air that field staffs had to move their HQs so frequently that communications between army and corps HQs and between corps and divisional HQs were so disrupted that they were lost in many cases. In practice, troops on the ground and formation HQs improvised as they tried to reach the Po. Jackson quotes the history of 278th Volksgrenadier Division, which noted that they 'received inadequate orders or none and came more and more to feel that they had been left on their own'.[25]

As we have seen, von Vietinghoff ordered the evacuation of Bologna on the evening of the 20th. In fact, he was ordering only the evacuation of the city's outer defences: Bologna was controlled by Italian partisans, and the only Germans in the city were deserters. Soon after daybreak on the 21st troops of 3rd Carpathian Division entered, 'their hackles up after a grim last fight with their opponents at Cassino, 1st Para, whose stores and paraphernalia they discovered and ground to bits beneath their tanks'.[26] Anders described that 'grim last fight'

> on the Gaiana river where, for the third time in the Italian campaign they encountered the 1st Parachute Rifle Division, the same that had defended Cassino. An unrelenting and merciless night followed, but the enemy was at length defeated and forced to withdraw during the night of April 20, pursued by our infantry and tanks.[27]

McCreery later wrote that the Poles 'fought magnificently, and on their front between the Senio and Gaiana over a thousand German dead were counted'. General Bohusz-Szyszko commanded the corps with Anders by his side 'most of the time'. After the liberation of Bologna, Anders described the advance from the Senio as 'Une belle bataille'.[28] On their way to Bologna, the leading Polish group came under heavy artillery fire along Highway 9. This did not come from Germans, but from Fifth Army's guns, the bombardment being laid down in the belief that the Germans were retreating along the Via Emilia; but, as Anders notes, 'the Americans ceased fire the moment their mistake was pointed out to them on the telephone and the centre of Bologna was reached at six o'clock in the morning of April 21'.[29] Two hours after the Poles' arrival, US troops of 34th Division arrived from the south at much the same time as Italian soldiers of Gruppo Friuli, from X British Corps, made their entry. The target that had mesmerized Clark for so long was now in Allied hands and, not surprisingly, the next day he held a parade 'through the well preserved streets of the city he had coveted so long'. However, he did write in his diary that 'Our most important objective remains the destruction of the enemy,' perhaps indicating that he had absorbed one lesson at least.[30] Two days later, McCreery paid special tribute to the efforts of II Polish Corps in a special order of the day. Having outlined their achievements, which he described as 'a decisive part in this great victory', he concluded:

> You have shown a splendid fighting spirit, endurance and skill in this great battle. I send my warmest congratulations and admiration to all ranks, and I wish you all the best of luck as you continue the march with Eighth Army until the enemy's final collapse in Italy is achieved.[31]

The liberation of Bologna marked the end of the Italian campaign for the Poles, as the corps was not called into action in the closing days on the plain. Sadly, the Poles, while contributing greatly to Allied victory in Italy, were not to see the liberation of their homeland as Poland exchanged one occupying power for another.

We have already seen how 1st Armored Division's Combat Command B had become engaged in battle with the defenders of Montombraro. This struggle lasted until the following day when the Germans were ousted and the town liberated, allowing CCB to advance to Ciano, and then more than a mile through the Castel di Samoggia area towards Castello di Savignano. Combined columns of Combat Commands A and C liberated Tiola and pushed on, only to be stopped at Zappolino; resistance from 194th Anti-Tank Battalion, plus man-portable weapons and mines, claimed twenty tanks. Although a considerable distance away, twenty Allied medium bombers struck at the bridge over the Samoggia at Vignola to disrupt movement of German reserves.[32]

This was the day on which 10th Mountain Division had cleared the Lavino valley, wrested Monte San Michele from a mixed force of defenders, engaged the rearguard at Mongiorgio and pushed forward to Fontanella by 8.00pm. Over on the left flank, the Brazilian I/6th Regiment advanced from Castel d'Aiano to Monte Righetti, following the overnight withdrawal of 114th Jäger Division to Zocca.[33]

Also in action and pushing ahead steadily were units of 6th South African Armoured Division. The left of the division's area was cleared by 4/13th Frontier Force Rifles, on loan to the division, and contact established with the Custermen. While this task was underway, 13 Motorised Brigade set off for the Setta valley; the brigade grouping also included the Special Services Battalion of 11 Armoured and the Royal Natal Carabineers of 12 Motorised Brigades. By the end of the day the brigade was stalled where Highway 64 crosses the Reno, having been engaged by enemy troops on Sasso Marconi (known as Praduro e Sasso or Sasso Bolognese before it was renamed in tribute to Bologna's famous son, Guglielmi Marconi, who had died in 1937).[34]

By now, the last German formations in the Apennines were withdrawing as quickly as possible. While 8th Gebirgs and 94th Infantry Divisions struggled manfully to stem Fifth Army's onrush, committing their last reserves to the line, both 65th and 305th Divisions were making an orderly retreat from the mountains. Although minus their fusilier battalions, both divisions were still comparatively fresh and would be available for combat on another day.[35]

In II US Corps' sector 91st Division came into action early on the 19th, taking over part of 88th Division's front, and command of two battalions of the latter. While 88th Division sidestepped to the west, 1/ and 3/350th Regiment, the battalions under 91st's command, took Monte Mario and began a north-westerly move down to the Reno valley. A similar drive was also being made by 1/361st and 1/362nd, both of the 91st, as they advanced to Monte Capanna. Elsewhere on II Corps' front, 34th Division was pursuing the retreating Germans, during which chase 2/363rd of 91st Division cleared Pianoro on Highway 65 and 1/133rd of 34th liberated Riosto.[36]

Gruppo Legnano had earlier been ordered to deploy its 9th Assault Battalion north-west to relieve 168th Regiment on 34th Division's right flank; this unit advanced in conformity with the Red Bulls. In fact, much of the gruppo was in action with the Piemonte Battalion of the Special Infantry Regiment attacking Hill 363 at 10.30pm. This hill sits on the ridge between the Idice and Zena valleys and the Piemonte attack was launched to enable the Goito Bersaglieri Battalion (the Goito name commemorated a Great War battle) to move on Póggio Scanno. To the east, the Aquila Battalion pushed into the Idice valley while 2/68th Regiment occupied the Pizzano positions and 1/68th maintained contact with Eighth Army's XIII Corps – and found the German defences manned and aggressive.[37]

On 15th Army Group's left flank, 92nd Division was also in action, having resumed its advance towards La Spezia. Since the 14th the division's progress had been stalled by a series of counter-attacks, each at battalion strength, by 361st Panzer Grenadier Regiment of 90th Panzer Grenadier Division. The German intention was not to stop the American advance completely but to allow their own forces to make a slow withdrawal into Sarzana and La Spezia. In addition to counter-attacks, the Germans had used the coastal gun batteries at Punta Bianca, about three miles south of La Spezia, to harass Massa and Carrara, now both in Allied hands, as well as the roads passing through and between both towns. The coastal batteries had defied all attempts to silence them, including fighter-bombers of XXII TAC, an 8-inch howitzer, and tank destroyers. The guns on the eastern side of the peninsula of which Punta Bianca is the tip finally fell silent on the 19th, presumably as a result of the Germans destroying them before withdrawing, but those on the western side continued firing until the following day.[38]

Although Fisher suggests that the abandonment of the guns at Punta Bianca was due to 'the necessity for a rapid withdrawal, because of the Allied breakthrough on the central front on both sides of Bologna', tough resistance still faced 92nd Division. In the mountains to the west, 442nd Regiment was advancing towards the village of Téndola, all approaches to which were covered by the determined defenders of a dominating hill. It was there that another Nisei soldier, Private Joe Hayashi, born in California, distinguished himself, skilfully leading his squad to a point within seventy-five yards of enemy positions before being detected and fired on:

> After dragging his wounded comrades to safety, he returned alone and exposed himself to small arms fire in order to direct and adjust mortar fire against hostile

emplacements. Boldly attacking the hill with the remaining men of his squad, he attained his objective and discovered that the mortars had neutralized three machine guns, killed 27 men, and wounded many others.[39]

This did not end Private Hayashi's display of gallantry and leadership. Two days later, while attacking Téndola itself, he manoeuvred his men along a steep, terraced hill to within a hundred yards of the Germans. Despite fierce fire, he crawled towards a machine-gun post, into which he threw a grenade that killed one defender and persuaded the others to surrender. Hayashi then spotted four other machine guns that were firing on his platoon and threw another grenade that destroyed one of their positions, before crawling to the right flank of yet another machine-gun post where he killed four soldiers and put their comrades to flight. However, as he tried to chase the fleeing enemy, he was hit by a burst of fire and wounded mortally, but 'his dauntless courage and exemplary leadership' had enabled his company to gain its objective. Private Hayashi received a posthumous award of the Distinguished Service Cross, which was upgraded half a century later to the Medal of Honor by President Clinton. He was also promoted posthumously to sergeant.[40]

In between Joe Hayashi's two acts of gallantry, another Nisei soldier, Second Lieutenant Daniel K. Inouye, also of the 442nd, distinguished himself at San Terenzo, not far from Téndola. Inouye, a Hawaiian, commanded a platoon with the task of attacking a defended ridge guarding a critical road junction:

> Second Lieutenant Inouye skilfully directed his platoon through a hail of automatic weapon and small arms fire, in a swift enveloping movement that resulted in the capture of an artillery and mortar post and brought his men to within 40 yards of the hostile force. Emplaced in bunkers and rock formations, the enemy halted the advance with crossfire from three machine guns. With complete disregard for his personal safety, Second Lieutenant Inouye crawled up the treacherous slope to within five yards of the nearest machine gun and hurled two grenades, destroying the emplacement. Before the enemy could retaliate, he stood up and neutralized a second machine-gun nest.[41]

Although wounded, Inouye engaged other enemy positions until a nearby grenade explosion shattered his right arm. Suffering great pain, he refused to be evacuated and continued directing his platoon until the Germans had been overcome and his men could consolidate their newly-won positions. Twenty-five Germans had been killed, and a further eight captured. Inouye was awarded the Distinguished Service Cross, the citation for which noted that his 'gallant, aggressive tactics' and 'indomitable leadership' had enabled the platoon to advance through determined resistance and was instrumental in capturing the ridge.[42] As with Private Hayashi, Inouye's decoration was upgraded to the Medal of Honor, which he received from President Clinton in 2000; by then Inouye had been a US senator, representing Hawaii on Capitol Hill for almost forty years.

By the time Hayashi and Inouye had earned their decorations, adding yet more lustre to the record of 442nd Regiment, the Allies had broken through on both sides of Bologna and the tipping point in the offensive had been reached. Clausewitz wrote that all action is directed to the destruction of the enemy, and that the fruits of victory are to be had in the pursuit. Fifteenth Army Group, well on its way to destroying Army Group C, would reap the fruits of victory in the pursuit to the Po and beyond. Fisher notes the significance of 20 April thus:

> The 20th of April marked the turning point in the Allied spring offensive across the entire front. From that point the operation was to become a pursuit with fighter-bombers of the MATAF flying in close support of wide-ranging Allied columns fanning out across the Lombardy plain. The aerial harassment, which would soon make of the Po River as much of a barrier to the retreating Germans as they had hoped it would be to the Allies, represented the culmination of 11,902 Allied sorties of all types, flown over the battle area since 14 April. The six days since the Fifth Army's phase of the Allied offensive had begun had witnessed the greatest single week's air support effort of the entire Italian campaign and was a fitting climax to the long months of Allied air operations in the theater.[43]

On Eighth Army's front, as we have seen, 6th Armoured Division was released from Army Reserve to come under command of V Corps on the 18th. Lieutenant General Charles Keightley, V Corps' commander, had first taken 6th Armoured to war in 1942. The division was now under Major General Horatius Murray, who had commanded a brigade of 51st (Highland) Division before being appointed to succeed Gerald Templer as GOC of 6th Armoured; Templer had been injured badly in a mine explosion in the Arno valley not long after assuming command. Murray had had the headache of commanding the division in Fifth Army in the Apennines, terrain hardly suited to tanks, where he had recognized quite early Mark Clark's antipathy towards the British. It had been a relief to transfer to McCreery's command, and the opportunity to see action in a break-out role was something to which Murray and his men looked forward. Murray's orders were simple: 6th Armoured was to pass through the left flank of 78th Division, swing to the north-east, advance to Bondeno, keeping the divisional left flank on the Reno, and link up with Fifth Army.[44]

At first, the division made only slow progress since the road to Argenta was congested. The war diary of 3rd Welsh Guards gives an insight to the scene facing the men of the division:

> Scenery singularly macabre and grim, barbed-wire entanglements, fosses, extensively flooded land, burnt out vehicles, dead animals etc., were to be seen littering the road.
> ... Move up [through the Argenta Gap] was interesting as such engines of war as arks, crabs and crocodiles were dispersed throughout the column and added to the novelty of the advance. The road was dusty, and bridges [were] utterly destroyed and reduced to twisted wrecks.[45]

Third Grenadiers' war diary comments on 'order and counter order all day' on the 18th before the battalion was sent to 'near Alfonsine'; the following day they moved to Boccaleone, where the Irish Fusiliers 'had nearly captured a German Div Comdr 24 hours previously'. It also noted an 'Air raid on Argenta while Bn passed through'.[46]

With both 56th and 78th Division using the same route to supply their units at the front, there could be no speedy move forward. Although McCreery had told Murray that Argenta was in British hands, he had also suggested confirming this with Keightley and so Murray went to see the corps commander. Keightley told him that he believed the way was clear. Murray then went forward to see Arbuthnott, GOC of 78th Division for confirmation:

> Unfortunately the 'gap' was even less obvious than we had thought, but two factors decided me in accepting this challenge. In the first place the opposing troops must have had quite a hammering in the previous ten days since the operation commenced and might well be reasonably disorganized. Secondly, we were now within striking distance of the Po, and in this area 6th Armoured Division would have its last chance of fighting an armoured battle. We would never have forgiven ourselves if that fleeting chance had escaped us: it was now or never.[47]

Val ffrench-Blake, CO of 17th/21st Lancers, describes the 'gap' as being 'literally only a few yards wide', but enough for an armoured division to pass through and seize the opportunity to carry out its role.[48] That role was to link up with Fifth Army and, in concert with elements of Truscott's command, destroy what was left of Army Group C 'caught in the noose of Bologna's defences'.[49] And so the battlegroups rode forth. Even though the congestion was nightmarish, by late afternoon on the 19th both the Lothians/2nd Rifle Brigade (LB/2RB) and the 16th/5th Lancers/1st King's Royal Rifle Corps (16/5L/1KRRC) groups were passing through the leading infantry and preparing to advance from Consandolo, ten miles from Argenta. (The third battlegroup, 17th/21st Lancers/7th Rifle Brigade (17/21L/7RB), as divisional reserve, was following.) As well as armoured regiments and infantry battalions, each battlegroup included a battery of 12th (HAC) Regiment RHA, a 1st Derbyshire Yeomanry squadron, a self-propelled troop of 72nd Anti-Tank Regiment, a half-squadron from 25 Armoured Engineer Brigade, a troop of 8 Field Squadron RE, and an augmented section of 165th Light Field Ambulance RAMC.[50]

Sixth Armoured Division passed through 78th Division with 8th Indian covering its left flank. As Murray's tanks began their north-westward exploitation role, 56th and 78th Divisions continued their advances from Argenta, pushing towards Ferrara and the crossings of the Po to the north of that city. With Fifth Army forces advancing to link up with 6th Armoured, defeat was facing those Germans caught in their pincer movement, while their comrades making for the Po were being harried from the air and the ground and, in McCreery's words, were being given no rest. The final phase of Operation GRAPESHOT was about to begin.

Notes

1. Starr, op. cit., p.405.
2. Ibid., pp.405–6.
3. Ibid., p.406.
4. Ibid.
5. Ibid., pp.406–7; Fisher, op. cit., pp.474–5.
6. Quoted in Duncan, op. cit., p.327.
7. Fisher, p.480.
8. Starr, p.407.
9. http://www.custermen.com/History85htm 4 Jan '14
10. Fisher, p.482.
11. Delaney, *The Blue Devils in Italy*, pp.203–4.
12. Starr, p.407; Orpen, op. cit., pp.286–7.
13. Fisher, p.482; Starr, pp.416–17; Belogi & Guglielmi, pp.266–7.
14. http://www.custermen.com/History85htm 6 Jan '14
15. Ibid.; Orpen, op. cit., pp.288–9.
16. Starr, p.408.
17. Belogi & Guglielmi, p.238.
18. Ibid., pp.238–9.
19. Starr, p.409.
20. Fisher, p.482.
21. Jackson, pp.284–5.
22. Ibid., pp.285–6.
23. Ibid., p.286.
24. Ibid.
25. Ibid.
26. Blaxland, p.271.
27. Anders, *An Army in Exile*, p.267.
28. McCreery, *RUSI Journal*, p.11.
29. Anders, p.267.
30. Blaxland, pp.271–2; *I Gruppi di Combattimento*, pp.221–2.
31. Anders, p.268.
32. Belogi & Guglielmi, pp.251–2.
33. Ibid., p.251.
34. Ibid., p.252; Orpen, p.288.
35. Jackson, p.287; Belogi & Guglielmi, p.252.
36. Starr, p.416; Belogi & Guglielmi, pp.252–3.
37. Belogi & Guglielmi, p.253; *I Gruppi di Combattimento*, pp.358–61.
38. Ibid., pp.344–6; Fisher, p.483; Jackson, p.323.
39. US Army Center of Military History, http://www.history.army.mil/medalofhonor 23 Nov '13.
40. Ibid.
41. US Army Center of Military History, http://www.history.army.mil/medalofhonor 23 Nov '13.
42. Ibid.
43. Fisher, p.483.

44. Donovan, 'A Very Fine Commander', p.172.
45. NA, WO170/4982, war diary, 3 W. Gds, 1945.
46. NA, WO170/4979, war diary, 3 Gren Gds, 1945.
47. Donovan, op. cit., p.180.
48. ffrench-Blake, 'Italian War Diary', p.48.
49. Blaxland, p.268.
50. NA, WO170/4456, war diary, 26 HQ Armd Bde, 1945.

Chapter Eleven

The Germans had intended the Genghis Khan Line to be a major obstacle to Eighth Army's advance. This intention was known to Eighth Army Intelligence, and 2nd New Zealand Division expected to meet fierce resistance along the Idice. Kay notes that Freyberg told a conference at 43 Brigade HQ on the morning of 17 April that:

> If the Idice proves tough I want to step back from it, and bomb and shell it. Halt 9 Brigade and 43 Gurkha Brigade, put the other two brigades [5 and 6] through to establish a bridgehead, tidy your two [9 and 43] brigades up and put you through the bridgehead, get right out beyond and try to make a break.[1]

Although Freyberg and his commanders did not expect to meet strong opposition before the Idice, this appreciation proved to be mistaken. As we have seen, the Germans fought hard along the Gaiana, and the artillery force arranged to deal with the Idice had to be brought into play there. Once over the Gaiana the New Zealanders set off for the Idice. Shortly after midnight on 19/20 April they reached the Quaderna and crossed it in spite of mines, heavy machine-gun fire and barbed wire; by daylight sappers had three bridges across and 5 and 6 Brigades were making for the Idice. Along that river 10th Indian Division had already established bridgeheads, with 25 Brigade's 3/1st Punjab and 3/18th Royal Garhwal Rifles and 10 Brigade's 3/5th Mahratta LI in the lead. As the New Zealanders made for the river their intelligence assessment was revised to suggest that the Germans would not be able to hold the Idice.[2]

That fresh intelligence assessment proved accurate. Although there was opposition, it was nowhere near as strong as had earlier been anticipated. It seemed that the Germans had made such an effort on the Gaiana that they could not defend the Idice as they had planned. When the New Zealanders crossed the river they found dumps of weapons and ammunition that had been part of the preparations to hold the Genghis Khan Line. However, the Germans had lost so many men on the Gaiana that this proved impossible. One New Zealand officer had written of the Gaiana encounter that 'ground was not what we wanted. We wanted to destroy the German armies in Italy this side of the Po, so that they could not get back into the Alps. At first it looked as if this time we had failed.'[3] However, the same officer was to revise his opinion when:

I went forward to the river line itself early the next day [and] I realised that this was not so. We had indeed hit the enemy as we wished. The first count of enemy casualties [about 200] had been too low. Along those banks in the stream, in their trenches, in houses and holes behind, lay the massed dead. Few battlefields in this war can have presented the picture of carnage which the banks of the Gaiana showed that day, this spectacle of Germans killed by the barrage, or caught crouching in their holes by the flame-throwers, or slaughtered in a hundred other ways. … There they lay in all their ghastliness, the youth of Germany, the pride of Hitlerism ….[4]

Brigadier Gentry, having walked over the ground flamed by the Crocodiles, commented:

it was quite clear that it had been held in adequate strength to prevent any successful attack in daylight except possibly with very heavy air and artillery support. There were more dead Germans on the battlefield than I saw in any of the preceding operations.[5]

Small wonder that the Genghis Khan Line was little more than a chimera. On the right of 5 Brigade's front, 23rd Battalion by-passed Budrio in its advance, which began at 5.30am, and reached the near floodbank of the Idice unopposed at 11.30am. However, 21st Battalion, on the left, encountered some German tanks and strongpoints but cleared Budrio and advanced to the Idice north of the town without further problems. Meanwhile, 23rd Battalion had reconnoitred the riverbank just after midday and encountered some enemy troops, who had arrived from Bologna and were not prepared for battle. At 1.00pm 23rd Battalion crossed the river, supported by Crocodiles and tanks. However, it was ordered not to advance any more than 100 yards to allow the tactical air forces to bomb the ground beyond.[6]

Meanwhile the Germans assailed the bridgehead with shells and mortars. At about 6.00pm a counter-attack was launched which interfered with the work of sappers who had begun bridging the Idice. By midnight, however, the bridgehead had been expanded with the support of an intense artillery bombardment that showered 16,000 rounds on the Germans. The advance was continued and tanks crossed the river and linked up with the infantry. On the 6 Brigade front the only ford over the Idice was secured by 26th Battalion at noon, even though this meant encroaching on II Polish Corps' ground and 24th Battalion crossed against opposition to take a firm grip of the far bank. By midnight the bridgehead was secure and tanks of 20th Armoured Regiment were supporting 6 Brigade. Meanwhile the Polish Rak Group and Rud Force had advanced to the ford secured by 26th Battalion. That the two Allied armies were coalescing was demonstrated when 1/ and 3/184th Regiment and Caorle Battalion of San Marco Regiment, all of Gruppo Folgore, linked up with the Goito Bersaglieri Battalion of Gruppo Legnano. Both regiments of Gruppo Friuli had reached Ozzano dell'Emilia and Castel dei Britti.[7]

Adolf Hitler's birthday was not a day of celebration for the German dictator. There was no good news for him from any front as his troops reeled back from the unrelenting pressure of the Allies. All along the northern Italian front, soldiers of Army Group C were fighting a battle without hope as Fifth and Eighth Armies tightened the vice of their assaults. With IV US Corps coming down out of the Apennines into the Po valley, Highway 9 north-west of Bologna cut by II US Corps, XIII British Corps across the Idice, and the Argenta Gap cracked open by V British Corps, von Vietinghoff knew that only withdrawal could save his armies from complete destruction; but the Allies were determined that complete destruction would be their fate.

On the eastern end of the front, the Comácchio sector, 162nd Division was beginning a retreat while, at 1.00pm, the partisan 28 Garibaldi Brigade attacked west of Porto Garibaldi. However, 29th Panzer Grenadier Division was still showing considerable spirit as its I/15th Regiment launched no fewer than three counter-attacks on 1st Scots Guards of 24 Guards Brigade on the Canale Diversivo, north of Portomaggiore. But 2/6th Queen's, also of 56th Division, and 56 Recce, of 78th Division, were attacking Gambulaga, which was defended by II/71st Panzer Grenadier Regiment while, farther to the west, 26th Panzer and 98th Volksgrenadier Divisions were taking up defensive positions along the San Nicolò canal.[8]

Near Runco, the Kangaroo Army of 2nd Irish Rifles and 9th Lancers, later joined by 10th Hussars, launched an attack and, west of the railway from Portomaggiore to Ferrara, 36 Brigade's 5th Buffs and the Irish Brigade's Inniskillings attacked Montesanto, which was defended by 198th Anti-Tank Battalion of 98th Volksgrenadier Division. The attacking battalions crossed the San Nicolò canal at 2.00am where they came under heavy artillery fire but pressed on to take Montesanto three hours later. However, German gunners continued firing on the area, delaying the sappers who were trying to bridge the canal.[9]

It was into this kaleidoscope of action that 6th Armoured Division entered on that Friday morning. In fact, the division's troops had already seen action the previous day when the leading battlegroups, 16th/5th Lancers and 1st King's Royal Rifle Corps and the Lothians and 2nd Rifle Brigade, had each encountered their first opposition. The groups were advancing down the Reno's eastern bank. On the first stage of their advance, two waterways fed by the Po crossed their axis, the Po Morto di Primaro and Fossa Cembalina. Both waterways converged with the Reno, where each was afforded a narrow passage in the shadow of the Reno floodbanks. On each, at the point where it met the Reno, also sat a village, Traghetto on the Po Morto and Passo Segni on the Fossa Cembalina. Beyond Segni at Póggio Renatico, some five miles distant, stood the last bridge across the Reno, the only avenue of escape from XIII Corps for those Germans south of the Reno. Naturally, Traghetto and Segni were the first objectives for Murray's battlegroups.[10]

There was no quick start to the advance since the ground over which they were to move was quite soft, forming an irregular grid of drains, some with high floodbanks that were major obstacles for the tanks. Away from the ditches were lines of vines, orchards and woods. Although it looks perfectly flat on a map, this was difficult country for tanks, and for the infantry's troop-carrying vehicles. In fact, the infantry had to abandon their own vehicles and take to riding on tanks before, eventually, having to foot-slog alongside the Shermans to be better able to deal with the many natural obstacles and the pockets of German resistance that impeded progress. The commanding officer of the Lothians, Lieutenant Colonel Gordon Simpson, later wrote:

> Some senior officers thought that tanks would run riot on the Plains of Lombardy as on the map they are quite flat. The trouble is that the drainage system, evolved after hundreds of years of cultivation, cuts up the plain into thousands of fields, some an acre, others of hundreds of acres. Most ... drainage ditches are antitank obstacles. Another problem affecting mobility is that many of the roads are elevated with ditches on either side. No map can show all these potential tank traps.[11]

Simpson's group reached the village of San Nicolò Ferrarese with its bridge across the Po Morto that night, having lost four tanks in scrappy fighting en route. However, the bridge had been blown and there was considerable resistance from 198th Anti-Tank Battalion while the Kesselring 2nd Machine-gun Battalion of 26th Panzer Division made a counter-attack. Better luck attended 16/5L/1KRRC on the left; they took Traghetto, 'totally burnt out by oil bombs dropped by our air force on 10 Apr',[12] with little difficulty and by morning had a bridgehead across the Po Morto. But when they pushed on from Traghetto they ran into a German anti-tank screen and had to stop. As a result, Val ffrench-Blake's 'Death or Glory Boys' and 7th Rifle Brigade were called forward to lead the way to Segni.

Since vision was restricted by hedges, orchards, buildings and a jumble of other obstructions, the tanks were ordered to shoot up every building and thicket with their main armament and machine guns. Rover David was called upon, and fighter-bombers strafed enemy anti-tank gun positions before the Shermans charged them, overran the guns and pushed on. Two squadrons were deployed in the lead and the Green Jackets of 7th Rifle Brigade advanced with them. Of necessity, it was a slow advance since German defenders had to be winkled out of many strongpoints. As they advanced, the lancers and riflemen evicted Germans from the shells of many buildings and some anti-tank guns were also dealt with, a few of which were captured. Thus by nightfall the leading squadron was some two miles short of the Fossa Cembalina. The decision was taken to rest for the night since the troopers and riflemen were tired but, an hour before midnight, ffrench-Blake received orders from Murray to continue his advance in the dark. Those who were already asleep were woken hastily and, once again, the Shermans and their accompanying riflemen set off.[13]

C Squadron of the Lancers with C Company 7th Rifle Brigade reached the Fossa Cembalina just before day broke. The bridge had been demolished, but the Green Jackets waded across the wide ditch to take the defenders so much by surprise that forty were captured. Tanks then moved out across the Fossa to the left to seek a way between the canal and the Reno at Segni. What followed is a typical example of the difficulties faced in the terrain of the northern plain. Segni was reached and taken but, on the far side, progress was impeded as the gap between the Reno and a canal to the right was covered by concealed anti-tank guns that defied the artillery's efforts to locate them for several hours. With other German artillery in action, any movement on the open ground was dangerous. Finally, the advance was resumed when the enemy anti-tank guns were pinpointed and attacked by fighter-bombers, which also targeted several German tanks. The battlegroup was then able to move behind a curtain of artillery fire and by 4.00pm Lancers and Green Jackets were in the enemy positions and dealing the *coup de grace* to the defences. Thereafter, B Squadron was sent into the lead towards Póggio Renatico, with orders to speed up and seize the village of Gallo.[14]

When Gallo was liberated, at 5.30pm, the bridge was found intact. When this news was passed back to HQ 26 Armoured Brigade the response was almost immediate: 'Push on to Póggio with all speed.'

> Push on with two squadrons and your infantry to Póggio Renatico (M0178). This is the chance of a lifetime. Leave one squadron on the bridge at Gallo and hold it at all costs until relieved.[15]

No more welcome order could have been received by an armoured regiment. Of this episode, Val ffrench-Blake writes:

> This was the chance of a lifetime. Leaving B Squadron ... at Gallo, I brought up C Squadron from reserve and ordered them to go for Póggio Renatico at full speed down the road. The significance of Póggio was that it contained the only bridge over the Reno for the main road from Bologna to Ferrara and the Po crossings – the chief escape route for all the Germans retreating in front of US Fifth Army. Maj James Maxwell drove his leading troops on at a fine gallop, followed by RHQ and A Squadron. Machine-gun tracer streamed into farms and woods beside the road; many burst into flames, as they contained hidden stores of petrol. As we approached Póggio, surrounded by a mile of open fields, anti-tank fire began to come in from the town, which was on our left. The enemy fire came from an anti-aircraft battery of four 88mm guns, but, unused to the anti-tank role, they did not score a single hit.[16]

The order from HQ 26 Armoured Brigade was like a visit from Father Christmas for cavalrymen who, for the first time in Italy, could demonstrate true cavalry panache. According to the brigade war diary, the Death or Glory Boys 'tore into Póggio Renatico down the main road with C Squadron leading and firing liberally as they went'.[17] In the course of their 'gallop' C Squadron knocked out many guns and vehicles and seemed almost oblivious to that battery of 88s that attempted to assail them for the last 2,000 yards of their charge; but, as ffrench-Blake points out, these were flak gunners attempting a role to which they were not accustomed, and trying to deal with fast-moving targets. By nightfall, the 17/21L/7RB group was four miles from Gallo at Póggio Renatico and in positions to block every exit, thereby cutting the sole alternative road from Bologna to Ferrara. The battlegroup had covered a remarkable eleven miles since leaving its start line.[18]

Some Germans attempted to continue the fight and the most stubborn of their number received the attentions of the Green Jackets; one stubborn infantryman had knocked out C Squadron's leading Sherman with a Panzerfaust. These were undoubtedly men of 278th Volksgrenadier Division, which had relieved 362nd Division, supported by some Nashorns of 525th Heavy Tank Destroyer Battalion.[19] Other Germans, however, were less determined and either tried to surrender or put up token resistance with little co-ordination; these included flak gunners and service and support personnel. In his history of his regiment, ffrench-Blake writes:

> At Corps and Army headquarters, the victory was now assured, but in the dark, under the walls of Póggio Renatico the Regiment felt very insecure. There had been heavy expenditure of ammunition on a large number of targets and possible enemy positions, petrol was down to below twenty-five miles, and there was no prospect of replenishment until the route was cleared of the enemy.[20]

There was certainly a surreal atmosphere about Póggio Renatico as haystacks blazed 'particularly well', Germans tried to surrender and the battlegroup assessed its stocks of ammunition and prospects for the morrow. At 6th Armoured Division's HQ, Murray and his staff were concerned about ffrench-Blake's battlegroup, especially when a company of 1st Welch Regiment, of 24 Guards Brigade, crossed the Fossa Cembalina but was then forced to withdraw by German infantry and armour, including some Tigers of 504th Heavy Panzer Battalion. However, there was more reassuring news when 1st Welch made a second foray across the Fossa. This time the attack was aided by a complete platoon of Germans deserting their posts.[21]

Once the Welch bridgehead was established it was enlarged by 3rd Grenadier Guards which, in turn, allowed the Lothians to embark at dawn on a reckless advance to Bondeno, in the course of which they lost eleven tanks, but failed narrowly to seize the bridge. By the end of their advance, the Lothians' leading tanks had clashed with two Tigers of 504th Heavy Panzer Battalion before trying to take the bridge by *coup de main*. The Shermans made their way across but the Tigers followed, firing at and knocking out the Shermans; an explosion also destroyed the bridge. The battlegroup was also counter-attacked by II/994th Regiment of 278th Volksgrenadier Division and, later, by a mixed force from 26th Panzer Division. In spite of all this, the Lothians and their Green Jackets reached the Po at 10.45am on the 23rd, St George's Day, where they were joined by 1st Derbyshire Yeomanry; 5th Royal West Kents from 8th Indian Division, now back in the battle, arrived within ten minutes of the Derbys. The Lothians' Shermans were the first tanks of Eighth Army to reach the river and they, and their Derbyshire comrades, were ordered to halt. They then spent their time harassing the many Germans trying to cross to the northern bank. The Lothians, Derbys and West Kents were not the first Allied troops to reach the Po: 10th Mountain Division had beaten them to it by a day.[22]

Of this day McCreery writes:

> Now an acute shortage of artillery ammunition cropped up. We had used 1,400,000 rounds of 25-pounder since 9 April, so it was lucky that the hard fighting was clearly at an end. The Eighth Army had now taken over 15,000 prisoners, and the Fifth Army no less than 25,000. The next day thousands more of the enemy surrendered south of the Po.[23]

ffrench-Blake's lancers were kept busy on the 24th as the fighting continued. There was house clearing to be done, the Germans continued to shell areas of the town into which the riflemen and tanks were moving and still more Germans, retreating from Fifth Army, tried to come through Póggio on their way to safety. Thus plans for a further advance by the 17/21L/7RB battlegroup that day were postponed.[24]

With more open ground across which to advance, 16/5L/1KRRC had reached Mirabello, putting them some distance ahead of their fellow lancers. Although not part of the battlegroups, in spite of having trained for the role, 1 Guards Brigade had kept pace with them, and we have noted how 1st Welch played a major part in protecting the flank of the battlegroup at Póggio Renatico. At Mirabello 3rd Welsh Guards also played a part in evicting the enemy from the town, their war diary noting that 2 Company 'beat up the unsearched part' of the town, using an M10 and a flamethrower while 'a Fascist headquarters was discovered and various curious people' detained.[25]

The Green Jackets of 7th Rifle Brigade were ordered to consolidate their hold on Póggio Renatico and take the bridge across the Reno, which they did before daybreak on the 23rd. In this action the riflemen clashed with a patrol from 2nd New Zealand Division, advancing on the other side of the river, and a soldier of 28th (Maori) Battalion was killed. Not all the battalion was left at Póggio Renatico as some accompanied 17th/21st Lancers who carried on the advance towards Sant'Agostino. Having passed though Sant'Agostino, where columns of retreating enemy transport were shot up and some rearguards engaged, the leading troop was approaching Pilastrello when tanks were spotted coming from the south and 'a seventeen-pounder shot was fired; fortunately it missed, since the target was American. For the 17th/21st, it was the last shot of the war.'[26]

Somewhat farther north, 16/5L/1KRRC were making for 26 Armoured Brigade's second key objective on the Panaro, the small town of Finale Emilia. Seizing Finale would close the German escape, and there was little surprise when a convoy of enemy vehicles was spotted. Not only did the lancers engage with their main guns, but they also called in an air strike and fighter-bombers caused devastation among the vehicles lined nose to tail along the road. The damage wrought by the Allied aircraft might have been even greater since the battlegroup had just made contact with the leading troops of II US Corps, who were approaching Finale from the south. When it was learned that II Corps' artillery was about to bombard Finale to cover an attack by the South African 12 Motorised Brigade, the Allied aircraft were called off and the artillery plan cancelled. Leading elements of the two 6th Armoured Divisions – British and South African – then made peaceful contact.[27]

Finale proved an appropriate place for the meeting of the two armoured divisions, since it also marked the end of the fighting war for 26 Armoured Brigade. However, both 1 Guards and 61 Brigades remained in action. So, too, did some Germans in the area of the 16/5L/1KRRC battlegroup, one of whom shot and fatally wounded the CO of 1st King's Royal Rifles, Lieutenant Colonel John Hope DSO MC and Bar. Hope, who had joined the 60th as a subaltern in 1940 and had taken over command on 1st March, was sitting in a 'sawn-off' Stuart (an American light tank, known as the Honey in British service, with its turret removed and used by the reconnaissance troops of armoured regiments) with Lieutenant Colonel Denis Smyly, CO of 16th/5th Lancers when he was shot in the back. Corporal Stanley Waring, the Stuart's commander, went to give Hope first aid but was also shot and killed. John Hope, an exceptionally popular commanding officer, was one of the very few veterans of Eighth Army's early days to have survived to this time.[28]

On Tuesday 24 April 1 Guards Brigade reached the Po where, following a speedy reconnaissance, 3rd Grenadiers made a nocturnal crossing in DUKWs and Fantails, setting off at 12.45am on the 25th. Their objective, Gáiba, on the far bank was secured by 1.45am. Guardsman Doggett of No. 1 Company was the first British soldier to cross the Po, and the only opposition was a single hit on a Fantail by a sniper. Deployed as a flank guard, No. 3 Company captured ten Germans and killed another eleven, mostly from 155th Training Division. Of 26th Panzer Division there was no sign. A 7th Hussars' squadron, operating DD Shermans, also crossed, but the Grenadiers noted that 'Their tracks were on the bottom all the way over'.[29] Both 3rd Welsh Guards and 1st Welch joined the Grenadiers later that morning and set off for the Adige, the next main water obstacle, and the basis of the Venetian Line. Freyberg's New Zealanders had also crossed, farther upstream, and joined in the advance to the Adige, the overall intention being to keep sufficient pressure on the retreating foe to prevent any stand there.[30]

The New Zealanders, still full of running in spite of having been in action since D Day, outstripped the Guards to the Adige and, in doing so, pinched 1 Guards Brigade out of the battle, leaving only 61 Brigade of 6th Armoured Division involved.

At this point a brief summary of the activities of 2nd New Zealand Division since the crossing of the Idice is appropriate. After 5 and 6 Brigades crossed on 20 April, Bailey bridges were in place next morning, allowing 18th Armoured Regiment to join 5 Brigade in the advance. Opposition was encountered at Cazzano and four Shermans of 18th Armoured fell victim to the ambush. The Germans held out in spite of intense artillery fire and attacks by fighter-bombers, and the advance was resumed by 28th (Maori) Battalion bypassing Cazzano to cross the Scolo la Zena at midnight. Six Brigade was also held up by small pockets of enemy while, in mid-afternoon, 20th Armoured Regiment also ran into German tanks at San Brigida.[31]

That evening the Germans began withdrawing, breaking contact with the attacking New Zealanders who found themselves in 'untouched countryside with no defences, although there were wired-up demolition charges on the bridges'.[32]

Crossing Highway 64, the division swung north for the Reno, bypassing San Giorgio and contacting elements of 91st Division of Fifth Army. Both leading brigades were to continue north-westwards, maintaining radio contact with the leading armoured cars of 12th Royal Lancers, assigned to the division by XIII Corps as a reconnaissance unit. By now some 3,000 Germans had surrendered to 2nd New Zealand Division, about 150 having been added that day.[33] On the 22nd the advance continued with soldiers of 23rd and 28th Battalions riding on tanks of 18th Armoured Regiment. When the brigade reached the Savena, a canalized stream flowing beside Highway 64, the infantry had to leave the tanks as the bridge had been demolished; 28th Battalion pushed on towards Bentivoglio on the Canale Navile while the tanks waited for an Ark and a bulldozer to prepare a crossing.

The Maoris met no resistance and took prisoner several groups of disorganized Germans. Although the bridge over the Canale Navile had been demolished partisans built a footbridge of planks over which the battalion passed and 'took position beyond the canal, scooping up an enemy RAP and directing batches of prisoners, some under escort and some under their own power, back to the rear'.[34] By midday the bridge had been repaired and tanks and other vehicles were across. With 23rd Battalion also across the Navile, Freyberg ordered 5 Brigade to get over the Reno if possible. Air OPs reported no sign of Germans for the next four miles but Lieutenant Colonel Awatere insisted that 28th Battalion should advance on foot

> and search every building on the way. About 20 enemy fled from a house before the Maoris could close with them. Elsewhere a Wasp flame-thrower assisted the partisans who were fighting a 'pitched battle' with some Germans. By midnight 28 Battalion had reached the Fosso Riolo, about seven miles beyond Bentivoglio and only one mile from the Reno.[35]

By now the danger of meeting any opposition seemed very slight and the infantry were told to climb aboard any available vehicle, in which style they followed the tanks to the Reno where Awatere waded across and, seeing empty trenches, called for B Company to follow. The battalion was then ordered to stand fast and await orders. On the left of 28th Battalion, 23rd had also made a speedy move to the Reno, bypassing San Pietro in Casale, and its German garrison, reaching the river by midnight and crossing unopposed. By dawn on St George's Day, which probably meant little to the New Zealanders, 5 Brigade had a bridgehead over a mile wide and almost a mile deep across the Reno. Sadly, both battalions were fired on by troops of 6th Armoured Division, a soldier of B Company 28th Battalion being killed by a patrol from Murray's division.[36]

Meanwhile 6 Brigade had also reached the Reno, encountering more opposition than did 5 Brigade. There was a determined pocket of Germans two miles north of San Giorgio who held up the advance for a time on the 22nd but the brigade was able to move on next morning with 26th Battalion, riding on tanks, reaching the Scolo Riolo, some six miles on, by mid-morning. Not long after the leading companies were across the Reno, contact had been made with 6th Armoured and 25th Battalion had also come up into positions between Sant'Alberto and the river. Finally, 9 Brigade arrived, B Squadron of 19th Armoured Regiment having had a brief encounter with the enemy en route in which some casualties were suffered from mortar and small-arms fire. On the night of the 22nd soldiers of 22nd Battalion were queuing for food when they were strafed by an enemy aircraft. The effect of the attack was to persuade

> four or five hundred men simultaneously to dive under trucks or into shelter of any kind … and whole containers of food were upset amid shouts of 'Put out those lights! You fools!' It was all over within a minute, and a badly shaken battalion queued up again for what was left of the food.[37]

The same, or another, aircraft also dropped butterfly bombs in the lines of the Divisional Cavalry Battalion, causing some casualties. Following this wholly unexpected attack, 9 Brigade's area was very quiet. At dawn the advance resumed and, after an almost-incident-free journey, the leading tanks and Kangaroos reached the Scolo Riolo about midday. The New Zealand Division was now ready for the advance to the Adige.

V Corps had also been advancing steadily with 56th Division's 24 Guards Brigade crossing the Po di Volano against stiff opposition at Finale di Rero at 8.00am on Sunday 22 April while 28 Garibaldi Brigade crossed the Canale di Volano and made for Codigoro, meeting determined resistance from the Nuotatori Paracadutisti Battalion of the Decima MAS Division. Next day the brigade secured Codigoro, through which 2/21st Regiment, two groups of 7th Artillery Regiment and engineer elements of Gruppo Cremona passed in an advance that took them to the west of Mezzogoro; the gruppo also took 28 Garibaldi Brigade under command. With the Guards Brigade across the Po di Volano, a Bailey was built, across which 27th Lancers and 2nd Coldstream, dubbed Steelforce, drove to liberate Tresigallo in the late afternoon, pushing on to beyond Formignana by nightfall. Steelforce, which was to make directly for the Po, linked up with 1st Buffs who had taken Sabbioncello in the early afternoon but were stopped by the enemy at Formignana at midnight. Steelforce reached Ambrogio on St George's Day after changing direction on being counter-attacked en route. The Buffs crossed the Po di Primaro and advanced to the Canale Bianco where they encountered *Kampfgruppe* Linnarz, composed of the surviving Panzer IVs of 29th Panzer Grenadier Division and the survivors of 26th Panzer Division. By 6.00pm the Buffs had reached Piumana.[38]

Arbuthnott's Battleaxe Division reached the Po di Volano at Fossalta and Viconovo at 8.00pm on the Sunday, with 5th Northamptons of 11 Brigade in the van; 2nd Lancashire Fusiliers, to the left, came up to the waterway at Contrapo where a German counter-attack was launched. With 11 Brigade on its right, the divisional left flank was secured by 8th Argylls, who crossed at Cona to occupy the triangle between that and the Diversivo di Volano canal. However, since this proved not to be a suitable axis of advance, the Argylls were stopped and 6th Royal West Kents took up the baton, making for Ferrara despite heavy enemy shellfire. The West Kents reached

San Bartolo at 6.00pm, although some of their supporting tanks had fallen victim to Tigers of 504th Heavy Panzer Battalion, slowing the advance somewhat.[39]

Eighth Indian Division's 1st Argylls had encircled the Germans at Galbanella on the 22nd and 5th Royal West Kents of 21 Brigade advanced to Ferrara airport by 6.00pm. That evening the pressure from the division compelled 67th Panzer Grenadier Regiment to quit the city.[40]

The Allied armies' attacks were now converging and the German armies were disintegrating, their cohesion breaking down under the relentless pressure applied by McCreery and Truscott. Both armies were now looking at ensuring that their advances did not clash: on the 22nd the US 91st Division established Task Force McAdams to ensure a successful link up with Eighth Army at Bondeno; this was built around 2/362nd Regiment, reinforced by 757th Tank, 804th Tank Destroyer and 346th Field Artillery Battalions. Ninety-first Division, on the extreme right of Fifth Army, re-organized at Bologna airport on the 22nd with 363rd Regiment on the right and 362nd on the left; 3/363rd was mounted on tanks and 2/363rd on lorries. Both deployed towards the Panaro, which they reached at midnight. Meanwhile, 362nd made a similar re-organization and encircled Castel d'Argile and Pieve di Cento from the south-east.[41]

The South Africans, having extricated themselves from traffic congestion in San Giovanni in Persiceto, moved off in a north-easterly direction towards Cento on the Reno with 11 Armoured Brigade leading. Cento was defended by 147th Regiment of 65th Division, which was also responsible for defending San Matteo di Decima. On Sunday afternoon the Imperial Light Horse/Kimberley Regiment (ILH/KimR) and the Special Services Battalion encountered 576th Regiment of 305th Division at the confluence of the Samoggia and Reno and, later, at San Matteo di Decima, but the advance continued. At noon 12 Motorised Brigade set off for the Panaro with the WR/DLR reaching Cavadecoppi eight hours later where they came under fire from the far bank.[42]

At 7.45pm Prince Alfred's Guard's tanks and the Royal Durban LI, with the Divisional Engineer Battalion, came up to the Panaro at Finale Emilia, only to come under counter-attack just over an hour later by a 4th Fallschirmjäger Division rearguard force. The Fallschirmjäger, with some Italian 149/19 howitzers of their artillery regiment in support, were fighting to maintain a corridor for a retreating German column. The howitzers were in concealed positions north of Cento, but, as the South Africans arrived, their detachments destroyed the weapons and remaining ammunition as fuel for their Breda 61 half-track gun-towing vehicles was all but exhausted.[43]

The Germans holding out in Finale Emilia were shelled by Allied artillery throughout the night but this did not deter the Fallschirmjäger rearguard from counter-attacking the RDLI and PAG an hour after midnight. An hour later the Germans blew the bridge and, at 3.30am, pulled back, but, at 7.00am, the ILH/KimR and the Special Services Battalion met strong resistance on reaching the town; this was only overcome finally at 9.00am. Ninety minutes later the entire town was in

Allied hands, as were many of its erstwhile defenders, although their tenacious stand had allowed survivors of I Fallschirmjäger Corps to escape; a surprise counter-attack by a few Tigers of 504th Heavy Panzer Battalion had also played a part. Later that morning the RDLI and PAG were sent back to Camposanto while the WR/DLR, already across the Panaro, were ordered to advance to San Felice sul Panaro. It was this unit that leading elements of 6th British Armoured Division encountered later that day, with the outcome we have already seen.[44]

In II Corps' sector both 85th and 88th Infantry Divisions were also making steady progress, each reaching Camposanto on the Panaro on the 22nd. In the case of 85th Division, its 337th Regiment was in Camposanto, where there was an intact bridge, by 6.00am; the 3rd and 1st Battalions, with 85th Reconnaissance Troop (Mechanized) covering their flanks, made entry to the town. A counter-attack by 1097th Security Battalion, retreating from Bologna, was rebuffed but it took an all-day battle, with the support of elements of 6th South African Armoured on the right, before the bulk of the regiment was able to cross the Panaro. However, by late morning 2/337th had cleared the defenders from San Lorenzo della Pioppa.[45]

On 22 April IV Corps was moving forward like an expanding flood with the Po as its objective. First to reach the river were the men of Task Force Duff of 10th Mountain Division. Once again, Hays' mountaineers were setting the pace.

Early on April 21st 1945 10th US Mountain Division, covered by a small armoured screen ..., launched forth from the foothills of the Apennines across the plain of the Po valley.

The decision to break out into open country had not been reached at Divisional HQ until midnight of April 20th/21st, with the result that the infantry ... were slow to start next morning. The Commanding Officer of 178th (Medium) Regiment with recce parties following him found the armoured screen bumping opposition on Route 9 at Ponte Samoggia ... with no artillery up to support them. The guns of both his batteries were quickly brought into action in a forward position, well ahead of the infantry whom they were supposed to support, but who had not yet started. This was a fortunate happening as it was obviously better to be with the tanks which advanced nineteen miles that day ... to Bomporto, covered the whole way by the fire of the Regiment. The speed was terrific, and the Regiment thoroughly enjoyed moving over clear roads unhindered by infantry vehicles. The splendid infantrymen of this American Division followed on foot, deployed across country mopping up and taking prisoners. When the foremost infantry reached Bomporto just before dark, they found the Regiment's guns already in action with one battery pointing north-east and the other north-west, as both flanks were open and no other artillery unit was up to defend the position that night. It was this day's operations which started the infantry cry, 'Say, Colonel, when are you going to put bayonets on the end of your guns?'

During the whole of the next morning a strong enemy rearguard held up the advance in the thick country beyond Bomporto, though a bridge over the river Secchia was captured intact. Contact was maintained by a troop commander with the reconnaissance regiment, but observation was too difficult and friends too near to foe for close support.[46]

At 8.30pm on 22 April, Task Force Duff finished a rapid advance from Bomporto to San Benedetto Po, followed by the battalions of 86th Regiment, which touched on the river between Moglia and Concordia. Later, 1/87th, on the left flank, linked up with Task Force Duff at San Benedetto, having passed through Novi di Modena and Moglia; 3/87th entered Carpi. Meanwhile, CCA of 1st Armored Division bypassed Modena, no place for tanks anyway, although the city had been taken over by partisans, on the way to the Po, striking towards crossing points at Guastalla and Brescello, 1st Tank and 14th Armored Infantry Battalions to the left and 13th Tank and 6th Armored Infantry to the right. CCB – 4th Tank and 11th Armored Infantry – also bypassed Modena, the tanks crossing the Panaro along Highway 9 and the infantry a little farther south.[47]

Both corps of Fifth Army were conforming with Truscott's plan for this phase of the offensive:

> On April 19th, when the advance of the IV Corps had caused the German withdrawal on the front of the II Corps, I had issued orders for continuing the pursuit to the Po River as soon as Bologna was isolated or in our hands. The two Corps, each with one armored and two infantry divisions, were to press on boldly and rapidly, seize the line of the Panaro River, and then press on to the Po to secure crossing sites and cut off German forces still south of the river. This plan was put into effect on April 21st.[48]

With both armies up to the line of the Po, the offensive was entering its final phase.

Notes

1. Kay, op. cit., p.464.
2. Ibid., pp.465–7; Belogi & Guglielmi, pp.220–2.
3. Quoted in Kay, p.478.
4. Kay, p.478.
5. Ibid.
6. Belogi & Guglielmi, pp.248–50.
7. Ibid., pp.263–5; *I Gruppi di Combattimento*. pp.290–2 & 363–4.
8. Jackson, p.291; Belogi & Guglielmi, pp.262–3.
9. Belogi & Guglielmi, p.261.
10. Ibid., pp.261–3; Jackson, pp.289–90.
11. Quoted in Ford, *Mailed Fist*, p.186.

12. NA, WO170/4982, war diary, 3 W. Gds, 1945.
13. Ford, pp.187–8; ffrench-Blake, *The 17th/21st Lancers 1759–1993*, pp.111–12.
14. Ibid.; NA, WO170/4456, war diary 26 Armd Bde, 1945.
15. NA, WO170/4456, op. cit.
16. ffrench-Blake, 'Italian War Diary', p.58.
17. NA, WO170/4456, op. cit.
18. NA, WO170/4629, war diary 17/21 L, 1945.
19. Belogi & Guglielmi, pp.292–3.
20. ffrench-Blake, *A History of the 17th/21st Lancers 1922–1959*, p.222.
21. Belogi & Guglielmi, pp.291–3.
22. Ibid., pp.307–8; Blaxland, p.273.
23. McCreery, draft memoirs, p.15.
24. Ford, p.188.
25. NA, WO 170/4982, op. cit.
26. ffrench-Blake, *The 17th/21st Lancers 1759–1993*, p.113.
27. NA, WO170/4456, op. cit.; Jackson, pp.291–2; Orpen, p.288.
28. Blaxland, p.270; Doherty, *Eighth Army in Italy*, pp.215–16.
29. NA, WO170/4979, war diary, 3 Gren Gds, 1945.
30. Belogi & Guglielmi, pp.320–1.
31. Ibid, pp.263–4.
32. Ibid., p.281.
33. Kay, p.496.
34. Ibid., pp.496–7.
35. Ibid., p.497.
36. Ibid.
37. Ibid., p.500.
38. Belogi & Guglielmi, pp.209–2 & 304; *DSM* Gruppo Cremona, p.121.
39. Ray, pp.218–20; WO170/5033, 5051 & 4988, war diaries, 2 LF; 5 Northants; 8 A&S Hldrs.
40. NA, WO170/5021, war diary, 5 RWK, 1945; *The Tiger Triumphs*, p.198.
41. Belogi & Guglielmi, pp.294–5; Starr, pp.424–5.
42. Belogi & Guglielmi, pp.295–6.
43. Ibid., p.296.
44. Ibid., p.309–10.
45. Belogi & Guglielmi, pp.296–7.
46. Freeth, in Duncan, pp.327–8.
47. Belogi & Guglielmi, p.297.
48. Truscott, p.491.

Chapter Twelve

Truscott's plan for operations north of the Po was co-ordinated with that of Eighth Army. Both army commanders were following an exhausting routine of visiting their commanders and formations at the front. Both spent much time in the air moving from headquarters to headquarters. There were also visitors to the army HQs, anxious to be shown around and 'entertained':

> Dick was now covering great distances to keep in touch with his army. He had a number of visitors, first Harold Macmillan, whom he took to see Anders, ecstatic after what he described as *'une belle bataille!'* and with the divisional flag of 1 Parachute Division in his possession. Alexander arrived on the following day and accompanied Dick to meet Keightley, Murray and 'Pasha' Russell, whose 8 Indian Division was entering the battlefield again on the right of 6 Armoured Division, and then Freyberg. The envelopment of Bologna was now complete, taking place at the appropriately named town of Finale on 23 April, where the advanced patrols of 16th/5th Lancers met their equivalents from 6 South African Armoured Division. The first Allied formation to reach the Po itself was 10 Mountain Division on the evening of April 22. 6 Armoured Division's long-serving reconnaissance regiment, the Derbyshire Yeomanry, and the 5th Royal West Kents from 8 Indian Division arrived on the south bank of the great river within 10 minutes of each other the next day.[1]

McCreery's time in the air was spent either in his C-45 or in an Auster Air OP of the RAF, which he referred to by its popular name of 'whizzer'. Truscott's flying time was spent mostly in his L-5 Cub, the US equivalent of the Auster (itself an American aircraft built under licence in the UK), but occasionally he flew in an adapted P-51 Mustang fighter with USAAF Brigadier General Thomas R. Darcy at the controls. This was the case on 23 April when, following his morning staff conference, he flew with Darcy in the Cub 'to Florence, transferred to Darcy's P-51, and took off for another survey of the battle area':[2]

> Some fighting was in progress on the II Corps' front and on the left of the IV Corps west of Modena. Occasionally we were greeted by bursts of flak. However, the German columns were now in a state of confusion and disorder. Columns were moving in opposite directions on adjacent roads, others were crossing routes. Hundreds of vehicles were streaming toward the river in a desperate effort to escape. A short distance west of San Benedetto ..., Darcy

circled, pointed downward toward a column of troops …, and shouted: 'Boche!'
I nodded agreement. The next I knew we were plunging earthward in a steep
dive and Darcy was strafing the Germans. In several attacks, he set a number of
vehicles on fire and dispersed the German column; then we turned eastward.
Below Ostiglia, we found several other German columns approaching the river
with none of our own troops in the vicinity. We circled over these, making one or
two strafing passes to keep them halted and dispersed, while Darcy called other
fighter-bombers to the area and directed them onto the target. While some of
the German forces had escaped to the north bank, vast quantities of weapons
and equipment had been abandoned on the south bank, for there was no means
of conveying it across.[3]

Although the Germans had made preparations for withdrawing across the Po,
the pressure of the Allied advance and the attention of the tactical air forces had
overtaken their plans. Many engineers who were to operate the crossing points
were ordered into combat in rearguard operations, thereby forcing commanders to
improvise without engineer support. And there had been another factor unforeseen
by either side: the weather. German engineers had selected a number of suitable
crossing sites, unsurprisingly the same ones their Allied opposite numbers would
choose, at which 'they had cached the necessary matériel, including large and small
ferry boats suitable for use with any of three possible water levels, for during early
spring and summer the Po in this was unpredictable'.[4] In 1945 it proved even more
unpredictable than usual with the river's level at its lowest in fifty years, leaving the
water too shallow for the larger ferries on which the Germans planned to move their
heavy equipment and vehicles:

> Often running aground, the [larger] ferries became easy targets for Allied
> fighter-bombers, leaving the Germans no choice but to use smaller, shallower
> draft ferries with greatly reduced carrying capacity. That inevitably meant
> abandoning much heavy equipment south of the river.[5]

Truscott had anticipated that II Corps would reach the Po first and its 39th Engineer
Group had been assigned to prepare the crossings, but it was Crittenberger's IV Corps
that took the lead and so most of the engineers were re-assigned to IV Corps. From
aerial and map reconnaissances, the engineers had already selected a dozen likely
crossing sites for assault crossings, another twelve for ferries, and nine for floating
bridges. All were along a twenty-mile stretch between Borgoforte and Ostiglia, with
San Benedetto about midway; the Borgoforte-San Benedetto sector seemed more
suitable than the eastern sector because of the large marshy rice-growing area close to
Ostiglia that would restrict operations in the vicinity, especially by armour.[6]

Some German formations did not even reach the Po, let alone cross it. Chief
among them was 94th Division, which had been wrong-footed earlier as we have
seen. General Bernhard Steinmetz had been ordered by HQ XIV Panzer Corps
to assemble the survivors of his division near Mirandola, about half-way between

Modena and the crossing point at Ostiglia, where the division was to establish a rearguard position. But it proved too late to do so. Even as Steinmetz was receiving his orders, 88th Division, the Blue Devils, entered Mirandola, leaving Steinmetz's men to try to make their way to the Po in small groups. Steinmetz was cut off from his troops and his operations officer wounded and captured while reconnoitring crossing points. Another German division to cease to exist south of the Po was 305th, about which the Blue Devils' historian writes:

> By the time the Po River was reached the 88th had bagged 15,000 prisoners with the 349th accounting for more than 9,000 of the total. Prize catch was Major General von Schellwitz, 305th Infantry Division commander, taken along with his headquarters staff by the 349th as it drove through Magnacavallo. The doughs who captured the Kraut 'brass' were Pfc Taylor Abercrombie of Hollywood, Calif., and Pfc Joseph Wells of Weippe, Idaho. His division all but wiped out, General von Schellwitz paid the Blue Devils one of their brightest compliments when he told interrogators that 'as soon as I saw where the 88th Division was being committed I realized where the main effort would be – they have always spearheaded Fifth Army drives'.[7]

Schellwitz, reputedly an ardent Nazi, was the first German general captured by the Allies in Italy, his fate providing 'a good example of how the relentless advance of Eighth Army had driven the enemy into the arms of the fast-moving Fifth'.[8] It was also excellent proof of how the careful planning of the two army commanders was bearing fruit. Such was the devastation wrought on German forces south of the Po that von Senger, XIV Panzer Corps commander, was left with no signals equipment to control his divisions and felt compelled to dismiss his staff, ordering them to re-assemble at Legnago, some ten miles to the north, on the Adige. Early on the 23rd von Senger and his staff 'joined the precipitate flight across the Po'.[9]

As already noted, the first Allied troops to reach the Po were from 10th Mountain Division. With his men moving rapidly against light opposition in the centre of IV Corps' thrust, Major General Hays had decided to take full advantage of the situation by creating a combined armour/infantry task force to spearhead his division. This force, under Brigadier General Robinson E. Duff, his assistant divisional commander, and therefore Task Force Duff, had been formed on 21 April with a battalion from each of 85th and 86th Regiments, 91st Cavalry Reconnaissance Squadron, a light tank company, an engineer company and a platoon of tank destroyers. At twilight that day Task Force Duff was up to the Panaro where it captured intact the bridge at Bomporto, although German engineers had prepared it for demolition, while 85th Division had also taken intact the bridge at Camposanto.[10]

However, Task Force Duff had one major setback on its advance from Bomporto to the Po: it ran into an ambush not long after leaving Bomporto. Having met little opposition the previous day, Duff had relaxed his flank security to increase the speed of his move to Ostiglia:

Allowing half of the column to pass, the Germans opened fire on the tanks and tank destroyers in the middle of the column with panzerfausts, destroying and damaging many vehicles. Infantry following in trucks quickly dismounted and deployed. Although the enemy detachment was dispersed within an hour, that meant that much more time for enemy forces to escape across the Po.[11]

From then on Duff hurried his column along the road to San Benedetto Po. Blaxland describes this as 'a tremendous feat of endurance and adaptability' since Hays' division had now

capped a week of gruelling fighting down the Apennines with an advance of 40 miles across the plain, carried out in two days, and in the process they had split apart [Fourteenth] Army as effectively as Eighth Army had split [Tenth] Army.[12]

But, an hour away from San Benedetto, Duff's jeep was caught in the blast from an exploding anti-tank mine and he suffered serious injury. Hays came forward to take command and, by 6.00pm, San Benedetto was in Allied hands. The remainder of 10th Mountain Division arrived during the night, deploying along the riverbank ready to cross the Po next day. Blaxland notes that the pace set by 10th Mountain was aided by the flank protection provided by Pritchard's 1st Armored Division, which reached the Po a few hours after Hays' men.[13]

On Eighth Army's front, leading elements of 8th Indian and 6th Armoured Divisions were on the Po:

It was an awesome experience for the troops to find that they could at last gaze across the 'mighty Po'. It was described as such in leaflets that the Germans had for long been showering upon the troops of Eighth Army by gunfire, with descriptions in racy jargon of the horrors – 'Oh Boy' – that were in store for the attacking troops, and certainly it was a huge river to cross, with floodbanks of much greater width, though of less height, than those of the Senio and its many parallels. But the charred remains of vehicles and equipment that were strewn around the southern bank in such profusion showed that there had been some misapprehension of the 'blanket of fire' promised by the enemy, and the surrender of stranded or disinterested Germans in large number suggested that there might be a shortage of men to put down the terrible fire.[14]

Plans had been made for a contested crossing of the Po, responsibility for which McCreery had given to John Hawkesworth and his X Corps headquarters but, on 21 April, he had decided that X Corps would not be needed as, clearly, there would be no serious opposition to an Allied crossing.[15] However, a Po Task Force to deal with bridging and other means of crossing was in being. Sixth Armoured Division was transferred to XIII Corps, and Harding and Keightley were ordered to make crossings as soon as, and wherever, possible. The rationale for the adjustment of orbats was to bring other corps headquarters back into action; by transferring Murray's command to XIII Corps from the left wing of V Corps, a second corps was being given a limited frontage along the Po.[16]

V Corps, meanwhile, was pushing up to the Po, having secured Ferrara without opposition, thanks to partisans who had taken control of the city. Both 56th and 78th Divisions had also made good progress so that, by the 25th, V Corps was up to the Po on a wide front. In spite of the pressure they faced, elements of LXXVI Panzer Corps had retained cohesion and fought tenaciously, blowing the Po di Volano bridges and ambushing a company of 2nd Coldstream, but they had been forced to abandon the defences around Ferrara by 8th Indian Division, whose Jaipurs led the advance to the Po. As they did so, they ran into a powerful block by a panzer group on a road junction at Pontelagoscuro that required calling in support from 78th Division.[17] That support was provided by 9th Lancers of the Kangaroo Army who attacked the Germans from the right flank:

> A tremendous battle developed across open march, which brought back memories of the Desert to many of the Lancers as they searched for folds in the ground from which to fire back at the dark forms belching tracer at them. There was the big difference that they wielded the heavier firepower, for the Tigers and Panthers had all been expended in isolated actions in support of the infantry, and only Panzer IVs were left to confront Shermans … armed in many cases with high-velocity 76mm guns. Only one Sherman was knocked out, and the blazes that raged long after the fall of darkness proved the loss they had inflicted.[18]

This was 26th Panzer Division's last stand. When the Jaipurs made unopposed entry to Pontelagoscuro next morning they found ten tanks destroyed by gunfire and thirteen abandoned.

By then, XIII Corps was across the Po. We have already seen how 3rd Grenadiers made their crossing, but the New Zealanders, who had completed the elimination of enemy forces north of Bologna, were also available and 'Harding gave Freyberg the option of joining Murray in the crossing. Freyberg stressed the many problems and accepted.' His men were to cross astride the remains of the bridge at Ficarolo, two miles on the left of 6th Armoured's crossings; as we have already noted, only one bullet struck a Fantail carrying the guardsmen. It was a different story for 8th Indian Division around Ferrara as shells and Nebelwerfer rounds descended on them. McCreery had also planned a descent by 2 Parachute Brigade but, as with thirty-one earlier planned airborne operations, this was cancelled due to the strength of German anti-aircraft artillery in the intended drop zones. However, the Italian F Recce Squadron, with additional volunteers from Gruppo Folgore, dropped in groups of three or four to carry out guerrilla operations. So well did they perform 'that the Partisans' Committee of Liberation declared a general uprising on this morning of April 25'.[19]

First to reach the Po, 10th Mountain Division was also first to cross the river. Hays was not going to let the opportunity slip and, on the morning of the 23rd, fifty M2 assault boats were brought up. There were no engines, 'so the engineers paddled the ungainly craft, each one loaded to the gunwales with ten to twelve infantrymen'.[20] Artillery support was to be provided by a battalion of M7 105mm howitzers and a battery of 178th (Lowland) Medium Regiment. The commander of 7 AGRA had reinforced the Scottish regiment with Q Battery of 17th Medium, which made it easier to support each of the American infantry regiments,[21] while retaining the power to concentrate:

> All three batteries of the Regiment were in action by 8 a.m., some 6,000 yards south of the river. ...the infantry were expected to attempt a crossing the following night, and the CO decided to go forward to Divisional HQ for breakfast, while the Regiment seized the opportunity for a shave, a wash and food. On arrival at HQ the CO found that the leading infantry regiment had suddenly decided to cross in boats in an hour's time, and a diversionary and protective fire plan had to be made in a hurry, while OP parties were hastily called forward to the river bank and Battery Commanders to their infantry regimental HQs. Fortunately the zero hour for the crossing was delayed until noon, when guns opened for the first time and the leading infantry started to cross in boats.
>
> The chief opposition came from devastating 88mm low air-burst fire over the forming-up area, and later over the crossing itself – delivered, as we afterwards learned, by no fewer than 20 enemy guns, which were firing flashless ammunition so that even the Air OPs could not see them. In desperation the CO drove his jeep through the enemy fire to the river bank. There he met three Austrian prisoners and an Italian youth, who had just been brought back by boats returning from the first flight. The Austrians only knew the infantry positions, but the Italian youth had actually helped to dig the gunpits of the German guns. He was able to give their position on a 1/50,000 map, and they were promptly engaged with air-burst, not only by 178th Medium plus Q Battery, but by 2nd Medium Regiment, which had by then closed up as well – a 'Yoke' target from 40 medium guns! This fire soon silenced the enemy guns and enabled the infantry to secure a firm bridgehead. It was later found that the enemy had blown up all 20 88mm guns in their pits.[22]

The first wave of soldiers to cross, 1/87th, was followed by the remainder of the regiment and, in spite of opposition from machine guns, mortars and small-arms fire, the mountaineers had established a 2,000-yards-square bridgehead by 5.45pm. Fifteen minutes later, 85th Regiment joined them and 86th followed during the night, with a battalion of DUKWs arriving as the ferrying operation was underway. Bridging equipment followed next day and the river was spanned with a floating pontoon bridge that allowed trucks, tanks and artillery to cross for the drive north.[23] A cable ferry was in service by the afternoon of the 24th. And Mark Clark also arrived:

At long last, General Clark caught up to the 10th. Once again he congratulated General Hays – the insubordinate cavalry charge out of the hills apparently forgiven. Clark pumped Hays' hand and, grinning, called him 'the conqueror of the Po'.[24]

With a speed that had shocked the Germans, Fifth and Eighth Armies had smashed the Po defensive line and the situation now called out for exploitation. The next formation to cross was 85th Division, the Custermen's 3/337th crossing at Quingéntole, followed by the Blue Devils of 88th Division. Both divisions skirmished with Germans along the Po at Revere, these being elements intending to cross in the Revere-Ostiglia area, unaware that Allied troops had beaten them to the river line. IV Corps now held all its stretch of the Po with a division already across the river.

His 'wildest hopes' exceeded by the bold thrust to the Po, General Truscott prepared to take advantage of it by bringing up the 34th Division from garrison duties at Bologna to free part of the armor to exploit the crossing of the Po.[25]

CCA of 1st Armored Division was then deployed to San Benedetto to take part in a race to the Adige and Verona with 10th Mountain and 85th Divisions. Liberating Verona, the city of Shakespeare's *Romeo and Juliet* and *Two Gentlemen*, would reduce still further the escape routes available to German forces in the western sector of northern Italy. While CCA was deploying on this rapid advance, CCB, with 81st Reconnaissance Squadron, assembled near Reggio, between Modena and Parma, to support the Brazilians in gathering in what was left of LI Mountain Corps between the Apennines and the Po.

As demonstrated by the hordes of Germans eager to surrender, by the debris of a once-proud German Army that choked the roads leading to the Po, and by the easy crossing of the river by the 10th Mountain Division, no need remained for any formal set-piece attack to get across the Po. With that in mind, General Truscott ordered all divisions to cross on their own as quickly as possible.[26]

So both McCreery and Truscott were issuing similar instructions to their commanders. Their plans for destroying Army Group C were close to completion. Of that there was further convincing evidence on the morning of 25 April when General Graf von Schwerin, commander of LXXVI Panzer Corps, surrendered to Eighth Army. A man disillusioned with the war, von Schwerin had expressed that disenchantment 'and [his] conviction that continued fighting merely deepened his country's misery, he had survived Hitler's wrath only because he was a member of the old German nobility'.[27] Although his corps retained some organization, he believed that nothing could save his command, and so ordered them to abandon their tanks, artillery and other heavy equipment, and save themselves by making for the Po and swimming to safety. In his last instruction to his men, issued through Eighth Army after his surrender, he wrote:

I know the situation. For German soldiers in Italy it is hopeless. My Corps had had it. Under these circumstances I cannot give further commands.

In full knowledge of the situation I have chosen the only way open to a soldier who has been honourably but decisively defeated.

It is now the duty of every officer, of every NCO and of every soldier bravely to look facts in the face and to realize that it is criminal to throw away more human lives.[28]

Asked about the dispositions of his forces, von Schwerin told his captors, 'You will find them south of the Po.'[29] The rout of LXXVI Panzer Corps was complete. With LI Mountain Corps it had passed into oblivion.

Starr writes that 'the whirlwind drive which followed was one of the most brilliant in the entire history of Fifth Army'.[30] The army was fanning out across north-western Italy, IV Corps to the left racing north on the axis San Benedetto–Mantova (Mantua)–Verona, aiming to seize the airfield at Villafranca and liberate Verona. The corps was also charged with pushing fast-moving strong forces directly northward to the foothills of the Alps before swinging westward along the northern side of the Po valley through Bréscia and Bérgamo to deny to the retreating Germans the escape routes from Italy through the mountains between Lakes Garda and Como. II Corps' task was to advance northwards along the axis of Highway 12, securing the Adige's west bank from Legnago to Verona. With these objectives secured, the Germans would find no escape routes between Verona and Lake Como and Fifth Army would be positioned to make a major assault on the Venetian Line.[31]

The German plans for retiring north of the Po had been predicated on the assumption that the Allied armies would pause to regroup and await supplies of ammunition and equipment before continuing the offensive, thereby allowing Army Group C's constituent formations to reform and assume defensive positions. But, once again, no rest was allowed to von Vietinghoff's men. As 15th Army Group continued without pause, the Germans were unable to turn the chaos of retreat into the disciplined order needed for defence.

Once again 10th Mountain Division led the way with a dedicated task force. With Duff out of action, command of this group devolved on Colonel Orlando Darby, who, at the behest of Lucian Truscott, had raised and trained the US Army's first rangers unit at Carrickfergus in Northern Ireland. Darby had been posted back to Washington on being promoted colonel and, in March 1945, when he was with the War Department General Staff, took the opportunity of joining an observation mission to Italy under General 'Hap' Arnold. When Duff was wounded, Darby was appointed in his stead as assistant divisional commander. The new task force, under Darby's command, included 86th Regiment, 13th Tank Battalion of 1st Armored Division, B Company 751st Tank Battalion, B Company 701st Tank Destroyer Battalion, 1125th Armored Field Artillery Battalion, and elements of 126th Engineer Battalion.[32] Although Task Force Darby was to lead the divisional pursuit, it had to await the completion of bridges. The first bound by Hays' division was made by 85th Regiment.

Moving off shortly after midnight of 24/25 April, 85th Regiment marched almost twenty miles to Villafranca airfield, which was reached by mid-morning, a praiseworthy feat in strange country without proper maps and with no support to the rear. Late in the day, Darby's force arrived at Villafranca and passed through 85th en route to Verona. Arriving at the city at 6.00am on the 26th, Task Force Darby found that 88th Division had preceded them by eight hours. (From the 26th, the division's left flank was protected by 91st Cavalry Reconnaissance Squadron.) Darby pressed on, and by dusk his force was moving up the east shore of Lake Garda. With 85th Regiment still at Villafranca, 86th resting at Verona and Task Force Darby at Lake Garda, 10th Mountain Division had sealed the escape routes to the Brenner Pass between Verona and Lake Garda.[33]

To the right of 10th Mountain, 85th Division had crossed the Po at Quingéntole, using assault boats, DUKWs and rafts, and set off to the north, eventually securing the hills above Verona. En route to Verona, the Custermen were overtaken by the Blue Devils, whose 2/351st Regiment reached Verona two hours before midnight on the 25th. The Blue Devils' advance had not been without incident. Pfc Marvin A. Noll, a Pennsylvanian, captured ninety-seven Germans and later, when his platoon was caught in an ambush, 'stood his ground in a cross-fire of machine guns and bazookas and killed four, wounded three and captured eight'.[34] Pfc Rodolpho Sanchez, of Idaho, a lead scout, was surrounded by Germans who demanded his surrender. However, Sanchez fired a rifle grenade into the ground at the Germans' feet, killing three and wounding four. Although wounded himself, Sanchez had warned his squad of the ambush, turning the tables on the thirty surviving Germans who soon found themselves prisoners. At Buttapietra, Magnano and Verona, well-defended roadblocks were eliminated by Staff Sergeant Erwin H. Bender, of Ohio, while Lieutenant William F. Brennan, of Long Island, and his platoon of C Company 349th Regiment, tackled a German position near Oppeano from which fire had been opened on the column. Although outnumbered, Brennan and his men overcame the ambushers, and captured an 88mm gun that had also fired on them.[35]

CCA of 1st Armored Division crossed the Po on the 25th while CCB and Task Force Howze were assembling, ready to follow CCA towards Highway 11 and then into north-west Italy. Until the 26th both CCB and Task Force Howze had been south of the Po, the former north of Réggio and the latter blocking possible escape routes as far west as the river Taro, to the north-west of Parma.[36]

Also in action was 34th Division, the Red Bulls, the most experienced US division in the European theatre. Its task was to cut off enemy forces still in the mountains west and south of Modena. To do so, it advanced up Highway 9 with 133rd Regiment taking Réggio late on the 24th while 168th, with 755th Tank Battalion, ousted a force of service troops with some SPGs at Parma late the following day. It was then the turn of 135th to make for Piacenza, about forty-five miles away. Reached on the afternoon of 26 April, Piacenza was held by a determined garrison of Italian SS and German troops who held off the Red Bulls for two days. However:

In less than three days the 34th Division had pushed its forces 80 miles from Modena to the Po crossings at Piacenza and had split the enemy in two. To the south of the thin divisional line – 40 miles long and 40 feet wide – were the 148th Grenadier and Italia Bersaglieri Divisions, trapped at the edge of the Apennines south of Highway 9; to the north was the 232nd Grenadier Division, which had managed to cross the highway west of Parma ahead of the 34th Division and assembled to defend itself in the Po loop south of Cremona while slowly negotiating the river by ferry. The 34th Division, strung out as it was between three relatively intact divisions, was in no enviable position, yet the very fact that we could get away with such a maneuver illustrates clearly the end of the German armies as an organized fighting force.[37]

Starr's comment that the German armies no longer constituted an organized fighting force was proved by the relative ease with which 34th Division sealed off the Piacenza escape route on the north-west between 26 and 28 April while simultaneously deploying both 133rd and 168th Regiments to deal with 232nd Grenadier Division south of Cremona. Only part of 232nd managed to cross the Po, the remainder surrendering on the 27th, having sustained heavy losses in men and equipment. Thereafter, 34th Division was moved from the Piacenza area and 1st Brazilian Division took over, accepting the surrender of the other Axis divisions a few days later.[38]

The Brazilians had reached the plain south of Modena on 23 April, then wheeled to the north-west, south of Highway 9 and parallel to that road – and 34th Division. The FEB's change of direction pinched out 371st Regiment of 92nd Division, which was then deployed to Modena to guard prisoners. On the plain the Brazilians made good progress against token opposition until the 26th when their reconnaissance units and Italian partisans working with them encountered elements of 148th Grenadier and the Italia Bersaglieri Divisions at Collécchio, south of Parma. With the grenadiers and Bersaglieri determined to resist, a sharp skirmish developed that ended with the arrival of reinforcements; some 300 prisoners were taken. An attempt by 148th Division to break through the Red Bulls south of Parma on the 27th failed and the Germans withdrew along the Taro valley into the hills around Fornovo where heavy fighting followed until, at 6.00pm on the 29th, the commanders of both 148th Grenadier and Italia Bersaglieri Divisions surrendered to the Brazilians. By the last day of April the Brazilians had a haul of over 13,000 prisoners, as well as 4,000 horses and 1,000 lorries. By then the Brazilians, having taken over 34th Division's zone, had deployed 1st Infantry to Piacenza while a battalion of 11th Infantry had moved to eliminate the enemy pocket south of Cremona.[39]

Also over the Po and operating against the retreating enemy was 91st Division, which had crossed at Sérmide and advanced towards Cerea and Legnago. At the former, the division's 361st Regiment fought what Starr describes as 'a weird night-long engagement' with a large enemy column of transport and artillery that was trying to move north through Cerea:

Fortunately, the Germans were more confused than the 361st Infantry, and by morning they had been cut to pieces with appalling losses in equipment and personnel. Movement from Cerea to the Adige was without further incident. The 2nd Battalion, 363rd Infantry cleared Legnago by noon on the 26th and began crossing the Adige River immediately.[40]

Another bridgehead over the Po had been established at Felónica on the 25th by 6th South African Armoured Division.[41]

Twelve days after launching Operation CRAFTSMAN Fifth Army had sliced Army Group C in two. IV Corps had 10th Mountain Division blocking routes to the Brenner Pass between Verona and Lake Garda, while 85th Division was heading from Verona to the Adige in the hills north of the city and CCA was making for Bréscia past Mantova before wheeling north-west towards Como. On the army's right, II Corps' 88th and 91st Divisions were along the Adige from Verona to Legnago and making crossings of the river while 6th South African Armoured, on the corps' right, was heading for the Adige crossings south of Legnago, although two of its brigades were still south of the Po. In its zone Eighth Army was also deploying forces towards the Adige. Over to the west, 92nd Division had eliminated the final Gothic Line position on the 25th and was moving towards Genoa.[42]

Truscott issued fresh orders on 26 April: Fifth Army was to cut off and destroy those German forces in north-west Italy and assist Eighth Army in liberating Pádova (Padua), a role assigned to II Corps, which was to wheel to the east on the axis Verona-Vicenza; this deployment was also intended to block routes to the mountains from the Adriatic that might be used by retreating Germans. However, the main effort was to seize the Adige defences before the enemy could man them. IV Corps, meanwhile, was to deploy a division northwards along the eastern shore of Lake Garda on the axis Verona-Trento-Bolzano to the Brenner Pass and into the so-called Alpine redoubt, in the existence of which Clark still seemed to believe. Underlying the operations of the final week of the war in Italy was a determination to capture as many of the enemy as possible, thereby preventing the creation of 'the Tyrolean army reportedly being organized in the mountains',[43] an army that was no more than a delusion. Meanwhile, 1st Armored's drive north-westwards to Lake Como was to continue while the Red Bulls and Brazilians mopped up south of the Po.[44]

With some notable exceptions, there was no organized resistance from German and fascist Italian formations, all cohesion above unit level having been lost. However, on 28 April, at San Pietro in Gu, north by north-west of Padua, the town was retaken in a surprise attack by a column of 26th Panzer Division, who took prisoner a number of Allied soldiers, including the entire personnel of a US artillery battery. Elsewhere, a greater problem was presented to IV Corps by the presence of 'an intact block of two divisions' of Lieutenant General Ernst Schlemmer's LXXV Corps in the western sector of the Po valley. These divisions, 34th Grenadier and 5th Gebirgs, had been deployed to guard the Italo-French border but were withdrawing north-eastwards past Turin and suffering persistent attacks from Italian partisans. Elements of IV Corps were deployed to ensure that they could not escape from the Po plain.[45]

No front lines existed north of the Po and Fifth Army's formations operated in high-speed mobile all-arms columns, ready to deal with any opposition. In many instances, US troops found themselves ahead of the retreating enemy and cutting them off from the Alps. Vicenza was in American hands at the end of the 28th, following some hard fighting by 350th Regiment of 88th Division. Once clear of the city, the Blue Devils again found themselves faced by mountains; 'in two weeks they'd traversed all the flat country in Italy'.[46] Ahead of them lay their last battles of the war and their foe was I Fallschirmjäger Corps, or some of what was left of it. Withdrawing into the mountains the Germans fought to slow the advance of Kendall's division:

> The Kraut had his back to the last wall. At 1250 hours on the 29th, the 351st Infantry secured the bank of the Brenta River at Bassano and made a crossing in strength on the 30th, clearing the town of Bassano and opening the gateway to the so-called Inner Fortress or Inner Redoubt, the area in which Hitler had been expected to make his last stand with picked SS troops.[47]

After the heat and dust of the past two weeks, it must have been a shock to the GIs when they were issued with winter clothing and snowpacs 'as the regiments crunched north through the snow and Dolomite Alps'.[48] Fonzaso was taken by the 351st while 2/349th liberated Feltre on 1 May, the 351st moving on to Borgo, which they secured by noon on 2 May, and the 349th advanced to Fiera di Primiero. More fighting was expected when fresh orders listed Innsbruck in Austria as the next major objective, to be reached via the Brenner Pass. Unknown to the officers and men of the Blue Devils the war in Italy was already over. Not until 4.00pm on 2 May did they have an inkling of this, and it came from a party of three officers of 1st Fallschirmjäger Division who approached 351st Regiment under a flag of truce, informing them that the war had ended officially, with unconditional German surrender, at 2.00pm. Unfortunately, Colonel Miller, commanding 351st Regiment, thought this might be a ruse, especially when he could not contact divisional HQ by radio. Giving the Germans an hour to surrender their own formation, Miller was confronted, before the hour expired, by a second delegation with the same story. On this occasion, he told the Germans that they had fifteen minutes to surrender. Although warned that the enemy would resist any attempt to advance, Miller ordered his men forward and the Germans fought back. Four men died and six were wounded in the subsequent short scrap. It was some hours before official news was received of the German surrender and it took until early on the 3rd to pass that news to all units of the 88th.[49]

The Custermen of 85th Division 'simply walked through the Adige Line north of Verona' on 26 April, before reverting to Army reserve, ready to support any of various thrusts if necessary.[50] Meanwhile, 10th Mountain moved up Lake Garda's east shore towards the entrances to the Brenner Pass. Hays' men ran into 'the most difficult fighting it had experienced since the breakthrough in the Apennines'.[51] Under direct command of HQ Fifth Army after 28 April, they made for the head of Lake Garda but met tough resistance. The Germans blew tunnel entrances, making a road approach almost impossible. With no mountaineering equipment to take to the mountains that come down to the lakeshore, elements of the division made an amphibious hook while others continued to fight along the shore. Two companies of 85th Regiment were carried by DUKWs across the lake to Gargnano, which they secured, and captured Mussolini's villa before continuing on the western shore through Limone sul Garda to Riva at the head of the lake. Still with the division was the British 178th Medium Regiment, which faced the problem of keeping its 5.5-inch guns close enough to support the forward troops. A masterpiece of improvisation ensued:

> By the afternoon of April 28th it was obvious that the advance could no longer be carried on by land. At the northern end of the lake the road ran through tunnels which had been very thoroughly wrecked. The infantry wasted no time in taking to DUKWs and, supported by the Regiment's fire on land, succeeded in outflanking the enemy rearguards by water. Q Battery of 17th Medium Regiment had by this time been withdrawn and the two batteries of the Regiment were in action as far north as possible, but only just within range of a bridgehead likely to develop on the northern shore of the lake. The CO decided that one battery would have to get to the bridgehead by water and went off to search for craft.[52]

With their usual thoroughness the Germans had destroyed the engines of all motor barges on the lake. However, three sailing barges were found at the little ports of Brenzone, Casteletto and Cassone and loading a 5.5-inch gun twixt main and mizzen masts of each looked feasible. Malcesine's small harbour became a port of embarkation, a troop was brought out of action and its gun detachments became dock labourers. After holds had been loaded with ammunition as ballast, Bailey bridge girder decking was laid from gunwale to gunwale. Difficulties overcome, the first barge, SS *Veronica*, sailed at 5.00pm on 30 April, and with a strong following wind covered eight miles in seventy-five minutes before berthing in Torbole, captured earlier that day. Two DUKWs winched the 5.5 on to dry land and it was in action before dark, after running the gauntlet of enemy 105mm concentrations during the move through Torbole.[53]

Next day, May 1st, the ships *Angela*, *Ardua* and *Isonzo*, (the last-named brought back from the northern port of Riva after a Focke-Wulf plane had been unloaded from her hold) ferried over three more guns. Each [sailing ship] made two trips, the wind providentially blowing south in the morning and north in the afternoon, [and] seven guns of this battery were in action before dark. The eighth gun and Advance HQ followed next morning. A half-track armoured OP, loaded in the stern of the second vessel, took the place of a tractor and hauled all the remaining guns to the position about 800 yards from Torbole. Thus the Regiment, with three OPs advancing in the bridgehead, was able to support the leading infantry as they moved forward up the three lines of advance north of the lake, up to the very last moment when, on the evening of May 2nd, the German armies in Italy and Austria gave up the struggle.[54]

In those final days, Colonel William Darby was killed. In Torbole meeting with Brigadier General Ruffner and other officers to plan the advance to Trento, he had left the hotel with the others and climbed into the back seat of Ruffner's jeep when an 88mm shell hit the building above them. A piece of metal tore into Darby's chest and he died instantly, as did a young sergeant major who was hit in the head. William O. Darby was promoted posthumously to brigadier general.[55]

By the time the Germans surrendered, elements of 86th Regiment were manning road blocks five miles north of the lake at Arco.[56]

First Armored had deployed its combat commands around Milan, which was liberated by Italian partisans; a task force from IV Corps entered the city on 30 April. Old Ironsides had hammered a wedge between enemy forces on the plain and those in the mountains; the line the division had formed was strengthened by 34th Division and Gruppo Legnano. Relieving elements of 1st Armored along the Ticino on 1 May, 34th Division liberated Novara the next day and, by so doing, trapped LXXV Corps north-east of Turin, which was liberated by partisans. Schlemmer had no alternative but to surrender.[57]

On the Ligurian coast, 92nd Division had broken what was left of the Gothic Line by 22 April, except for the stronghold at Aulla, thereby forcing a hasty enemy withdrawal. Inland, 370th Regiment advanced down Highways 62 and 63, behind 148th Grenadier and the Italia Bersaglieri Divisions, who were also under pressure from the Brazilians and 34th Division. Meanwhile, 442nd and 473rd Regiments raced to Genoa on Highway 1, where the garrison had surrendered to partisans on 26 April, although a detachment of marines on a hill overlooking the harbour, and the port garrison, held out, until threatened by an American and partisan assault when the two regiments arrived on the 27th. Driving around Genoa, 442nd moved north onto the Lombardy plain, liberating Alessandria, capturing its 3,000-strong garrison next day and establishing contact with the Brazilians; contact with IV Corps had already been made at Pavia. On 30 April 473rd Regiment made contact with French colonial troops on the coast. With American troops pushing down into Italy from the north, the Germans were surrendering almost everywhere.[58]

Eighth Army's General Staff had concluded that the Germans would defend the Po strongly until LXXVI Panzer Corps had been evacuated and that they would have difficulty manning the Venetian, or Red, Line.[59] On Eighth Army's front the Venetian Line extended from the Euganean Hills in the west to the Adige in the east but the central, flat, sector was considerably weaker than the flanks. Beyond the Venetian Line there were no further prepared positions in Eighth Army's sector. From the Po two axes of advance were possible: for XIII Corps, to Badia Polesina on the Adige, or, for V Corps, to Rovigo along Highway 16, Via Adriatica. The General Staff preferred the former, western, axis since it could less easily be obstructed, but the latter was needed as the army's main supply route. Since an advance on the western axis might not be speedy enough to cut off a retreating force on Highway 16, McCreery decided to continue with both XIII and V Corps up. Bridging equipment was divided between the corps, as were DUKWs, LVTs, assault rafts, boats and DD tanks. The Po Task Force would build the planned high-level Bailey near the Via Adriatica.[60]

We have already seen how 1 Guards Brigade of 6th Armoured Division crossed and, with the New Zealanders, pursued the retreating Germans from the Po. The battlegroups of 6th Armoured were well back but an improvised group was formed from C Squadron 7th Hussars with DD Shermans, D Squadron 12th Lancers with armoured cars and A Squadron 1st Derbyshire Yeomanry with Sherman and Stuart tanks. Commanded by Colonel W. R. Nicolson DSO, this was Nicforce which snapped at the Germans' heels so effectively that it captured about a hundred men, killed between forty and fifty, knocked out sixteen vehicles and an armoured car, captured three 105mm howitzers and two other artillery pieces and some forty 'machine rifles and *faustpatronen*', although this haul was considered 'a very conservative estimate'.[61] Its task complete, Nicforce was disbanded on 27 April. The New Zealanders, still with 43 Gurkha Brigade under command, had pinched out the Guards to cross the Adige at Badia Polesina on the night of 26/27 April, having met no opposition. Freyberg spent the 27th consolidating his command before moving off at dawn next day to advance to the Venetian Line. Probing ahead were 12th Lancers, acting as the divisional recce regiment. Again no opposition was encountered and Blaxland describes how the 'troops surged forward like hounds in full cry, jostling each other, blasting aside spasmodic opposition, and often speeding across bridges proudly preserved for them by partisans'.[62]

In V Corps' sector, 8th Indian Division crossed the Po west of Ferrara and 56th Division a dozen miles to the east. The Indian 17 and 21 Brigades met little opposition in doing so on the night of 25/26 April. On the 25th leading elements of 56th Division met 'brisk opposition' while probing the river in daylight, but the Queen's Brigade crossed almost unopposed in LVTs that night, supported by a squadron of DD Shermans, and advanced to within three miles of Rovigo, the corps objective. On the extreme right of V Corps, Gruppo Cremona also crossed, improvising with whatever abandoned boats and rafts they could find, to liberate Adria early on 26 April, after which, with 28 Garibaldi Brigade still under command, they made their way along the coast to Venice.[63]

During the 26th both corps reached the Adige, the Queen's Brigade north of Rovigo and the New Zealanders close to Badia Polesina. Although Herr had intended that Tenth Army would stand on the Venetian Line, this proved impossible: Eighth Army was moving so fast that the Germans could not regain any equilibrium, and had lost so much equipment and heavy weaponry before crossing the Po that they lacked the wherewithal to fight. Although elements of I Fallschirmjäger and LXXV Panzer Corps had escaped, the Adige proved another disaster for them, as they had to abandon much of what little equipment was left.[64] Even so, there was some fight left in some Germans at least:

Entering Rovigo late on 26 April, the Queen's found that the German garrison had already been incarcered in the gaol. But next day the 2/7th Queen's were strongly counterattacked after crossing the Adige and had a grim fight to retain a bridgehead.[65]

Italian partisans were very active, saving several bridges from demolition, a boon to Allied engineers who were pushed to keep up with the advance. Because of the shortage of bridging equipment, crossings were being made by LVTs and DUKWs and the swimming Shermans were much prized. Keeping an eye on the advance from his Auster, Sir Richard McCreery was able to see 7th Hussars' DD Shermans crossing both Po and Adige.[66] Meanwhile the sappers toiled to ensure that the leading elements could be maintained: an 1,100-foot-long Bailey pontoon was open in XIII Corps' area, at Ficarolo, early on the 27th while, by midnight, a similar bridge at Pontelagoscuro was aiding V Corps.[67]

McCreery had been compelled to ground some of his formations: in addition to II Polish Corps and 10th Indian Division, both now out of action, 78th Division was brought to a standstill, as were 24 Guards and 167 Brigades of 56th Division. After the Adige 8th Indian Division was also grounded; only 61 Brigade of 6th Armoured remained in the race. In fact, Freyberg's New Zealand Division, still with 43 Gurkha Brigade under command, was the largest Eighth Army formation still operating. The New Zealanders had a new task: advance to Trieste 'at top speed'. This was to ensure that Trieste and the surrounding area remained Italian rather than falling under Yugoslav control; Tito's Yugoslav Fourth Army was also making for the city. Since the province of Venézia Giúlia was also coveted by the Yugoslavs, 56th Division was directed to Venice, as were elements of 2nd New Zealand Division.[68]

On the morning of the 28th, as day broke, 12th Lancers moved off for Trieste 'on what was to become the regiment's most exhilarating episode of the whole war'.[69] Freyberg chose to move with the van, travelling in a scout car and, by 3.00pm, 'they were in Este and by midnight in Padua. The advance moved so fast that the regiment ran out of maps and was compelled to equip itself with a collection of Baedeker guide books and atlases.'[70] Eighth Army's war diary notes that:

> During the day rapid advances were made by our troops from the two bridgeheads across the Adige and by last light leading elements were reported at MONSÉLICE 2330 and ESTE 1529.[71]

Those 'leading elements' at Este and Monsélice were the armoured cars of D Squadron, 12th Lancers. A Squadron made contact with 6th South African Armoured Division at Montagnana, west of Este.[72] At Freyberg's behest, B Squadron was diverted to Venice, the main objective for 169 (Queen's) Brigade, since the GOC was determined to be in the city first, so as to liberate the Danieli Hotel where he had spent his honeymoon, as also had McCreery. B Squadron, leading a small battlegroup of 9 Brigade, crossed the causeway on the afternoon of the 29th, reaching Venice about two hours before the Queen's Brigade, who dealt with a rearguard at Mestre before pipping 44th Reconnaissance Regiment to make 56th Division's entry into Venice. About 3,000 captive Germans were handed over by partisans. A New Zealand officer, with eight men, travelled by boat to the Lido and the islands of Murano and Burano to take the surrenders of the local German garrisons.[73]

Along the way both formations found that Italian partisans had been at work. Jackson pays tribute to their work:

> A notable contribution to the fragmentation of both German armies was made by Italian Partisans. After the Allied breakthrough came with the crossing of the Po a general insurrection had been ordered by the CLNAI in Milan on 25 April. Most of the big cities of northern Italy thereafter fell into Partisan hands before Allied troops could reach them and important facilities, such as hydro-electric works, were thus saved from German demolition. In the field Partisan forces obstructed the Germans' withdrawal routes and waylaid the despatch riders who often represented the sole means of communication between headquarters. 26th Panzer and 29th Panzer Grenadier Divisions had both to fight off attacks from strong bands as they tried to move across country into the Venetian Line. Their dispersed and exhausted units were continuously beset during the subsequent withdrawal to and across the Brenta.[74]

In Padua 12th Lancers found that the 5,000-strong German garrison had been imprisoned by partisans, who, to their credit, carried out no major reprisals against German soldiers. Another thousand Germans, including the local commander, were captured by 43 Gurkha Brigade, which also entered the city. Udine had been liberated by 61 Brigade of 6th Armoured Division and, while 56th Division remained in Venice, the New Zealanders were again on their way to Trieste; 1st Scots Guards had been added to their strength.[75]

Freyberg's men were under orders to make all speed on the seventy-five-mile journey to Trieste and, on the afternoon of 2 May, A Squadron led the way into the city centre. The German garrison surrendered to Freyberg rather than to the Yugoslavs, whose political ambition was to include Trieste and the surrounding region in Yugoslavia. The day before, at Monfalcone, Freyberg had met the Yugoslav partisan commander, General Drapsin, whom he told that his command was but the advance guard of a powerful force of armour and infantry. Nonetheless, Yugoslav partisans entered Trieste on 1 May, bringing terror to many of the city's population. Freyberg's soldiers were called upon to act as diplomats and protectors while their commanders attempted to create good relations with the Yugoslavs.[76]

Resolution of the Trieste problem was not something that soldiers could achieve, but the western Allies' determination to uphold Italy's claim – Trieste, once part of the Austro-Hungarian Empire, had been ceded to Italy in 1915 – could only be shown by a demonstration of force, and an American division deployed to Trieste in May. In 1947 the city became part of a free territory under United Nations protection until Italy and Yugoslavia agreed frontiers in 1954 when the city again became part of Italy and British and US troops finally left.[77]

There were also problems with the Yugoslavs and Soviets in Austria but these are outside the scope of this book, although many of those who had fought from the Senio onwards were witnesses to them.

As the New Zealanders raced for Trieste the final phase in surrender negotiations was underway. 'Peace' negotiations had begun as far back as February when Karl Wolff, SS commander in Italy, had made approaches to Allen Dulles, a US diplomat, and later head of the CIA, through a Swiss intermediary. Liaison continued, although Kesselring, as overall commander in the west, had taken a diehard stance. While an agreement was reached on 29 April for the unconditional surrender of all German and Axis forces in Italy and the Austrian provinces of Vorarlberg, Tyrol, Salzburg and parts of Carinthia and Styria, this was pre-empted by von Vietinghoff when he learned of Hitler's suicide the next day and ordered his soldiers to surrender. However, his orders only brought forward the time for the formal surrender by an hour. All fighting was to cease by noon on 2 May. Kesselring's reaction was to order von Vietinghoff's arrest, but events soon outran him and von Vietinghoff was released.[78]

Inevitably, there were some problems with the surrender. We have already noted the misunderstanding between 88th US Division and the fallschirmjäger who attempted to surrender to them. The opposite problem faced 27th Lancers who came up against Germans on the road to Klagenfurt who considered that the surrender order did not apply to them, as they were part of Army Group South-East and not under von Vietinghoff's command. In the clashes that ensued at least one lancer was killed some two hours after the surrender hour. A truce was agreed but the Germans did not capitulate for several days.[79] Green Jackets of 2nd Rifle Brigade had a similar problem. They encountered Germans who wanted to continue the fight against Bolshevism and suggested that they be allowed to cross the border into Austria. However, the problem resolved itself as those who were keen to continue fighting were allowed to cross the Austrian border where they surrendered on 7 May.[80]

While the surrender was being finalized on 29 April, the weather broke. Having been fine and dry for Eighth Army since operations began 'we had a few days of heavy showers and thunderstorms' at the end of the month which caused some rivers to rise very rapidly, but 'they fell again equally quickly'.[81]

The experiences of 27th Lancers, 2nd Rifle Brigade and 351st Infantry of the Blue Devils, as well as that of the New Zealanders in Trieste, illustrate how wars never end cleanly, irrespective of how history records their ends. Operations GRAPESHOT, BUCKLAND and CRAFTSMAN were over, and with them the war in Italy, but many results of the war had still to be resolved. These included displaced persons, the attempts by the Soviets and their Yugoslav allies to seize territory, the clearing of minefields and unexploded munitions, and the repair of wrecked or damaged essential infrastructure. The infrastructural problems could have been worse had it not been for Italian partisans who prevented the Germans from sabotaging or destroying many facilities, such as pumping stations, electricity-generating plants and bridges. But the damage was still huge and would take many years to repair.

The end of fighting prompted a flurry of congratulatory messages. Even before that, Nap Murray, GOC of 6th Armoured Division wrote:

The Division has just concluded a brilliant action and I wish to congratulate you all on the magnificent way you exploited the fleeting opportunity which presented itself on April 18th. We fought non-stop for five days and our success was entirely due to the magnificent fighting qualities of the forward troops and the untiring efforts of those behind. Our reward was over 3,000 prisoners and considerable quantities of guns, ammunition and stores. Moreover, we were the first British Division to reach the Po.

At the conclusion of the battle we had the honour of a personal visit by Field Marshal Alexander and General McCreery, the Commander of Eighth Army. They asked me to congratulate you all on their behalf.

Well done everybody![82]

That message was issued on 24 April but, after the German surrender, Murray issued a further message on 5 May:

Seldom in a campaign of the magnitude of the Italian campaign has one formation contributed in such great measure to final victory.

Our fighting qualities and our outstanding teamwork have made this possible. It is indeed a privilege to command you.[83]

Other commanders, at corps, divisional and brigade level, issued their messages, while McCreery sent special orders of the day to the corps of Eighth Army, including versions in Italian and Polish. From far off Washington DC, the new US president, Harry S. Truman, sent a message that Clark passed on to 'each American officer and enlisted man':

On the occasion of the final brilliant victory of the allied armies in Italy in imposing unconditional surrender upon the enemy, I wish to convey to the American Forces under your command and to you personally the appreciation of the President and of the people of the United States. No praise is adequate for the heroic achievements and magnificent courage of every individual under your command during this long and trying campaign.

America is proud of the essential contribution made by your American Armies to the final victory in Italy. Our thanks for your gallant leadership and the deathless valor of your men.[84]

While Clark and Truman seemed to have forgotten that there were personnel other than Americans in Fifth Army, no complaint could be made about chauvinistic bias in Winston Churchill's message to Alexander:

I rejoice in the magnificently planned and executed operations of the Fifteenth Group of Armies which are resulting in the complete destruction or capture of all enemy forces South of the Alps.

That you and General Mark Clark should have been able to accomplish these tremendous and decisive results against a superior number of enemy divisions after you had made great sacrifices of whole armies for the Western front is indeed another proof of your genius for war and the intimate brotherhood in arms between the British Commonwealth and Imperial Forces and those of the United States.

Never I suppose have so many nations advanced and manoeuvred in one line victoriously. British, Americans, New Zealanders, South Africans, British Indians, Poles, Jews, Brazilians and strong forces of liberated Italians have all marched together in the high comradeship and unity of men fighting for freedom and for the deliverance of mankind.

This great battle in Italy will long stand out in history as one of the most famous episodes in this second world war.

Pray give my heartfelt congratulations to all your commanding and principal officers of all Services and, above all, to the valiant and ardent troops whom they have led with so much skill.[85]

Churchill's message was much more appreciative of the efforts of the many nations that had contributed to victory in Italy. Of course, he had had a closer interest in the campaign than other leaders, having been a chief architect of it and a supporter of the Allied efforts in Italy, whereas the United States' commitment to the theatre reduced greatly after the Normandy landings in June 1944.

For soldiers on the ground there was little time for celebrations as many tasks faced them in the weeks and months ahead. The author of the history of the Indian Army's divisions in Italy wrote of the experience of 8th Indian Division when the war ended, by which time the division had been grounded (although a squadron of 6th Lancers deployed into the Alps to confront the remnants of 1st Fallschirmjäger Division; the German commander refused to surrender to anyone other than an officer of equal rank and so an American general was found). For the rest of the division:

In the fields, around the village fountains, in the billets of the towns, the sepoys told the civilians, 'Guerra è finita'. The volatile Italians cheered and cried and celebrated; the Indians were kissed and embraced and wined and fed. They took it all gravely. It had been such a long road that it was a little difficult to realize that the march was over. It was hard to believe that a man might walk upright and openly in the daylight without death seeking him. That night hereafter would be a time for sleep instead of for bitter marches and grim encounters – this too seemed a strange thing.[86]

What celebrations there were in Eighth Army were muted. It would take time for men to adjust to peace, but no one regretted the end of the war. The day before war ended in Italy, the Catholic padre of 38 (Irish) Brigade discovered the bodies of three soldiers of 2nd Irish Rifles who had been reported missing the previous winter during a patrol in the Apennines. Jim Trousdell of 1st Royal Irish Fusiliers recalled feelings that must have been shared by many:

> the end of the war was celebrated with a tremendous barrage of Very lights, parachute flares and everything else that was luminous and noisy. The opportunity to dispose of these items that had been carried for so long could not be missed. It was difficult to realize that the war really had ended and it took some time to adjust to the unusual experience of peace. I had gone straight from school in 1939 into the Army and now a new life was about to begin.[87]

Neither the history of Fifth Army nor the US Official History of the Italian campaign record any American celebrations. None is mentioned in the history of the Blue Devils, but that of 34th Division reflects Jim Trousdell's feelings:

> There was no shouting or cheering, no demonstrations whatsoever. Perhaps this was because these battle-weary men had for many months foreseen that the enemy's collapse was inevitable. Perhaps too, they were sobered by a feeling that this awful war was not to end all wars. Certainly, one heard much talk of probable future wars. So, while there was a great sense of relief that the fighting was over, nevertheless, a peculiar atmosphere of depression seemed to pervade our troops.[88]

Peace seemed to be a hard concept to grasp.

Notes

1. Mead, op. cit., p.184.
2. Jeffers, op. cit., p.251.
3. Truscott, op. cit., p.492.
4. Fisher, op. cit., pp.490–1.
5. Ibid., p.491.
6. Ibid., p.490.
7. Delaney, op. cit., p.207.
8. Blaxland, op. cit., p.273.
9. Fisher, p.492.
10. Jenkins, op. cit., p.227; Starr, op. cit., p.421; Rottman, op. cit., p.37.
11. Fisher, p.493.
12. Blaxland, p.272.
13. Jenkins, pp.231–2; Rottman, p.38; Blaxland, p.272.
14. Blaxland, p.273.
15. Jackson, p.315–16.

16. Ibid., p.316.
17. Jackson, pp.316–17; *The Tiger Triumphs*, p.198; Belogi & Guglielmi, p.276.
18. Blaxland, p.275.
19. Jackson, p.317; Blaxland, pp.274–5.
20. Shelton, op. cit., p.250.
21. Freeth, in Duncan, p.328.
22. Ibid., pp.328–9.
23. Ibid., p.329.
24. Shelton, p.252.
25. Fisher, p.495.
26. Ibid., p.496.
27. Ibid., p.498.
28. Scott, op. cit.
29. Ray, p.226.
30. Starr, p.429.
31. Fisher, p.499; Jackson, pp.322–3.
32. Fisher, p.500; Rottman, p.32.
33. Starr, p.430.
34. Delaney, op. cit., p.211.
35. Ibid., p.
36. Starr, p.430.
37. Ibid., p.431.
38. Ibid.
39. Maximiano & Bonanume Neto, op. cit., pp.33–4; Starr, pp.431–2.
40. Starr, p.433.
41. Belogi & Guglielmi, p.332; Orpen, pp.301–2.
42. Starr, p.433.
43. Ibid., p.434.
44. Ibid.
45. Belogi & Guglielmi, pp.353–4; Starr, pp.434–5.
46. Delaney, p.218.
47. Ibid., pp.218–19.
48. Ibid., p.219.
49. Ibid., pp.219–20.
50. http://www.custermen.com/History85htm 8 Feb '14;
51. Starr, p.435.
52. Freeth, in Duncan, p.329.
53. Ibid.
54. Ibid.
55. Shelton, pp.272–3; Belogi & Guglielmi, pp.354–5; Jenkins, p.243.
56. Starr, p.435.
57. Ibid, pp.435–7; *I Gruppi di Combattimento*, pp.365–6.
58. Starr, pp.272–3.
59. Jackson, pp.323–4; NA, WO170/4180, war diary, HQ Eighth Army (G, Main), Apr '45.
60. Jackson, p.319.
61. NA, WO170/4456, HQ 26 Armd Bde, 1945.
62. Blaxland, p.276.

63. Belogi & Guglielmi, pp.328–9; *DSM*, Gruppo Cremona, pp.123–4.
64. Jackson, p.321.
65. Blaxland, p.276.
66. Mead, p.187.
67. Jackson, pp.317–19.
68. Ibid., p.324.
69. Mead, p.187.
70. Ibid.
71. NA, WO170/4180, HQ (main) Eighth Army, Apr '45.
72. Kay, p.517.
73. Kay, p.525; Williams, op. cit., pp.119–20.
74. Jackson, pp.321–2.
75. Kay, pp.526–8; Jackson, pp.326–7; NA, WO170/4626, war diary 12 L, 1945; Blaxland, p.277.
76. Jackson, pp.324–6.
77. Ibid., pp.336–9; Doherty. *A Noble Crusade*, p.318.
78. Jackson, pp.329–32.
79. NA, WO170/4630, war diary, 27 L, 1945.
80. NA, WO170/5062, war diary, 2 RB, 1945.
81. McCreery, draft memoir, p.16.
82. NA, WO170/4456, war diary, HQ 26 Armd Bde, 1945.
83. Ibid.
84. *Finito*, p.64.
85. Ibid., p.65.
86. *The Tiger Triumphs*, p.201.
87. Trousdell to author.
88. *History of 34th Division*, unpaginated (p.189 of text).

Epilogue

For most people today the Italian campaign is summed up in two words: Cassino and Anzio. Little is known about the many other battles, whether before or after Cassino and Anzio. So little has been written of the war north of Rome that the sacrifices of Allied soldiers in the Gothic Line battles are almost unknown. The same may be said of the campaign covered in this book. The author is aware of only one book on Operation GRAPESHOT in the UK – that by Brian Harpur, published in 1980. Why this amnesia?

Six days after the German surrender in Italy, the Allies celebrated VE Day. Just as the liberation of Rome on 4 June 1944 had been overshadowed by the landings in Normandy two days later, so victory in Italy was overshadowed by victory in Germany; the term 'Victory in Europe' was to become associated popularly with the fall of the German homeland. In the United Kingdom the image of Montgomery accepting the German surrender on Lüneberg Heath is much better known than that of Alexander's Chief of Staff, General Morgan, accepting the German surrender at Caserta, or of Mark Clark accepting that of von Vietinghoff. The same is true in the United States where Eisenhower's name is much better known than those of Clark, or Truscott, although in part that is due to Eisenhower's two terms as president. It seems that the Italian campaign began to slip from public consciousness even while its final phases were being fought in the northern Apennines and on the plain of Lombardy.

However, those final days in Italy should be remembered for several reasons, not least the sacrifice made by all who fought and died in the last weeks of war in Italy. But there are other reasons. Those include the planning and execution of the campaign, which bear comparison with anything in north-west Europe. As we have seen, both armies involved in Operation GRAPESHOT had lost considerable manpower to other theatres and did not greatly outnumber the enemy, thus requiring their commanders to devise plans to overcome their lack of mass. Sir Richard McCreery and Lucian Truscott produced plans that did just that. Using specialized armour, much of it produced in workshops in Italy, gave the attackers a positive advantage. So too did the use of new methods of transporting infantry into the attack, as the Kangaroo APCs and the Fantails demonstrated. Combined with McCreery's decision to attack from a totally unexpected direction, across Lake Comácchio and the neighbouring flooded land, such machines ensured that the attackers reaped a harvest of surprise, with the Kangaroos also permitting rapid pursuit of the enemy, giving him no opportunity to consolidate fresh defences.

The role of artillery was critical, as so often in Italy. Most of 15th Army Group's artillery was British; and the performance of the artillery generally was summed up succinctly by Brigadier Tom Howard, commander of 6 AGRA, who commented of the closing weeks that 'It was like giving the final tap to a truly driven nail with a nicely balanced hammer'.[1] The shell famine overcome, both armies' gunners wielded considerable muscle to which the Germans could not respond effectively. With Air OPs over the battleground, and FOOs accompanying advancing formations and units, artillery support could be provided almost immediately. Rare indeed were the occasions when gunners could not respond effectively to a call for support.

Like the gunners, the engineers were on top of their game, having honed and enhanced their techniques and skills in the harsh university of the Italian campaign and, in the case of the British sappers, even earlier in North Africa. The work of the New Zealand engineers in Operation BUCKLAND exemplified the skills, professionalism and flexibility of sappers in Italy, and their quick responses to every call made on them ensured that the two armies could move rapidly throughout GRAPESHOT. That the New Zealand engineers could put a Bailey across a stream or small river in less than an hour is ample testimony to their abilities.

Both armies worked as teams, as did both tactical air arms, while co-operation between ground forces and air forces reached new levels. Granted there were still errors, in which lives were lost, but those were few when related to the number of sorties flown and the complexities of operations. General McCreery wrote that:

> The Desert Air Force gave the Eighth Army magnificent support. Not only on the banks of the Senio, but often during the next twelve days the fighter-bombers of Desert Air Force were accurately bombing strong points, such as farms, only two to three hundred yards ahead of our leading infantry. They also frequently located and knocked out single tanks or SP guns. In the difficult terrain of Italy this brought out once again that success was always achieved by good team work; good team work between the fighter-bomber, the tanks, the Crocodile, the artillery, the infantryman and the sapper. It was essential to have mutual confidence between the various arms, and this was always achieved when the various arms knew each other well and had trained together beforehand.[2]

McCreery was generous in his praise of those who made up Eighth Army's team, which included the personnel of Desert Air Force, a formation he described as 'the best trained Air Force in the world'.[3] That description is no exaggeration. The same may be said of the various elements of his own command, whether infantry, tank crews, gunners, engineers, medics or the many others who came together to form the most famous of British armies, Eighth Army, which included an international mix of British, Indian, Italian, Jewish, New Zealand and Polish troops among the many races to be found in its ranks.

Fifth Army too had reached a high state of efficiency by the opening of the final offensive and there could surely have been few troops in any army to match those of 10th Mountain Division, whose advance through the mountains onto the plain split a German army in two and knocked it off balance completely. With Brazilian, British, Italian and South African troops in the order of battle, it was another truly multi-national formation. Fifteenth Army Group reflected fully the title the Allies had adopted more than two years earlier: United Nations.

While there is no doubt that such an eclectic mix of nations – Alexander reckoned that he had about thirty different nationalities under his command – could cause problems, these were overcome by good leadership, Alexander himself proving an ideal commander for such a multi-national force. Although much British and American equipment differed, there was also much that was common, the Allied armies having standardized on the American M4 Sherman as their principal battle tank, while American artillery was also used across the army group; some British artillery was also common, the American 75mm anti-tank gun being the British 6-pounder. The Germans had similar problems although Clark believed the German armies to be homogenous; this was not true, since they included several other nations as well as Germans – Russians and Poles as well as ethnic Turks, Azeris and refugees from the Caucasus. There were also individuals caught up in the maelstrom of war, such as the Tibetan pedlar captured by Eighth Army who had been in the ranks of 162nd Turkoman Division. This unfortunate had left his homeland with a small caravan of animals to ply his trade near the Russian border when

> men in brown uniforms seized him, gave him a brown uniform and forced him to fight men in grey uniforms who captured him and put him into a grey uniform and now he finds himself fighting in a grey uniform against a new lot of men in brown uniforms. He wants to know what is happening and is very worried about his caravan of animals and asks how soon he can get back to them.[4]

The predicament of that unfortunate Tibetan was typical of the aftermath of war.

The planning of Operation GRAPESHOT, and its many components, was a masterpiece of the planners' art. To many casual observers the military staff officer is either a figure of fun or someone who is not at all understood. However, to him falls the onerous task of ensuring that plans are made with painstaking care, the tasks of the various arms and services are dovetailed correctly, and that inter-service co-operation is treated in like fashion. All this becomes ever more demanding when dealing with a multi-national force with, for example, demands for different foodstuffs, not only to meet national tastes but also to satisfy religious and cultural demands. The British Army, with long experience in India, and elsewhere, was used to meeting the needs of Hindus and Muslims. The US Army may have had less experience in dealing with many cultures but had adapted well in Tunisia and Italy.

The complexities of the staff officer's tasks are best illustrated by the opening phases of both Operations BUCKLAND and CRAFTSMAN. These will not be rehearsed here, but the reader will appreciate the need to ensure that friendly artillery, or heavy mortars, were not firing while friendly fighter-bombers were attacking ground positions. The awful consequences of errors in the timing of these phases need no spelling out. Likewise, the tragic consequences of mistakes by attacking heavy bombers is illustrated only too well by those that bombed Polish and New Zealand troops on D Day of BUCKLAND. The South Africans found that, although 'coloured reflecting plastic strips were used for the first time to ensure that aircraft could identify South African units' vehicles in the forward area', there were still 'unfortunate incidents' that resulted in deaths and injuries.[5] Nonetheless, the fact that there were so few incidents indicates the professionalism of planners and those who executed their plans. On a more mundane level, those same planners ensured that there were sufficient roads for the traffic that would move forward for D Day, and that those roads could bear the loads imposed on them; the provision of additional roads and the supply of surfacing materials was among the many tasks carried out by the engineers.

If the work of the sappers has been unnoticed largely in the history books, that of the Royal Army Service Corps and their American counterparts is all but taken for granted. We have seen in this book how the RASC manned the LVTs used by V Corps but this was only a small part of their contribution to success; the Corps' history notes that, in Italy, there was a great diversity of nations in its ranks – Sinhalese, Cypriots, Mauritians, Basutos and Arabs from both Arabia and North Africa – as well as Italian volunteers, many of whom had been prisoners of war, and anti-aircraft units that had been converted to GT companies.[6] American supply and transport units likewise played an important but often unrecognized role. There were many others whose roles were critical but who do not appear in the headlines of history: medics working frequently under fire, military policemen ensuring that traffic flowed smoothly, ordnance personnel, chaplains, cooks, and clerks, and others keeping the machinery of war running. In short, the planners of both armies had mastered the art of bringing combat and combat support arms and combat service support elements, to use modern terminology, into close harmony.

Since most of the Italian campaign after the liberation of Rome has become obscured by events in north-west Europe, little is known of Operation GRAPESHOT generally and the achievements of Eighth and Fifth Armies in that final month of war are not part of the popular memory of the Second World War. As a result, few appreciate that the finest example of manoeuvre warfare by western Allied armies in the Second World War was carried out in northern Italy rather than in France, the Low Countries or Germany. Most of the Italian campaign had been attritional, although there had been an attempt to develop manoeuvre warfare immediately after the breakthrough of the Gustav and Hitler Lines and the break-out from the Anzio bridgehead. This had come to naught, largely because of Clark's desire to be seen as the man who liberated Rome. It had also ended north of Rome with the hardening of German resistance as the Allies approached the Gothic Line. Thus Operation GRAPESHOT represents the only true example of manoeuvre warfare in Italy.

The identifying elements of manoeuvre warfare include surprise, targeting the enemy's command, control and communications, using air and artillery assets to reduce his ability to react, and rapid deployment of ground forces to out-manoeuvre him. Binding these together is the glue of accurate, up-to-date intelligence, knowing exactly where the enemy's forces are situated, the locations of his command, control and communications centres, and those of his logistic support. All of these, plus an element of deception, can be seen in the planning of GRAPESHOT.

In the popular perception of the Second World War German forces are often credited with the greatest strategic, operational and tactical skills, with the 1940 campaign in the Low Countries and France cited as an outstanding example of manoeuvre warfare. Indeed, the popular belief is that this was based on a German strategic theory known as *blitzkrieg*, or lightning war, itself an outworking of Germany military genius. However, *blitzkrieg* was not a word familiar to German generals before the war. It seems to have been coined by a journalist to describe the rapid campaign in Poland in 1939 and became linked inexorably with the German forces thereafter. Irrespective of its origins, it is an understandable description of the German concepts of war developed in the inter-war years, which owed much to their existing concept of *Vernichtungsschlacht*, or battle of annihilation. What is not known generally is that the concept of swift-moving forces, using armour and supported by artillery and aircraft, was employed by the British armies in France and Flanders in 1918 to bring about the end of the First World War.

Does GRAPESHOT bear comparison with the German campaign in France in 1940? While the answer to that is affirmative, it has to be qualified by stating that 15th Army Group went further than the German forces in 1940. Eighth and Fifth Armies achieved the *total* destruction south of the Po of Army Group C, whereas the German army groups of 1940 failed to prevent the escape of the British Expeditionary Force from France. It can also be argued that the French armies of 1940 had never possessed either the will to fight or the organization needed to defeat the Germans. Thus, using mobile infantry, tanks, self-propelled guns and the Luftwaffe as long-range, rapid-response airborne artillery, the Germans wrote themselves into the history books as masters of manoeuvre warfare. And it is as masters of such warfare, *blitzkrieg* in the popular view, that Germany's armies of the war are best remembered. Thereby, we are left with a very inaccurate image of German soldiery.

What the Germans did for most of their warfighting time in the twentieth century was retreat. And they became masters of the defensive battle, as they demonstrated again and again in Italy. Consider the almost 120 months between August 1914 and May 1945 that German armies were in the field and it will be seen that, brief periods in 1914, early 1916, spring 1918, September 1939, May 1940 and several months of 1941 excepted, most of those armies were either holding defensive positions or retreating; over a hundred months were spent 'on the back foot'. Thus it was Europe's most experienced defensive army that 15th Army Group had to defeat in April 1945.

Did Army Group C have to be defeated? Would not the Germans in Italy have surrendered once the Reich itself had been forced to surrender? The answer to the second question is, almost certainly, yes. However, that does not mean that the answer to the first question is 'no'. What has to be taken into account here is the German myth that the Second Reich's field armies had not been beaten in battle but betrayed by politicians at home. Although it was clear to any objective observer that the German armies had been defeated in the field, and the country was all but starved into surrender, the myth grew, providing a powerful boost to the rise of Hitler's National Socialist Party and the birth of the Third Reich. An undefeated German army group in northern Italy might have encouraged a similar myth after the Second World War and perhaps had a destabilizing influence on post-war Germany. (There is a parallel with the *U-bootwaffe* which received a signal from Dönitz that suggested that it had not been defeated; British reaction was to order a formal surrender at Lisahally in Northern Ireland on 14 May 1945.) Thus it is reasonable to state that this final campaign had to be fought with all the risks implied in any such offensive. McCreery pondered the necessity for it, but came to the conclusion that it had to be undertaken to prevent the German creation of 'a legend of never having been really beaten'.[7]

In the execution of GRAPESHOT the Allied armies demonstrated a professionalism that matched anything seen elsewhere during the war, so much so that the Eighth Army of 1945 may be described as the best ever British field army. At all levels, this was true. Not only did both armies disrupt the enemy's plans by striking into their depth but they displayed the ability to conduct operations at a fast pace and with tremendous effect. Command and control was devolved to corps, divisional and brigade commanders, all of whom rose to the occasion, while both army commanders placed their trust in their subordinates. Looking at some of the Allied formations shows how they fitted in to the overall plan, and how effective they were.

In Eighth Army the sole formation involved from H Hour to the German surrender was 2nd New Zealand Division, which included three infantry and one armoured brigades. Such was the proficiency of their field and combat engineers that the New Zealanders were over the Senio so quickly that the Germans could not regain their equilibrium in time to take advantage of the Santerno defences, which the New Zealanders all but 'bounced'. The speed of their advance was maintained over the next river lines. They fought their last major battle at the Gaiana, although they had expected this encounter to take place later on the Idice, before crossing the Po and pursuing remnants of the German armies into the north-eastern region of Italy and finally to Trieste where they interposed themselves between Yugoslavs and Germans who would surrender only to the New Zealanders. The New Zealand Division had been in action since 1941, having fought in Greece, Crete and the desert and Tunisian campaigns with Eighth Army. Rejoining Eighth Army in Italy, it had served in most of the major battles of the campaign. All of this had been achieved under one GOC, Major General Sir Bernard Freyberg VC. Before GRAPESHOT the division had re-organized with a third infantry brigade and had absorbed reinforcements from home. Nonetheless, it is remarkable that this formation had endured almost four years of war under one commander and was still capable of fighting as it did across the river lines from the Senio to the Po and beyond.

In contrast Fifth Army's veteran 34th Division, the Red Bulls, had caused concern to its corps commander, Keyes, as we saw in Chapter Two (page 29), since many of its experienced officers and men felt they had done enough. The Red Bulls first saw action in Tunisia in November 1942 and fought throughout that campaign. Like the New Zealanders they did not fight in Sicily but returned to action with Fifth Army at Salerno and were engaged heavily thereafter, including the first battle for Cassino and the Anzio bridgehead. The Red Bulls are credited with more days of front-line action than any other US formation – a total of 517 days with some elements seeing over 600.[8] Although it also fought well along the Arno, it seems to have suffered a morale crisis and to have lost the confidence of higher commanders. Certainly, its role in Operation GRAPESHOT was a supporting one, in marked contrast to that of the New Zealanders. It may be that a change of command in July 1944 contributed to the loss of morale: Major General Charles L. Bolte who succeeded Major General Charles W. Ryder seems not to have been as inspiring a commander as Ryder. In contrast, 442nd Infantry Regiment, which joined the 34th for a time in Italy, had a remarkable record, fighting in Italy, then in France and returning to Italy for the final campaign. We have seen that one of its soldiers, Pfc Sadao Munemori, earned a posthumous Medal of Honor, which was awarded in 1945, while others were recognized retrospectively as having performed acts of gallantry worthy of the Medal of Honor. Moreover, the regiment's 1st Battalion, formerly 100th Battalion, of Nisei soldiers, was probably the outstanding US Army infantry unit of the war, earning the soubriquet the 'Purple Heart Battalion', and contributing to the 442nd's record of twenty-one Medals of Honor and almost 9,500 Purple Hearts.

One other US soldier was awarded the Medal of Honor in 1945, Pfc Magrath of 2/85th Mountain Infantry Regiment. The last US infantry division to enter action in Europe, 10th Mountain may be compared to the New Zealanders. Hays' mountaineers were in constant action from D Day of CRAFTSMAN until the German surrender and harried the enemy out of the mountains, across the plain and into the Alps. It may be argued that they were fresher than the Red Bulls but the New Zealanders had seen even more action than 34th Division and it was more likely the morale and leadership of 10th Mountain that contributed to its outstanding record.

Although GRAPESHOT was a 15th Army Group operation, the original inspiration for which came from Alexander when he was army group commander, the two army commanders, McCreery and Truscott, provided the dynamo for success. Both were cavalry officers, which may have contributed towards a different style of thinking and planning, but both were also men with a keen eye for ground – as McCreery demonstrated on taking over Eighth Army in 1944, and both he and Truscott showed to full effect in spring 1945; Truscott's decision to use 10th Mountain Division as he did, and his ignoring of Bologna as an immediate objective, coupled with McCreery's identification of the Argenta Gap as an avenue of advance and Comácchio as an opportunity rather than an obstacle, were critical to GRAPESHOT's success. Their analysis of the problems facing them, and their solutions to those problems, mark them as the best British and American field commanders in Europe.

McCreery was admired greatly by his corps and divisional commanders, some of whom noted that he could be found even farther forward than they were. All his subordinate commanders appreciated McCreery's professionalism and knew that he was the man who could bring a final success to Eighth Army. He was

> the leader who turned a dispirited army into the highly effective force which achieved one of the most complete victories of the war. The Battle for the River Po should be taught at all military academies and staff colleges as an example of a brilliant plan and a faultless execution.[9]

And a man with 'the rare gift of being leader and servant at the same time'.[10]

Truscott was the perfect teammate for McCreery. They knew that together they could destroy Army Group C and that was their aim. Neither craved public acclaim, but both cared greatly for their soldiers. Addressing a Memorial Day service at Anzio in May 1945, Truscott spoke not to the living gathered for the occasion but to the dead who lay there and he turned to face the rows of graves as he did so. Of him his biographer wrote that:

> No one in the war contributed more on the front lines to defeating Germany than the raspy-voiced ex-schoolteacher, ninety-day wonder and tight-lipped general who liked meals with flowers on the table and did not give a damn if his name was in newspapers or written large in history books.[11]

It is worth recording the opinion of one British officer who served for a time on Truscott's staff. Kendal Chavasse, a Royal Irish Fusilier who had commanded 56th Reconnaissance Regiment for much of the war, was Deputy Chief of Staff (British) at HQ Fifth Army and wrote that Fifth Army 'had a most excellent Army Commander, who had succeeded General Mark Clark. He was General Lucian Truscott. I got on very well with him when I met him.'[12] He also told the author that Truscott was a gentleman who got the best out of his staff whom he inspired.

Sadly, both army commanders walked into history in the shadow of lesser men, such as Montgomery and Clark, who managed to bring the spotlight on themselves. Both deserve more from history as the architects of the most outstanding victory by Allied forces in Europe in the Second World War.

Finito!

Notes

1. Quoted in Duncan, op. cit., p.622.
2. *RUSI Journal*, op. cit., p.13.
3. Ibid.
4. Doherty, *A Noble Crusade*, p.328.
5. Orpen, op. cit., pp.277–8.
6. Sutton, *Wait for the Waggon*, p.200.
7. *RUSI Journal*, p.5.
8. *History of the 34th Infantry Division* www.minnesotanationalguard.org 29 March 2014.
9. Mead, op. cit., p.236.
10. Bishop Victor Pike, quoted in Mead, p.326.
11. Jeffers, op. cit., p.309.
12. Chavasse, 'Some Memories of My Life', p.82.
13. Chavasse to author, Oct 1991.

Appendix

Outline Orders of Battle, April 1945

15th Army Group
(General Mark Wayne Clark)

Eighth Army
(Lieutenant General Sir Richard McCreery)

V Corps (Lieutenant General C. F. Keightley):
    56th (London) Division (Major General J. Y. Whitfield)
        24 Guards Brigade (2 Cldm Gds; 1 Scots Gds; 1 Buffs)
        167 Brigade (9 R. Fus; 1 London Scots; 1 LIR)
        169 (Queen's) Brigade (2/5, 2/6 & 2/7 Queen's)
        2 Commando Brigade (2 (Army); 9 (Army); 40 (RM) & 43 (RM) Cdos)
        9 Armoured Brigade (27th Lancers (armoured cars) less sqn; Composite LVT Regt; 4th
        Hussars (Kangaroos, with capacity to lift two battalions); (less 7th and 14th/20th Hussars))
    78th Division (Major General R. K. Arbuthnott):
        11 Brigade (2 Lancs Fus; 1 E. Surrey; 5 Northants)
        36 Brigade (5 Buffs; 6 R. West Kent; 8 A&S Hldrs)
        38 (Irish) Brigade (2 Innisks; 1 RIrF; 2 LIR)
        2 Armoured Brigade (Bays; 9 L)
    2nd New Zealand Division (Lieutenant General Sir Bernard Freyberg VC):
        4 NZ Armoured Brigade (18, 19 & 20 Armoured Bns)
        5 NZ Brigade (21, 23 & 28 (Maori) Bns)
        6 NZ Brigade (24, 25 & 26 Bns)
        9 NZ Brigade (2 Bn (Cav), 22 (Mot) & 27 (MG) Bns)
    8th Indian Division (Major General D. Russell):
        17 Brigade (1 R. Fus; 1 FFR; 1/5 RGR (FF))
        19 Brigade (1 A&S Hldrs; 3/8 Punjab; 6 RFFR; Bn Jaipur State Infantry)
        21 Brigade (5 R. West Kent; 1 Mahratta LI; 3/15 Punjab)
        21 Tank Brigade (12 RTR; 48 RTR; NIH)
    Cremona Combat Group (Brigadier General Clemente Primieri):
        21st Infantry Regt
        22nd Infantry Regt
        28 Garibaldi Brigade (partisans)
Under Corps Command:
    1st Army Group Royal Artillery
    6th Army Group Royal Artillery
    6th Armoured Division Artillery
    54th Super Heavy Regiment Royal Artillery (less two batteries)
    Two squadrons Special Boat Service
    Two troops Raiding Support Regiment

II Polish Corps (Major General Z. Bohusz-Szyszko):
    3rd Carpathian Division (Major General B. B. Duch):
        1 Carpathian Brigade (1, 2 & 3 Carpathian Rifle Bns)
        2 Carpathian Rifle Brigade (4, 5 & 6 Carpathian Rifle Bns)
        3 Carpathian Rifle Brigade (7, 8 & 9 Carpathian Rifle Bns)
    5th Kresowa Division (Major General N. Sulik):
        5 Wilenska Brigade (13, 14 & 15 Wilenska Rifle Bns)
        6 Lwowska Brigade (16, 17 & 18 Lwowska Rifle Bns)
        4 Wolynska Brigade (10, 11 & 12 Wolynska Rifle Bns)
        2 Warsaw Armoured Brigade (1 Bn Polish Armd Cavalry Regt; 4 Bn Polish Armd Regt; 6 Bn Lwowska Armd Regt)
        7 Armoured Brigade (6 RTR & 8 RTR)
        43 Gurkha Brigade (2/6 GR; 2/8 GR & 2/10 GR; 14/20 H; 2 RTR)

Under Corps Command:
    Army Group Polish Artillery
    Battery 54th Super Heavy Regiment Royal Artillery

X Corps (Lieutenant General J. L. I. Hawkesworth):
    Friuli Combat Group (Major General Ettore Cotronei):
        87th Infantry Regt
        88th Infantry Regt
    Jewish Brigade Group (Brigadier E. F. Benjamin):
        1 Palestine Regt
        2 Palestine Regt
        3 Palestine Regt

XIII Corps (Lieutenant General Sir John Harding):
    10th Indian Division (Major General D. W. Reid):
        10 Infantry Brigade (1 Durham LI; 2/4 GR; 4 Baluch; Bn Jodhpur Sardar Infantry)
        20 Infantry Brigade (2 Loyals; 3 Mahratta LI; 2/3 GR; 1/2 Punjab; Nabha Akal Infantry)
        25 Infantry Brigade (1 KORR; 3/1 Punjab; 3 RGR; 4/11 Sikhs)
    Folgore Combat Group (Brigadier General Giorgio Morigi):
        Nembo Regt
        San Marco Regt
Under Corps Command:
    Lovat Scouts
    2 Highland LI

Army Reserve:
        6th Armoured Division (Major General H. Murray):
        26 Armoured Brigade (16/5 L; 17/21 L; 2 L & B Yeo)
        1 Guards Brigade (3 Cldm Gds; 3 W. Gds; 1 Welch)
        61 Brigade (1 KRRC; 2 RB; 7 RB)

        25 Armoured Engineer Brigade (less detachments with assault formations)

        2 Para Brigade (4, 5 & 6 Para Bns)

Under Army Command:
>   16th Army Group Royal Engineers
>   20th Army Group Royal Engineers
>   22nd Army Group Royal Engineers
>   7th Hussars (DD tanks)
>   Sqn 12th Royal Lancers (armoured cars)

Fifth Army

(Lieutenant General Lucian Truscott Jr)

II Corps (Major General G. T. Keyes):
>   34th Division (Major General Charles Bolte)
>>   133rd, 135th and 168th Infantry Regiments
>   88th Division (Major General Paul W. Kendall)
>>   349th, 350th and 351st Infantry Regiments)
>   91st Division (Major General William G. Livesay)
>>   361st, 362nd & 363rd Infantry Regiments
>   6th South African Armoured Division (Major General Evered Poole)
>   11 Armoured Brigade (Prince Alfred's Guard (PAG); Special Service Bn (SSB); 4th/13th
>>   Frontier Force Rifles)
>   12 Motorised Brigade (First City/Cape Town Hldrs (FC/CTH); Royal Natal Carabineers
>>   (RNC); Witwatersrand Rifles/Regt de la Rey (WR/DLR))
>   13 Motorised Brigade (Imperial Light Horse/Kimberley Regt (ILH/KimR); Natal Mounted
>>   Rifles/South African Air Force Regt; Royal Durban LI (RDLI))
>   Legnano Combat Group (General Umberto Utili)
>>   68th Infantry Regiment
>>   69th Infantry Regiment

Under Corps Command
>   752nd Tank Bn
>   757th Tank Bn
>   804th Tank Destroyer Bn
>   805th Tank Destroyer Bn

IV Corps (Lieutenant General W. D. Crittenberger):
>   10th Mountain Division (Major General George Hays)
>>   85th, 86th & 87th Mountain Infantry Regiments
>   1st Brazilian Division (*Força Expedicionária Brasiliera*) (Major General Joao Batista
>   Mascharenas de Moraes)
>>   1st Infantry Regiment (Sampaio Regiment) (I/, II/, III/1st Infantry)
>>   6th Infantry Regiment (Ipiranga Regiment) (I/, II/, III/6th Infantry)
>>   11th Infantry Regiment (Tiradented Regiment) (I/, II/, III/11th Infantry)
>   1st Armored Division (Major General Vernon Pritchard)
>>   6th, 11th & 14th Armoured Infantry Battalions
>>   1st, 4th & 13th Tank Battalions

Under Corps Command:
>   751st Tank Bn
>   Coy 760th Tank Bn

701st Tank Destroyer Bn
part 894th Tank Destroyer Bn
365th Infantry Regiment (from 92nd Division)
371st Infantry Regiment (from 92nd Division)

Under Army Command:
85th Division (Major General John B. Coulter)
337th, 338th & 339th Infantry Regiments
92nd Division (Major General Edward M. Almond)
370th Infantry Regiment
less 365th and 371st Infantry Regiments
Attached: 442nd (Nisei) and 473rd Infantry Regiments

758th Light Tank Bn
760th Tank Bn (less two companies)
679th Tank Destroyer Bn
894th Tank Destroyer Bn (less two companies)

Army Group C

(General Heinrich von Vietinghoff-Scheel)

Tenth Army

(Lieutenant General Traugott Herr)
LXXVI Panzer Corps (General Gerhard Graf von Schwerin):
42nd Jäger Division (Major General Walter Jost)
98th Volksgrenadier Division (Major General Alfred-Hermann Reinhardt; Brigadier General Otto Schiel from 11 April)
162nd (Turkoman) Division (Major General Ralph von Heygendorff)
362nd Division (Major General Alois Weber)
I Fallschirmjäger Corps (Lieutenant General Richard Heidrich):
26th Panzer Division (Major General Alfred Kuhnert; Major General Viktor Linnarz from 19 April)
278th Volksgrenadier Division (Major General Harry Hoppe)
305th Division (Major General Friedrich von Schellwitz)
1st Fallschirmjäger Division (Brigadier General Karl-Lothar Schultz)
4th Fallschirmjäger Division (Major General Heinrich Trettner)

LXXIII Corps (Lieutenant General Anton Dostler)
This formation, which controlled only minor defensive units, was responsible for coastal defence between the Po and Venice.

XCVII Corps (General Ludwig Kübler)
188th Gebirgs Division (Major General Hans von Hößlin)
237th Division (Major General Hans von Grävenitz)
This corps was transferred to Army Group E on 10 April.

Army Reserve
155th Training Division (Major General Georg Zwade)
29th Panzer Grenadier Division (less 15th Panzer Grenadier Regiment, which was east of Ferrara) (Major General Fritz Polack)

Fourteenth Army

(General Joachim Lemelsen)
XIV Panzer Corps (General Fridolin von Senger und Etterlin)
    8th (formerly 157th) Gebirgs Division (Major General Paul Schricker)
    65th Division (Major General Hellmuth Pfeifer)
    94th Division (Major General Bernhard Steinmetz)

LI Mountain Corps (General Friedrich-Wilhelm Hauck)
    114th Jäger Division (Major General Hans Joachim Ehlert; Major General Martin Strahammer from 15 April)
    148th Division (Major General Otto Fretter-Pico)
    232nd Division (Major General Eccard Freiherr von Gablenz)
    334th Volksgrenadier Division (Major General Hellmuth Böhlke)
    1st Italia Bersaglieri Division (Major General Mario Carloni)

Army of Liguria

(General Alfredo Guzzoni)

Corps Lombardia (Lieutenant General Kurt Jahn)
    3rd (San Marco) Marine Division (less elements detached to Kampfgruppe Meinhold) (Major General Amilcare Farina)
    Kampfgruppe Meinhold (Fortress Brigade 135 and elements of Italian Monte Rosa Division)

LXXV Corps (Lieutenant General Hans Richard Schlemmer)
    2nd Littorio Division (Major General Tito Agosti)
    4th (Monte Rosa) Alpine Division (Colonel Giorgi Milazzo)
    5th Gebirgs Division (Major General Hans Steets)
    34th Division (Major General Theobald Lieb)

Army Group Reserve
    90th Panzer Grenadier Division (Major General Heinrich Baron von Behr)

Glossary

AA	anti-aircraft
AAA	anti-aircraft artillery (American use)
AASC	Army Air Support Control
AGRA	Army Group Royal Artillery
AGRE	Army Group Royal Engineers
ANR	*Aeronautica Nazionale Repubblicana* – Italian National Republican Air Force
AOP	air observation post
APC	armoured personnel carrier
AWOL	absent without official leave
BEF	British Expeditionary Force; also Brazilian Expeditionary Force
CIGS	Chief of the Imperial General Staff (British)
CRA	Commander Royal Artillery (of a division)
CRE	Commander Royal Engineers (of a division)
DD	duplex drive tank
Doughs	from Doughboys, a name for US Army soldiers dating from the Civil War and their ration of dough cakes
DUKW (duck)	US six-wheeled amphibious lorry, capable of carrying a field gun
Faughs (pronounced Fogs)	Nickname of the Royal Irish Fusiliers, from their regimental motto Faugh A Ballagh! – Clear the Way! in Irish Gaelic.
FDLs	forward defended/defensive localities
FEB	*Força Expedicionária Brasiliera* (Brazilian Expeditionary Force)
Flak	German anti-aircraft fire, from *Flugabwehrkanone*, anti-aircraft cannon
FOO	forward observing officer (artillery)
GI	US Army soldier, said to originate from the term 'Government Issue'
GOC	General Officer Commanding (a division)
HAA	heavy anti-aircraft
HAC	Honourable Artillery Company
HQ	headquarters
Jawan	a young soldier (Indian Army)
Kapok bridge	floating infantry assault bridge, using kapok-filled canvas floats supporting a timber pathway
LAA	light anti-aircraft
LI	light infantry
LVT	landing vehicle, tracked
M7	American 105mm howitzer mounted on the hull of an M3 tank (Lee/Grant) and known in British service as a Priest from the pulpit-like AA machine-gun position

M10	American tank destroyer, a 3-inch anti-tank gun mounted in an open-topped turret on the hull of an M4 tank. Known as Wolverine in British service where it was also up-gunned with a 17-pounder anti-tank gun and renamed Achilles
MAAF	Mediterranean Allied Air Forces
MACAF	Mediterranean Allied Coastal Air Force
MASAF	Mediterranean Allied Strategic Air Force
MATAF	Mediterranean Allied Tactical Air Forces
MM	Military Medal (third-tier gallantry award until 1993)
OKW	Oberkommando der Wehmacht – overall command of the German armed forces – Army (Heer), Navy (Kriegsmarine) and Air Force (Luftwaffe)
OP	observation post
PIAT	projector, infantry, anti-tank – British man-portable, spigot-launched anti-tank weapon
PR	photographic reconnaissance
SAEC	South African Engineers Corps
Skins	Nickname of the Royal Inniskilling Fusiliers
SPG	self-propelled guns, known as assault guns to the Germans
SR	strategic reconnaissance
Tac/R	tactical reconnaissance
USAAF	United States Army Air Forces
Viper	flexible hose filled with explosive used to clear a path through a minefield
Window	strips of metallic foil dropped by aircraft to confuse radar operators
Yoke target	an artillery fireplan involving all the guns of an army group

Bibliography

Alexander, Field Marshal Sir Harold (Ed: John North), *Memoirs*, (Cassell, London, 1962)

——, (Supreme Allied Commander, Mediterranean), *Report on the Italian Campaign, Pts I – III* (HMSO, London, 1946–1948)

Anon, *Finito! The Po Valley Campaign 1945* (Headquarters 15th Army Group, 1945)

Anon, *History of Task Force 45 (29 July 1944 to 28 January 1945)* (Combined Arms Research Library Digital Library, 2011)

Anon, *The Story of 46th Division 1939–1945* (np, Graz, 1945)

Anon, *The History of 61 Infantry Brigade* (np, Klagenfurt, 1945)

Anon, *The Tiger Triumphs* (HMSO, London, 1946)

Anon, *The London Irish at War* (Old Comrades' Assn, London, 1948)

Anders, Lt Gen W., CB, *An Army in Exile. The Story of the Second Polish Corps* (Macmillan, London, 1949)

Arthur, Max, *Symbol of Courage: A History of the Victoria Cross* (Sidgwick and Jackson, London 2004)

Ascoli, David, *A Companion to the British Army 1660–1983* (Harrap, London 1983)

Badoglio, Pietro, *Italy in the Second World War* (Oxford University Press, London, 1948)

Bailey, Lt Col D. E., *Engineers in the Italian Campaign 1943–1945* (Central Mediterranean Force, 1945)

Barclay, C. N., *The History of The Royal Northumberland Fusiliers in the Second World War* (William Clowes and Son, London, 1952)

——, *History of the 16th/5th Queen's Royal Lancers 1925–1961* (Gale and Polden, Aldershot, 1963)

Barzini, Luigi, *The Italians* (Hamish Hamilton, London, 1964)

Beale, Nick, D'Amico, Ferdinando, Valentini, Gabriele, *Air War Italy 1944–45: The Axis Air Forces from the Liberation of Rome to the Surrender* (Airlife Publishing Ltd, Shrewsbury, 1996)

Beckman, Morris, *The Jewish Brigade. An Army with Two Masters 1944–45* (Spellmount, Staplehurst, 1998)

Belogi, Marco & Guglielmi, Daniele, *Spring 1945 on the Italian Front: A 25 Day Atlas from the Apennines to the Po River* (Roadrunner by Mattioli1885spa, Fidenza, 2011)

Bernstein, Jonathan, *P-47 Thunderbolt Units of the Twelfth Air Force* (Osprey Publishing, Botley, 2012)

Bidwell, Shelford & Graham, Dominick, *Tug of War. The Battle for Italy: 1953–45* (Hodder & Stoughton, London, 1986)

Blaxland, Gregory, *Alexander's Generals. The Italian Campaign 1944–45* (William Kimber, London, 1979)

Blumenson, Martin, *Mark Clark* (Jonathan Cape, London, 1984)

Bourhill, James, *Come Back to Portofino: Through Italy with the 6th South African Armoured Division* (30° South Publishers, Johannesburg, 2011)

Bowyer, Chaz & Shores, Christopher, *Desert Air Force at War* (Ian Allan Ltd, Shepperton, 1981)

Bryant, Sir Arthur, *Triumph in the West. Completing the War Diaries of Field Marshal Viscount Alanbrooke* (Collins, London, 1959)

Bullen, Roy E., *History of the 2/7th Battalion The Queen's Royal Regiment 1939–1946* (np, 1958)

Burns, E. L. M., *General Mud* (Clark and Irwin, Toronto, 1984)

Carver, Field Marshal Lord, *Harding of Petherton: Field Marshal* (Weidenfeld and Nicolson, London, 1978)

——, *The Imperial War Museum Book of the War in Italy 1943–1945* (Sidgwick & Jackson, London, 2001)

Churchill, Winston S., *The Second World War*, Vols VII & VIII: *The Hinge of Fate*; Vol IX: *Closing the Ring*; Vol XI: *Triumph and Tragedy*; (Cassell, London, 1951, 1952, 1954)

Circolo Filatelico 'Vincenzo Monti' di Alfonsine, *Diario storico militare del Gruppo di Combattimento Cremona* (Bacchilega Editore, Imola, 2009)

Clark, General Mark W., *Calculated Risk: His Personal Story of the War in North Africa and Italy* (Harrap, London, 1951)

Clarke, Rupert, *With Alex at War from the Irrawaddy to the Po 1941–1945* (Leo Cooper, Barnsley, 2000)

Cooper, Matthew, *The German Army 1933–1945. Its Political and Military Failure* (Macdonald and Jane's, London, 1978)

Cox, Geoffrey, *The Road to Trieste. The story of the fall of Trieste, told by a member of General Freyberg's staff* (Heinemann, London, 1947)

Cunliffe, Marcus, *The Royal Irish Fusiliers, 1793–1968* (Oxford University Press, Oxford, 1970)

Danchev, Alex, and Todman, Daniel (eds), *War Diaries 1939–1945 Field Marshal Lord Alanbrooke* (Weidenfeld & Nicolson, London, 2001)

Daniell, D. S., *History of the East Surrey Regiment* (Ernest Benn, London, 1957)

Delaney, John P., & Sloan, John A., *The Blue Devils in Italy. A History of the 88th Infantry Division in World War II* (Infantry Journal Press, Washington DC, 1947)

Doherty, Richard, *Clear the Way! A History of the 38th (Irish) Brigade, 1941–47* (Irish Academic Press, Dublin, 1993)

——, *Only The Enemy in Front: The Recce Corps at War 1940–1946* (Tom Donovan, London, 1994)

——, *A Noble Crusade. The History of Eighth Army 1941–45* (Spellmount, Staplehurst, 1999)

——, *The North Irish Horse. A Hundred Years of Service* (Spellmount, Staplehurst, 2002)

——, *Ireland's Generals in the Second World War* (Four Courts Press, Dublin, 2004)

——, *Eighth Army in Italy 1943–45: The Long Hard Slog* (Pen & Sword, Barnsley, 2007)

——, *Ubique: The Royal Artillery in the Second World War* (The History Press, Stroud, 2008)

——, *British Armoured Divisions and Their Commanders, 1939–1945* (Pen & Sword, Barnsley, 2013)

Dole, Bob, *One Soldier's Story. A Memoir* (HarperCollins, New York, 2005)

Donovan, John (ed), *'A Very Fine Commander'. The Memoirs of Sir Horatius Murray GCB KBE DSO* (Pen & Sword, Barnsley, 2010)

Durnford-Slater, John, *Commando* (William Kimber, London, 1953)

Evans, Bryn, *With the East Surreys in Tunisia and Italy, 1942–1945: Fighting for Every River and Mountain* (Pen & Sword, Barnsley, 2012)

——, *Decisive Campaigns of the Desert Air Force* (Pen & Sword, Barnsley, 2014)

Feuer, A. B., *Packs On! Memoirs of the 10th Mountain Division in WWII* (Stackpole Books, Mechanicsburg PA, 2004)

ffrench Blake, R. L. V., *A History of the 17th/21st Lancers 1922–1959* (Macmillan, London, 1962)

——, *The 17th/21st Lancers 1759–1993* (Leo Cooper, London, 1993)

Fisher, Ernest F., Jnr, *United States Army in World War II: Mediterranean Theatre of Operations: Cassino to the Alps* (US Army Center of Military History, Washington DC, 1977)

Ford, Ken, *Battleaxe Division. From Africa to Austria with the 78th Division 1952–45* (Sutton, Stroud, 1999)

——, *Mailed Fist. 6th Armoured Division at War 1940–1945* (Sutton, Stroud, 2005)

Fowler, William, *The Secret War in Italy: Special Forces, Partisans and Covert Operations 1943–45* (Ian Allan Publishing, Hersham, 2010)

Fraser, David, *Alanbrooke* (Collins, London, 1982)

——, *And We Shall Shock Them: The British Army in the Second World War* (Hodder & Stoughton, London, 1983)

——, *Knight's Cross. A Life of Field Marshal Erwin Rommel* (HarperCollins, London, 1993)

Fox, Sir Frank, *The Royal Inniskilling Fusiliers in the Second World War, 1939–45* (Gale & Polden, Aldershot, 1951)

Frederick, J. B. M., *Lineage Book of British Land Forces 1660–1978* (Microform Academic Publishers, Wakefield, 1984

French, David, *Raising Churchill's Army. The British Army and the War against Germany 1919–1945* (Oxford University Press, Oxford, 2000)

Gaylor, John, *Sons of John Company, The Indian & Pakistan Armies 1903–1991* (Spellmount, Staplehurst, 1992

Gore, Enid A., *This Was The Way It Was. Adrian Clements Gore* (privately produced, 1977)

Graham, Dominick, & Bidwell, Shelford, *Tug of War. The Battle for Italy: 1943–45* (Hodder & Stoughton, London, 1986)

Gunner, Colin, *Front of the Line: Adventures with The Irish Brigade* (Greystone Books, Antrim 1991)

Greene, Jack, and Massignani, Alessandro, *The Black Prince and the Sea Devils: The Story of Valerio Borghese and the Elite Units of the Decima MAS* (Da Capo Press, Cambridge MA, 2004)

Hallam, John, *The History of The Lancashire Fusiliers 1939–45* (Sutton, Stroud, 1993)

Harpur, Brian, *The Impossible Victory. A personal account of the Battle for the River Po* (William Kimber, London, 1980)

Hinsley, F. H., *British Intelligence in the Second World War (Official History of the Second World War) (Abridged Edition)* (HM Stationery Office, London, 1993)

Hogg, Ian V., *British & American Artillery of World War 2* (Arms & Armour Press, London, 1978)

——, *Allied Artillery of World War Two* (The Crowood Press, Marlborough, 1998)

——, & Weeks, John, *The Illustrated Encyclopaedia of Military Vehicles* (Quarto, London, 1980)

Holland, James, *Italy's Sorrow: A Year of War, 1944–45* (St Martin's Press, London, 2008)

Horsfall, John, *Fling Our Banner to The Wind* (Kineton Press, Kineton, 1978)

Hougen, John H., *The Story of the Famous 34th Infantry Division* (Battery Press, 1979)

Howard, Michael, *Grand Strategy, Vol IV (Official History of the Second World War)* (HM Stationery Office, London, 1972)

——, *Grand Strategy, Vol V – Strategic Deception (Official History of the Second World War)* (HM Stationery Office, London, 1990)

Howarth, Patrick, *My God, Soldiers. From Alamein to Vienna* (Hutchinson, London, 1989)

Jackson, W. G. F., *The Battle for Italy* (Batsford, London, 1967)

——, *The Mediterranean and Middle East, Vol VI: Victory in the Mediterranean, Part II – June to October 1944 (Official History of the Second World War)* (HM Stationery Office, London, 1973)

——, *The Mediterranean and Middle East, Vol VII: Victory in the Mediterranean, Part III – November 1944 to May 1945 (Official History of the Second World War)* (HM Stationery Office, London, 1984)

Jeffers, H. Paul, *Command of Honor: General Lucian Truscott's Path to Victory in World War II* (NAL Caliber, New York, 2008)

Joslen, Lieutenant Colonel H. F., *Orders of Battle Second World War 1939–1945* (HM Stationery Office, London, 1960)

Kay, Robin, *From Cassino to Trieste, Vol II, Italy: History of New Zealand in the Second World War* (Department of Internal Affairs, Wellington, 1967)

Keegan, John (Ed), *Churchill's Generals* (Weidenfeld & Nicolson, London, 1991)

Kesselring, Field Marshal Albert, *Memoirs* (William Kimber, London, 1953 & Lionel Leventhal, London 2007; with introduction by James Holland)

Kippenberger, Maj Gen Sir Howard, *Infantry Brigadier* (OUP, London, 1949)

Lamb, Richard, *War in Italy 1943–1945. A Brutal Story* (John Murray, London, 1993)

Lett, Brian, *SAS in Tuscany 1943–45* (Pen & Sword, Barnsley, 2011)

Linklater, Eric, *The Campaign in Italy* (HMSO, London, 1959)

Lunt, James, *The Scarlet Lancers. The Story of 16th/5th The Queen's Royal Lancers 1689–1992* (Leo Cooper, London, 1993)

Macksey, Kenneth, *Kesselring. German Master Strategist of the Second World War* (Greenhill Books, London, 1996)

Maximiano, C. C. & Bonalume Neto, R., *Brazilian Expeditionary Force in World War II* (Osprey Publishing, Botley, 2011)

Mead, Peter, *Gunners at War 1939–1945* (Ian Allan, London, 1982)

Mead, Richard, *The Last Great Cavalryman: The Life of General Sir Richard McCreery, Commander Eighth Army* (Pen & Sword Books, Barnsley, 2012)

Merewood, Jack, *To War with The Bays. A Tank Gunner Remembers 1939–1945* (1st The Queen's Dragoon Guards, Cardiff, 1996)

Messenger, *The Commandos 1940–1946* (William Kimber, London, 1985)

Mitcham, Samuel W., Jr, *Hitler's Field Marshals and their Battles* (William Heinemann, London, 1988)

Molony, C. J. C., *The Mediterranean and Middle East, Vol VI: Victory in the Mediterranean, Part I – 1st April to 4th June 1944 (Official History of the Second World War)* (HM Stationery Office, 1974)

Nicholson, Lt Col G. W. L., *Official History of the Canadian Army in the Second World War, Vol II: The Canadians in Italy 1943–1945* (Queen's Printer, Ottawa, 1956)

Nicolson, Nigel, *Alex: the life of Field Marshal The Earl Alexander of Tunis* (Weidenfeld & Nicolson, London, 1973)

Oland, Dwight D., *North Apennines: The US Army Campaigns of World War II* (US Army Center of Military History, Washington DC, 1995)

Olivia, Gianni, *Soldati e Ufficiali: L'Esercito / Taliano Dal Risorgimento a Oggi* (Arnalolo Mondadori Editore S.p.A., Milano, 2009)

Orgill, Douglas, *The Gothic Line: The Autumn Campaign in Italy, 1944* (Heinemann, London, 1967)

Orpen, Neil, *Victory in Italy* (Official History of South Africa in the Second World War) (Purnell, Cape Town, 1975)

Pal, Dharm, *The Campaign in Italy: Official History of the Indian Armed Forces in the Second World War* (Orient Longmans, 1960)

Parkinson, C. Northcote, *Always A Fusilier* (Sampson Low, London, 1949)

Pitt, Barrie (Ed), *The Military History of World War II* (Hamlyn, London, 1986)

Petacco, Arrigo & Mazzuca, Giancarlo, *La Resistenza Tricolore: La Storia Ignorata Dai Partigiani con le Stellete* (Arnaldo Mondadori Editore S.p.A., Milano 2010)

Place, Timothy Harrison, *Military Training in the British Army, 1940–1944. From Dunkirk to D-Day* (Frank Cass, London, 2000)

Platt, Brigadier J. R. I., *The Royal Wiltshire Yeomanry 1907–1967: Britain's Oldest Yeomanry Regiment* (Garnstone Press, London, 1972)

Popa, Thomas A., *Po Valley: The US Army Campaigns of World War II* (US Army Center of Military History, Washington DC, 1996)

Ray, Cyril, *Algiers to Austria. The History of 78 Division, 1942–1946* (Eyre & Spottiswoode, London, 1952)

Rosignoli, Guido, *The Allied Forces in Italy 1943–45* (David & Charles, Newton Abbot, 1989)

Rottman, Gordon L., *US 10th Mountain Division in World War II* (Osprey Publishing, Botley, 2012)

——, *World War II River Assault Tactics* (Osprey Publishing, Botley, 2013)

Routledge, Brig N. W., *Anti-Aircraft Artillery, 1914–55* (Brassey's, London, 1994)

Ryder, Rowland, *Oliver Leese* (Hamish Hamilton, London, 1987)

Saunders, Hilary St G., *The Green Beret: The Story of the Commandos 1940–1945* (Michael Joseph, London, 1949)

Senger und Etterlin, Frido von, *Neither Fear Nor Hope: the wartime career of General Frido von Senger und Etterlin, defender of Cassino* (Macdonald, London, 1963)

Shelton, Peter, *Climb to Conquer. The Untold Story of World War II's 10th Mountain Division Ski Troops* (Scribner, New York, 2003)

Shepperd, G. A., *The Italian Campaign 1943–45. A political and military re-assessment* (Arthur Barker, London, 1968)

Short, Neil, *German Defences in Italy in World War II* (Osprey, Botley, 2006)

Smyth, Sir John, *The Story of the Victoria Cross 1856–1963* (Frederick Muller, London, 1963)

Stafford, David, *Mission Accomplished: SOE and Italy 1943–1945* (The Bodley Head, London, 2011)

Stato Maggiore Dell'Esercito Ufficio Storico, *I Gruppi Di Combattimento: Cremona, Friuli, Folgore, Legnano, Mantova, Piceno (1944–1945)* (SME, Ufficio Storico, Roma, 2010)

Squire, Lt Col G. L. A., and Hill, Maj P. G. E., *The Surreys in Italy* (Queen's Royal Surrey Regiment Museum, Guildford, 1992)

Stack, Wayne & O'Sullivan, Barry, *The New Zealand Expeditionary Force in World War II* (Osprey Publishing, Botley, 2013)

Starr, Lt Col Chester G., *From Salerno to the Alps. A History of the Fifth Army 1943–1945* (Infantry Journal Press, Washington DC, 1948)

Steer, Frank, *To The Warrior his Arms* (Pen & Sword, Barnsley, 2005)

St John, Philip A., PhD, *Thirty Fourth Infantry Division* (Turner Publishing, Paducah, KY, 1989)

Strawson, John, *General Sir Richard McCreery* (Published privately by Lady McCreery, 1973)

——, *The Italian Campaign* (Secker & Warburg, London, 1987)

Sutton, John (ed), *Wait For The Waggon: The Story of The Royal Corps of Transport and its Predecessors 1794–1993*, (Leo Cooper, Barnsley, 1998)

Truscott, Lucian K., *Command Missions* (E. P. Dutton, New York, 1954)

Vokes, Maj Gen Chris, CB, CBE, DSO, CD, *My Story* (Gallery Books, Ottawa, 1985)

Wake, Sir Hereward & Deedes, W. F, *Swift and Bold: The Story of the King's Royal Rifle Corps in the Second World War 1939–1945* (Gale & Polden, Aldershot, 1949)

Wallace, Sir Christopher, *The King's Royal Rifle Corps … the 60th Rifles. A Brief History: 1755 to 1965* (The Royal Green Jackets Museum Trust, Winchester, 2005)

Williams, David, *The Black Cats at War. The Story of the 56th (London) Division TA, 1939–1945* (Imperial War Museum, London, 1995)

Williamson, Hugh, *The Fourth Division 1939 to 1945* (Newman Neame, London, 1951)

Wilson, Lt Gen Sir James, *Unusual Undertakings. A Military Memoir* (Pen and Sword, Barnsley, 2002)

Unpublished

National Archives, Kew, Richmond, Surrey

ADM202/87 – war diary 40 Commando Royal Marines, 1945.

ADM202/88 – war diary 43 Commando Royal Marines, 1945.

AIR23/1750 – Photo reconnaissance for Mediterranean Allied Tactical Air Force and 15th Army Group.

WO170 – Records from this series covering Army formations and units in Italy. These are too numerous to list but include war diaries of formations from army group level down to brigades and individual units. Among the latter are the British Liaison Units (50, 51 & 52 BLUs) with the Italian combat groups. Many of these documents, but not all, are included in chapter notes.

WO204/12291 – Gruppi di Combattimento Friuli and Folgore

WO204/7588 – Gruppi di Combattimento Legnano and Mantova

W204/1774 – Gruppo di Combattimento Piceno; Training of Italian Army and Carabinieri

WO204/ 8066 – Gruppo Cremona, January 1945

WO204/7050/7060/7586/8066 – Gruppi Friuli and Cremona attached to auxiliary units.

Records from series CAB106

CAB106/339 – Italy: account of operations of 2nd New Zealand Division 9–16 April 1945, including crossing of the Senio.

CAB106/405 – War Office memorandum on the Neo-Fascist Republican Army, September 1943– May 1945.

CAB106/427 – Italy: Operations of British, Indian and Dominion forces, September 1943 to May 1945: Part III – The Campaign in the northern Apennines, 10 August 1944 to 1 April 1945. Section A: Allied strategy

CAB106/428 – Italy: Operations of British, Indian and Dominion forces, September 1943 to May 1945: Part III – The Campaign in the northern Apennines, 10 August 1944 to 1 April 1945. Section B: Eighth Army – the Gothic Line and Romagna battles.

CAB106/429 – Italy: Operations of British, Indian and Dominion forces, September 1943 to May 1945: Part III – The Campaign in the northern Apennines, 10 August 1944 to 1 April 1945. Appendices.

CAB106/430 – Italy: Operations of British, Indian and Dominion forces, September 1943 to May 1945: Part III – The Campaign in the northern Apennines, 10 August 1944 to 1 April 1945. Section C: V Corps operations.

CAB106/431 – Italy: Operations of British, Indian and Dominion forces, September 1943 to May 1945: Part III – The Campaign in the northern Apennines, 10 August 1944 to 1 April 1945. Appendices I-II.

CAB106/432 – Italy: Operations of British, Indian and Dominion forces, September 1943 to May 1945: Part III – The Campaign in the northern Apennines, 10 August 1944 to 1 April 1945. Appendices III-IV.

CAB106/433 – Italy: Operations of British, Indian and Dominion forces, September 1943 to May 1945: Part III – The Campaign in the northern Apennines, 10 August 1944 to 1 April 1945. Section D: X Corps operations.

CAB106/434 – Italy: Operations of British, Indian and Dominion forces, September 1943 to May 1945: Part III – The Campaign in the northern Apennines, 10 August 1944 to 1 April 1945. Section E: Canadian Corps operations.

CAB106/435 – Italy: Operations of British, Indian and Dominion forces, September 1943 to May 1945: Part III – The Campaign in the northern Apennines, 10 August 1944 to 1 April 1945. Section F: II Polish Corps operations.

CAB106/436 – Italy: Operations of British, Indian and Dominion forces, September 1943 to May 1945: Part III – The Campaign in the northern Apennines, 10 August 1944 to 1 April 1945. Appendices.

CAB106/437 – Italy: Operations of British, Indian and Dominion forces, September 1943 to May 1945: Part III – The Campaign in the northern Apennines, 10 August 1944 to 1 April 1945. Section G: XIII Corps in the mountains.

CAB106/438 – Italy: Operations of British, Indian and Dominion forces, September 1943 to May 1945: Part III – The Campaign in the northern Apennines, 10 August 1944 to 1 April 1945. Appendices.

CAB106/439 – Italy: Operations of British, Indian and Dominion forces, September 1943 to May 1945: Part III – The Campaign in the northern Apennines, 10 August 1944 to 1 April 1945. Section H: German strategy.

CAB106/440 – Italy: Operations of British, Indian and Dominion forces, September 1943 to May 1945: Part III – The Campaign in the northern Apennines, 10 August 1944 to 1 April 1945. Section I: principal administrative aspects.

CAB106/441 – Italy: Operations of British, Indian and Dominion forces, September 1943 to May 1945: Part III – The Campaign in Lombardy, 1 April to 2 May 1945. Section B: Eighth Army final offensive and appendices A-D.

CAB106/442 – Italy: Operations of British, Indian and Dominion forces, September 1943 to May 1945: Part III – The Campaign in Lombardy, 1 April to 2 May 1945. Section B: Eighth Army final offensive and appendices E-L.

CAB106/443 – Italy: Operations of British, Indian and Dominion forces, September 1943 to May 1945: Part III – The Campaign in Lombardy, 1 April to 2 May 1945. Section C: V Corps operations.

CAB106/444 – Italy: Operations of British, Indian and Dominion forces, September 1943 to May 1945: Part III – The Campaign in Lombardy, 1 April to 2 May 1945. Appendices.

CAB106/445 – Italy: Operations of British, Indian and Dominion forces, September 1943 to May 1945: Part III – The Campaign in Lombardy, 1 April to 2 May 1945. Section D: XIII Corps operations.

CAB106/446   Italy: Operations of British, Indian and Dominion forces, September 1943 to May 1945: Part III – The Campaign in Lombardy, 1 April to 2 May 1945. Section E: X Corps operations.

CAB106/447 – Italy: Operations of British, Indian and Dominion forces, September 1943 to May 1945: Part III – The Campaign in Lombardy, 1 April to 2 May 1945. Section F: II Polish Corps operations and appendices.

CAB106/448 – Italy: Operations of British, Indian and Dominion forces, September 1943 to May 1945: Part III – The Campaign in Lombardy, 1 April to 2 May 1945. Section G: German strategy.

CAB106/449 – Italy: Operations of British, Indian and Dominion forces, September 1943 to May 1945: Part III – The Campaign in Lombardy, 1 April to 2 May 1945. Section H: principal administrative aspects.

CAB106/451 – Italy: Operations of British, Indian and Dominion forces, September 1943 to May 1945: Part IV, O2E papers (i) disbandment and conversion of personnel of other arms to infantry, (ii) work of 'X' RTD re-allocation centre, (iii) statistics.
CAB106/453 – Italy: Operations of British, Indian and Dominion forces, September 1943 to May 1945: Part V, Desertion, VI, leave, VII, rest camps, VIII, compassionate postings, IX, marriage, X, repatriation, XI, employment of co-operators, XII, veterinary service, XIII, medical.

Archivo dell'Ufficio Storico dello Stato Maggiore Esercito, Rome
Boxes 2173, 2196 and 2205 – war diaries, Gruppo Cremona
Box 2260 – war diary, Gruppo Folgore

Websites
http://www.comune.alfonsine.ra.it/…/Musei/Museo-della-Battaglia-del-Senio Museum of the Battle of the Senio Line, Alfonsine, Ravenna, Italy
http://www.irishbrigade.co.uk 38 (Irish) Brigade of 78th (Battleaxe) Division. Includes documents, maps, photos, personal stories and a Roll of Honour
http://www.royalirish.com The Virtual Military Gallery of the Royal Irish Regiment includes information related to its antecedent regiments, three of which fought in Operation GRAPESHOT in 38 (Irish) Brigade.
http://aad.archives.gov National Archives and Records Administration, USA.
http://www.history.army.mil/medalofhonor US Army Center of Military History, Medal of Honor website.
http://www.history.army.mil/brochures/Po US Army Center of Military History, brochure on the Po valley campaign.
http://www.custermen.com/History85htm US Army divisional histories.
www.minnesotanationalguard.org *History of the 34th Infantry Division*

Other unpublished material
Bredin, Major General H. E. N. (Bala), CB DSO** MC*, 'An Account of the Kangaroo Army'.
Chavasse, Colonel K. G. F., DSO*, 'Some Memories of My Life'.
Duane, Major John, MC, Notes on the Italian Campaign.
ffrench-Blake, Colonel R. L. V, DSO, 'Italian War Diary 1944–45'.
Owens, Squadron Leader James, BSc MA RAAF, 'How influential was aerial intelligence on the Battles of El Alamein?' (MA dissertation, 2014)
Skellorn, John, 'What did you do in the War Grandpa? (An account of his service with 16th/5th Lancers.)
Trousdell, Colonel P. J. C., OBE, Notes on his service with 1st Royal Irish Fusiliers in Italy.
Scott, Brigadier T. P. D., DSO, 'Narrative of the service of the Irish Brigade'.

Index

General